More Old Tales of the Maine Woods

Ezekiel,

Have fun with
these old stories,

Steve Pinkham

More Old Tales of the Maine Woods

Steve Pinkham

Merrimack Media

Cambridge, Massachusetts

Published by Merrimack Media, Cambridge, Massachusetts
ISBN: 978-1-939166-39-5 (print)
ISBN:978-1-939166-38-8 (ebook)

Library of Congress Control Number: 2014930593

Manufactured in the United States of America, or in Great Britain, when purchased outside of North or South America.

Merrimack Media
For further information, contact info@merrimackmedia.com
www.merrimackmedia.com

Cover design by Merrimack Media

This book is dedicated to my many Chiltern friends with whom I have hiked, paddled and camped with in the past thirty years. It is especially dedicated to the "Canoe Group," with whom I have enjoyed many annual trips and great friendships – Joe, Ken, Chai, Andy, Bill, Dave, J. T., Mike, David J., Kirk, Greg, and others who have adventured with us.

CONTENTS

Acknowledgements

The journey that created this book took me from Northern Maine to Washington, D. C. and introduced me to many wonderful people who helped me along the way. Outside of Maine I visited many research facilities and am especially grateful to the librarians and staff members who helped me find so much material – The Library of Congress, New York Public Library, New York Historical Society, Yale University, Brown University, the Providence Athenaeum, University of Massachusetts at Amherst, the American Antiquarian Society in Worcester, the University of New Hampshire at Durham and Dartmouth College.

Much of my initial research was done in institutions in Greater Boston where I found a great wealth of material in old bound volumes and microfilms. I am especially indebted to the staffs of the Boston Public Library, New England Historical Genealogical Society, the Appalachian Mountain Club, the Thomas Crane Library in Quincy and the Lamont, MIT Archives and the Lamont, Widener and Ernst Mayr Libraries at Harvard University. Special thanks to Mary Sears, reference librarian at the Ernst Mayr Library at Harvard, who tracked down and scanned much obscure material and numerous photos for my many projects.

In Maine I am thankful for the use of materials and generous assistance at the public libraries of Portland, Skowhegan and Bangor, as well as the Longfellow and Hawthorne Library at Bowdoin College, Mallet Library of the University of Maine at Farmington, the Maine State Library and the Maine Archives at Augusta.

Valuable assistance came from the staffs at Bethel Historical Society, Maine Historical Society, the Old Canada Road Historical Society, Moosehead Historical Society, the Registry of Deeds at Houlton and the Maine State Archives. And I am forever grateful to State Historian Earle Shettleworth who allowed me access to the wonderful collections at the Maine Preservation Commission.

There were also individuals who helped and stood by me on this decade long project and I am thankful for their unconditional love and everlasting friendship. Thanks to my Mother, Charlie, Chai and Joe Cove, who helped and supported me in many ways to see this project through to the end.

Introduction

Ten years ago I began collecting articles for my first book, "Mountains of Maine," and started finding wonderful stories of the Maine Woods that were not about mountains, but were nonetheless, fun and exciting tales. Quickly getting the idea of collecting stories of the Maine Woods for a separate volume, I went back to the beginning and started over, methodically perusing through all the old sporting magazines, journals, newspapers and other periodicals for any and all articles about the Maine Woods. I soon found that if I looked for mountain articles, I would find stories; if I looked for stories, I would find mountain data.

This journey has taken me from northern Maine to the Library of Congress and to numerous libraries and historical societies to locate the stories and to date I have collected, copied and filed over 22,000 articles and photographs on the Maine Woods, choosing the best stories for this volume.

Running from 1845 to 1905, many of the stories came from *Forest and Stream*, the foremost sporting magazine of the latter 1800s. After 1910 most regions of the Maine Woods had been visited and written about and stories about the Maine Woods became sporadic and often redundant. Also, as the nation expanded, the focus of the sporting magazines also turned westward, and less and less was written about Maine.

The tales in this book are separated into specific regions of the State of Maine, running east from the New Hampshire border to the northern tip of Maine and Down East, and include exciting tales of hunting and encounters with wolves, catamounts, bears, moose and other wild animals as well as great fishing tales. The majority of tales are the adventures of known authors, while others are fictional stories, written in the ever popular juvenile books and novels and collections of stories.

If you ask anyone today, who went to the Maine Woods in the 19th century, most people would mention Henry David Thoreau, the man credited with coining the title "Maine Woods." But thousands of others including well-known and lesser known individuals ventured into the woods and also penned articles about their experiences. Some of the well-known authors are Seba Smith, Henry David Thoreau, James Russell Lowell, John Burroughs, Lucius Hubbard, Thomas S. Steele, Charles A. Stephens and Fannie Hardy Eckstrom.

Where the author is known, we have included some biographical information and a photograph, and in the case of an unknown individual, or an unknown pseudonym, we have often included some appropriate information on the region, setting, or if a story has been extracted from a longer narrative, and have included appropriate old photographs.

Finally, in *Old Tales of the Maine Woods*, the reader was provided with an introduction to each region that showed how the area developed as a sporting and lumbering region. In this volume I have provided the reader with many short anecdotes and information about each region, gleaned from my vast collection.

May you enjoy these stories as much as I did discovering them.

STEVE PINKHAM

Chapter 1

THE ANDROSCOGGIN AND
MAGALLOWAY RIVERS

In June of 1772, Henry Tufts, a notorious criminal who spent most of his life in and out of New England jails, was wounded in a fight, and after a meeting with Capt. Josiah Miles, the great Indian fighter, began a three-year residency with the Pigwacket Tribe in the Fryeburg area, in an attempt to get cured. Falling in in love with Polly Sussap, niece of old Tumkin Hagen, who lived at Umbagog Lake, Tufts spent some of the time hunting and trapping around Umbagog Lake. His adventures were published in 1807 in *A Narrative of the Life, Adventures, Travels and Sufferings of Henry Tufts*.

Fryeburg, most noted for the battle between Capt. John Lovewell's men and the Pigwackets in 1725, was first settled 1763, there being no settlements north of it until the spring of 1774, when Nathaniel Segar of Newton, Mass. settled in Bethel. He returned after the Revolution, and in 1781, the last Indian incursions in Maine occurred in Bethel, then called Sudbury Canada, when a small band of St. Francis men killed several settlers and took Benjamin Clark and Nathaniel Segar captive for sixteen months.

Along the Androscoggin River, Hanover was settled in 1774, Newry in 1781, Rumford in 1782, Andover in 1789 and Dixfield in 1793. Towns north of the Androscoggin were not settled until the nineteenth century with Byron being first inhabited in 1814, Upton 1823 and Grafton in 1830. The Magalloway River, being so inaccessible, was settled much later: Lincoln Planation in 1825.

In November of 1826 Waters Holman, a young man, was engaged in making shingles at a camp near Dixfield, and was so exhausted from the work, that he lay down to sleep. The camp, full of shavings and other debris, quickly caught fire. His companions found him dead, his body nearly half consumed by the flames.

A new stage route was established in late 1826, connecting Portland with Bethel, which met the White Mountain Stage from Jefferson, New Hampshire, creating a direct link from Jefferson to Portland, 110 miles.

Francis Parkman, the well-known American historian, visited the Magalloway region in 1842. Recording his adventures in his diary, the small band of adventurers explored the river and mountains, staying in homes and then lumber camps during their week in the woods.

Mr. J. Soule and friends of Errol, New Hampshire went out hunting one day in 1849 near Lake Umbagog, checking on the line of traps he had previously set. When his companions returned to get him, they found his body torn in pieces. From all appearances Soule came across two catamounts (panthers) in a tree. Quickly retreating to his cabin, he made half the distance when he fell over a tree and was leaped upon immediately by the big cats.

In 1852 the New York Times published a long article, *A Trip Down East*. It was written anonymously, the author using the pseudonym, Quahaug, chronicling a trip to Grafton and Upton, Maine, mentioning how good the fishing and hunting were. He also made a trek to the summit of Baldcap Mountain.

In July of that year Zenas T. Haines of Phillips, Maine, published a long report in the Portland Transcript, called *Sports of the Umbagog*, lamenting the fact that the snows were so deep the previous winter, that moose were slaughtered in great numbers, and lauding the Legislature for appointing commissioners in several of the counties to stop this lawless destruction. He also praised the fishing opportunities at Umbagog and the Rangeley Lakes.

Eight years later, Harper's Magazine published a long account in February of 1860, called *Coos and the Magalloway*, in which a small group of men came through New Hampshire and pushed up the Magalloway River to Lake Parmachenee and climbed Camel's Hump. The article included sketches of their adventures, being some of the earliest views of that region.

The following year Marshall Tidd, a lithographer from Woburn, Massachusetts, who helped produce some the earliest sportsmen's maps of the Maine Woods, made a long trip to Lake Parmachenee, producing a very detailed description of the region in his journal. This diary, which includes many watercolors of the area, was deposited in the Bangor Public Library and later printed in *Appalachia* in 1957, titled, *Up the Magalloway River in 1861*. In November 1864 Harper's published another anonymous excursion to the same region, titled *Exploring the Magalloway*. It chronicled the adventures of another small group of explorers, who lauded the marvelous fishing opportunities they found.

In 1863, Mr. Washington French of Albany, just south of Bethel, had been annoyed by bears all summer, killing a number of his sheep. Setting a trap, he finally caught the bear, which weighed about 300 pounds.

A WINTER CAMP ON THE MAGALLOWAY

By J. A., from *Forest and Stream*, March, 5, 1874

*In the Wilderness
(Currier & Ives)*

This is one of our earliest descriptions of the Magalloway region and certainly the first narrative of a winter trip. They approached from the west, passing Rump Mountain, which they called Camel's Hump. As there were no cabins in that region for a few more years, they camped out, though their guide was able to get them to a warm and welcome lumber camp.

It was at Island Pond, on the Grand Trunk Railroad, that N. and I struck off from the confines of civilization *en route*, for the head-waters of the Connecticut River, to hunt moose in winter. We had never explored this region and had only a vague idea of the locality in which to find our game, intending to cross from the lakes that feed the Connecticut to the Magalloway and trusting to chance to obtain a guide from among the hunters or settlers thereabouts. With our Indian snow shoes and a blanket, we were prepared to enter the woods, taking only such provisions and clothing as could be carried in a pack, a hatchet in the waist belt, a pistol and rifle. The common racketts used by the natives are not to be compared with Indian snow shoes, which are woven with fine strings of carribou or moose hide. Carribou strings are best, as they shrink and become tightened by wetting while moose hide loosens.

We were assured that we should find a cabin used by hunters on the shore of First Lake, one of the two in which the Connecticut takes its rise. Our guide was a certain Bill Lewis, whom we found at his log cabin, and who was induced to go with us for a money consideration and a share of the provisions. About noon we started into the woods for the camp with no misgivings about reaching it before dark, as the road we were to follow had been "blazed." Four miles we sped along without snow shoes on a firm crust. The afternoon was waning, dusk coming on, but still no signs of the camp; and stranger yet, the blazes were so indistinct that it required very close inspection to find them. In fact we had not gone far before all traces of the road were gone. Still no camp, and the sky overcast with rain! Yes, we were lost, that was sure, when we could find no more blazed trees. As darkness approached, it was a question of a few minutes either to find the cabin or to sleep where we were in the snow. None but a hunter's expedients were of use. So we looked about for sleeping quarters; the rain made it useless to attempt to build a fire, but shelter at least must be had. No friendly pine spread its sheltering arms for us, but a huge tree trunk, fallen and heaped with snow, under which it was possible to dig a hole and burrow after the manner of hibernating bears, was the only lodging that offered. So thus we snatched a few hours of sleep. I shall never complain of a hard bed again if it be under a roof and dry. The dog contributed some warmth, but of a shivery, moist, doggy nature.

With the morning light, we set off again, not much refreshed by our night's lodging in the snow; and not relying on blazed trees, we soon reached First Lake, where we built a fire and dried our clothing. Though somewhat *discouraged* by the follies of a night, we were bound to find a moose. Our guide exerted himself. The ice was several feet in thickness, but he cut a hole and caught some trout, which were soon done brown and served on spruce chips, and garnished with frizzled bacon. A flock of snowbirds or crossbills of brilliant hue twittered about our camp, regarding us perhaps as a second edition of "Babes in the Wood." On our way from First and Second Lakes to the Magalloway we met two moose hunters, natives, going out to the clearing after a successful hunt. They had killed a moose and left the meat covered with snow, which information was encouraging. Bill Lewis was a poor guide, as we had already discovered, but he proved to be a worse hunter; in fact we preferred that he should tend camp while we hunted.

Stalking the Moose is uncertain business, and requires all

one's patience and skill to be successful. Many a moose we tracked through the snow for miles only to hear the animal break away amongst the spruces when within half shooting distance. These cunning animals often make a circle and approach their own back track, where they await the hunter's appearance in safety.

Our snow shoes were bound with flannel on the wooden frames to muffle the sound. Signs of moose are found on the trees and shrubs where they browse, or where the bark is worn off by the rubbing of the antlers while in the velvet. Their tracks in snow can be detected even after they have been filled up with fresh snow, and when carefully cleared out with the hand the hunter feels the direction in which the game was moving by the shape of the holes made by their cloven feet. When near the game, only whispers or signs are used, and each footstep must be carefully considered. The moose may be behind the nearest snow covered spruce, or lying under a thick pine. If not wounded when he starts, he will plunge away and soon put miles between you. The Indians rarely abandon the chase, although it may take several days to run down a moose. We found tracks plenty, but soon discovered that other hunters had been after them. The next day we took a course towards Camel's Hump Mountain, near the Magalloway, where we built a good brush camp, and after a hard chase killed a young bull moose. N. was off alone the next day, but I decided to rest in camp. During the day I visited a small pond with an outlet near the river, and caught some brook trout through the ice, using pork for bait. We were now well supplied with provisions; moose meat and trout were a welcome change after a diet of bacon and biscuit.

We followed down the Magalloway stream on the ice until we came to Parmachenee Lake where we were delighted to meet some lumbermen fishing on the lake, which we crossed, and arrived at the lumber camp before dark, where a bountiful supply of bread, hot biscuit, baked beans and apple sauce, was set before us. Your entertaining correspondent, Jacobstaff, has already described the achievement of one hungry hunter in a lumber camp, where he surrounded a "brown stone front." So that I need not dwell on a similar experience.

The head waters of the Connecticut and Magalloway Rivers have been a good hunting ground for moose and carribou, but like the region about Moosehead Lake, an indiscriminate slaughter of this noble game in season and out, has made them very scarce, although I am glad to see by the communication of W.E.S. that moose and carribou are getting back to this section.

Until the Game Law is enforced the hunter must penetrate the wilds of New Brunswick or Cape Breton, if he would kill large game.

ON THE MEGALLOWAY

By Wm. Warren Greene, M.D., from *Forest and Stream*, October 22, 1874

William Warren Greene (1831-1881) was a famous surgeon from North Waterford, Maine. He began his career by teaching at Bethel and then opened the first high school in Waterford. He attended Bethel Academy from 1848 to 1851 and began a medical tutelage under Dr. Seth C. Hunkins, attending medical lectures at Berkshire College in Pittsfield, Mass. and graduating from the University of

William Warren Greene, M. D.

Michigan in 1855. He returned to Maine, spent several years as volunteer surgeon in the Federal army, and then in 1862 was offered a position in Pittsfield accepting the chair of theory and practice of medicine. But his talents lay in surgery, so he transferred to that department and in 1865 took over the professorship of surgery at the Medical School of Maine, was Professor of Surgery at Long Island College Hospital a few years, then in 1880 was elected president of the Maine Medical Association.Ironically Dr. Greene died on a return trip from England, as the ship did not have the facilities to treat his urinary attack. He is remembered in the medical community as a surgical genius. Dr. Greene loved the outdoors, and took many fishing trips in Maine and Michigan.

On the 15th of October 1871, my guide and I were paddling in Megalloway River. About noon we reached lower Metallochis Pond, a sheet of water about a mile long and a half a mile wide, which empties into the river by a narrow channel only two rods in length. As we reached this locality our attention was arrested by a peculiar sound, resembling the tinkling of bells. I had already heard the old hunters in this region speak of "sleigh bell ducks," but had never seen but one who had shot them, while no other of my acquaintance had seen them, except my guide "Spoff." The moment we heard this peculiar noise, "Spoff" says, "Doctor, I think there are 'sleigh bell ducks," in which opinion his brother George, another veteran guide, entirely coincided. You can easily imagine the feelings excited by such novel sounds, the origin of which was soon to be determined. Drawing the boat noiselessly to shore we carefully surveyed the surface of the pond, and saw a flock of birds, probably a hundred fifty in number. At this moment, opportunely, Lewis Brown, Esq., of Portland, and his guide, came down the river in his canoe and joined us. Immediately "Spoff" and George in my skiff and Brown and "Ed." in his canoe pushed into the lake, the two former carrying each a double-barreled gun, while I with my breech loader stood upon the shore. An hour's shooting secured thirteen birds, which Mr. Brown took in his canoe and left us. After another hour's intermission for dinner we resumed work, and at sun down brought in twenty-three more, making in all thirty-six as the result of the afternoon's shooting.

Now comes the principal points of interest. At the first round two birds were killed and several so crippled as to be unable to fly. The remainder of the flock rose and circled over the lake in two sections, forming in the manner of wild geese, but either from the lack of a leader, or because attracted by the wounded, they soon broke up and settled upon the water. These maneuvers were repeated again and again after successive shots until the close of the afternoon, when the remnant of the flock rose high in air, divided in two parts, and going South and the other North, in the same harrow-like form already indicated. Our attention was then directed to the dead and wounded, and in retrieving the latter we had an excellent opportunity of studying the peculiarities of these, to me, novel ducks.

The veteran hunter, Nahum Bennett, who alone had shot them in this region, and that only once, had told me that the peculiar noise which, when produced by a considerable number together, resembles closely the jingling of small sleigh bells, was caused by the motion of the wings; found however, it was purely a vocal note, uttered both when swimming and flying, and easily produced upon the dead body by sudden, sharp compression. Their sudden dive and rapidity of motion, both upon and under the water, was remarkable, no more so, however, than the wonderful amount of shooting necessary to bring them to bag. This was explained by an examination of the recovered birds. Their size was intermediate between that of the black and wood ducks, their shape resembling the latter. Feet and legs like the black duck; plumage universally jet black and so thick and dense as to explain the fact that in no instance was the body wounded, the head and neck being the only parts penetrated by the shot; under mandible, pure black like the feathers, upper mandible, bright yellow. A thick layer of fine fat intervened between the skin and the flesh, which was tender and of a delicious flavor.

The peculiar note which these birds utter has already been referred to, and it is easy to conceive how anyone hearing the combined tones of a large flock would apply them to the term "sleigh bell ducks," while the note of a single bird is a short, plaintive, monosyllabic whistle.

On the 16th of the present month, about 2 P.M., while rowing at the head of Umbagog lake, in company with my friend, N. C. Brown, of Portland, and my old guide "Spoof," we saw a flock of ducks, about one hundred in number, flying northward in the same goose-like order already mentioned, a mode of flight never adopted by any known species of duck, so far as I am aware. If you or any of your contributors can inform me whether this is a new variety, or whether I have overlooked them in examining the classification of Wilson and Audubon, you will greatly oblige myself and my friends.

I had fully intended to preserve specimens of these remarkable birds, but by the failure of an expected means of transportation was prevented from so doing. I should add in this connection that Mr. Bennett, the hunter referred to, informs me that one year ago he found a small flock of the ducks in a small pond in this locality, but was unable to secure a specimen after several shots at near range, still further demonstrating the impenetrability of their loon-like plumage.

I presume this region is familiar to many of your readers as one affording fair opportunities for exercise of rod and gun. The localities for camping cannot be excelled, and to the kindness of the settlers no one can bear more hearty testimony than myself; but while game is sufficiently abundant for all legitimate purposes at present, it cannot

long remain so if a certain set of gentlemen(?) whom the settlers characterize as a particularly *noyesy* party, often repeat such a ruthless slaughter as required them last year to *bury* one hundred birds in one day.

I would add in reference to the birds under consideration that, except the few needed for our own use, they distributed among various friends, several of who are well versed in Natural history' but to all of them they were *rara avies*.

THE NORTH WOODS OF MAINE

By G. T. Ridlon, from *The American Sportsman*, Vol. 5, January 2, 1875

Gideon T. Ridlon Sr., (1841-1928), born in Hollis, Maine, left the farm at age fifteen, going to the city to learn the iron machinist's trade, traveling throughout the eastern U.S. introducing the new cotton-spinning machinery. After serving in the Seventeenth Regiment of Maine Volunteers, he became an evangelical minister in 1865, serving for a few years in Harrison, Maine, Salisbury and Amesbury, Massachusetts, then returned to Harrison. An avid historian, he published "The Early Settlers of Harrison, Maine," a Ridley-Ridlon genealogy and his most famous work, "Saco Valley Settlements." In 1878 he produced a series of stories of his adventures in the Maine woods, which he published in "The American Sportsman" magazine. This is his first story.

G. T. Ridlon

For many years I had spent much of the time during the Autumn months among the grand old timber in the north-woods of my native State, and such a relish had I for the "tramp and camp" that when the nights grew frosty, I would rise early, and, looking toward the hills, snuff the morning air and like the dog, really "whine" to be let loose from the dull haunts of monotonous labor, that I might "beat" in the woods.

It was in the month of October 1864, that I broke away from the shop, visited the country-home of my father, and commenced to gather traps for a two-month's camp-out. The hunting-frock–a thick woolen one–was put in trim; the hunting-knife ground; the belt and pouches filled; the moccasins oiled and mended; the gun cleaned and oiled; the small axe ground; two dozen steel traps packed; and then came the "nick-nacks," such as extra gun nipples, pocket screw-driver, extra buttons, needles and thread, leather strings, woolen shirts, thick socks, pouch of salt, fry-pan, tin plate, spoon, knife, ham of bacon, box of herring, and what *must not* be forgotten, plenty of good friction matches. The above-named "kit" connected with the expectation of "hard knocks and greasy chin" will do very well for the fall months, but is not all that is needed for a winter camp. When the blankets were packed and the knapsack filled; when the belt was buckled and the frying-pan slung, we two–for there were two of us–shouldered our "shooting irons" and tramped for the north, "determined for a country that was out of sight to find."

After pushing forward nearly all night, and growing foot-sore, we opened a field-gate, rolled in our blankets, and lay down for a "nap." We were soon asleep, and rested sweetly until awakened by some girls on their way to school. They had discovered our guns, and looking through the bushes concluded that we were Indians. We frightened them somewhat as we jumped from our blankets, for they ran down the road screaming as only girls can. After a breakfast of "plain fare" we resumed our tramp, camping when weary, until the third afternoon, which found us at the mountains near what is known as "Brickitt's Notch." At the foot of these mountains–they are the boundary between Chatham and "Batchelder's Grant"–was a farm-house, at which we called for directions. The good woman informed us that it "seven miles up and seven miles down," going across the mountains, before we should reach "Bisbie's," which was a small farm on the other side. It was a "hard pull," and we expected to camp on the mountains that night; consequently we bought a loaf of bread, and a chicken, and commenced the ascent through a narrow foot-path. It was raining and the rocks were very slippery, causing one who was inexperienced in tramping, as was my companion, to fall down frequently. I shall never forget the persuasion and encourage-ment I had to use that evening to get that fellow along. After pass-ing the highest point of land, and commencing the descent, weary and wet, hungry and cold, the poor "greeny" begged me to camp. "No," I would reply, "I shall reach 'Bisbie's' before I sleep if I can keep the path." I "led the van," and would occasionally hear him exclaim, "damn it all, I won't go another step," and looking behind would find he was down. The path was very steep, and the mossy rocks so wet that none but a real "tramp" could keep his footing. My chum would fall, and being loaded with traps and knapsack, these would sometimes be thrown over his head. He was an inveterate smoker, and found some consolation with his pipe. But he declared he knew we were *lost* and would never get out. He did not dare remain behind and pressing forward, he was soon to follow me.   At length we were on the bank of a swift running river, which being very low, we were able to cross on the rocks. A herd of deer were drinking under the bank-bushes, and when we stepped down the bank they snorted and away they went, the hard thump of their hoofs being heard for some distance. When that old buck snorted I presume my chum thought his hour had come, and that some awful denizen of the woods was about to crunch his marrow-bones, for a groan was extorted from him which would have done justice to a converted sinner in a camp meeting.

We soon discovered the glimmer of a light through the trees, which inspired courage; and after following a path across a small clearing, we stood before the door of a large log-house. "Now," said Bill, "it will be presumption to ask them to let us in, for we are *so wet,* and besides it's not *at all* likely that they have much to eat or an extra bed." But I gave a sharp rap at the door, and soon saw before me a thick-set man with shaggy hair and beard, holding a candle in his hand. "What's wanted out there," he asked. I informed him that we were hunters from "down east:" that we had come from "Brickett's," that we were weary, wet, and hungry, and would like to tarry with him through the remainder of the night.

"Come right in, boys," said he; "throw yer traps down there by the chimney and draw up to the fire. Why, boys," said he, "never mind bein' wet, we don't very often have company, and if you can git on with our coarse fare ye are jist as welcome as can be. Jerry, stir that are fire a bit, will ye, and roll on a big log, or two. Mother and Jane, cum now, you jist fly round and set on some warm grub for these fellers; they must be mighty tired and hungry afore now. Cum, boys, now you pull off them moccasins and socks, and them wet duds, and we'l hev them all dry afore mornin'; now won't you fellers just act as if you was ter home. We folks in here are rough kinder folks, but we're allers glad to 'comerdate travellers." As soon as we had hung our clothes around the fire food was ready, and we were invited to "set round." There, you poor, pale-faced dyspeptic city fellows, if you can dig out of your counter-corners, throw away your linen, and climb the mountains awhile, then set down to a supper like the one we had that night, you would know how to appreciate life, and get new blood. Plenty of hot coffee, hot barley bread, nice fried ham and eggs, yellow butter, and nice rich milk, and a steam rising from the table like a locomotive ready for a move. My jolly, how we fellows did "hoe in" and test our "bread baskets!"

Supper done, we took a survey of our quarters. The room was very large and without plaster; the beams were huge round logs; the chimney was of rough stone, and contained a fire-place some six feet wide. Sitting near the fire, we could look through the roof and see the twinkling stars. The table was of rough boards, "home manufactured;" the chairs were basket-bottomed, and every article of furniture or house hold utensil were in perfect keeping with the place. On hooks which hung from the beams, overheard, were suspended guns, rifles, powder-horns, and pouches, and around the wall-corners stood the small farm implements. This family consisted of a man and wife, about forty-five years of age, a daughter some sixteen, and a lame boy. The man was a real woodman and hunter; he could tell of adventures and hair-breadth escapes in which he enacted a part, from morning until night. He was generous, kind-hearted and full of fun—running over with good nature all the time. His wife was a true specimen of the frontier Yankee woman—a tall, broad-shouldered, masculine creature, and as ignorant of the ways of the outside world as she was secluded from it. After telling stories until toward morning, the old gent said, "Wal now, mother, I spect these ere fellers are mighty tired and want a bit of rest; Jane, you take the candle and lead them inter 'tother room, where they can sleep." Upon this the tall, slim, green, shy looking creature took the light, and we followed her into another unfinished room. She set the light upon a little red stand, and was about to dodge out when I said. "Now, Jane, I must kiss you good night," and sticking a "down East" smack upon her mouth, she went blushing from the room. We slept until late in the morning, and were awakened by hearing the old lady calling her fowls, "Bid, Bid, Bid; come and get your corn."

With haste we presented ourselves in the kitchen. The old man was leaning against the wall, in his chair, reading a dingy old paper—the Oxford *Democrat*. The daughter was preparing the table, while the mother was "at milking." As soon as she saw us she commenced laughing. Then my "chum" chimed in, which attracted the attention of her father, who, laying aside his reading, said, "Now, Jane, I'd just like ter know what in time yer laughing at, for I never seed yer act so kinder quear in all yer lifetime. Hev yer fell in love with one uv these Easters?" By this time she had taken refuge in the pantry, and shut the door with a nervous demonstration. I saw that affairs were assuming a serious aspect, and hearing the tramp of the mother at the door, concluded to explain the whole affair, and trust to the good nature of the old gent for safety. So I acknowledged that for "sport" I had kissed the daughter "good night," and hoped it would give no offense. This was enough. "Well, well," said the father. "Now, Jane, come out here and face the music. I'll be darned if I'd run just for that. Come out here." The mother coming in, he told her, and the whole company engaged in a hearty, side-shaking laugh. Jane could not be persuaded to show herself, and the old man declared he believed she never was kissed before.

After a hearty breakfast we felt much refreshed, and being directed by our host, we crossed the Wild River and made our way through the forest to the town of Shelburne, N.H. and to the Androscoggin river valley. Following the river road we reached Gorham that evening. Here we were to find our guide, procure some provisions, see that our traps were already, and move straight onto our hunting grounds. We tarried in the village a few days, saw "Merrit" play with the "Alpine house" bear, and having employed "Old Griffin" as guide, we went on our way to the woods. Following the course of the river to Berlin Falls, we struck boldly to the right and entered the deep, unbroken forest. We had hired a man to take us and luggage as far as a horse could go, and having reached that point, which was on the bank of a deep brook, and at the end of an old logging-road, we unharnessed the team and prepared to camp for the night. Old Griffin said if we would build a fire he would furnish some trout for supper, and, arranging his line and bait he went down to the brook. We were soon seated around the bright fire, which so lighted up the forest that one could have seen to read at some distance, and after recounting the transactions of the day and discussing the prospects of the future, we rolled in our blankets and were soon in the land of dreams.

The night was clear and cool, but, being near a roaring fire, we kept warm enough. We had been sleeping but a short time when our teamster, who had been city born, and was not used to the woods, commenced to whistle and sing with all his powers. "What ails you," asked Old Griffin, as he raised his head from his blanket. "Why don't you hear the wolves and wild-cats howling on the mountains?" replied the "greeney," "and do you think I shall lay there on the ground and have a pack of them come down on me. I tell you what, gentlemen, that box of herring must be nailed up and put out of the way, for I have heard it said that they will *draw* bob-cats." Old Griffin replenished the fire, called the teamster a "milk-and-water fop," and went back to his blanket; but there was no more sleep for us; the poor, timid fellow, climbed into his wagon and whistled to drive the cats away until he could not keep on a pucker; and as soon as a streak of daylight could be seen, he hitched up his team and turned homeward.

After a hearty breakfast we strapped our baggage, broke camp, and commenced one of the hardest marches I have ever endured.

We were informed by our guide before breaking camp that we had a rough path to tread, and that being loaded so heavily we must "take it fair and easy." I have taken many a forced march upon Southern fields, "laden with the rations," but never called upon my legs to support such a load as I carried on my way to the northern hunting grounds. We could not proceed more than a mile at a "pull" before resting, and didn't accomplish more than twelve miles the first day after entering the unbroken forest. We had killed some fine, fat birds on our way, and finding a protected camping place we soon had our fire going and meat upon the "spits." We were now far from the haunts of men, in the deep primeval forest. The land was covered with ledges and huge granite boulders, and these with soft, green moss. The trees were very large and tall, and there being but little "underbrush" one could see a long distance between their giant trunks; yet their branches overhead were so interwoven and dense, that they formed a canopy so complete that we could hardly see the stars, as we lay looking upward from our blankets. Oh, how grand are the woods, and what pictures the lively imagination will draw under circumstances like ours! We seemed shut out from the world, in which we had been living, and were alone with God in his great house. Such a solemn stillness as brooded there; a stillness broken save by the note of the lonely night-bird, the loons upon the lake, and the distant scream of some wild beast; these sounds, with the whispering zephyrs which moved through the bowered courts above us, were all that disturbed the awful silence of our retreat. At times nature put the finger of silence to her lips, and then we seemed to have passed beyond the province of time and sense to an uninhabited kingdom. If one would have grand conceptions of the Creator, and the glory of His work, let him be in the deep, still forest at night, resting on the lap of mother earth, and looking upward to the sparkling heavens.

Having no city "greeney" to disturb us we found a refreshing sleep, and were early up for a tramp. We saw game frequently while on our way, and killed birds as we needed them. At about noon of the second day's march we reached the borders of a lovely lake, nestled among towering mountains, and were informed by our guide that we were at our "headquarters." "Now boys," said Griffin, "unstrap your traps and pile them on this beaver dam, and we will look round a bit." Standing upon an eminence with this silver-bosomed lake stretching far away, and tree-capped mountains towering to the clouds on either hand, he pointed to a small wooded island in the lake, and said: "There, boys, you see that clump of trees running toward the east shore; well, there is plenty of water fowls; that is the feeding ground of ducks and geese; and there—pointing toward some granite rocks which stood out in the water—is the place to take your trout." He then called our attention to the many musk rat houses on the meadow around the lake; to an immense beaver dam at its outlets, and then said, "Well, boys, we had best look for a good camping spot."

We found a small elevation near the "Blackstrap" river, and only a short distance from the lake, and there commended the erection of our camp. Perhaps some of our friends, who live in the warm summer climate, would like to know how a northern hunter's camp is constructed. Well, we drove some small posts into the ground near each other, and filled these with small logs, "chinking" the seams with moss; then having two side walls of about six feet in height; completed, we put on the cross beams, over which were laid small straight poles, their lower ends touching the ground and forming the roof; this was well "shingled" with hemlock, and our camp was done. Of course the front was open to our fire. This would not have been suitable for winter, but with a deep bed of cedar boughs, and a roaring fire in front, was warm enough for the season. Just in front was a large log, against which our fire was built. We had now got ready for housekeeping, dedicated our camp with songs and stories, which made the old woods laugh with echoes, and, paying our guide, we were left alone in the 'northwoods" of Maine.

As soon as our camp was completed, and a large pile of dry wood secured, we drew up our order of exercises and commenced business in earnest. We intended to make our tour, not only pleasurable, but remunerative; and hence determined not to "eat the bread of idleness." Our guide–"old Griffin"–had pointed out many "signs" of sable along our way while entering upon our hunting grounds, and had thrown out many valuable hints about trapping this beautiful little animal. As we were not to hunt upon snow, we must adopt the forms of trapping adapted to the bare ground. Our northern sable are a shy little fellow, and seldom seen by the hunter until in his trap. They secret themselves during the daytime in hollow trees, logs and in crevices of the rocks. I have only seen two or three sable in daytime during all the time I have spent among the forest haunts. I was once waiting for a shot at some "hatchet-head" duck, and, hearing a slight movement in the dry weeds near the water's edge, saw one of them drinking; but a movement of my hand caused him to disappear so quickly that I could not tell where he went to. In setting traps for this animal the hunter establishes a "sable-line"–that is, drags a piece of meat along the ridges of rocky land, and then builds his traps about twenty rods apart on the "line." This line usually extends some three or four miles in circumference–forming a circle–and on one side approaches the camp. The "ground traps" are made of billets of wood driven into the ground on a circle with a diameter of ten inches. This is arranged with a "bed-stick" and "fall and set," either with a "rolling spindle" or a figure "4," with the bait inside the enclosure; which the sable, attempting to get, crawls between the "bed" and "fall," and is crushed between them when the trap is sprung. The reason for dragging the meat is obvious, for, as sable commonly associates in "droves," when they strike the scent of meat, they will be sure to follow it until they come to a trap, and sometimes they will follow the "line" until the whole drove are taken in one night. The hunter will go along his "bouts"–follow his line–once in two or three days, and if in a good "sable beat," frequently returns to his camp with his sack full of pelts. I have known two hunters to take sixty sable in two nights, upon a three-mile line, in winter. The traps are then made by three wide spruce chips, cleft from a "riff-tree," and stuck into the snow. When making our "bouts" and tending to our traps, we gathered spruce gum as we found it along the "line," this we "bagged" in the "rough," and on rainy days cleaned it in camp, ready for market. Some of the large trees have been "seamed" by lightning from top to stump, and the gum oozes out, thickly studding the "seam" in large, clear lumps. On some of these we gathered five pounds of merchantable gum–gum which sold for seventy cents the pound.

Inside of the old beaver-dam was a meadow of one hundred acres. This was once covered with water, flowed by the dam previous to the breaking through of the streams which formed the outlet of the lake. This meadow was formed with tall "flat-grass," and was literally alive with musk-rat–a thickly populated city of animal inhabitants. Their cone-like houses were thickly clustered along their water-roads, giving the whole scene an enterprising and industrious appearance. The water-roads above mentioned were narrow channels cut through the grass, leading from the body of the lake to the rat-houses. These were filled with water and had a passage into the houses, which they entered under water. It was sport to sit upon the beaver-dam during the clear moonlight evenings and shoot the rats as they were swimming through these water-roads. We could look in no direction upon that meadow after daylight without seeing musk-rats. I have no doubt there were a thousand of them in that lake when we commenced shooting and trapping them. We took these animals in small steel traps; these were set in their "roads" at the entrance of their huts, or inside the hut, by carefully removing a few tufts, which were replaced after the trap was put in. The chain was made fast to a stake outside. Care must be used in setting the traps for musk-rats, or they will wind them up in the grass and twist their legs off; thus the trapper will get more paws than pelts. After learning their habits we wound the jaws of our traps with strips of cloth, which saved breaking the bone of the leg, and afterwards lost none of our rats. Those caught in the huts would always dig out, and would be sitting on the outside when we found them. There were a few mink among the streams and shores of the lake, which were taken in "log-traps," or in steel traps set in holes along the water's edge. Steel traps must be so set that the mink will jump into the water and drown, or they will twist their legs off, and escape. The old story about animals *gnawing* their legs off when trapped is a foolish one, and I think without foundation, in fact.

As we were frequently upon the lake, fishing until nearly dark, or tramping along the "sableline," we could not always reach the camp until the shades of night had fully settled around us; and had it not been for our "beaten paths," we should have lost our way. We had been out on the raft fishing one rainy afternoon, and having left our guns upon the shore of the lake, found them so damp that they refused fire. On reaching the beaver dam–our landing place–we found ourselves in wet clothes, without matches and the rain coming down copiously. It was so dark that we could almost *feel* its density, and it was with difficulty that we found our camp; and could not have found it, but the path from the lake to the camp was shaped by the winding of the stream, upon the bank of which the camp was erected. When we had reached our camp, Bill said if I would cut some dry wood for the fire, he would crawl in and get some matches–these were kept in a knapsack, in the rear of the camp–to kindle with. I had found the axe, and was about to prepare the "kindling" when I heard Bill exclaim, "Good Lordy," followed by hearing him jump over the "fire-log" down the bank of the brook. I knew that something was "in the wind" and as soon as I could, hailed him: "What's up, Bill? Are you dead or alive?" All the answer I received was an indistinct muttering as he came climbing up the muddy bank; but when he was convinced that he *was* really alive, he vented himself somewhat as follows: "As true as there's a sun in heaven there's a bear in our camp." I remarked that he must be mistaken; but he declared that he was not, "for," said he, "I was down on my hands and knees, reaching out for the knapsack, when I put my hand square in his fur; he is eating our herring, and if you hark you will hear him." Here our conversation ceased for the time, and we both prepared to "hark;" and we did not have to wait long, for, true's I live we could hear him crunching the bones of our herring. "Well," said Bill, "I think this is pretty cool, anyway; he has taken possession and means to hold it; and our guns water-soaked, and no matches for a fire." I had no idea of yielding our cozy cabin to a wild beast, especially on a rainy night, and began to cast about in my mind how we should dislodge him. That we were in a poor predicament for battle we both knew, and Bill, having "felt the hair" of the critter, was inclined to retreat and leave the field. I found some pitch-knots and commenced throwing them into the camp, hoping thus to drive the beast, or whatever it was, out; when one of these hit him, he would stop eating and for a few seconds be quiet; but soon after commenced his supper again as though nothing had disturbed him.   After having tried the virtues of clubs, we pulled a pole from the camp-side, and after a few bunters against his ribs, the creature went out, under the roof poles and down through the brush-wood, crashing as heavy as an ox. What it was we could not learn until morning, when we found tracks in the soft clay along the brook, which represented the feet of a panther or lynx-cat. He had devoured nearly half a box of herring, leaving their tails neatly piled in a bunch. When satisfied that the camp was clear, matches were brought out, a fire kindled, supper cooked, and leaving a roaring fire which illuminated the mountain-side, we rolled into our blankets and were soon dreaming of wild beasts of the most frightful kind.

"WHO'S AFRAID OF A LYNX?" AND "A RIDE ON A BUCK"

By Capt. Frederick Barker and John Danforth, from *Hunting and Trapping on the Magalloway River and Parmachene Lake, A Winter in the Wilderness*, 1882

Fred Barker & John Danforth

In the fall of 1876, Capt. Fred Barker and John Danforth went up the Magalloway River, leaving the comforts and securities of civilization at Capt. Wilson's house during the duration of the winter. With plenty of provisions, traps and tools, they paddled to Parmachenee Lake, refurbished an old abandoned logging camp and spent their days trapping, hunting and exploring the Upper Magalloway River and its tributary streams seeking martin, otter, beaver, lynx and more. They explored the headwaters of the river, climbing as far as Poacher Ridge, on the Canadian Border. Collecting enough furs to finance further careers, they vowed to return the following year. Capt. Barker became a well-known figure on the Rangeley Lakes and wrote another book about this adventures, while Danforth opened a set of sporting camps on an island in their beloved Parmachenee Lake.

Who's Afraid of a Lynx?

When we got to the brook where the trap was left under the suspended partridges, we found it gone. The tracks, though dim, owing to the melting snow, we could see, and we were sure it was the lynx. But he was nowhere in sight. We drew our load to camp, then looked for the trap. The track of it we could only occasionally see in the snow; this showed that it was in the air most of the time. We looked for the stick which had been fastened to it, and found it just where we left it. It was frozen fast in the ice; evidently the first jump the lynx made had broken the chain, leaving nearly all of it attached to the stick,.

It was so near night that we postponed our search until morning. We left all of our skins outside to freeze, and before starting on the trail in the morning, put them inside to keep them from the sun, so that they should not dry any until we got to the home camp, where we could stretch them.

The trap, after leaving the partridges, evidently had gone straight for the thickest growth of scrub-trees in sight, which was about ten rods up the brook on the south side; at this point it seemed to have amused itself for quite a long time by knocking the bark off the trees and breaking small branches; then it had started along, getting behind every stick and upturned tree, thus causing itself and the lynx a great deal of delay until it reached higher ground, where the open growth had less attractions for it. At this point we began to understand its motive. There was a pile of huge granite boulders about half a mile beyond. There we expected to see the trail end of the entrance of some big hole. And we were right in our conclusions.

Sure enough, under one of those big stones the trail went. The hole was large enough for one of us to crawl into; but either we did not want to go, or through politeness one waited for the other. Finally we introduced a long pole, which was seized when it had been pushed in about eight feet, and we could hear fierce growls. Then we cut another pole, and cut off one limb, so as to make a hook, trimming all the others close. This we tried for a long time to hook into the trap; but at last we found our hook bitten off, and the end of the pole chewed to splinters. Then we tried a smoking-out process, similar to the way in which we smoked the fisher.

Our fire had hardly been lighted when we could hear the rattle of the trap, as though it was getting uneasy. Yet it did not come forth. We stood away from the mouth of the hole, not caring to meet the trap too unexpectedly. We looked on all sides, to see if any other hole would betray itself by sending forth smoke, but there was evidently no other.

Our fire burned low, and we replenished it with a good stock of pine wood from a dry stub which stood near. Instantly the flames more than filled the hole; they climbed up the rocks and licked the overhanging snow. The heat was so great that we had to step back in order not to burn our faces; and it was fortunate for us that we did; for at that instant our fire shot out of the hole as though a keg of powder had exploded behind it, and the lynx, with open mouth and glaring eyes, came too through the whirling embers, deprived of this side whiskers, and the tassels on his ears, which did not improve his looks in the least.

We both fired at him, but this did not stop his headlong career. The trap was an impediment, and caused him many a tumble, but did not delay him so that we could get a second shot before he was out of sight, under another rock.

It was hard medicine for the lynx, but we could not help laughing at the sight which must forever remain in memory. His long hair was all burned off, which made him look leaner than is usual with a lynx; and besides, the fire had taken all the fight out of him.

We had spoiled the skin, yet we wanted the trap; so we tried him the second time. The place where he had gone in was where several boulders about twenty feet in diameter, lay close together, forming, with the great amount of snow, deep, dark alleys, thus giving him a good lot of room to operate in. It was no use to try the smoking process here. We must contrive some other means to drive him out. The plan we adopted was to follow him into his ice-bound cave with birch-bark torches, and either shoot him in there or drive him forth.

The first thing was to gather the bark, which did not take long; then we rolled it into as close rolls as we could, then pushed it onto the ends of split sticks. We made three of these torches, but it being inconvenient for the one which had the rifle, to carry anything else, we left one outside. Then with a light in one hand, and a fresh torch in the other, we began our search for the trap.

The passage was not wide enough for us to go side by side, nor high enough to walk upright. We were obliged to crawl along and keep close together as we could. But we had little to fear of the lynx giving us a battle, for we thought he had got fire enough to give the torch a wide berth if he could.

After going in about twenty feet, we found the cave would not amount to much in summer, as the sides, and also the roof in many places, were nothing but snow and ice; and we also saw that deep holes ran back, made by fallen trees which held the snow from the ground, and that these would give the lynx plenty of chances to hide himself from us for a long time.

But we kept on, the torch giving light enough to see some distance ahead. We proceeded for some time without seeing any signs of him. The torch was nearly burned out, and we were obliged to light the other. Still we had not reached the end of the passage. We pushed along faster, to reach the end and return before this last torch burned out. But we had not gone far when a cold feeling suddenly crept over us, and it was not owing to the damp atmosphere, but to the sound that reached our ears, the unearthly yells of the frightened lynx as he got sight of the torch. It is needless, perhaps, to say just how quick we reached the opening, where we instantly changed the torch for a rifle, and proceeded directly to camp. We were full convinced that we did not want the trap.

It was past noon when we got home, so we did not leave until the next morning; but before night we had taken up all the traps in the vicinity and hidden them. If anyone had been near us that after- noon, they would have heard this question asked many time: "Who's afraid of a lynx?"

A Ride on a Buck

The high range of mountains which runs down from the north on the west side of Parmachenee Lake, seems to stop to let a deep cove in beyond what should have been the shore, were the lake regular in its shape at the south end. Beyond this cove, a ridge some forty or fifty feet high stops the water from running on through a swamp to reach the Little Magalloway. A mile and half beyond, where it widens out and runs through a flat country, it is known to a few as Long Pond; and whoever fished at Parmachenee Lake, usually spent a day at Long Pond, for it is alive with fish.

It was for that pond we started the next morning after we got our meat to camp. We took along a few traps, our hatchets and rifles. The morning was fine, and as we walked out upon the lake from the river, the sun came over the mountains and shot his rays over us into the head of the deep cove, spreading there a pale red light, and still farther on toward the west the ice-covered top of Bose Buck Mountain shone like sheets of silver.

The trees, which had got nearly rid of their winter's load, looked gray. The birds seemed to increase in number each day, and while crossing the lake we saw the first migratory bird of the season – a crow.

The walking on the lake was splendid; we carried our snow-shoes slung on our rifles until we got to the head of the cove. There we were obliged to put them on, for the snow in the woods where there was no track, would not bear us without them.

Partridges were plenty, sunning themselves on the branches of the dead cedars which lay along the edge of the lake partially buried in snow and ice. They would allow us to approach within thirty feet before they would fly. We did not shoot any, as we did not like them to eat, because their meat tasted too much of the buds on which they had lived so long. The few we shot up river had satisfied us on that point. As soon as we entered the woods, we began to set traps wherever we saw a good and likely place for animals. We could not judge of this by the tracks, as the crust would not bear them up.

On the ridge which formed the cove, deer paths were very plenty; and we had just reached the top of it when we came upon a drove of them.

They had no paths to run in except the ones we were traveling along. The unfortunate creatures were caught in a trap by being at one end of their yard, while by chance we had come between them and their only way out. The ground was covered with spruce and fir-trees, with branches high enough for us to look under for some distance. Thus we could see the frightened creatures wildly looking in all directions; they seemed to know that they could not escape through the untrodden snow, and also that that was their only chance.

It did not take them long to decide. Away they went, clearing the snow at every bound. But their strength was not sufficient to carry them far, and the sharp crust, through which they broke at each bound, cut their legs and breasts. They slackened their speed by the time they had gone twenty rods. As soon as we understood the trap they were in, we gave them chase; and our snow-shoes carrying us over the snow in a growth where there was no underbrush, gave us all the advantage.

It was not more than ten minutes before we were up with them. The poor creatures were so frightened that many of them uttered the most plaintive bleating, while a few of the older ones turned and gave us battle by jumping straight for us, with ears laid back, and wild-looking eyes, at the same time striking with their forefeet. But we still had all the advantage, for one step to the right or left let them bury themselves in the snow at our side; and it took them some time to get up, swing around, and strike again.

During all this time we were whooping and yelling at the top of our voices. Taking it all together, there was a curious noise; the bleating of the frightened deer, the snort and whistle of the furious buck as he made charge after charge, and all the noise we could make. It caused the mountains and valleys which usually sent back clear echoes, to do nothing but rumble and roar.

After the big bucks had jumped at us several times, they seemed to fear us less, and would stand beside us where they plunged in the snow for several minutes at a time before renewing the attack.

At one of those lulls in the conflict we decided that each of us would jump astride one and take a ride. We were about forty feet apart, and on the brow of the ridge where it pitched toward the Little Magalloway at a point where the descent is much more abrupt than the ascent from the lake. At the signal we both mounted, and instantly found that we had no way of carrying our rifles, so they went into the snow under the deer's feet. The feet did not stop to trample upon them, but forced the deer and its rider into the air high enough to carry them about fifteen feet down the steep hillside.

When we struck, we found we had still more about us than we needed for such a ride; and that was our snow-shoes; they seemed to be particularly huge and unhandy things, but we had no time to un- fasten them, as our hands were locked tight under the deer's necks, and unless we had ridden enough, it would not do to part them.

And doubtless we both thought it was no lynx affair, at least on our part, so we let the snow-shoes take care of themselves, and after the first bound they went behind and did not get under the deer again. Our ride was not long, yet it was exciting, and our minds were not upon anything else; and after the performance was over, one could not laugh at the other, for he did not see him. About ten rods from where we mounted the deer was level ground; and once on that the mighty bucks were at our mercy. They tried several times to jump, but their strength was too far gone, and they could not clear the snow.

As we lay on them, we could hear their hearts beat through their violent exertions. Then came the question, "What was to be done with them?" And we agreed that when they got quiet we would let them go. It was not long before they gave up and sank into the snow completely conquered.

When we got off they did not bounce away, but swinging their heads around, they gave us a look as much as to say, "What next?"

We left them and went back up the hill, picked up our hats, and our rifles. We looked around to see if there were any more deer to ride back down the hill, but they all had gone back into the yard. We then took our course again for Long Pond, very well satisfied with buck-riding for the season.

CAMP CARIBOU, SATURDAY, DECEMBER 13TH

By Daniel Heywood, from *Parmachenee Guide at Camp Caribou,*
Parmachenee Lake, Oxford Co. Maine, Fall of 1890

Daniel Ellsworth Heywood (1869-1911), a native up
Errol, New Hampshire and Upton, Maine, removed
further up the Magalloway River where he hunted,
fished, trapped and was employed as a guide at
Camp Caribou on Parmachene Lake for many
years. Heywood wrote many articles for sporting
journals, publishing many in "Shooting and Fishing,"
from 1895 to 1906, and "Arms and the Man," from
1906 to 1907. It was most likely a well-to-do guest of

Daniel Heywood

the camps that urged Heywood to keep a diary of his
day to day adventures and more than likely financed the publication of
the book. The diary spans from October to December, 1890, chronicling
his work as a guide, trapper and handyman for his boss, John Danforth,
the noted owner of Camp Caribou. While most of the entries are short,
Daniel would often give us a short story of some adventure, this one from
his childhood.

I also remember an incident that occurred to me when I was not
over seven or eight years of age. It was nearly the first time I had
been away camping out. It was in May. The ice was still in the
main part of the lake, but the river and around the outlet of the
lake, where my oldest brother George had a hunting and trapping camp, was open. I had begged to go with him and been
allowed to do so. We started early in the morning from home,
as we were going to go on the ice most of the way and draw our
boat on a sled. The morning on which we started was a clear, cold
morning in spring. The ice had frozen during the night, so we
were able to walk on it, drawing our boat and provisions without any difficulty. The woodpeckers could be heard drumming on
the hollow stubs, and the birds were flitting merrily about in the

trees, while the crows flew in pairs and even in small flocks, calling to each other from a long distance. Everything seemed to be busy, and feeling that one day in the spring, on such a morning, was worth three in mid-summer; but before we reached the open water, where we must use our boat, the sun which had been filling the whole eastern horizon with crimson for more than an hour, rose, causing the surface of the ice to grind under our feet and the sled runners, like four inches of corn, and our march became a tiresome one; but at last with a breath of relief, we reached the open water, and I got in the boat and George ran it into the water, springing into it with me, as the ice broke under his feet.

The object of this hunt was to capture two hundred rats, which were very plenty around the outlet and up the Magalloway. As we reached the shore at the landing, by the camp, we found a large spruce tree which had stood near the water's edge, and near the path, had fallen into the water, blocking the landing. George ran the boat into the top and I stepped out on it and held the boat, steadying myself all the time in fear of falling into the cold water. George stepped out of the boat, made it fast, and taking an ax went ashore on the tree, cutting off the branches on the upper side of the tree as he went. When he reached the shore he called to me to follow which I did, though in great fear of falling in, but I reached the shore in safety. Then we went up to the camp, and on opening the door which had been many times nearly ruined by hedgehogs gnawing their way into the camp, we noticed that they had been occupying the camp regularly, and the boxes and table and various other articles had been badly damaged by them lately.

George took a survey of things, talking a great deal, very much alike in person, and finally remarked: "Well, let's go down and get a load of stuff for the boat." As we emerged from the camp we heard a crackling of brush beside the camp, and looking over saw two large hedgehogs hurrying away towards a large tree. "Ah!: exclaimed my brother, "Here is the fellows that have been raising h—l with our camp stuff. Your go for the gun and I will watch them till you get back. I feared very much to venture alone on the log, which lay between our boat and the shore, but the fear of being called chicken-hearted prevented my making any hesitation; so I turned and ran for the boat, and if I should fall in returning with the gun, I should probably lose it. I wished I was already wet for an excuse for not bringing the gun; but I only waited a moment before I was nervously edging along the log. I had nearly reached the boat and began to gain courage, when I lost my balance and went feet first in to the ice cold water. I could not swim, and it was some ten feet deep, but I must have caught a branch as I went down, for I went ashore hand over hand alongside the log, in much less time than it takes to tell it. Then all dripping with water I hurried up to camp to tell of my accident, which needed no explanation only that I fell in going instead of coming back with the gun. My brother regarded me a moment with a curious smile and then said: "Well, you stay here and I'll try it." And as the hedgehogs both had taken to a tall spruce tree, I only had to stand and shiver a few moments when my brother came running back with the gun, and aiming at the lower hedgehog, sent a heavy load of No. 2 shot through it, bringing it lifeless to the ground. He instantly cocked the other barrel and threw it to his shoulder, when a thought struck him. Being a kind-hearted fellow, he was going to let me shoot the other one to cheer me up. So loading the barrel already fired, with a lighter charge than was formerly in it, as one of them "old rat charges" would have rolled me in the brush, or caused my head and feet to change places, he handed it to me, put me in a position where I could see my mark which had climbed nearly to the top of the spruce, and said: "now take good aim and I guess you'll fetch him, and don't be afraid of the gun." I accidentally cocked the wrong barrel, and looking as smart as I could, took aim and fired. I lost the fun of seeing the hedgehog come tumbling down through the branches, as I was at that time engaged in extracting myself from an old spruce top. Fortunately my brother watched the gun and saw where it landed. That was the first hedgehog I ever killed, and the first time I was ever laid on my back by the recoil of a gun, but by no means the last time. We got a fire going in camp, and I dried my clothes and was once more comfortable.

That night my brother set his gun close by the berth where we slept, also have a lamp and matches handy. I, being very weary with my day's work, slept soundly, but my brother always slept with his ears at half cock. Along in the night, when I was sleeping soundly, I was terribly startled by a thundering roar from my brother's gun, and as I demanded, "what in the world has happened," he chuckled a moment and then pointed to hedgehog which just filled the hole in the corner of the door, with his had all blown away by the charge of shot. Thus by these and other experiences, I may say my brother, George, first broke me into the realization that a hunter's life was not all cream and honey.

A GOOD BEAR STORY

Anonymous, from *History of Bethel, Maine* by William B. Lapham, 1891

William Berry Lapham (1828-1894), a doctor and historian who was born in Greenwood, Maine, was educated at Gould Academy and Colby College, later attended lectures at the Maine Medical School, Dartmouth College and completed his studies in New York in 1856. After serving in the Civil War, he settled in Bryant Pond, serving that region in the Maine Legislature in 1867. An avid researcher, he moved to Augusta in 1871, from where he published histories of five western Maine towns.When Lapham wrote and published his "History of Bethel" in 1891, he went around to the local farm and families collecting stories from the local farmers. As every good story book must have a "good bear story," he included the following tale, which is evidently true, and which occurred a few miles from Bethel on the side of Puzzle Mountain.

William B. Lapham

It was in the year eighteen hundred and forty-six, on the sixteen day of September that Orrin, son of Enoch Foster, a boy of about sixteen years of age, was sent by his father to look up some cattle which had strayed away from the mountain pasture into the woods. His route took him up the side of Puzzle Mountain, through pasture and forest, and when about two miles from home, he came across a path, which led to a brook. Thinking he had found the path of the lost cattle, he pressed on, and soon heard the sound of some animal in the bushes nearby, and going toward the point from which the sound seemed to proceed, he was surprised and alarmed at the appearance of a huge bear, which, with eyes flashing fire and gnashing teeth, sprang toward him from thicket not three rods away. Foster tried to encourage a small dog which accompanied him to attack the monster, but he cowardly slunk away and hid himself in the bushes. Foster then turned and went about two rods to a sappling beech, which was the only tree in the vicinity and which was about seven inches in diameter at the ground. The body of the tree was smooth, and the lower limbs were about eight feet from the ground. The bear with jaws distended and eyes glowing like fire, was close upon him, and his only chance was in being able to climb the tree. He sprang with all his strength and tried to grasp the lower limbs, but failed, but he seized the trunk of the tree with both his hands and drew his feet up. The bear comprehending his intentions, sprang after him, but happily falling a little short of his aim, he struck at the root of the tree. Foster succeeded in reaching the limbs, and as the bear recovered, he again sprang and raked Foster's foot as he was drawing himself into the lower branches. He came very near drawing Foster down, but with all his strength, he broke away and ascended the tree with the bear in close pursuit. He went up nearly thirty feet from the ground where the tree was so small that he could easily clasp it in his hands, and the bear foaming with rage and disappointment, was about four feet below him. The tree began to bend under the great weight, and Foster tried to balance it, but the bear kept slowly advancing. In this moment of extreme peril, it occurred to Foster to try and shake his pursuer from the tree. Securing his hold with a vice-like clutch, and with all his strength, quickened and increased by the fear of a horrible death, he shook the tree, and the bear being unable to sustain his weight on the underside, fell to the ground. His fall of twenty-five feet momentarily stunned him, but he soon sprang up and made several unsuccessful efforts to re-climb the tree, but each time fell back. While Bruin was trying to climb up a second time, Foster was not idle. Taking out his jack knife, he descended the tree a short distance, and cut off a large limb about five feet long, which he whittled to a point at one end, intending to make an attempt at the bear's eyes, should he succeed in re-climbing the tree. Being foiled in his attempts at climbing, he watched Foster's motions for a few moments and then went for the dog. But the dog was not pleased with Bruin's attentions and kept himself at a safe distance from his bearship and finally left for home. The bear then returned to the foot of the tree and vented his anger in dismal howls and in gnashing his teeth. He would then follow the cattle path for twenty rods or more, and then return to the tree, thinking probably that Foster had availed himself of his absence and had descended from the tree. He tried this ruse again and again, but at last he became discouraged at the prospect of an evening meal in this direction, and about sunset, with a howl that seemed to shake the mountain and reverberate through its dark ravines and caverns, he slowly retired.

When Foster rushed against the beech he bruised his stomach, and after the immediate danger from the bear had passed, his chest began to pain him severely, and he found it was badly swollen. He was without coat, and exposed on the north side of a mountain, to the chilly blasts of an autumn night. He also began to suffer from hunger and thirst, having neither ate or drank since morning. His hands and feet were badly swollen by holding onto the tree, and the blood rushed to his head and throat so as to almost produce delirium. He had called for assistance until his voice had failed him, and after the bear left him, he did not dare to leave the tree, fearing the monster might be lurking near, ready to pounce upon him. This occurred on Sunday, and his parents had attended religious services at some distance from home, and had stopped with a friend to take tea. Returning at night, they found the dog had returned without his master, and from his uneasiness, they felt certain that Orrin had met with some accident and was detained on the mountain. The news quickly spread through the neighborhood and some twenty persons assembled with lanterns and tin trumpets, and with lighted torches. Dividing into small squads, they ascended the mountain, blowing their trumpets and building bonfires, so much of which young Foster from his elevated perch in the treetop, was a silent spectator. But he was so debilitated that he could neither go down from the tree nor make himself heard. It was eleven o'clock when three persons approached the tree, and among them he recognized the voice of his father. The hour of deliverance had come and he was soon in the midst of his friends. After having his limbs chafed for a while, he was able, with the assistance which he received, to descend the mountain and reach his home, but it was more than a year before he was able to perform much labor. To him, his deliverance was like a renewal of life. While the hungry bear was exerting all his strength to reach him, he expected to be torn to pieces, and when the monster left him, death still seemed to hover near him in the fearful forms of cold, hunger and exhaustion. While in the tree, when hope had nearly abandoned him, Foster started the blood from his arm with the point of his knife, and with a pointed stick as pen, and the blood as writing fluid, he inscribed upon his pocket handkerchief the words, "Killed by a bear," and then tied the handkerchief to the tree, that should he never return, his friends might learn of his terrible fate.

REMINISCENCES OF A SPORTSMAN

By Joel Parker Whitney, from *Reminiscences of a Sportsman*, 1906

Joel Parker Whitney

Joel Parker Whitney (1835-1913) left New England at the age of seventeen and traveled to California, where he made a fortune in the hunting market and purchased a sheep ranch in Rocklin, which he built from 320 acres in 1856 to 27,000 acres. He became a powerful and wealthy businessman in the wool and fruit industries and built his mansion, "The Oaks" in Rocklin. An avid traveler, Whitney maintained a lodge at Whitney's Point in Upper Richardson Lake in the Rangeleys, which he would visit several times a year. The house is now gone and the point is a popular camping spot. In his autobiography, Reminiscences of a Sportsman, Whitney recalls his hunting and fishing adventures throughout the United States, particularly hunting in the Rocky Mountains, but relates his adventures in Maine in several chapters.

I came into a deer yard in the winter of 1859–the first winter trip after the fishing excursion–in the early morning with my hunting guide, Nay Bennett, and his mongrel undersized dog–but clever with moose and deer,–and we spent the whole half-day searching for the deer which we had clear evidence were in the yard. It was some two mile long by a mile wide, and indicated the holding of a goodly number by the numerous fresh tracks, twig browsing, and other signs, and though we hunted industriously for it for four or five hours, no deer could we find, and as we had an objective point to reach that night several miles off, we concluded to lunch and push on. So, with a brisk fire, and some made with water from melting snow, and a rasher of broiled salt pork and bread, we relieved our somewhat fatigued legs by a rest.

We had one gun, a half blanket, and some pounds of bread and salt pork, some tea and a small pot and cups, extra thick socks, and a few other incidentals, including a few hooks and lines for catching trout through the ice. We were in a wilderness of forest where we could go a hundred miles or more without seeing a settlement, and were bound for Parmachene Lake, the headwater of the Androscoggin River, some thirty mile distant. What more could we desire than the prospect before us? I was reluctant about giving up further search for the deer, and not joining Nay in his accustomed smoke after eating, I left him to pack up our extensive holdings, with the gun, and follow, and taking a compass line in the direction we were to go, started on accompanied by our canine, which bore the euphonious name of Zip. I was passing out the yard north, when up sprang a dozen deer from their beds in the snow and in mass broke from the yard and down the somewhat steep hill in the direction I was heading. They were soon out of sight, leaving a deep furrow which Nay afterwards said looked as if a loaded cart had gone down there.

There was no time to lose as they should be hard pressed at the start before they could recover from the first fright, and settle down to a steady, moderate pace, or separate. So calling loudly to Nay, uncertain if he could hear me, I hastened on with Zip, who already was about out of sight ahead on the trail. He was a knowing dog, this mongrel Zip, who has served his apprenticeship for some years with Nay, his master being a noted hunter, and fonder of moose and deer hunting and life in the woods than work on the small farm he had at the Magalloway settlement. I was quite light and quick on the snowshoe, and I soon overtook and passed Zip, who occasional slumping in the snow retarded his progress, but gave no cessation of his excited yelping. I soon left him far behind, but had no discouragement in his bones, and afterwards came up in good season.

Not more than half a mile more did I go, before I had the deer in sight ahead; they, being confused and floundering in the deep snow, were still together. Pitiful sight was it not? I think so, but not then, as I was too eager for the killing and fresh meat. But as I came up to them they parted in different directions, as was their habit when close pressed. Hastily selecting the largest of the herd for my particular attention, and holding as best I could only until he came up, I pressed him to bay, for he could not make progress equal to mine, so he beat down the snow about him and faced me, and I was holding him when Zip arrived full of fury and yelping.

My quarry upon this broke off again, when Zip, with still more frightful yelps, fastened momentarily on the rear, letting go in season to avoid the front-foot stride so habitual with the deer at close quarters. A dog of this character is more efficient with moose and deer at bay, and in face with bear or other large animals belonging to the dangerous class, than a large and courageous one depending upon his power untaught by experience, which often occasions his sudden exit from the scene, and consequent peril to his master.

I noted lately an account of the escape of a hunter in the mountains from a wounded grizzly bear by the active distracting work of a fox-terrier which accompanied him.

All the rest of the deer had broken away out of sight, and I saw no difficulty in holding mine until Nay should come up with the gun. But he was slow in arriving, and my buck kept moving along, and I kept after him, impeding him with Zip as much as possible, which worked him up into a great fury in which he would charge at his tormentor with a hissing sound, striking at him with his feet, which Zip managed to keep well clear of, but came very near being trodden under several times owing to the broken snow, which troubled him as much as the buck.

I worked up pretty closely with my cheering on, but thought prudent to have my long-bladed knife in hand in case I should receive a charge, and sure enough it came rather unexpectedly, and so suddenly that in my haste to avoid it, I locked my snowshoes and came down in a heap with the buck on top of me, but whose sharp feet I managed to avoid as he came down. Zip managed to get in on the rear, but I lost sight of him in the flurry, and had no way to avoid an up-and-down churning, excepting to throw my arms up over the neck of the deer, still retaining my knife in my hand. In this situation I was lifted up and down very quickly several times with no ability to use my knife, and I saw that something would have to result very shortly, or I should be *hors de combat*, as my weight and strength seemed of slight avail in contrast with the apparently increasing strength of my adversary, who was hissing with fright and rage and whom I would have been glad to cry quits with, if I could only have been relieved from him. But the combat ended in a moment. I managed with my left arm hooked over the neck as I came down to get a handful of hair and skin, to hold at, and support my weight, and as quickly liberated my right arm and hand, and thrust my knife to the hilt in the chest of the deer at the neck. It was a lucky thrust, splitting the windpipe and heart, and we came down together, but I had to turn in the snow to avoid the ruddy flow from the nostrils of my dying victim. I had now to find if I had received any injury, and found I had but a few scratches to show, though my snowshoes had more serious damages, requiring more or less patching up during the balance of the trip.

When Nay came up we dressed and hung up the buck after taking a few choice strips for present use, and the deer remained for ten days or so frozen. Being but a few miles from a logging camp, we had the buck afterwards dragged out by the camp tote-sled, and on to the Megalloway settlement to take back with us, and its weight dressed up was one hundred and eighty-seven pounds.

Upon another occasion I killed with the same knife a still larger buck which came suddenly upon me in the snow when wounded. We pushed on for Parmachene Lake at the headwaters of the Androscoggin area of drainage, being situated near the Canada line twenty-five miles from the Megalloway River settlement, passing nearly two weeks on this my first snowshoe excursion to that region, which I was so much delighted with that I made four more excursions to the same region in the following winters with the same guide, meeting with many adventures and minor experiences too numerous to give much mention of at this time. These were made in the months of February and March, when the snow was from four to seven feet deep on the level, and when the conditions were favorable for securing large game.

Chapter 2

THE RANGELEY LAKES

One of the earliest views of the Rangeley Lakes was made by Ephraim Ballard, a surveyor from Hallowell, who in the summer of 1794 made a survey line, establishing the south line of Redington, Dallas and Rangeley townships. Starting at the end of Mt. Abram Township, he worked his way west over the summit of Saddleback Mountain, which he named in his report, and dropped "144 rods down to a lake, one mile across." This was Rangeley Lake, originally called Oquossuc Lake, for the blue-backed trout found there, but currently had no known name. Continuing west, he came to another unnamed lake, which was Mooselucmeguntic. Squire Rangeley, for whom the lake was named, did not arrive for another twenty-five years.

In the fledgling town of Phillips in 1813 a sudden cry of an Indian attack aroused the settlers. Wagons came in from the surrounding areas, loaded with families, people rushed from their homes and everyone made their way to the top of a hill, where they made the summit house of Elder Wilbur into a makeshift garrison, and the boys dug a make-shift trench. It was later ascertained that the alarm had been given by an individual who only wished to elude a sheriff who had come to apprehend him.

In 1839 Josiah S. Swift, a minister and farmer from Madrid, who later became editor of some of Farmington's first newspapers, ascended Saddleback Mountain and left us with a complete narrative of his journey.

Having removed to Maine from Roxbury, Massachusetts,

Joshua G. Rich made his first trip to Rangeley Lake in August of 1843. He and his brother-in-law, Fairfield Golder of Strong, "put up at Haley's and procured a boat. We were directed to South Bog Stream...We found the brook full of trout which would average a pound each, some nearly two pounds..." The next winter Rich went back to Rangeley Lake, accompanied by Mr. Allen, a merchant of Boston. "So we tramped over the ice to South Bog, dragging a hand-sled with supplies for a regular siege. We however only found enough trout to eat." On their return trip they got lost in trip a blinding snowstorm, wandered around for a day without sighting land, and finally found the small house of Mr. Frazier. This was the old trapper's first camping trip. He later moved to Upton, where in 1866 he operated a store, and was "killing more bears than any other man living in the State."

In January 1846 an anonymous writer gave a description of Indian Rock, which sits at the convergence of the Rangeley and Kennebago Rivers, and which was named for the St. Francis tribe that had previously hunted and camped in that region. He found that the ledge, which jutted out into the lake, was fast becoming celebrated as a great trout fishing spot, and that boats were kept there to accommodate the anglers who were coming from afar to enjoy the marvelous fishing prospects. If you take a boat up the Kennebago a short distance, around a bend, to a neck of land that jutted out into the river, this was the site of the Indian Burial Ground. Later an old hermit named Smith camped there, and sold out to Mr. C. T. Richardson, who built a rough camp for the accommodation of fishermen. Richardson sold it to the newly-formed Oquossuc Angling Club, who built a much larger camp, and hired him as their first superintendent.

Two months later two wildcats were captured in Weld, and were so ferocious that they could not be kept together. Subsequently one was killed, and the other, which measured three feet in length and twenty-two inches in height, was put on exhibit in Portland.

By 1847 there were two hotels at Phillips, one, operated by Mr.

D. Howard, and the other recently purchased by George Toothaker. A tri-weekly stage connected the valley to Farmington. In 1853 F. V. Steward established a new stage line that ran through Avon, Strong, Farmington, Wilton and Jay.

One of the first description of sporting at Rangeley was written by Zenas T. Haines of Phillips, when he took a trip to the lakes in August of 1850. Calling Rangeley Lake, "Ocwossuck," they rowed over to South Bog Stream, then over to the "old supply road, extending from this, to the lake below. This road was cut for the use of the logging companies, and over it was formerly transported their hay and provisions. For many years it has not been used, and at present, on nearly it entire length, it supports a luxuriant mass of blueberry bushes." The following year Haines reported that three or men had "just returned from the region of the Cupsuptuck and Kennebago, having killed six moose and one deer, within the past week."

In 1869 the Franklin Chronicle reported that there was a great rush of sportsmen to the Rangeley Lakes, and that Barden's Hotel in Phillips "is crowded every night, with parties from Boston and New York...a party of three came out Monday, bringing with them 200 lbs. of trout."

The next winter, Abner Toothaker and Company employed men to cut and land logs for $3.00 to $4.00 per thousand. They were scheduled to cut some ten million square feet, and run them down the lake and river to Berlin, and other places on the Androscoggin River.

The summer of 1870 saw a large destruction made by wildfires. It was so windy, that fires were multiplying by the hour. By four o'clock the large fire that stretched from Rangeley City four or five miles north to Spotted Mountain, met another fire, which was working its way down from Dead River. Sweeping down through Dallas Plantation, the inhabitants had to flee the smoke and lost many homes. At eight that evening thunderstorms began, saving the region from more destruction.

The Oquossuc Angling Club, which was formed by George

Shephard Page and other men of New York, New Jersey, Philadelphia and Massachusetts about 1865, was incorporated February 15, 1870. They built Camp Kennebago near Indian Rock, which became one of the first hostelries on the Rangeley Lakes. Page, along with I. N Crounse and H. M. Hutchinson, lease two townships from the lumbermen, and built Camp Bema on the eastern shore of Mooselucmeguntic Lake, two miles from the outlet of Bemis Stream.

In July of 1873 five men were out on Haley's Pond at Rangeley in a sail boat. By some means the boat capsized and two drowned, the other three making it to the shore.

The ice was still thick on Rangeley Lake, that on May 12, 1875, a six-ox team loaded with boards, was driven across the lake.

George Soule, who was considered the oldest trapper in Rangeley, had a small house on Rangeley Lake, from which he guided many of the early sportsmen. This building was later purchased by H. T. Kimball, proprietor of the Greenvale House, who erected the Mountain House in 1875 and attached Soule's cottage to the end of the hotel.

TROUT FISHING IN MAINE

By D. H. E., from *The American Sportsman*, April 2, 1873

 *Kennebago Lake, which means "long lake" or "large lake," in Abnaki, is a long slender lake lying due north of Rangeley about ten miles distant. In the 1860's the few sportsmen who visited this lake had to pack everything in on foot and camp out as there were no cabins or lodges to be had. This was a small inconvenience for the hearty sportsmen as the good fishing was just reward.*

It was in the middle of September, 1863, when being worn out with business, and tired of the turmoil of the carriage shop, myself and three companions, all genial good fellows and true disciples of "old Izaak" started for a two week's cruise among the wild woods of Maine. We had determined to break away from the usual haunts of sportsmen, and make our camp where the foot of man seldom trod, and where the lazy sportsman would not be likely to find us.

We selected for our rendezvous Lake Kennebago, a beautiful sheet of water situated some twelve miles from the settlements, and right in the heart of the vast forest and mountain region that separates us from the Canadian frontier.

We left the city of P– without regret by noon train to Farmington, thence by stage to Phillips, a charming country village, nestled down among the hills. Resting here for the night, we took an early start in the morning in a vehicle drawn by one horse–did I say? Well, "Don Quixote's" Rosinante was a beauty to him. But he proved a great deal better than he looked, and dashed away over hill and down dale in a manner that would have put Peerless to shame, and caused envious feelings in the bosom of the owner of that famous steed. All we could do was to hold on and let him go. O, the exhilarating effects of the ride in the clear morning air; the trees were just donning their autumnal dress of russet brown and gold, and the dark green of the fern and hemlock formed a striking background for the picture. But Rosinante dashed swiftly on and gave us but little time to study nature or indulge in sentiment. And in less than six hours after leaving the village of Phillips we had reached the remotest bounds of the settlement. Quickly dispatching our dinner, we made ready our packs for a start into the woods, being determined to sleep no more, for the present, beneath the roof of civilization.

Guns and fishing rods, frying pan and kettle, hard bread, coffee, pork and beans, etc., all of which we had provided before leaving home, we soon made up into snug packs, and having engaged a pack horse, the traps were stowed in position and we started. In a few minutes we had crossed the opening that separated us from the woods and struck the "tote path" or trail that led to John's Pond, nine miles distant, and upon the shore of which we intended to camp for the night.

I will not describe the tramp. The rough, narrow trail crossed two mountains, winding its way up their steep sides and thence down again in the valley, making hard traveling for man and beast.

Once our poor horse slipped and rolled completely over, and all hands had to be piped to the rescue, and the packs removed before we could establish him on firm footing again, a little worse for the wear. However, we must push on, as the sun was beginning to sink below the tree tops, and we had yet three miles to make before reaching the shore of the lake. We had now reached the top of the last mountain, and from thence to the lake it was all descending ground. This was soon gone over after some grand and lofty tumbling by some of the party, which would have done credit to the Hanlon Brothers. Our canine friend, Jack, came in for his share of duty and succeeded in flushing a fine covey of partridge, five of which were quickly brought to grief; and when our camping ground was reached we were well provided with game for supper.

One of our party was pretty used up by this time with the hard travelling, and the medicine chest as brought forth and its contents examined, and thimble-full of "Extractus cannabis," prescribed the medicine man. Its effects were truly astonishing, and it was voted that the same dose be taken all around. No sooner said than done and then all hands turned to, to making preparations for the night.

The first business was to make a fire, it being the main comfort of the camp, whether in summer or winter. It is liked as well for its cheerfulness as for warmth and dryness. We soon felled some large trees, which stood convenient to our intended camp ground, and quickly had a nice fire in progress.

We next proceeded to build a brush camp or hut. This was done by planting some stakes firmly in the ground, and placing a pole across these, then some more poles extending back from this with one end resting on the ground, forming the rafters. These we covered with the branches of the hemlock and the house was completed. Then we made our bed. The small twigs of hemlock and fir were selected and carefully laid up as one would shingle a house, the butt or twig being covered by each next layer, these we piled up to the depth of eight or ten inches at the head, and sloped down to the foot, making a very fragrant and soft bed.

While this was in progress the Dutchman was preparing supper, and when all was ready we gathered round the festive board (said board consisted of a hemlock log) and partook of broiled partridge, fried pork, brown bread, and coffee; and our appetites well sharpened with our unusual exertions, did ample justice to the supper. The cook was voted "shuts so good a feller as never was." A short pull at the "dudeen" followed our repast, the fire was replenished with some huge logs, and being too tired and sleepy for storytelling, our blankets were brought out, and one by one we rolled ourselves up in them, feet to the fire, and were soon oblivious to everything around us.

How long I slept I know not, but when I awoke the fire had burned low, and one of my companions was up to replenish it. I lay and watched his shadowy form, now suddenly appearing from out of the darkness as he brought fresh fuel, which, thrown upon

the smoldering embers sent up showers of sparks, then disappeared again in the gloom of the forest like some phantom. The
somber stillness of the night was broken only by the hoot, hoot
of the solitary owl, and watching the stars peep down through
the branches of the trees, I gradually lost myself and when I next
awoke the day was breaking. Rousing my still sleeping companions, we made our toilet at the lake and then prepared our breakfast. This partaken of we discharge our guide and pack horse, and
cut loose from all that was civil or civilized, being determined to
go the whole thing alone.

The pond must next be crossed and a raft made for that purpose. This was soon done from logs we found lying on the shore,
left there in the spring when the water was high. We rolled several
of these together and bound them securely, then placed some
boughs on top for a flooring to put our traps on. All being in
readiness, we embarked and pushed out into the lake, which lay
spread out before us like a huge mirror, reflecting in its clear,
sparkling bottom, the surrounding mountains and forest, making
it seem as though we looked upon another world, the counterpart
of the one we were in.

The morning air was sharp and bracing, and the sun just
showing his beams above the mountain tops in the direction we
had traveled, and as we slowly paddled along, we raised our voices
in song, and made the mountains ring and echo back again in joyful notes.

Nearly one hour was passed in accomplishing this delightful
part of the journey, after some little delay in finding the proper
landing place, we disembarked, made our raft fast in a safe place
to be ready for our return, and shouldering our packs, we pushed
boldly into the woods in the direction of the Kennebago lake, two
miles distant.

Each man's pack weighed about one hundred pounds, beside
gun, rod and equipments, and we started off quite cheerily. Before
our first half mile was gone over my pack felt as thigh I had two
hundred pounds in it and at the end of the first mile I felt sure I

had enough there to supply a small army. But onward we pushed, the packs growing almost unbearable, and the travelling rougher, until the tote path turned up the side of a hill, and seemed to lose itself in a tangled mass of fallen trees and brush and thick under-growth. Breaking through this, we found ourselves on the top of a hill, and there, at our feet, lay the longed for haven of rest. There was the log hut that was to be our home for a while, and further on was the lake and the stream just visible through the trees, while the huge mountains in the back ground showed the dividing line between us and the Canadas

This picture was greeted with three cheers and a "tiger," that must have made the denizens of that region think a menagerie had broken loose. We hastened forward to camp, and depositing our packs, a short rest was taken the "pipe of peace" was freely passed around. Then the rods were brought out and put together, the flies overhauled and carefully selected, and part of the compa-ny went down to the stream to try their luck for trout. I remained to fix up camp and get things in shape for the night; this occupied some time, and when it had grown dusk I thought I would go down to the stream and try my luck. Putting together my fly rod (weighing 12 oz., that had done me good service on former excur-sions) I selected for my fly, a white miller, as being adapted to the twilight and season of the year. .

A few rods from the cap as a log bridge across the stream, and thither I went as the most favorable place for fishing. The pool was still and deep, and clearing my line, with a long sweep well back, and quickly turning forward, I sent the fly full thirty feet from where I stood, before it struck the water. Scarcely had it done so, when with a plunge that sent the blood quickening through my veins, a noble trout rose to it. A sharp, quick turn of my wrist, and I felt that I had struck him, and prepared for what was to follow.

For one second of time he remained motionless; then with the swiftness of the wind he darted down stream. I let him go until I found my line was fast running short, and his pace was slack-ing a little; than I gently check and gradually tuned him towards me, at the same time keeping him well in hand and reeling up my line as he advanced. When within fifty feet of me he started with the speed of a bullet from a rifle, directly for the bridge upon which I was standing, intending to go under it. Should he do this, I feared he was lost to me. Quickly divining his purpose, I put on the check, and now came the tug of war. My rod bent nearly double, until I could easily take the tip on one hand while still holding the butt in the other. My line was of the best Irish linen, my leader of the whitest of gut, and my fly new and strong. Would they hold the strain?

It was a moment of intense excitement. Was I to lose him? Slowly the flexible rod began to spring back, the pressure and strain upon my arm and wrist relaxed, and I knew he was giving way and would turn down stream again. I was ready with him, as with a plunge he started in his career. Again I checked and turned him; this time before he had run off seventy-five feet of line, and as I gently led him towards me I saw that he was beginning to feel the effects of my efforts in his behalf, but I well knew that I was to have one more trying time before I conquered him. He turned on one side and I could dimly see his glistening form, then with a desperate plunge, he went straight to the bottom of the pool and gave a few sudden jerks at the line; then as quick as a flash of light, he reappeared and commenced a series of evolutions, that called all my skill in requisition,–throwing himself his length out of water and lashing with his tail, endeavoring to catch a bight in the line and break it or unhook it. Such tumbling could not last long, and indeed proved to be the final struggle of this game fish, and as I found myself the victor, I breathed freer. Slowly I led him to the bank, where he was skillfully netted by one of my companions and landed.

A noble fish he was, and as game a one as it had been my fortune to kill. 'He had fought a good fight,' but to man belonged the victory. His length was 19 1-2 inches, and he weighed 3 1-2 pounds. Darkness was now fairly settled down upon us, and well satisfied, we returned to camp for supper and rest.

This was the commencement of rare sport, and many such noble trout graced our table, cooked all the various ways that we could devise. For one week we wandered up and down the streams, rod in hand, in pursuit of this most beautiful of fish. Well do I remember a dark, deep pool at the foot of the rapids, some half mile below camp, where in one short hour we landed six trout weighing a total of twenty-one lbs.

But all such things must have an end, and so one rainy morning we picked up our traps and turned backs on one of the pleasantest places it has ever my lot to see. A long day's tramp and the settlement was reached, the gun and rod laid aside, and we were ready again to commence our labor in the carriage shop with renewed health and strength.

– FROM THE HUB.

TWO HOURS ON RANGELEY RIVER

By Thomas S. Steele, from *Forest and Stream*, August 6, 1874

Returning to Rangeley for another summer vacation, Thomas Sedgewick Steele (1845-1903) once again pursued his hobby of fly-fishing. This time he fished in the Rangeley River, a short river that connects Rangeley and Mooselucmeguntic Lakes, relating how he caught the big one. Later he took trips to northern Maine and illustrated his books, "Paddle and Portage" and "Canoe and Camera," with many etchings he made while on the trip.Steele retired from jewelry work in 1875 and began painting, almost

Thomas Sedgewick
Steele

ruining his eyes by painting by gaslight. His paintings were featured at the National Academy of design in 1877 and later at the Union League Club of New York City. He was also elected to the Boston Art Club and had his celebrated trout painting "Net Results" etched by a local publishing company in that city. His still life entitled "Day's Catch," became a popular painting and hung in many of the parlors and club halls of fishermen throughout the northeast.

It would be impossible to say that the weather selected for my ramble along the banks of Rangeley River, Maine, was all that could have been desired. Those beautiful mornings, described by writers, do not always fall to the lot of every angler, and when camping in the woods it often seems as if it "never rained but it poured," and that a greater portion of the time. Great heavy clouds of vapor hung down the mountain sides almost concealing them from view, while heavy showers of rain accompanied by thunder and lightning, would strike our camp, carrying away all that was moveable along with it.

So the morning and the first part of the afternoon had been occupied in cleaning my gun and putting numerous other traps in order, but at four o'clock the storm having abated, I called my guide, and buckling on my invincible "Mackintosh wading pants," we strolled up the stream.

We found "Indian Eddy" was as well patronized as usual, and at that time many a speckled beauty was leaving its ripples to be soon transferred to the caufs dancing attendance at the stern of the boats. So on we pushed, occasionally taking fish, until we reached a certain position on the stream. Oh! Shall I whisper where? I well know the object of the FOREST AND STREAM is to give the location of good fishing resorts, but a description of each stone and tree is seldom resorted to. Suffice it to say, that is was beside a certain overhanging bank, near a certain number of handsome fir trees, and that an old dead stump around which you can just clasp your arms, reflects itself in the stream, and furthermore, that said stream at this time, in June, is about four feet deep; and if by this description you can discover my secret, you are welcome.

Getting to the lee of a "smudge," built by the guide to get rid of the angler's pests, the black flies, whose supply always more than equals the demand, I fastened to my line the most tempting treasures from my fly book, and made a cast far over the shining waters. Thinking the flies did not alight on the water to my satisfaction, I was about making a back cast when a gleam of silver far down under the dark waters, a rush, a splash on the surface, and the next moment my stretcher fly was fast in a pound trout. Placing my finger on the line above the reel, I realized he was firmly hooked, and I prepared myself for the battle which was sure to follow. A pound trout is not much to handle with plenty of room, but take overhanging boughs, a slippery bank and a wild rushing river, and the odds are frequently in favor of this fish.

The Rangeley River flows from the Rangeley Lake, which is ten miles long, through the woods a distance of two miles, and empties itself into the Mooselucmaguntic Lake, another large body of water some twelve miles long by four miles wide, and with such velocity that in the spring, at which time this incident occurred, it was with difficulty you could maintain your foothold when only a short depth in the water. Many an angler has mistaken its hidden force, and while wading that stream capsized in its turbulent waters and risen to the surface "a sadder but wiser man." So, with the fish tugging away at my line, (as a trout only knows how,) it required great skill and careful management not to lose him, or be upset myself. A few wild rushes up and down the stream, occasionally showing his gleaming sides near the surface of the water, bending my eight-ounce rod as if it were a twig, and with mouth wide open, he soon lay exhausted on the bank. Then another cast, and another fish of about the same proportions, followed by others still of 1 1/4, 1 1/2 and 2 pounds each, my flies hardly touching the foaming surface before they were eagerly taken by the voracious fish. Sometimes two and three would spring for the enticing flies at the same time, and my past ideas of the delicate sense of a trout was badly shocked by their selfish exhibitions of character. For two hours, the shortest I ever experienced, these trout kept me busy, and sometimes when giving them the first blow, bending my split bamboo three feet below the butt, while my faithful guide stood at my side, net in hand, transferring the fish to the cauf as fast as possible. You who take no zest in outdoor sports, or rambles by forest and stream, and think with the old adage "that angling is merely a stick and a string with a fish at one end and a fool at the other," what wouldn't I have given to have placed you suddenly in my position, and if the blood in your veins didn't course more freely after such excitement, then you must be as dead to all enjoyment as the Egyptian mummies in the museum at Niagara Falls. But as "all thing have an end" so did these joyous moments, which were finally brought to a close in a more hasty manner than I anticipated.

For the last ten minutes the trout had ceased to rise, and we had concluded that we had either exhausted the pool, or by repeated casts had frightened them away, (for we had not moved three feet from our first position during the whole time,) when letting my flies float slowly under the big stump, I was immediately reminded that one fish at least was left to tell the story. Taking the fly greedily, as if he meant business, he dashed up the stream with lightning speed. Checking him in his wild career by "giving him the butt," I succeeded in turning his head towards me, when away he went backwards and forwards across the stream, (which is some twenty feet wide,) and then down in to the most turbulent and rapid of the water, making my reel hum like a buzz saw. Now I tried to hold him a little, which brought the tip of the rod at the water's surface; now he would sulk under some mossy bank or overhanging rock, from which I was obliged to rouse him, until finally he dashed for the middle of the stream, where he wound the line around and around an immense boulder. Plunging into the water up to my waist, I roused him from his fortress, when away he started down stream around a curve in the river, dragging my line through the alders and brush which lined the water's edge, while over the slippery stones and through numerous holes I followed till he had exhausted over one hundred feet of my line. Then I finally succeeded in stopping him, but against the wild rushing water, which boiled around me, I could only hold him. The guide now hastened to my side, and held my rod, which following the line through the middle of the stream I held it firmly half way between the guide and trout. Guide then reeled up the line to where I stood, and handed me the rod, and I congratulated myself on having gained fifty feet. But it was only a moment, for I again started the fish, and away he dashed down the stream, carrying with him the fifty feet of line I had just gained. I was now determined to net him at all hazards, and "giving him the butt again" I brought him to bay. My guide now went ashore, and with net in hand, disappeared among the bushes to look up his lordship's headquarters, while I followed carefully down stream, full of anxiety and suspense. Some time after the slackness of the line told me I had either lost the prize or "William" had secured him for me; the line was free, at all events, and I patiently waited the result. Finally, to my delight, the guide appeared, triumphantly bearing the net with my treasure safely secured in its meshes. He had captured him over one hundred feet from where he left me. The trout turned the scales at 2 ½ lbs., and was one of the finest specimens of the *salmo fontinalis*, as regards color and proportions, that I ever landed. We reached camp at 6 ½ o'clock, P.M., having been absent only two-and-a-half hours of which I was occupied in going and returning from camp.

Throwing back into the water a number of the smaller fish, we weighed the remainder, which numbered forty-eight, and they turned the scale at fifty-six pounds. Since that day I had caught my two, three or even six pound brook trout, and have experienced a variety of emotions while enjoying their capture, but I look back to the time when I landed with an eight-ounce rod, forty-eight trout weighing fifty-six pounds in two hours' fishing, as the most successful day in my whole experienced.

THE RICHARDSON LAKES IN WINTER

By Nedlam, from *Forest and Stream*, March 7, 1878

Charles A. J. Farrar

This story, which was penned by Capt. A. J. Farrar (1842-1893), a man who grew up in Edgecomb, Maine, then moved to Cambridge, Mass., where he worked under the tutelage of his uncle, a newspaper publisher. An avid sportsman, Capt. Farrar often visited the Rangeley Lake region and soon purchased a steamboat and small house at the South Arm of Lower Richardson Lake, from which he carried goods and people to Middle Dam Camps, Whitney's Camp and Upper Dam as well as to the many private camps on Upper Richardson. It was from this venture that he acquired the title of Captain. Winters were spent at his home in Jamaica Plain, creating new books, guides and maps, as well as updated editions. Summers were spent at the Rangeley Lakes. This article offers detailed information about J. Parker Whitney's many annual trips to the Rangeley lakes. It also offers precise information on Whitney's Camp on Mollechunkamunk, or Upper Richardson Lake. Interestingly, it also reminds us how uniformed they were in those early years, mentioning that the two mountains seen from the camp are over 4,000 feet above sea level, when Observatory Mountain is actually only 2,515 feet, and its higher neighbor, Mount Aziscohos is only 3,186 feet.

Our party consisted of Merrs. P. Adams Ames, one of the proprietors of Camp Whitney, H. P. De Graf, of New York, and myself. One Thursday morning early in December we left Andover for the lakes. Our team consisted of three horses and a bob-sled, driven by Charlie Cushman, who was bound to see us on our way. Milton Cushing, one of the oldest and most experienced of the Andover guides, had been sent ahead to find out the condition of the ice. The lake road was in fair condition, and we reached the Arm about noon. Here we met Milton, who reported that he had been up the lake a mile, and that there was ice as far as he could see. We congratulated ourselves on our good luck, and after lunch drove out on the ice. It cracked considerably when the horses began to trot, it being not over four or five inches thick. But, proceeding carefully, Charlie drove up about a mile and a quarter, just beyond Bailey's Point, and there left us. A little way beyond the ice was thinner, and although safe for foot travel, was dangerous for a team. We had a couple of hand-sleds, and upon these we loaded our traps and pushed valiantly forward, two men to a sled, while the guide went before, ax in hand, trying the ice. Reaching the foot of Spirit Island, we found that beyond it the lake was open from shore to shore, and there was no farther progress without a boat, unless we made a *cache* of our things and took to the woods where we would have the roughest kind of traveling. It was determined to return to the Arm and stay overnight in the camp there, a small frame shanty, but vastly superior to a brush camp. We left the things we did not need on the shore of the lake, and in a blinding storm, made our way back to camp. Luckily for us, the store of wood that I had kept for the steamer was piled up within a few rods of the camp, and we had the guide bring us in a generous supply.

A true sportsman is always a philosopher, and we made the best of the situation. The most that troubled us was the rapidly fading daylight, for the prospect was that we would eat our supper in the dark. But even this little difficulty was removed; for Ames suddenly started to his feet with the air of a man who means business, and commenced exploring the hidden recesses of his traveling-bag. Now, that bag was a peculiar one—almost equal to Aladdin's lamp, and its supplies were apparently inexhaustible. After turning over the few thousand things it contained, he at last produced a wax taper about four inches long. He told us that he had bought the candle some fifteen years before in Europe. It had been in his bag ever since, and had traveled thousands of miles with him. A dozen times he had been tempted to throw it away, but some good genius had prevented. And now the time had come for its use. After traveling half around the world, it was doomed to be burned in a little hut in the wilds of Maine, to furnish light for our first supper in the woods, proving beyond a doubt how much better it is to save a useful article than consign it to wanton destruction.

The candle gave up the ghost early in the evening, a gentle hint for us to retire, and each one of us crawled into a bunk, and lay, not upon a bed of down, but down upon a bed of limbs about the size of average cord wood. We covered ourselves with our overcoats, and told Milton his life was forfeit if the fire went out during the night.

The wind had now blown a hurricane, and found its way into the camp through numerous cracks and crevices, chilling us through and through. With the earliest dawn we sent Milton to Andover to have Cushman bring on some more supplies and blankets. After he had gone we divided what was left of the provisions into four equal parts, each one taking his share. We had really come down to an allowance.

The windstorm continued all day, and it was so rough that we stopped in camp and kept warm. It was quarter of seven before we heard the welcome sound of the sleigh-bells, and it being dark as a pocket in camp, the first article we called for was candles! And several were lit at once. Then followed oysters, beefsteak, bread, coffee, tea, milk, sugar, etc., and we soon sat down to supper. In the morning, everything being ready for a fresh start, we rode down and found that the lake, which was open the day before, was now frozen over. We packed upon the two hand-sleds all they could carry and sent two men ahead to try the ice, while the others followed behind with the sleds. I offered to draw one and Milton took the other, while Whitney and Ames went ahead with the ax, sounding the ice. In this order we left Spirit Island, keeping near the eastern shore of the lake, and creeping carefully along on our moccasins, as the ice was very thin.

It was a beautiful morning, clear, frosty, sparkling, and was perfectly calm, with the thermometer only two degrees below zero. The scene before us was magnificent; the glassy surface of the lake, the snow-covered mountains, the dark firs on the hillside, the gnarled and twisted cedars by the shore, and even the huge boulders on the points, all combining to make the picture.

As we neared Hard Scrabble we found the ice growing thinner and thinner, but it was wonderfully tough and elastic, bearing us up, although it cracked in every direction as we passed along, sometimes buckling an inch or more under us, and I expected every moment to go through. It was as clear as crystal, and being only three-quarters of an inch thick we could see through it as one would a window-pane, and see every grain of sand, every pebble, and every weed with the utmost distinctness.

Reaching the point we found the ice broken up a little near the shore, and we had to take to the rocks. We fastened long lines to the sleds, and then with poles pushed them farther out on the lake, where the ice still remained whole. Crawling along the ice-covered rocks that formed the line of the shore, I dragged the sleds, while the guide kept them out with a pole. It was slow work, but we stuck to it and made about half a mile above Hard Scrabble, where we took to the ice again. We went on for half a mile further, and then were brought to a standstill by a ripping, crashing and cracking that sounded like salvos of artillery.

Looking in the direction of the sound we beheld a singular sight. The ice at the eastern shore had commenced bulging up, and arose to the height of a foot or more above the water, forming a reef that in a few moments had extended entirely across the lake. We stood and watched it as it was hove up, snapping, cracking and breaking, rumbling and thundering, until at last it settled back to the level of the field ice, leaving an open channel from shore to shore some twenty feet in width. A half-mile above we noticed a second open channel, also extending the entire distance across the lake, and beyond that another that reached about half way across. Between the lower and upper channels, a distance of about a mile, the ice had also broken away from the shore, leaving an open passage all the way some twenty feet in width.

Here was a dilemma, the firm ice being too far from the shore to drag the sleds upon, even with the aid of our lines and poles, with the shore for the next mile above us, was lines with huge boulders, fallen trees, and a *debris* of broken ice and driftwood. To drag the sleds loaded over such obstructions was simply impossible, while if we unloaded and carried the things along the shore to the firm ice, a mile or more beyond, there would not be the slightest possibility of reaching camp that night, as we should be obliged to make several trips if we undertook a portage. I thought best, therefore, to cache the traps where we were, and after doing this in the best manner possible, we took lunch, had a smoke, and proceeded on our way.

About three-quarters of a mile below the Narrows we reached old ice, several inches in thickness, and across this we pursued our way with increased speed. The snow on the ice was soft, and had drifted to a depth of nearly a foot in some places, making the walking very hard. When we reached Metalic Point I was surprised to find the upper lake frozen over, with the exception of a little strip extending from the mouth of the river to the half-way point, and reaching into the lake about a mile.

The exercise in the morning of putting the sleds around rocky point and broken ice, combined with the long tramp, had begun to tell upon me, and I walked considerably slower than I had in the early part of the day. I longed earnestly for a sight of the camp, and finally I saw its hospitable roof looming up before us, the smoke curling gracefully from the chimney.

In a few moments more I was welcomed by my fellow voyagers, and was soon resting before the large open fireplace in the sitting-room exchanging our adventures. They had both broken through the ice and had reached the camp in a soaked condition. About six o'clock we sat down to one of Capt. Cole's excellent dinners, and after dinner, around the huge fireplace in which mammoth four-foot logs were merrily blazing, sending out snapping embers on the hearth, we enjoyed our cigars and pipes, recounted the incidents of the day, and laid our plans for the future.

Camp Whitney, which I consider a model camp in every sense of the word, occupied a lovely site on the eastern shore of Lake Mollechunkamunk, near the mouth of Mosquito Brook, in the immediate vicinity of excellent fishing grounds. It fronts the lake and sits about eight rods from the shore. The whole upper part of the lake is visible, with its winding and irregular shores.

The house overlooks Observatory and Aziscohos, two mountains of remarkable symmetry at the head of the lake, forming a barrier between it and the Magalloway River. Observatory is a sugar-loaf peak, rising to a height of some 4,000 feet above the sea, and is heavily wooded to the top. On the northeast it sweeps down to the Upper Richardson Pond. Aziscohos, which is several hundred feet higher than its neighbor, lies a little southwest of it, and has two peaks about a mile apart, with quite a depression between them. It is a grand old landmark, visible from almost any part of the lake region, and overlooking the whole of this section of the country. Several persons who have made the ascent of both mountains, declare that it commands a finer view than Mount Washington. Eastward it descends toward the lake, while on the west its base is washed by the wild and turbulent Magalloway. Through and beyond this valley, between Aziscohos and Observatory, several mountains appear Bennett and Emery's Misery attaining the most prominence.

Opposite the camp, on the western shore, a range of wooded hills, of no mean pretensions as to height, sweep away to the south. Southwest the view is enhanced by two little islets–Ship Island, so called from three old pines that grow upon it, suggesting the masts of a vessel, and Half-Moon Island, crescent shape in form. South one can scan the lake to the Narrows, where the silvery waters disappear, lost in the emerald green of the forest. Beyond the foothills the greater part of the White Mountain range appears walled against the sky; Washington, Jefferson, and Adams being easily distinguished from the other peaks–sharp, clear, and well defined. From our piazza with an ordinary glass the buildings upon the summit of Mount Washington may be distinctly seen, and in some of the extraordinary clear days of late June they were visible to the naked eye, although forty miles distant, an indication of the wonderful rarity of the atmosphere.

Camp Whitney is thirty by fifty feet on the ground, two stores and a half in height, and covered with a pitch roof. An eight-foot wide piazza, with its sloping roof, extends the entire distance in front, and furnishes a delightful place for lounging.

Indoors, on the lower floor, in front is the sitting and dining room combined, a generous apartment over twenty-eight feet square. A space of five feet wide, directly back of the sitting room, is divided into a closet, a pantry, and stairway leading to the chambers on the second floor, all of which are accessible from the sitting room. The kitchen takes up the balance of the ground floor. There is an excellent cellar. On the north side of the sitting-room is an enormous brick fireplace that will take in at one mouthful a good half cord of wood. The room is filled with comfortable, and what in some cases might be termed luxurious furniture for a camp in the back woods; one of its chiefest charms in my eyes being a well-filled library, containing, besides works of fiction, travel and adventure, all of the best known books on sporting matters. Over the fireplace is a rack made of deer's feet, elegantly mounted, on which in the fishing season the rods are hung when not in use, and the walls are decorated with pictures and sets of mounted deer and caribou horns. The whole camp is plastered and is painted inside and out. A well-filled ice-house and a large boat-house, containing half a dozen boats of various descriptions, are near the camp. A trail through the woods leads to Trout Cove, on Lake Mooselucmeguntic, a mile and a third distant from camp. At the cove Mr. Whitney had another boat-house, containing four fishing boats. A second trail, running through the woods in a different direction, leads to the upper dam, two miles north of the camp.

The camp was christened Camp Whitney, in honor of J. Parker Whitney, Esq., formerly of Boston, but now a resident of San Francisco. Mr. Whitney visits the camp every season, and has only missed one year out of the last twenty-two. He is one of the oldest habitués of these lakes, and the present one is his forty-fifth trip. He has fished some forty other lakes in Maine, as well as the waters of Colorado and the Pacific coast, and had taken many a basket from the streams of England and the lochs of Scotland. He has bagged game in all these places, and shot twenty-three deer as well as other large animals. He has an inexhaustible fund of interesting anecdotes at his tongue's end. Associated with him in the ownership of the camp are George T. Rice, Esq., of Worcester, Mass., who has visited the lakes for several years, and T. Adams Ames, Esq., of San Francisco, formerly of Boston. The present is Mr. Ames' twelfth trip to the camp. Capt. Benjamin Cole, of Byron, Maine, the present superintendent, is an excellent fisherman, a fine cook, and capital fellow. He is one of the oldest and best guides in the lake region, and has been here about nine years.

Sunday we passed comfortably in camp. During the day we were witness to one of those sudden exhibitions of elemental strife peculiar to this latitude. The sun, shining with unwonted brilliancy, quickly disappeared from view beneath a mass of dull, leaden clouds that came floating from the northwest. The leaden pallor of the air increased until nearly the darkness of the night prevailed. The wind moaned and shrieked. Then an immense white sheet of feathery snowflakes, that drove and tossed before the whirlwind, completely enwrapped everything in its blinding mantle. The storm passed on as quickly as it came, and in half an hour we had sunshine again.

Speaking of the weather here, a native with whom I was talking one day abut the remarkable atmospheric change, remarked, "Wall, yes, we have lots er weather here in winter." A fact I can endorse, for in the few days since our arrival we have had all sorts, while the thermometer has ranged from ten degrees below to forty above.

Friday Mr. Whitney and one of the guides took their rifles and started off. A mile west of the lake they came upon the tracks of caribou. Near it were the remains of a rabbit that had lately been killed and eaten by a wild cat. It had be literally torn to pieces, and the bits of the skin, bones and hair, all bloody and scarcely cold, were scattered over the rock. A mile beyond they came to a smooth stream where the game had taken to the ice, and it was some time before they found where the animal had left the brook. After an hour's valuable time lost in searching for the tracks they found them, and again started in pursuit.

After following the trail for several hours they approached the Cranberry Bog, and proceeding with the utmost caution, they caught sight of the animals. The wind was in their favor; sinking down on the snow they crept carefully toward the game and finally worked themselves within five hundred yards of the animals, who were contentedly feeding on moss. Being afraid to approach nearer they agreed to both shoot at the bull, who had a fine set of horns. It was a long shot, but they took careful aim, and then the guide whispered, "Fire!" Two rifles cracked simultaneously, and the caribou started off across the pond in the middle of the bog.

The bull soon dropped, while his mate disappeared beneath the shelter of the forest. When the hunters reached the bull he was dead, having received both bullets. They took off his head and skin as trophies and returned to camp. The guides were sent with a hand-sled to bring back the meat. As near as we could judge he would weigh a little over three hundred pounds.

Saturday afternoon, between coffee and breakfast, we devoted to skating, the ice on some parts of the lake being in first-rate condition. After breakfast we all went on a scout, returning to camp a little before five. Whitney and myself came in empty-handed. Half an hour afterward Ames made his appearance, staggering under the weight of a young doe that he had shot on Black Point, scarcely half a mile from the house. He told us that, while making his way back to camp, feeling rather tired he sat down on a rock at the end of the point to rest. After a few minutes stop, he arose to go on, when he heard a snapping behind him. Cautiously turning, and at the same time cocking his rifle, he caught sight of some animal in the woods, about three hundred yards distant. Without stopping to make any investigations, ha banged away and then rushed to the game, which proved to be a young doe. Its death had been almost instantaneous. The doe weighed seventy-five pounds and was put away in the icehouse with the caribou.

Sunday, Whitney, not being satisfied with a cold sponge bath indoors, had Captain Cole go down to the lake and cut a hole in the ice about twelve feet square, a request that caused the worthy captain to roll his eyes in astonishment. As soon as the hole was cleared of ice, Whitney went down o the lake and throwing off his shirt, drawers and slippers, took a header into the lake. Ugh! It makes me shiver to think of it now. Climbing out, he tumbled into his things, and rushing up to camp, rubbed himself vigorously with coarse towels and experienced no ill effects for his swim.

Monday morning, Whitney, Ames and myself took our rifles and went on a scout for game. Result – five partridges, one rabbit, and an eight-mile tramp. The weather and country here now were very unfavorable for hunting. We are having what the natives call an open winter; about six inches of snow in the woods on an average, and we have had no occasion thus far to use snow-shoes, our thick boots and moccasins answering every purpose. First it thaws and then it freezes, precluding chances for deer or caribou.

Christmas Day came, and we sat down to a royal repast. Every dish was prepared by Mr. Whitney, and all the cooking was done under his immediate superintendence. By the side of each plate was a Christmas card and a copy of the bill of fare, written in pencil on some novel French dinner cards, suitable for the most nobly occasions:

CHRISTMAS, 1877–MENU.
Black bean soup; sherry and sercial Medeira; caribou a la chasseur; macon fleury; chablis; poulet a la Mollechunkamunk; roast turkey; roast chicken; oyster sauce; champagne and muscatel; currant jelly; roast onions; baked potatoes; plum pudding; au rhum and cold sauce; fromage de neuf-chatel; spiced peaches; crab apples; café noir; curacoa; cigarettes a la russe.

I fancy that there are not many camps in the backwoods where you could get Christmas dinner that would excel ours. We passed three hours very pleasantly at table, indulging toasts, songs and speeches, which were sandwiched in between the courses. I never passed a jollier or pleasanter Christmas evening in my life, and that was the opinion of the all present. I doubt if any of us ever forget it.

The following Wednesday morning we arose early, packed our things and took our seats on the sled, which had come to convey us back. It was a lovely morning, just cool enough to be agreeable. The horses were in good spirits, and they trotted away at a lively pace. At the lower end of the Narrows we found a large piece of open water, but by hugging the eastern shore, passed by it without trouble. After reaching the lower lake we found the ice smooth. The air was very clear, and we had a fine view of the White Mountains and could easily distinguish the buildings on the summit of Mount Washington.

Here I must chronicle the death of old Barney, the horse who had drawn the baggage across the Middle Dam Carry for a number of years, and who was well known to all the frequenters of the Angler's Retreat. He was coming up the river from Lake Umbagog, a short time ago and broke through the ice. Although not a very valuable animal, he was very intelligent, and there are many who will remember his pranks. Among his eccentricities was a decided relish for trout, which he could eat raw or cooked. Another habit was that of stealing pies from the kitchen window. He would devour them with all the gusto of a hungry schoolboy.

Before reaching Andover the sleighing gave place to bare roads. A friendly backboard bore us, not without mishaps, the rest of the way, and, arriving at Andover, the party who had together spent the Christmas holidays in the woods of Maine separated for their homes.

– C. A. J. F., BOSTON, JAN. 1877.

ON THE MOOSELUCMEGUNTIC

By E. T. Whitemore, from *Forest and Stream*, September 11, 1884

Edmund T. Whitmore (1828-1909) was born in the tiny village of Killingly, Connecticut, but lived most of his life in Putnam, where he was a successful shoe manufacturer. An active member of the community, in 1907 at the age of 79 he was serving as Chairman of the Board of Relief for the city. Whitmore was an enthusiastic fisherman, who took numerous vacations to Maine and wrote about some of his experiences.

It has been my intention for several years to spend a week or two on the above named lake, but I never had that pleasure until the present season. Seven of us met at the railroad station on the morning of June 3, equipped with rods, reels, lines, and all the needed outfit for camp life in the woods, and as the train moved north we felt more like boys just out of school than business men on a vacation, and after a two days' ride on cars, buckboard, stage and steamer, we found ourselves unpacking our traps in the very pleasant camps owned by Capt. Fred Barker, at the mouth of Bema stream.

Our party was composed of merchants, manufacturers, mill superintendents, insurance agents, bankers, lumber dealers and designers. It would be strange if out of them all some would not be found full of fun and frolic, and in this case we were favored with two or three of the most fun-loving, side-splitting jokers that ever struck in the Maine woods, and no man has any business with such crowd as this was unless he has a double fastening put on to his trousers and vest buttons before he leaves home.

We had been in camp two days and some of us had taken several large trout, which were put into the fish cars that were fastened to a boom of logs. Some of our party who had stayed behind a day or two now came into camp and, of course, had to take a look at the big fish, and this was just the place where the fun began. Out walked the new-comers to the end of the boom, and craning their necks to peep into the car, the log on which they stood began to roll. Now, no one but a first-class "river driver' can stand on a log turning at the rate of twenty times a minute. So in they plunged waist deep into the cold water. To say that yells, screeches and roars of laughter filled the air would be putting it light, for one of the party, "who should have been a minister," actually danced a jog on a flat rock nearby in the presence of the whole company. This was a good send off as it acted as a cooler on a hot day and the jig gave unlimited sport for all that were fortunate enough to see it.

The next day some of the mugwumps of the tribe went down on the steamer to Upper Dam to meet some friends they expected in to join the party, as they wished to give them a proper reception and a little surprise also, at the same time. They besmeared their face and hands so they were just dripping with tar and oil, but as they neared the landing they looked for their friendly hands. In their stead a crowd of admirers followed them around with such exclamations of delight as, "Big Ingun-waugh! Much red man! Caroin achin chemokana!" and pet and endearing names. It was noticed, however, that they took the first boat back to camp, and they were whiter if not wiser men.

The "great joker" of the party weighed 114 pounds, and it was surmised by some that Capt. Barker imported this same fellow to keep us from eating him out of house and home, for at every meal some of us had to leave the table or burst at his jokes and queer sayings; but we always forgave him, for he was a splendid follow, take him as a whole. We did, however, have no really "troublesome customer" in the party. We christened him the "infant," on account of his size and his terrible hankering after milk. He weighed 246 pounds "when quiet," but when "stirred up" he would swing nearly 1200 pounds; this is no joke, for he would actually "clean out " the whole camp when in his tantrums. As this was his first trip to the Rangeleys, we used to tag him with a large pasteboard tag, as he had a habit of wandering off in the woods, and with all our care of him he strayed away over the mountains and was gone all day, but finally turned up all right with about a bushel of small trout in a bag strung across his back, which in part compensated us for the trouble he made us. He tried fly-fishing with a bait rod, but when he saw some of the old veterans kill some large trout with a 9-ounce split bamboo, he declared he was "converted," threw his bait rod into the lake, borrowed a spare fly-rod that was in camp, and fished like a little man ever after. When he was fairly "domesticated" he proved to be the "very best fellow" in the whole camp.

I think some of the old campers ought to come in for their share of "pigheadedness," but for want of space will only mention one or two brilliant feats. One day while the writer was trolling, he leaned over the side of the boat to change the water in the minnow bucket, and just at this instant an old "sockdolager" of a trout struck the bait. To grab the rod and strike the fish took but a few seconds, but turning to take the bucket into the boat again, "lo and behold, " the bubbles that came to the surface of the water was the only indication of where the bait and bucket was to be found, i.e., on the bottom of the lake. There was no "cuss words" about it, but that boat was "yanked" about a mile to camp in double quick time, and the old man shut himself up in his room for about two hours.

I was down at the pier the next morning about 6 A.M., laying the flies out across the stream when "gewhitcker!" what a trout rolled up at my fly but missed it. The blood went to my fingers' ends with a rush, and my heart thumped my breast like a triphammer, and every instant I expected he would come up again. Hearing a rattling of the stones on the pier I turned to meet the gaze of one of the old veterans, who with disheveled hair and eyeballs glaring wild and wide, spake thusly: "Did you–did you–hear that moose?" Moose be darned, you squash head, did you not know that Barker's cow got lost in the mountains yesterday and has not been found yet?" It is needless to say I was instantly left alone on the pier to meditate on moose and my bit trout.

We chartered Barker's small steamer *Oquossuc* one day, and arranged for a trip up the Mooselucmeguntic to Cupsuptic Lake, across that to the river, then up the river to Cupsuptic Falls and the head of a navigation, and only twelve miles to Parmachenee Lake. It is impossible for me to describe the trip up this river, just wide enough for the little steamer to follow its snake-like channel. I think the steamer headed to every point of the compass going up. The trees were covered with white, long-hanging moss, and just in the background the grand old mountains reared their heads heavenward. At 11 A.M. we ran the bow of the Oquossuc into the bank below the falls and tied her to a small tree, and off we scrambled up the stream to test the trout fishing.

For myself, I selected a long reach of rapid water, which I think is called the Second Falls. As the old and tried split-bamboo pitched the flies outward and upward and finally settled on the rushing current the golden sides of two noble trout came gleaming up through the water, and with a splash took the dark-winged Montreal and silver doctor. The usual merry song of the reel is heard as they rush down the stream and the fight begins. At this instant I hear shouts from just above me up the river, and turning I see one of our party with his rod bent to a half circle and his face beaming with smiles and a satisfied expression, which means much with a genuine trout fisherman. We spent two hours taking plenty of fish, then adjourned to the steamer where we partook of a good dinner of fresh broiled trout, boiled eggs, fried potatoes, fresh bread and plenty of good coffee. After dinner the steamer was headed down the river, and we arrived in camp at 8 P.M. We decided that this trip was the most enjoyable one we had while on the lakes.

There are four ponds upon and between the mountains three miles back of Barker's camp, and boats are kept there for the use of sportsmen. These ponds are clear as crystal and swarming with trout. Barker has built a good log camp on the shore of the largest of the ponds, which makes it the best and jolliest place to camp in the Maine woods.

So I start in my boat, casting the flies over the clear sparkling waters, with a cool breeze from the northwest, and a snow bank of half an acre on the south side of the ponds on the 25th of June, taking trout two at a cast and weighing from ¼ to ¾ pounds each. I thought of the people at home, sweltering in the hot sun with the thermometer at 90° in the shade. As I filled my lungs with the exhilarating air, redolent with balsam and pine, I muttered to myself, "How foolish some people are who can come to such a place as this as well as not, and still neglect it year after year for the sake of losing a few dollars for someone to wrangle about hereafter." I know some have not a taste for trout fishing and do not care to enthuse over beautiful mountain scenery, cool brooks or the lovely wild flowers that grow in such profusion in the wild woods, but with me it is different. As the body begins to weaken and the eyesight to fail, the mountains seem to take on new beauties and more majestic forms as tier after tier looms up in the dim distance. Once I used to pass by the tiny flowers, but now I often stoop and gather a few of these gems of the woods, to sniff of their fragrance and admire their wonderful beauty, and as the memories of the many happy days come crowding upon me I long for the time to come when I can again hie away to that haven of rest and enjoyment, the Maine wilderness.

– E.T.W., PUTNAM, CONN,. SEPT. 1.

MY FIRST BEAR HUNT

By Bruin, from *Forest and Stream*, October 7, 1886

In the year 1862, while trapping with a friend on Richardson's Lake, in Northern Maine, after a very pleasant fall, during which we had explored every stream and pond for many miles around, setting traps wherever signs indicated any chance for fur, and the season being near its close, snow having begun to fall, we made a trip to the settlement of Magalloway, a distance of eight miles through the forests without a track on the way. In passing a large rock, some ten feet high, we surprised a Canadian lynx which was crouched upon the top ready to spring upon a rabbit or fox that might pass nearby. He leaped down upon the opposite side and escaped without giving us a chance shot. Soon after we came upon the fresh track of a bear, and as I stood beside that noble track in the fresh snow, so soft and resplendent in the morning light, I felt a thrill pass over me such as I remember having experienced when, a small boy; from time to time I would venture to the edge of the forest after a light snow and let my eyes to feast upon the track of a fox or rabbit. To stand for the first time beside the track of our most noble game will awaken every dormant feeling and create a strong desire to follow the trail and see the home of a bear, at least that was my feeling, so after arriving at the settlement I sought a man, Mr. Leavitt, who had had some experience with bears, and found him very willing to go.

Early the next morning we started. Upon coming to the river the ice was found too thin to bear us, so we got some boards which we pushed along one after the other and were enabled to cross. In due time we came to the track in about four inches of snow. It led due south toward Moose Mountain, and over a hardwood ridge which divides the waters of the Umbagog from those running into Richardson Lake. We had two dogs; one a good bear dog about half bull, the other a fine hound. When we crossed the ridge the dogs shot ahead like an arrow and routed several deer, which struck directly for Cranberry Bog Pond, which lies about a mile north of this ridge. They were soon out of hearing. The hound was never seen afterward. We supposed he broke into the pond or was killed by the deer. The other dog found his way to the settlement. We continued to follow the bear's track, which led us, after many turns, down into a low cedar swamp; and just as darkness began to close around us we came to an old logging road that leads to Lake Umbagog and called B. Carry. We decided to follow it to camp at the foot of Richardson's Lake and camp for the night. Soon after we came to a trail crossing the road; we made out to see in the darkness that it was an enormous bear's track, the creature having but three feet and one stub, or as we afterwards found, a fore foot gone except the ball. He stepped only about ten inches and must have made slow progress. Mr. Leavitt said he would have that bear at any rate, so we made our way to camp, which we soon had aglow with a good fire; and after passing a comfortable night we took an early start for the trail.

We seen found that is old veteran was not so fine to follow as our young dandy bear of yesterday, for the latter chose the best walking ground, while this old fellow wallowed and crawled through the most inaccessible swamps, along the Lake shore to the marsh. No one can imagine what one was to encounter following a bear's trail unless he had once had a taste of the sport. We crawled through thickets of dead cedars and over old logs and rocks for miles, then we came to a great tract of burnt land where the pine trees lay across each other in some places ten to fifteen feet deep. We had some hard falls crossing on these logs, but as everything has an end we came to better ground at last, and were soon surprised to see a great fine stub having rotten wood newly thrown out over the snow for many feet around. We felt that we had got our bear at last, but upon passing around the stump we saw that he had rejected it and left. With much disappointment we pulled on his track. He turned to the west and crossed the deer's trail near the pond. Many times since I have wished we had followed to the pond and seen what had occurred there to have caused the death of our noble hound, had we known that he was lost we should have done so. Our big bear soon crossed the small bear's track along the side of Moose Mountain; there we found where he had been eating mountain ash berries, having broken the trees down in many places, and that he had made a bed upon a flat rock, but after resting awhile, he had taken his leave. We followed him to within two miles of the settlement, then as night came on we struck for home and came out soon after dark at a clearing. We were very tired; with clothes well worn out, and our courage not little dampened.

After a good night's rest and plenty of food we started upon the morrow, took the track and followed it south to a ledgy hill, where bruin had tried for a den, but could not suit himself. Then he had plunged into a shaky bog and wallowed in sloughs so deep we felt sure he must get mired; but they will go through mud that would mire an alligator. At last, after an endless tramping backwards and forward, he came to the Magalloway River and swam across. We set to work and made a raft. After breaking away the thin ice so that we could draw it along a narrow canal toward the other shore. The river here is deep and has but little current. We had the old bear dog again. In attempting to cross on the ice he broke through and came near drowning; his strength was so nearly exhausted by the breaking of the ice and a long cold bath that we had to build a fire and rub him to revive his energies. We were soon again on the trail. After much the same experience, from hill to swamp and through all the bad places he could find, we stood at the close of day upon the shore of the Androscoggin River, and saw a newly frozen track from shore to shore where our game had gone across. As we stood there we held a council of war. I had had enough of it. I did not believe the bear would ever den; and so I thought it of little use to follow him further. Had I known what I have since learned, I should have felt sure of finding him snugly housed. Mr. Leavitt said probably he was just across the river, and that we could go down to Errol, cross there, and, after stopping overnight, go up upon the other side and get our bear; but I was anxious to go the lake to attend to my traps, so I left my companion to go to Errol, while I returned to Magalloway.

The remainder of this hunt I will relate as I got it from Mr. Leavitt. After passing the night at Errol, he took with him a boy with a shotgun, he himself having an axe only, and proceeded to take up the trail on the opposite side of the river. He had gone only a very short distance when he saw the bear's head protruding from a hole in an old pine stub. The dog rushed up and snapped at him while he struck with the back of the axe at his head. The bear struck the dog upon he back and took him up on his paw, fastened by his claws to the skin, and was about to take him in his mouth when a severe blow with the axe caused him to drop the dog and make an effort to escape. This he did by breaking through the backside of the stump. A heavy blow administered upon his rump cause the axe to rebound, the thick fur making a complete protection. The boy fired his gun to no effect, while the bear disappeared in thick cover. Mr. Leavitt sighed for my heavy repeating rifle, and took the road nine miles for home. When he reached home his courage and energies were well-nigh exhausted, but upon relating his story to his brother-in-law, Mr. West, he was persuaded by him to go and try it again. So they started the next day with the dog, which had a large wound in his back. They followed the track into New Hampshire, up among the Diamond River Mountains; found lodgings at a lumberman's camp and started again the next morning. About noon the dog, being ahead, came up with the bear on the side of a hill, and while the dog and bear were engaged the men ran up and shot him in the side of the head with two balls in a little quill gun, which killed him at once. They found a coat of about 3in. of fat covering the whole body. They took the skin and fat and reached the lumber camp (where they had stayed the last night) at dark and returned the following morning for the meat, which proved a valuable addition to the supplies at the camp. All was left there except a fine piece which was awaiting my return when I arrived at the lake. The fat made nine gallons of oil.

I never have recovered from the disappointment that I felt when I learned how near I was to that bear when I turned back. Many times since I have remained firm when others have given up. Just a thought of it will cause me to rally when otherwise my courage would falter. I have since followed several bears, but none so large as that one. It was found that all the toes of one forward foot had been taken off by a trap.

– BRUIN.

A STORY OF TROUT LUCK

By W.K. Moody, from *Forest and Stream*, July 25, 1889

William K. Moody (1840-1902), who was born and raised in Strong, Maine, attended school at Hebron Academy and later graduated from Colby College. After teaching school a short time, he

Royal Sport (With Rod and Gun)

entered the newspaper business as editor of the Winthrop Gazette and two years later removed to Mechanic Falls, where he published the Androscoggin Herald. Four years later he purchased half of the interest in the Somerset Reporter of Skowhegan and became sole owner for a few years.In 1875 Moody moved to Boston where he became editor of the Weekly Advertiser, Women's Journal and held a position at The Boston Commercial Bulletin. After writing a series of articles on banking methods for the Boston Herald, he became a regular member of that paper.

An avid fisherman, Moody had a camp on Richardson Lake and visited there annually. Writing numerous articles on hunting and fishing, and being a preservationist, he worked tirelessly to get the State Game Laws amended to protect the game of his native state. He was also an amateur photographer, and left many photographs of Maine that he took during his vacations.

Camp Stewart

I sit down to write a big trout story; a story in which I am interested only to the extent that my wife, who has been on many trouting trips with me, caught the next largest trout, and a friend who, by the way, had never before dipped a line in Maine waters, caught the largest. I brought up the rear with a six-pounder. It was a very quiet little party that started from Boston, on the morning of the 24th of May, for a few days fishing on Richardson Lake. There were only three of us. Sickness kept back the others, who were to make up the party. Slowly we wended our way to the lake by way of

Andover, Maine. We had been told that the fishing was dull. The news was good. Always tell us that the fishing is poor, and we will bring out the big trout. We reached camp Stewart without special incident, except that some of the hand baggage was one day behind, and of course the fishing rods, though a small amount of tackle happened to be at hand. We reached camp at 4 P.M. of Saturday. It did not take long to don the old clothes that are always ready in that camp, and with an improvised rod, ten handsome trout were ready to be served for supper. Col. H. M. Fitch, the third member of the party, considered this a rather remarkably feature of the party, though he has fished in the Rocky Mountains and in many parts of the world, and he has now gone to Sitka, Alaska, with his fish rod in his trunk. But for those who know there are always trout to be had for the table there; that is enough. The next day was Sunday and the delayed fish rods did not arrive till night; hence one member of that party was saved from breaking the Sabbath–except with a cedar pole.

On Monday the rods were in and fishing began in earnest that is when the weather permitted; the wind blew most of the time during the middle of the day, and our fishing was put in at sunset and before 8 o'clock in the morning, at which time the lake was comparatively mild. Our success was good each day. A plenty of trout, all the way from ½ to 3lbs., but up to Wednesday morning no large ones had been caught. With Chas. Cutting of Andover, as guide, Mrs. M. went out that morning to see what could be done. They were absent from the camp about an hour, when they came rowing slowly back. The little boat touched the wharf in front of the camp. The water had begun to be boisterous, and Madam is afraid of very rough water. She called me to come down and help her out of the boat. Naturally lazy, I suggested that Cutting should assist her. But nothing would do but what I must go down to the boat. Mrs. M. had "caught a curious trout." She had "caught a little one." She paints trout pictures, and I calculated that she had caught a trout of fine coloring. Down I went to the wharf. There, in the bottom of the boat, lay a trout 24in.

in length, with a weight of 7 ¼lbs. Madam had caught it all her own self. She had conquered it with that little lancewood rod of mine, only weighing 9oz., and not even the tip was broken. The reel and line are as good specimens of tackle as the present age affords–the celebrated extension reel invented by Henry C. Litchfield of Boston. Was she a happy woman? Ask Charles Cutting, the guide. It may be stated right here that the same Charles Cutting told Col. Fitch that he was more pleased to have Mrs. Moody take that trout than any other person in the world. The trout was hooked fully half an hour before it could be brought to the top of the water. Then when Mrs. Moody saw its size the force of her arms gave out, and Cutting had to take the rod for a minute or two, when the lady finally brought the fish to the net.

That evening I went out fishing. The wind had died away and the surface of the lake was a beautiful mirror. I had the same rod and tackle that had conquered the big trout in the morning. All of a sudden I had a strike that nearly took the rod from my hands. The reel sung out twenty feet more of line in an instant. Cutting remarked that "you have a big one." I was ready for him. The little rod proved all that I had ever expected of it,. Scarcely an inch of line could I get. The trout sounded for the bottom and evidently found it. Then he sulked. I could not start him. The boat was slowly drifting toward the shore, where the snags were numerous and bad for a hooked trout to get among. Neither Cutting nor I had noticed the fact, so intent were we in watching that rod and line, till all at once a big snag, an ugly treetop, was not fifty feet from the boat. I called Cutting's attention to the danger. "We must try and tow the trout out into clear water," he remarked, and took up his oars. I expected trouble, but curious enough the trout then made an attempt to go under the boat, and we succeeded in getting him into deep water, safe from snags. Again he begun the operation of sounding and running out the line. At times the rod was bent up nearly double, till the reel was released and more line taken. But at last he was drawn exhausted to nearly the top of the water. He had been hooked twenty-five minutes by the watch when he was brought to the net, and he weighed plump six pounds. I was satisfied. I am satisfied to-day with my spring fishing trip. I had caught up to that evening nearly sixty trout, and had counted nor saved nothing under half a pound, except in cases where they were so badly hooked as to kill them. I had also caught nearly two-thirds of these trout with the fly, though it was very early for fly-fishing.

If one desires to see the eyes of a happy man, let them take Charles Cutting, as a guide, and hook in a big trout. It is worth the trip to see. He has grown old in guiding, but the man who employs him gets trout, if there are any to be had. Col. Fitch and Madam came down to the wharf to congratulate me as we came leisurely rowing in that evening. We told them that we had caught a little one–we had several little ones. You should have seen the expression on their faces when they saw that 6lb. fish. The Colonel's congratulations were hearty, but alas! There was a tone of sadness. His trout were all only fair sized. I had told him, at the outset of the trip that the trout of the world were to be found in the waters we were to fish. We were to break up camp the next morning. We advised the Colonel to try the trout in the morning. His trunk was all packed the evening before and the little steamer would not come for us till 9 o'clock. Reluctantly he promised to do so. I was up early–half past four. There was Cutting at the wharf, with the bait–minnows–all caught. He was strapping his hands to keep them warm. The mercury, though it was May 31, was down to 44. Col. Fitch came down rather reluctantly. He had little confidence in any good luck for his that morning. He had broken his rod all to pieces on a 3lb. trout the day previous, but had saved the fish by means of the reel. "I fear that I shall break it, he remarked, "and I told him that I did not fear his breaking it, and Cutting remarked that there was not the least danger, provided he handle it fairly well; for already it had bent double under the struggles of big trout. He took the rod and they paddled away. In about an hour and a half they came back. I saw by their motions that something was to pay. The Colonel shouted that he had "caught a little trout," which was again true. But that little trout story was played out with me. I ran down to the wharf, Madam followed.

They were just coming up alongside. Could I believe my eyes? There was a tout 27in. in length, and full 9lbs. in weight. The Colonel caught my hands. A happier angler I never saw in all my experience of more than 30 years. His face was a study. He had made a record that he need never hope to be beat. The trout was one of the most perfect specimens of *Salmo fontinalis* I have ever seen. The vermilion spots were very numerous and the sheeny sparkle was a sight to behold. Best of all, the little rod was as perfect as when he had started out. It had stood the strain of that giant trout for nearly three-quarters of an hour, and to-day it is as perfect as when it was made. Not a tip has been broken. When any one attempts to a reader of the FOREST AND STREAM that there is no difference in rods, or that a cheap rod is as good as a fair priced piece of workmanship just tell him that he does not know whereof he speaks. Mrs. Moody's trout is to be painted, and Chas. Cutting is to have the picture. Good reader, are there any trout in the Rangeleys? If you are preparing to say no; that big trout are scarce there, then I will tell you that I learned on my way in that the Stevens party, Mr. Shattuck and Mr. Smart, had taken a 7 and an 8-lbs. trout. Will Shaw of the Andrews House, South, Paris, Me., too a 9lbs. trout above the Narrows a few days before we went in. His wife got a big landlocked salmon. A gentleman from Portland had taken a 9-pounder. Mrs. J. P Whitney went out trolling only a few days before our visit. She had bet with some of their guests that she could take a bigger trout that day than any one of them. After fishing a little over an hour she returned with a trout that more than tipped the scales at 8lbs. But a curious feature of this trout was that soon after it was weighed there came out of it's mouth a sucker that weighed over a pound. These great trout swallow fish nearly as large as themselves.

– W. K. MOODY

INCIDENTS IN MY HUNTING LIFE.–II.

By J. G. Rich, from *Forest and Stream*, June 6, 1889

Joshua Gross Rich was born in New Sharon and attended high school in Farmington. After spending over five years at sea, he came home, married and lived for a number of years in Roxbury, Massachusetts, working as a book dealer.Rich began coming back to the Rangeley region in 1846, where he began trapping and hunting around Richardson and Mooselucmeguntic Lakes. He moved his family there, first settling on the Adams farm on Mooselookmeguntic. By 1849 he had relocated to Metallak Point on Upper Richardson, where he continued trapping and set up a store for trappers, hunters, fishermen, loggers and anyone who came into the area.

Joshua G. Rich

I was camping one night late in the fall of 1849, at the head of Mollechunkamunk Lake, near a stream, which runs from the ponds known as Richardson Ponds, and within ten rods of the lake. It was a dark and windy night, threatening a storm, so I put my night wood inside my shed camp and reloaded my gun, standing it in a convenient place, built up a cheerful fire outside, ate a hearty supper of broiled trout and other fixings and lay down for the night. How long I slept I cannot tell, but when I awoke I as on my knees peering out into the darkness, the rain was pouring and the fire was just about gone. And just then a tremendous yell or screech saluted me in the direction of the lake, not over a gunshot away. My hair stood on end. The situation was alarming and my nerves crystallized. But I did not lose my presence of mind. But holding on to my gun I at once set about kindling a fire, and of the few coals in sight I soon got a blaze with my kindling wood and birch bark. I consider a fire in a dark night the best protection against wild beasts. I heard several more of these fearful screeches, but the animal evidently did not like my fire, for he steered eastward toward the mountain, giving me a stunner of a good-bye yell.

There was no more sleep for me that night and as soon as day broke I went to the lake, and there deep in the sandy shore were the foot prints of a large panther, with toe nails or claws full 2in. long, and the creeping tracks near to each other when he passed my camp showed that he was wicked. When he came to the stream he leaped across some 25ft., sinking his feet deep into the sand, showing that he was a heavy animal.

I have no doubt this was what hunters term the Indian Devil, a creature with which a man in the woods alone has no business. I have tracked a creature like this since, but never heard his voice and never want to.

After 1840 for nearly twenty years moose were abundant in Maine, and it was lawful to kill them with dogs or at any time of the year; so almost everybody laid in a supply of moose meat each winter for the year, which was saved by smoking, drying or salting. Those farmers who did not care to hunt them, usually had enough given them by their neighbors or bought it cheaply.

At one time four of us were chasing a moose on the side of a mountain west of Rangeley Lake, when, on coming out into an open place in the woods, the moose stopped and "sulked" as we termed it. In our party was a 16-year-old boy who was a brave lad and like to show off pretty well, so when the old bull stopped, this fellow, Dan, ran into the open place near the moose to get a better look at him. But no sooner had Dan showed himself to the moose than the moose started for him. There was about 4ft. of snow and we all had on snowshoes. Only one of the party carried a gun, and he was a few paces back, just coming up. We all sang out, "Bring the gun! Bring the gun, quick!" So the gun soon got there, but not so quick as the moose, for four or five good strides brought the moose and the boy too near together. The boy was not idle for he turned and made for a big knole of hillock of snow a few yards away, and seeing the moose upon him he dove into the snow bank, out of sight, but not until the moose had trampled a beat where the lad was last seen, and in less time than I can write it had a standing place as hard as frozen ground, and under his feet we could see one of the boy's snowshoes.

As soon as it was possible that moose was shot and fell in his tracks, and we all ran to pull the dead body of the boy out from under the moose, where we expected to find him. We soon got the snowshoe, but the boy's foot was not in it; and while digging away the snow searching for him we heard him cry out. We all looked in the direction of the sound, and along the bank of snow about 100ft. the boy stuck up his head through the snow. The bank of snow was formed by a tall tree, blown up by its roots, the snow covering it out of sight, and under the tree was an open space, as the tree lay up from the ground, and under this the boy dove, as the moose reared to crush him down, just coming down on his snowshoe, which in the struggle broke from the boy's foot.

That was a scared boy, but he was a wiser boy. Much of his conceit had left him.

– J. G. RICH., BETHEL, ME.

A FATAL SUCCESS

By Henry Van Dyke, from Fisherman's Luck and Some Other Uncertain Things, 1889

Rev. Henry Van Dyke

Henry Van Dyke (1852-1933) graduated from Princeton in 1873, then received Theology Degree from that institution the following year. He was minister of the Brick Church in New York City for sixteen years, then returned to Princeton, where he taught English Literature from 1899 to 1923, and was ambassador to the Netherlands from 1913-1916.Van Dyke, a clergyman professor and author, wrote several books and numerous poems of candid wisdom, which exemplified his wonderful homespun philosophy. Remembered especially for his Christmas story "The Other Wise Man," his other books included "Little Rivers," and "Fisherman's Luck."

The following story, while it begins in the Adirondacks, it ends at the world-famous trout pool at the foot Upper Dam at the outlet of Mooselucmeguntic Lake.

It was in the second summer after the wedding that Beekman admitted to a few of his ancient Petrine cronies, in moments of confidence (unjustifiable, but natural), that his wife had one fault.

"It is not exactly a fault," he said, "not a positive fault, you know. It is just a kind of defect, due to her education, of course. In everything else she's magnificent. But she doesn't care for fishing. She say's it's stupid,–can't see why anyone should like the woods,–calls camping out the lunatic's diversion. It's rather awkward for a man with my habits to have his wife take such a view. But it can be changed by training. I intend to educate her and convert her. I shall make an angler of her yet."

And so he did.

The new education was begun in the Adirondacks, and the first lesson was given at Paul Smith's. It was a complete failure.

Beekman persuaded her to come out with him for a day on Meadow River, and promised to convince her of the charm of angling. She wore a new gown, fawn-colored and violet, with a picture-hat, very taking. But the Meacham River trout was shy that day; not even Beekman could induce him to rise to the fly.

What the trout lacked in confidence the mosquitoes more than made up. Mrs. De Peyster came home much sunburned, and expressed a highly unfavorable opinion of fishing as an amusement and of Meacham River as a resort.

"The nice people don't come to the Adirondacks to fish," said she; "they come to talk about the fishing twenty years ago. Besides, what do you want to catch that trout for? If you do, the other men will say you bought it, and the hotel will have to put in a new one for the rest of the season."

The following year Beekman tried Moosehead Lake. Here he found an atmosphere more favorable to his plan of education. There were a good many people who really fished, and short expeditions in the woods were quite fashionable. Cornelia had a camping-costume of the most approved style made by Dewlap of Fifth Avenue,–pearl-gray with linings of rose-silk,–and consented to go with her husband on a trip up Moose River. They pitched their tent the first night at the mouth of Misery Stream, and a storm came on. The rain sifted through the canvas in a fine spray, and Mrs. De. Peyster sat up all night in a waterproof cloak, holding an umbrella. The next day they were back at the hotel in time for lunch.

"It was horrid," she told her most intimate friend, "perfectly horrid. The idea of sleeping in a shower-bath, and eating your breakfast from a tin plate, just for sake of catching a few silly fish! Why not send your guides out to get them for you?"

But, in spite of this profession of obstinate heresy, Beekman observed with secret joy that there were signs, before the end of the season, that Cornelia was drifting a little, a very little but still perceptibly, in the direction of a change of heart. She began to take an interest, as the big trout came along in September, in the reports of the catches made by the different anglers. She would saunter out with the other people to the corner of the porch to see the fish weighed and spread out on the grass. Several times she went with Beekman in the canoe to Hardscrabble Point, and showed distinct evidences of pleasure when he caught large trout. The last day of the season, when he returned from a successful expedition to Roach River and Lily Bay, she inquired with some particularity about the results of his sport; and in the evening, as the company sat before the great open fire in the hall of the hotel, she was heard to use this information with considerable skill in putting down Mrs. Minot Peabody of Boston, who was recounting with details of her husband's catch at Spencer Pond. Cornelia was not a person to he contented with the back seat, even in fishing-stories.

When Beekman observed these indications he was much encouraged, and resolved to push his educational experiment briskly forward to his customary goal of success.

"Some things can be done, as well as others," he said in his masterful way, as three of us were walking home together after the autumnal dinner of the Petrine Club, which he always attended as a graduate member. "A real fisherman never gives up. I told you I'd make an angler out of my wife, and so I will. It has been rather difficult. She is 'dour in rising. But she's beginning to take notice of the fly now. Give me another season, and I'll have her landed."

Good old Beekman! Little did he think– But I must not interrupt the story with moral reflections.

The preparations that he made for his final effort at conversion were thorough and prudent. He had a private interview with Dewlap in regard to the construction of a practical fishing-costume for a lady, which resulted in something more reasonable and womanlike than had ever been turned out by that famous artist. He ordered from Hook and Catchett a lady's angling-outfit of the most enticing description,–a split-bamboo rod, light as a girl's wish, and strong as a matron's will; an oxidized silver reel, with a monogram on one side, and a sapphire set in the handle for good luck; a book of flies, of all sizes and colours, with the correct names inscribed in gilt letters on each page. He surrounded his favorite sport with an aureole of elegance and beauty. And then he took Cornelia in September to the Upper Dam at Rangeley.

She went reluctant. She arrived disgusted. She stayed incredulous and returned– Wait a bit, and you shall hear how she returned.

The Upper Dam at Rangeley is the place, of all others in the world, where the lunacy of angling may be seen in its incurable stage. There is a cozy little inn, called a camp, at the foot of a big lake. In front of the inn is a huge dam of gray stone, over which the river plunges into a great oval pool, where the trout assemble in the early fall to perpetuate their race. From the tenth of September to the thirtieth, there is not an hour of the day or night when there are no boats floating on that pool, and no anglers trailing the fly across its waters. Before that last fishermen are ready to come in at midnight, the early fishermen may be seen creeping down to the shore with lanterns in order to begin before cockcrow. The number of fish taken is not large,–perhaps five or six for the whole company on an average day,–but the size is sometimes enormous,–nothing under three pounds is counted,–and they pervade thought and conversation at the Upper Dam to the exclusion of every other subject. There is no driving, no dancing, no golf, no tennis. There is nothing to do but fish or die.

At first, Cornelia thought she would choose the latter alternative. But a remark of that skillful and morose old angler, McTurk, which she overheard on the verandah after supper, changed her mind.

"Women have no sporting instinct," said he. "They only fish because they see men doing it. They are imitative animals."

That same night she told Beekman, in the subdued tone which the architectural construction of the house imposes upon all confidential communications in the bedrooms, but with resolution in every accent, that she proposed to go fishing with him on the morrow.

"But not at that pool, right in front of the house, you understand. There must be some other place, out on the lake, where we can fish for three or four days, until I get the trick of this wobbly rod. Then I'll show that old bear, McTurk, what kind of animal woman is."

Beekman was simply delighted. Five days of diligent practice at the mouth of Mill Brook brought his pupil to the point where he pronounced her safe.

"Of course," he said patronizingly, "you haven't learned all about it yet. That will take years. But you can get your fly out thirty feet, and you can keep the tip of your rod up. If you do that, the trout will hook himself, in rapid water, eight times out of ten. For playing him, if you follow my directions, you'll be all right. We will try the pool tonight, and hope for a medium-sized fish."

Cornelia said nothing, but smiles and nodded. But she had her own thoughts.

At about nine o'clock Saturday night, they anchored their boat on the edge of the shoal where the big eddy swings around, put out the lantern and began to fish. Beekman sat in the bow of the boat, with his road over the left side; Cornelia in the stern, with her rod over the right side. The night was cloudy and very black. Each of them had put on the largest possible fly, one a "Bee-Pond" and the other a "Dragon;" but even these were invisible. The measured out the right length of line, and let the flies drift back until they hung over the shoal, in the curly waters where the two currents meet.

There were three other boats to the left of them. McTurk was their only neighbor in the darkness on the right. Once they heard him swearing softly to himself, and knew that he had hooked and lost a fish.

Away down at the tail of the pool, dimly visible through the gloom, the furtive fisherman, Parsons, had anchored his boat. No noise ever came from that craft. If he wished to change his position, he did not pull up the anchor and let it down again with a bump. He simply lengthened or shortened his anchor rope. There was no click of the reel when he played a fish. He drew in and paid out the line through the rings by hand, without a sound. What he thought when a fish got away, no one knew, for he never said it. He concealed his angling as if it had been a conspiracy. Twice that night they heard a faint splash in the water near his boat, and twice they saw him put his arm over the side in the darkness and bring it back again very quietly.

"That's the second fish for Parsons," whispered Beekman, "what a secretive old Fortunatus he is! He knows more about fishing than any man on the pool, and talks less."

Cornelia did not answer. Her thoughts were all on the tip of her own rod. About eleven o'clock a fine, drizzling rain set in. The fish were very slack. All the other boats gave it up in despair; but Cornelia said she wanted to stay out a little longer, they might as well finish up the week.

At precisely fifty minutes past eleven, Beekman reeled up his line, and remarked with firmness that the holy Sabbath day was almost at hand and they ought to go in.

"Not till I've landed this trout," said Cornelia.

"What? A trout! Have you got one?"

"Certainly; I've had him on for at least fifteen minutes. I'm playing him Mr. Parson's way. You might as well light the lantern and get the net ready; he's coming in towards the boat now."

Beekman broke three matches before he made the lantern burn; and when he held it up over the gunwale, there was the trout sure enough, gleaming ghostly pale in the dark water, close to the boat, and quite tired out. He slipped the net over the fish and drew it in,–a monster.

"I'll carry that trout, if you please," said Cornelia, as they stepped out of the boat; and she walked into the camp, on the last stroke of midnight, with the fish in her hand, and quietly asked for the steelyard.

Eight pounds and fourteen ounces,–that was the

weight. Everybody was amazed. It was the "best fish" of that year. Cornelia showed no sign of exultation, until just as John was carrying the trout to the ice-house. Then she flashed out:–"Quite a fair imitation, Mr. McTurk,–isn't it?"

Now McTurk's best record for the last fifteen years was seven pounds and twelve ounces.

So far as McTurk is concerned, this is the end of the story. But not for the De Peysters. I wish it were. Beekman went to sleep that night with a contented spirit. He felt that his experiment in education had been a success. He had made his wife an angler.

He had indeed, and to an extent which he little suspected. That Upper Dam trout was to her like the first taste of blood on the tiger. It seemed to change at once, not so much her character as the direction of her vital energy. She yielded to the lunacy of angling, not by slow degrees, (as first a transient delusion, then a fixed idea, then a chronic infirmity, finally a mild insanity,) but by a sudden plunge into the most violent mania. So far from being ready to die at Upper Dam, her desire now was to live there–and to live solely for the sake of fishing–as long as the season was open.

There were two hundred and forty hours left to midnight on the thirtieth of September. At least two hundred of these she spent on the pool; and when Beekman was too exhausted to manage the boat and the net and the lantern for her, she engaged a trustworthy guide to take Beckman's place while he slept. At the end of the last day her score was twenty-three, with an average of five pounds and a quarter. His score was nine, with an average of four pounds. He had succeeded far beyond his wildest hopes.

RANGELEY BROOK TROUT

By James A. Williamson, from *Fishing with the Fly; Sketches by Lovers of the Art, with Illustrations of Standard Flies*, edited by C. F. Orvis and A. N. Cheney, 1889

Fly Fishing (Currier & Ives)

James A. Williamson, an avid fisherman, was staying at the Equinox House in Manchester, Vermont, being a friend of the proprietor, Franklin Orvis, brother of Charles F. Orvis, the famous fly rod maker. Charles Orvis and A. Nelson Cheney, a fish culturist, collected stories of fly-fishing and produced a well-loved book in 1889. Here Williamson discovered R. G. Allerton's book, "Brook Trout Fishing, an Account of a Trip of the Oquossuc Angling Association to Northern Maine, in June 1869." He was so elated with his success at Upper Dam, that he soon joined and became secretary of the Oquossuc Angling Club.

About twelve summers ago, when spending a delightful vacation in Manchester, Vermont, under the shadow of Mt. Equinox, my attention was called to a little book which gave a description of the exceptionally large brook trout inhabiting the waters of the Rangeley Lakes.

Never having heard, heretofore, of a fish of that species that weighed more than three pounds, and never having caught any over a pound and a half (although I had dropped the line in many waters and exerted my utmost muscle in casting a line for fingerlings), I could not bring my mind to believe that such fish as were described really existed, and at once pronounced it another fish story. Although much interested in the narrative I finally threw the book in disgust, and as I did so, observed for the first time that the author, was Robert G. Allerton, a very old friend, whom I had always esteemed a man of veracity. I at once took a new interest in the subject and determined to investigate the matter personally. I came to New York, had an interview with Mr. Allerton, who was the Treasurer of the Oquossuc Angling Association, and by his advice joined the club, and in due time started for the promised land of mountains, lakes, and large trout, and after the usual vicissitudes of travel reached my destination at Camp Kennebago about the middle of September.

The forests were just developing their autumnal hues, the air was fresh and bracing, and all nature seems to conspire to make one realize that there was health in every breath inhaled, and beauty in every phase of land and water. Having secured a first-rate guide and boat, and partaken of a trout breakfast, which was relished immensely, such as can only be appreciated by one who has left the haunts of civilization and gone into the wilderness for recuperation, I considered my first duty was to pay my respects to Mr. Allerton who was in camp at Bugle Cove. From this location Lake Mooselucmeguntic lies spread out before you, while Mt. Washington in the distance rears its snowy peak, overshadowing Jefferson, Monroe, and the other giants of the White Hills of New Hampshire.

The crystal waters of the lake tempt us to cast a fly, and a suitable place having been secured, we proceed to business. After making several casts in a manner more or less scientific but without success, my former unbelief came creeping over me, and as my arm became tired and almost refused to do its duty, a sense of despondency overcame me, which I am sure sensibly affected the beauty if not the efficiency of my casts. But suddenly I am awakened to the realization of the fact that a big fish has seized the fly and is making the reel hum in its frantic endeavor s to secure its liberty. Fathom after fathom of the dainty line disappears beneath the water, and at last prejudice dictates a gentle snub, which finally terminates in a decided check to the mad career of the quarry. Having succeeded in turning his head in a different direction, another rush is made across the stream, making the line whiz as it cuts through the water; then suddenly he takes a downward course and ceases from all apparent effort to free himself. He now sulks for a long time, and impatience begins to take the place of excitement with which the fight began. The guide, who during the fray had hoisted his anchor, got ready his landing-net, and was now holding his boat in position with the oars, suggested that I had better send him a telegraphic message, which was accordingly done by striking the rod with a key. The first few strokes seemed to make little or no impression, but presently he convinced us that he was still there, although we had some forebodings that he had escaped by winding the line around a log or some other object at the bottom of the stream. He was up and alive in every sense, and performed the same tactics for liberty, with apparently more vigor than at first. These were kept up for about an hour, when he again took a turn of sulking, but this time of shorter duration, and when he again began his rushes it was with an evident loss of strength, but no diminution of determination and pluck.

A friend who was watching and timing me from his boat came over to inquire how the battle was progressing, and pertinently asked, "Whether the fish was going to take me, or I the fish." At last the strength of the tackle, the pliability of the rod, and the determination of the rodster overcame the pluck and strength of the fish, and he was brought to the boat turned upon his side, and was beautifully landed by the guide. The scales were at once applied, with a result of eight pounds full weight.

My inquiring and interested friend informed me that I had been two hours and twenty minutes in the fight and as I sat down in the boat, I, for the first time, realized that I was tired.

Now, my dear reader, do not think that this kind of sport is of common occurrence, far from that time to this, I have taken but two fish of equal weight; the average, however, has been much larger than trout from any other locality in which I have fished. Any fish under half a pound is considered unfit to land, and is again committed to the water to grow larger. The number of trout does not seem to be falling off, but this can be accounted for by the annual plant of fry from the Hatching House of the Oquossuc Angling Association, who have for years past turned about one million fish into these waters, and now contemplate increasing the amount to five million; still I think there is a sensible diminution of the size of the catch, which now run from one-half to four pounds, and anything over that weight is the exception. This would seem to confirm the supposition of Professor Agassiz, made many years ago, that these large fish possibly may have reached an age from 100 to 200 years, as they were evidently very old.

Anyone who has been thrilled with the vigorous strike of one of the ordinary sized fish would be almost beside himself when one from three to five pounds rose to his fly, and if his tackle was good, the sport derived therefrom would serve him a lifetime; and when the shades of night had fallen upon the camp, and he with is fellow-fishermen collected around the great fire, point and vigor would be given to his recital of how he caught and played the monster he that day had brought to his creel.

HUNTING IN MAINE

By A. K. P. Cushman, from *Maine Outings*, Feb, 1896

Before the "enterprising Yankee," so-called, changed the admirable ways of Nature to those of his own, before the axe of the woodsman had long been heard slashing through the forest, probably but few places could be found in America that would please the hunter of to-day as well as the Androscoggin Lakes region of Maine. It was, in fact, a paradise for large game such as the deer, caribou, moose, and bear, as well as for the hunter. The white, sandy beaches and the overhanging branches of the evergreen trees, that once made the lakes so handsome, are no longer as nature designed them; but the large dams which have been built between the lakes to hold water for the large mills on the Androscoggin River, have risen the water, thus killing all trees that had their roots covered and hiding the once lovely beaches, so that now, except when the water is very low, the shore is covered with rocks and dead-wood.

In the forest, too, far back from the lake's shore can be seen what has been and what is still being done to the Maine woods by the enterprising and restless Yankee. These lakes and forests were once the home of the red man, who well knew that it was a rare good place for him to hunt, fish and trap. It was here, too, that Metalluck preferred to spend his days; he lived in the vicinity of a pond which now bears his name. The Androscoggin River Region still retains deer enough to afford good sport on the first snows of autumn; but moose and caribou are not very easily found.

It was in the fall of '93 that A. E. Rowell, T. A. Cushman and myself decided to try our luck, as we had often done before, deer-hunting. We concluded to go to the lakes, and set Nov. 22d as the date to meet each other at our home camp, as we called it, near the Upper Dam. The day came at last, and by half-past in the afternoon we were all in camp, with rifles, cameras, sleeping bags, and a good supply of provisions. The next morning we packed our knapsack with about a week's supply of food, took our trusty rifles and started in a boat for Beecher Camp, which is situated near the Richardson Ponds. We rowed to the head of Mollechunkamunk Lake, took our luggage and walked the rest of the way. Arriving at camp about noon, we found it occupied by its owner, Henry Swett, an old hunter and trapper and one of the best guides to be met around the lakes. After eating a lunch we all started off to learn the lay of the land so that we could hunt to better advantage on the following day; returning to camp quite early, supper was soon prepared, and in the evening we listened to some thrilling tales of adventure.

The next morning, as soon as it was light enough to see, we were all in the woods, travelling together until we found signs of game, then it was each one for himself. Mr. Swett went off on one of his long lines to look at some traps. Avery, Albert and myself took a deer's track. I had not been following my deer but a short time when I heard three or four shots fired in rapid succession; the first deer had been started. I jumped the deer that I was after, two small ones, in an hour or so, and just caught sight of them as they were going behind an old tree-top; I did not shoot, thinking that by following them an hour or two I might get a standing shot. This was a good lesson for me and I learned from it, that when you see a deer shoot at it. Shoot, too, as long as you can see it and don't be afraid that the bullets will injure the meat. These deer led me through swamps, blow-downs, etc., till finally they came to a cedar swamp that was so tracked up be deer that I lost the trail completely. Retracing my steps to the trail that we came upon in the morning I was not greatly surprised to find where someone had dragged a deer along the trail, towards camp. I gave a yell and hurried on, overtaking Avery near the camp, with a handsome spike-horn buck which he had shot, and dragged nearly three miles. We found Mr. Swett at home, having got some sable to pay for his day' work. Albert had not yet arrived, but we had not been waiting long, however, when he gave a hoot, and came into camp dragging a male deer that Avery had shot. We hung the two deer up in front of the camp, and they formed, indeed, a handsome picture for the sportsman. Thus ended our first day's hunt.

The bill of fare at Beecher Camp was potatoes, fresh pork, white bread, baked beans, tea and coffee; and what was most refreshing of all, after returning from a day's tramp, was a drink of clear, cool water taken from the little brook in front of the camp, which came tumbling down from the mountain. I would rather have a glass of that pure water, dipped from Beecher Brook, than any drink I can conceive of. Before retiring, Albert and Avery, like every good sportsman that's returned from a successful day's hunt, had a story to tell in regard to their day's work.

At five o'clock the following morning we were up and had breakfast well under way; after eating we concluded to go back to the place where the two deer were shot the previous day, and as soon as it was light we were off. Within two hours we found some quite fresh tracks of deer. Avery and Mr. Swett struck off to the right of the trail, while Albert and I hunted on some higher ground which was on the left of the trail. I traveled and traveled, over ridges, up ravines, through swamps and thickets, but to find a deer I couldn't, so I returned to camp. Mr. Swett had got home and he immediately informed me that "Rowell has shot an 'old lacing buck' and is trying to get it out of the woods," also that "I fired a bullet, smash, into the largest doe that I ever saw, but she got away from me after all." I started off to help Avery, but I found him near the camp. He had dragged the buck part way to camp, but finding that he was too much of a load for one man, had hung him up in the woods until he could have some help. Albert, having arrived in the meantime, had been through nearly the same maneuvers during the day that I had, and with equally as good luck, to wit, to find that the camp wasn't lost when it began to grow dark at night.

The next morning we followed Avery to where he left the buck; it was a medium-sized deer with a splendid set of antlers. Albert and Avery started with the buck, and took it down on the east side of the pond nearly opposite our camp. Mr. Swett and I kept up on the trail to our old hunting ground, but finding no fresh signs of deer we returned to our camp. This was our last day's hunting at Beecher Camp. It being Saturday and the stock of provisions getting low, we decided to go back to our camp, which we did on the following Sunday morning, Mr. Swett coming down later. Albert had shot one deer, Avery had shot two, and I had shot—not a blamed thing. As I made up my mind to shoot some game before returning home, my courage was still very good.

Six o'clock Monday morning found us ready for business. I was going to try deer hunting again, and Albert decided to go with me. Avery, having got deer enough, concluded to stay at camp to-day and Mr. Swett stayed with him. Albert and I took an easterly course until we came to a ridge, then we separated, Albert taking the north side of it and I the south side. We were to meet on the east end which we did in the course of an hour, without seeing any fresh signs of deer. Then we started in a southeast direction, and inside of twenty minutes we found two quite new deer tracks; Albert took one of them, and I the other. The deer that I was after traveled in a direct course towards the sun nearly, which was one point in his favor, he also kept on low, bushy ground, which was another point against me. I had walked about an hour, apparently, when I came up from the low land and on to the north side of a hill, and keeping on up the hill I soon came to two large tracks, which at first I thought were made by caribou, but on further investigation proved to be those of moose.

I gave up deer hunting immediately, and found myself trespassing on the feeding-ground of moose before I knew it. As I stood looking at the spruce and fir trees which the moose had pushed over to feed on, I hardly dared to move for fear of starting the game. Suddenly I heard a noise, and looking up the hill, saw two large black animals tearing through the woods. I threw up my rifle into position and when I caught a glimpse of anything black was rather inclined to shoot at it. I use the '86 model Winchester rifle, 40-82 caliber, and fired four or five shots before the moose got out of sight. Hurrying up towards where the two animals were when first shot at, I was greatly disappointed not to find a moose kicking in the snow. But on going still farther up the hill to the tracks, I found one of them sprinkled with blood, and taking the back track for a few steps, found two tufts of hair, one on each side of the track; this told me plainly that one bullet, at least, had passed clear through the moose. Was it my lot to have the luck of killing a moose, the largest species of the deer family? Pondering this and little realizing the danger of hunting the moose, I started in pursuit of the wounded animal.

The moose left the hill at once and traveled in low, swampy ground, lying down every ten or fifteen minutes, and keeping far enough in advance of me so that I caught sight of it only once, during the first half hour. Following on in this way for an hour or so, I had just come out a thick cedar swamp, on to the side of a hill, where the loggers had worked years before, when I heard a prolonged hoot. Knowing well what the call was, I answered back and sat down on a stump to wait. In about ten minutes Albert came rushing up and says, "Where is the caribou? Where did you hit him?" and "He is our meat, sure," etc., etc. I had not seen the animals distinctly enough to tell what kind they were, moose or caribou; but judging by their mode of feeding, and by the track, I knew without doubt that it was a moose. I took the lead, with my rifle ready to fire on short notice; Albert was close at my heels and prepared for business, too.

We kept on in this manner for nearly an hour, coming every five or ten minutes to where the moose had lain down, and were expecting to see it any time. We concluded to stop for a little while to see what effect it would have on our game; and, on following up the trail, we came in a few minutes to where the moose had lain down last, as we thought. Starting into a fast walk and from that into a run soon heard the animal crashing through the woods, a little way ahead of us. This put new life into our muscles, and we now hurried on faster than before. I soon caught sight of the moose and fired; but the huge animal kept on going so that I fired one or two more shots before bringing it to a halt. The moose stopped in such a position that I could not see its head distinctly, so I fired two or three shots, which were the last ones I had, as near to the heart as I could; but still the old moose managed to keep on its feet. Albert came up immediately, and meantime, the moose had swung its head so as to give me a clear shot at the brain. This, Albert did not appear to see quickly, so he passed his rifle to me, and one shot in the brain dropped the noble animal to the ground. We worked rather cautious at first but soon had the moose dressed (hunter's style), and thoroughly cleaned inside with snow. I put the heart, which was very large, into a bag that was attached to my belt, hung a red handkerchief over the carcass, and we were ready to "strike" for the camp.

We thought that a northwest course would bring us out near the camp, so I took the compass and followed that direction, while Albert, with the hunting axe, blazed a line until we reached a territory that we were familiar with. On our way home we devised a way to surprise Avery and Mr. Swett. Arriving at camp soon after dark, I took off my belt at once and hung it up. Albert and I were questioned sharply, but most in regard to deer. Oh, yes we had been deer hunting. Albert said that "I jumped a large buck this morning, and fired one farewell shot at him as he quickly disappeared in the brush, but I guess that the bullet didn't hit him." I had followed an old buck too, and he had led me straight away from camp so far that I was about disgusted with deer hunting. Presently I went to my belt, took the heart out of the bag and placed it on the table, and the shout that went round the camp will be one of the reminiscences of this trip.

On the following morning we all started with cameras, to pay our last respects to the fallen "monarch of the forest." Arriving at the scene of action in about two hours, Avery and Albert set their cameras at once and exposed a few plates, and the photographs taken from them a few days later, proved to be quite interesting. The next task in order was to skin the moose. Avery and Mr. Swett cut a trail through to the Big Lake, while Albert and I were at work on the moose. The trail to the lake was soon finished. We decided to hang up the meat before leaving it, fearing that some wild animal might try and eat it up before we had a chance to go after it; this we did by cutting a stout pole fifteen feet long, placing one end in the crotch of a tree and raising the other end up side of a tree, it fastened into position by means of a forked stick; the meat was cut up, and by attaching a strong cord to each piece, we had the meat (all that was good to eat, and some that wasn't).

THE MAINE TRAGEDY

Special, from *Forest and Stream*, March 24, 1900

"The Barker Hotel" on Mooselucmeguntic Lake

On the morning of October 4, 1899 Richard M. Knight, a young man from Boston, went with his friends up Bemis Stream to hunt deer, and when the group gathered together, there was no sign of Mr. Knight, he being evidently lost. Capt. Barker made his hotel and camps the center of command and several weeks were spent combing the woods, but no sign was ever seen of the young sportsman. In desperation, Mr. and Mrs. Knight put up a large reward for anyone who could find their son.The next early spring a Sioux Indian arrived, saying he was hired by Buckskin Sam, to find the hunter and produced a skull which he said was probably that of Mr. Knight, but Dr. Blake identified it as the skull of an older person with a disease and the teeth did not match those of the lost hunter. Soon after, a backwoodsman said that a few days after his disappearance, Knight appeared in Grafton, New Hampshire, but his was never proven. Finally, as a last resort, the grieving parents agreed to hire a Boston medium and this is the story produced by the editors of Forest and Stream-

BOSTON, MARCH 10.–No traces of the missing your hunter, Knight, who went out from Bemis, Me., early last October, have yet been found. Still the hunters and guides will make further trials as soon as the weather becomes warmer, and the snow begins to melt. The foxes are fond of digging down to dead bodies as the snow is melting in the spring, and it is hoped that by following their tracks the searchers may be led to where the body lies. Capt. Barker, with his men, has located a spot where firing was heard the second night after young Knight disappeared. It seems that a couple of trappers or hunters were camped at Four Ponds, three or four miles from Bemis, at the time, and heard a gun fired six or eight times in succession just at nightfall. They remarked that someone must have wounded a deer; but, on the firing continuing, they decided that someone was shooting squirrels or firing at a target. They thought little of the matter, however, till the next day, when more firing was heard in exactly the same direction. They again remarked that the hunter must be shooting squirrels. They did not know that anyone had been lost in the woods till they went out to the settlement sometime after, though they plainly heard the whistling of Capt. Barker's steamers as they were plied up and down the lake day and night., whistling being to guide young Knight into camp if possible. Later Capt. Barker has found these men and gone with them to the place where they were located when they heard the firing. Leaving them there with signals prearranged, he has gone into the woods in the direction of the shots heard. Firing his gun every few rods, the men at the location have directed him by shots from their own guns. If moving too far to the left, they fired one shot; if too far to the right, two shots. In this way he kept on into the woods, firing his own gun at regular intervals till the signal from the men agreed upon told him that he had gone far enough. When they signaled him to stop, he found himself in the very worst sort of a tangle and blow-downs, buried deep in snow. He searched here all that it was possible to search, in the hope of finding some signs of foxes or other animals having dug down through the three or four feet of snow for the body, but found nothing. Later this location will be much more thoroughly searched.

Still the spirit mediums continue to communicate with the parents of the lost boy, with Capt. Barker, with Mr. Wilson, the man who went out hunting with Knight the day he was lost, and with others. Each pretends to be able to locate Knight or his body. The communications now go unanswered, but at first it was not exactly so. Some very interesting stories might be told of what these mediums were ready to pretend to do during the time that the most active searching was being done. Always they demanded their pay in advance. Some of them even went to Bemis, though Capt. Barker and the friends and parents of the lost boy kept

the medium matter as quiet as possible. But one or two good stories have leaked out. In one case the medium, a woman, went to
Bemis, with the understanding that her expenses were to be paid,
and if she found the boy the reward of $500 was hers. When they
got there she frankly admitted that she was totally unable to travel
the rough woods, but from a trance or inward sight she gave a party of searches the directions, and told them they would find the
boy under a certain tree by a fallen log. The hunters traveled all
day as directed, but returned at night and tired and hungry. The
medium had sat by the fire all day, absorbed in a novel. When they
came in she flatly told them that they had searched "too far to the
east." The next day they took a direction further to the right–"to
the west," she called it; but at night they came in again without
success. Then she told them that "they had gone too far to the
west," Now, the fact of the matter was that traveling to the west
was exactly into the lake, while to the east was directly from Bemis
over the mountains. The medium had not even got her point of
compass right. The searchers declined to follow her directions
another day. Another woman medium was more courageous, and
even started the searchers on a course that was going to find the
lost boy. The searchers hunted all day, but found nothing but a
piece of paper, dropped by some searcher or hunter. There was
some writing on it, and they passed it to the medium to read.
She immediately began to search for her spectacles; she could not
read the paper without them. She did not find them. She would
have to go into a trance to find her glasses, and did so–just a little
short trance. She could see them. They were up in the woods, just
where she had left the searchers when giving them directions in
the morning. Would not one of the men go and get them? He was
willing to accommodate, but the lost glasses were reposing quietly
pushed back on the woman's head. The men had seen them there
all the time medium also went home the next day. No more have
since been employed.

– SPECIAL

Chapter 3

THE DEAD RIVER, UPPER
KENNEBEC AND MOOSE RIVER
REGIONS

The earliest history of this entire region is dominated by the early exploration, the Revolution and the Bingham Purchase. In 1767 Col. John Montressor, starting in Canada, paddled down the West Branch into Moosehead Lake and down the Kennebec to Fort Halifax in Winslow, the first building he encountered. He then went back up the Kennebec, across the Great Carry into the Dead River and followed this back to Quebec. Eight years later Col. Benedict Arnold used Montressor's journal to go to Quebec, a disastrous expedition chronicled in diaries, fiction and poetry.

Few people know that in 1772, between these two monumental events, two trappers worked their way up the Dead River and built a hut at Stratton Brook. One trapper was killed by a mountain lion and the other barely escaped with his life.

After the Revolution the State of Massachusetts needed money to pay its veterans and came up with the idea of selling large tracts of the Maine Woods through a lottery. William Bingham, a wealthy Philadelphia lawyer, ended up buying over two million acres in Maine, one tract along the upper Kennebec River, the other Down East. The Kennebec purchase included the eastern townships of Dead River and the towns along the Kennebec from Bingham to Parlin Pond.

In the winter of 1792 Samuel Weston of Skowhegan, with a group of hired men, made a survey of the east boundary of the

Bingham Purchase. This proved to be very expensive and exceedingly dangerous due to the amount of snow and harsh conditions, forcing Weston to ask for more pay to aid his assistants when he wrote his report.

Laying out the Canada Road started in 1817, when one of the Commissioners for Eastern Lands and General James Irish, the surveyor, began "laying out a road from Kennebec to our northern line, to meet a similar one from Quebec." Col. Jewett of Norridgewock undertook the clearing of the roadway, which was expected to be completed that year.

In June of 1818 Asa Redington of Waterville and a crew of lumbermen arrived at the forks of the South and North Branches of the Dead River, built a cabin, and commenced cutting many of the tall, virgin pines that grew along the riverbanks. They sent the logs down the river the following year, taking only 48 hours for them to travel from Stratton Brook to Waterville. At this time Caleb Stevens of Kingfield became the first settler of Eustis, in the employment of Mr. Redington.

Capt. Samuel Holden became the first settler of Moose River, when he brought his family north along the Canada Road in March of 1819 on snowshoes, including his 80 year old mother.

In 1830 Eleazer Coburn and his sons Abner and Philander began their extensive lumbering operations on the Kennebec and its tributaries. Abner would go on to become one of the wealthiest men in the State and Governor of Maine during the Civil War.

In the first week of February 1832, Hiram Rockwood took a trip up to the Dead River Region, going up both the South and North Branches, checking to see if any trespassers had cut wood on any state lands, but found no indiscretions. He returned to Anson and went up the Kennebec the following week on the Canada Road, stopping at The Forks, where John Rockwood joined him. They overnighted with Mr. Stevens at Parlin Pond, describing the travelling as very difficult walking. The next three days were spent checking townships around Moose River and Long Pond, but they found no roads into the woods, concluding no logging was done, and stayed with Capt. Holden. They then snowshoed to "Little Brasway Pond, "and on to Moosehead Lake to check that region. The following year Rockwood explored Jim Pond Township on the North Branch of the Dead River, estimating that it contained enough pine for fourteen million square feet of lumber, exclusive of saplings, which would amount to an additional ten million.

Martin Lockyere, an Englishman by birth, attended Oxford University. He was apparently involved in a love affair, causing his father to disown him. The young lady died soon after, causing Lockyere to immigrate to Canada, but finding it too populous, he went over the border in 1846 to Jackman and went to live as a hermit on an island, with his six cats, six miles from his nearest neighbor.

In April of 1850 William Churchill of New Portland, who was then 74 years old, killed a four-year old moose on the borders of the Dead River. He went into the woods with two young men, all on snowshoes, and came into a mooseyard and startled a moose. The old man outran the younger men, shot the moose and cut his throat some time before the young men caught up.

Mr. Blackden, the stage driver, reported in 1854 that two men were drowned in the Dead River when their boat hit a rock and was staved in. Two other river drivers were rescued.

A group of seven men from Farmington took a trip to the Chain of Ponds region in 1867, giving us a detailed picture of the lumbering camps and endeavors of Steward & Eames, whose lumbering domain extended all over the Chain of Ponds and back six miles. This region was also lumbered by Abner Coburn.

Bears were quite plentiful in this section in 1868 when it was reported that two gentlemen who had hunted at Mt. Bigelow, passed through Farmington with the skins of five bears they had trapped, 118 partridges and the skins of eleven foxes.

ANIMALS OF THE MAINE WOODS: THE CARIBOU

By Joshua G. Rich, from *Wild Animals of Maine* in *Forest and Stream*, March 25, 1886

Joshua Gross Rich (1820-1897) operated his store and camps on the Richardson lakes for many years, but finally retired to a farm in Greenwood. He later became a respected citizen of Bethel, continued writing and died there February 18, 1897. A strong and athletic outdoorsman, Rich was also educated and began writing articles of his adventures and encounters with wild animals as early as 1860 when he published a series in the Bethel Courier. Writing tales of lynx, caribou, bear, and other wild animals, he continued to publish in American Angler, American Sportsman and later in Forest and Stream. His writings give us detailed information about the fauna of the region, but more importantly Rich weaved much of the early history of the lakes into his narratives, leaving us with an insight into the earliest history of the Rangeley Lakes region.

...In the spring of 1862 I went with an Indian of the St. Francis Tribe – named Prince Bashola – on a hunting expedition from Canada down by the forks of the Kennebec River and over Moxy Township, in the northern part of Somerset County. On the borders of Moxy Pond we discovered a herd of caribou of nearly thirty individuals. With sheets spread over our heads and bodies we slowly advanced toward them on the lee side, so they could not scent us by the wind, and were favored by a light falling snow. We struck their sloat on the pond and followed up carefully within sight of them. I was highly excited. The woods seemed alive with them. Some were reared high up against the trees feeding on the moss; others digging away the snow from evergreens on the ground; others were walking about making a low moaning noise in short grunts; others were lying down, and others still fauning each other in the most affectionate manner. Presently I heard

Bushy fire (I called my Indian guide Bushy for short), and very soon after heard him shout, and at the same time the very woods seemed alive with caribou – the roaring sound of a large herd on the travel, and the sonorous grunts of the old males, together with the lively shouts of Bushy, who was an eighth of a mile to the north of me, made the woods ring with exciting interest. I started toward the Indian, but it was with the greatest difficulty I could reach the spot from which the shout arose, and on my way shot, right and left, an old buck and a year old doe.

The whole herd were now fairly aroused and on a lively scare, running hither and thither. Bushy had shot a large doe, and several old males were after him, and he had jumped into a beech top and had dropped his ammunition. On my approach they scattered, and Bushy, being relieved, soon reloaded and let drive at the nearest.

As one came near in their circuit, we would shoot until we had killed seven, when the whole herd made off to the northward at a tremendous pace, and we with tumplines and fir boughs dragged our game together on the shore of the pond and then enjoyed the realization of our successful hunt over a pot of tea and roast venison.

We camped on the shore of Moxy Pond that night and the next day we made some moose sleds and loaded on each a whole animal and slowly made our way out of the woods to the militia road, made more than a hundred years ago by Arnold, while on his disastrous expedition into Canada, six miles distant, thence back to camp and soon until we hauled them all out. Bushy then returned to Moxy where he trapped a few weeks for fishers and sables. I took the caribou to Boston, whole, hired a room at the foot of Cambridge Street on Charles Street, where, after due notice in the daily papers, I was visited by Prof. Agassiz and gentlemen from the Boston Society of Natural History and agents from Yale College, and others who examined my stock in trade with much interest, and made purchases – some for skeletons, others for mounting, and others for both – and the most of the same caribou can now be seen, prepared and preserved, in the above museums.

Thus a relic of that herd of twenty five years ago is being hand-ed down to future posterity – possibly in the future years when the original animal shall be extinct.

NOTES FROM A WINTER CAMP

By H. and A. from *Forest and Stream*, January 21, 1886.

 *Since the 1840's logs have been harvested in the Moose River Valley and floated down the river, through Brassua Lake and on to Moosehead Lake. Here they would be hauled across the lake to continue their journey down the Kennebec River to the waiting mills. Early on, a wooden dam was built at the outlet of Brassua Pond, creating a larger lake as storage for the water needed on the spring drive. All winter long, the lumbermen would spend long, lonely nights around the warm stove and one anonymous logger ventured to give the editors and readers of Forest and Stream magazine a small glimpse into their life in the northern Maine woods throughout the year and especially at Christmastime.Editor Forest and Stream:*

As long ago as July when we pitched our tent on the shores of Brassua, we promised you as well as ourselves to write a series of letters for your excellent journal; but it is no easy task for a man of the woods to take his pencil and ponder over the phrasing of sentences for critical eyes to read. He may not hesitate, nay, he enjoys to take his corn cob pipe between his teeth, and after locating himself in good range of the hindmost log of the fire-place, a half dozen old mountain salts as his companions, and spin out lies about the size of the trout he caught the day before, or the height of a windfall that a buck deer that he was chasing last winter jumped over. Should he now and then in his narrative stray away from his old-time time teachings of Lindley Murray, there is no unkind comment, nothing confronts him at the finish but gaping mouths and dilated eyes, for it is almost a religious dictum among those big-hearted men of the forest to believe, or pretend to believe, every lie that's told them; and the bigger the lie, the more unbounded this seeming credulity. But when one puts himself in print he calls forth, not alone criticism on his literary effort, but the wrath of the conflicting witness. With this fear before our eyes we have postponed our advent into your columns until a sufficient number of incidents should really occur to build up a letter that should at least be free from parry and thrust from a letter.

Our cabin is on the south shore of lake, Norway Point, with its rugged pines, affording excellent shelter from the north winds. The famous deer park, extending from Lower Moose River to Brassua Stream, is within five minutes' walk of camp. This territory, six miles square, presents a sight at present that could not fail to enrapture the eye of any lover of a deer chase. The fall of snow is not yet sufficient to drive the deer to yarding, and their roamings have literally beaten down the snow covering nearly the entire park. The tracks are so numerous that it is impossible to select any particular one and follow it. Reports from all parts of the lake region, however, proclaim deer to be more numerous this season than ever known before.

The fact that deer are plentiful and trout scarce in this section is not a hard one to understand to any one spending a year here in camp. Just as soon as the spring season opens for trout the boats plying the lake are crowded with sportsmen, and the Mount Kineo Hotel, which affords accommodations for five hundred persons, is soon crowded to overflowing. Not a day is to be wasted. On the evening of their arrival they arrange their rods and tackle, and, although many of them make a three-months' stay of it, the next morning bright and early finds them en route to the alleged best fishing grounds. The waters of the different streams are kept in a foam by constant fly-whipping until the law kindly interferes and leaves barely enough grown trout to carry on preparations for the next season's sport. And even the law has no terrors for some of these men, as a neighboring magistrate's docket will bear witness. Many of these self-styled sportsmen catch as many as one thousand trout in a season, and they are proud of it, too; but it costs them persistent hard work every day.

Mount Kineo is the best center for nearly all sportsmen intent upon the streams and forests of Northern Maine, affording as it does, large facilities by steamer and canoe for fifty miles in any direction. It is curious to note how the preference runs toward summer, rather than winter sports. During the summer Mr. Dennen, of the Kineo House, is constantly at wit's end to know how to provide for his great number of guests. Yet, almost the first blast savoring of winter that comes from the north overcrowds the homeward bound steamboats, and within a week all is solitude. During the summer, a dozen canoes might be seen on Brassua Lake any day, and its banks dotted with tents, which now, just at the zenith of the real sport of this action, Camp Annie contains the only remnants of the summer boarder. Why is this? Do sportsmen really not care for the larger game? It is certainly more conductive to health, more pleasurable to spend a few weeks of a winter in the woods, especially where game is so abundant and deer can be had for the going for them, than to sit in a canoe with the thermometer in the nineties, engaged in constant battle with black flies, midgets and mosquitoes, with the phantom hope of an occasional trout. And this is the same thing day after day, while in the winter woods, with trapping and shooting, there is always an occurring novelty.

We have thus far, killed one moose, one caribou and two deer—just enough to satisfy our fancy in the way of hides and horns and supply us with fresh meat. We do not exaggerate when we say that with persistent hunting we believe we could have killed fifty of these animals since the open season came in. Our moose weighed 1,100 pounds and had a fine pair of horns, as did our caribou, which weighed 550 pounds. The deer were small.

Although we have all the romance and solitude pertaining to a howling wilderness, yet we are not, as the uninitiated suppose, and shut off from civilization by any means. Mt. Kineo, our post office, affects a telegraph office and a very good store where all articles necessary to camp life are purchasable. It is a ten-mile trip, on snowshoes, from camp, and is taken fortnightly. We append a bill of fare for our Christmas dinner. Of course we brought many of the delicacies from New York, but most of the articles were obtained here. It will prove to many of your readers that winter camp life is not all bacon and beans, as Nessmuk would lead them to suppose; but that with a little care exercised in the selection of a location and the forethought to lay in a varied supply, much solid comfort may be experienced within the logs of a winter cabin. Our thermometer has registered 15 degrees below zero, and for a month has clung constantly near the dividing line; yet we have never experienced a day when the closing of our cabin door has been essential to our comfort, so perfect is our shelter. We are comfortable and happy in our seclusion.

CAMP ANNIE—CHRISTMAS, 1885

MENU

OYSTERS
Canned   Cider
SOUP
Vegetable   Claret
FISH
Baked Trout.   Boiled Togue.   Herring, Smoked.
GAME
Caribou, Cranberry Sauce   Rabbits, Champagne
ROAST
Deer   Turkey
ENTRÉE
Giblets a la Allison, Camp Annie Fritters
Stewed Kidneys   Huntingtonian Maccaroni
VEGETABLES
Onions   Corn   Peas   Tomatoes   Cabbage.
Rice.   Hominy

MY WIFE'S VACATION

By A. G. McK., from Forest and Stream, June 30, 1887

 An article in the FOREST AND STREAM by "Special," dealt with the advisability of sportsmen taking the lady members of their families with them upon their camping out expeditions. Another article closed with the query why this is not oftener done. I suppose some wretches will reply that it is because they go for pleasure. I propose to tell you my experience.

In 1885 I promised my wife she should go with me, but later she agreed to wait a year if I would certainly take her then. So I went with a pair of fellows, had a good time, and on my return told her I thought she could stand such a trip. Last winter I took her out with me on one of my trips to fish for pickerel through the ice. The fact that I never saw her before in such good spirits as on that day led me to think that there might be as much "Indian" in her as in me. But another year came around, I dreaded for her the eight days of travel by rail, stage and buckboard which the round trip would necessitate, and I presented the tediousness of it to her in a manner which made her weaken.

One day in the early part of August, 1886, I went out to a neighboring village a few miles from here to see a friend with whom I have spent many happy hours in quest of sport and health, and when I returned I had concluded arrangements with him to camp out during September in the eastern part of Maine, close to the scene of the deer warden tragedy. At the dinner table that day, I told the "party of the second part" of my plans; and I thought they were received with rather an ominous silence. I felt quite sure of her opinions next noon, for when I came home she notified me that I "might make my plans to go to Maine, where I promised to take her last year, as soon as I pleased, for she was going." That seemed to me to settle the whole business, and I so remarked.

I was more than pleased with the idea of having her with me though, and I knew that once there, all right, she would enjoy such a vacation, better than any other, but as she had never been strong I dreaded the experiment. There seemed to be a pretty good prospect, however, of settling the question.

We started Aug. 29, stayed that night in Boston and the next day went via the Boston and Maine road to Kingfield, Me., arriving there very late. At the Portland transfer station I counted over twenty men with guns and rods.

We stopped at the new hotel which had been erected during the past year, and found accommodations quite in the modern style. I kept a close watch upon Madame, but to my surprise she said she was not tired in the least. The next day we took the stage for the thirty-mile ride up in the Dead River country. A light rain was falling, and the fog had settled into the valleys, so that the fine views of Bigelow and other mountains were wholly obscured. Still the ride was enjoyable and the passengers all proved to be charming company. What lots of fine fellows we meet when cruising around in this way. One of our party was a New Yorker, a Mr. Beck, who was going into the woods from Eustis for a month's "solitary confinement," except for the company of his guide, it being his seventh successive yearly trip to this place. At night Madame declared she had had a splendid ride, and was in perfect order. I could not quite see how this could be, for at home a walk of half a dozen blocks was liable to tire her out. All right, my lady, you may pretend to me that you are as good as new, but I know a seven mile buckboard ride to-morrow that will surely lay you out or I am no prophet. Although it was not cold and raining hard, and only and hour or two before dark, she was for going on at once; and only strong resistance on my part, and good advice from some ladies who know what such a ride in such a storm meant, induced her to change her mind. I had walked over the road several times, but had never ridden. The next morning I thought I would ride a short distance, and when she had become accustomed to this style of locomotion I would get off and walk. Before we had gone ten rods I had one arm around her and was holding on "for all I knew how," or she would have been thrown off as fast as she could get on again. It was an awful road. At one time three wheels would be in the air and one in a hole, and perhaps in a minute this order would be reversed. But all things generally come to an end, and so did the road. This was the point at which I was to carefully lift my exhausted wife from the buckboard and help her into a camp. But I didn't do it. She was off before I could shake myself together, and my word for it, I never was so surprised in my life as I was then to find her not in the least tired or lame, but in every respect in as good condition as myself. Although it made me out a false prophet, it was very gratifying. We found a good dry camp and a bed of boughs, the best an expert could make, and with sheets on it too. Think of that.

We spent two weeks here in solid happiness, fishing perhaps a couple of hours a day, and reading, resting, gunning and rowing about the lake, or passing time in any manner that suited us best. Madame saw lots of things that were new to her, such as ducks, loons, rabbits, etc., and one day she was lucky enough to see a deer while she was sitting in the door of the camp. She will not admit that she was disconcerted, except once, and that was one night about midnight, when a tremendous "hooter" came close to camp and awoke everyone in it with his dismal crying.

All who have ever been in this region will remember Kennedy Smith, at least by reputation. A week before our arrival he had been crushed by a tree, and we found him in camp here making a big struggle for life, and laying plans for a new camp another year, which he said would be by water never yet fished, and at the same time easy of access. Good luck to him.

The fishing seemed better this year than ever. I have thought many times if I were running a camp of this kind, I would allow no one to fish who did not take a small car along with the boat and keep the fish alive if possible, and put them in a larger one I should have near the landing at night. This could be drawn upon for food and emptied when too full, and a useless waste of fish prevented. I saw a party bring in 289 dead trout one day which were not needed for food, am I am sure the boys would have been full as willing to have brought them in alive as dead. In my last three days fishing I brought only five trout to camp, returning to the water all others caught, while the party I mentioned brought in 571 in the same time, all dead. Such a reckless waste as this could easily be prevented, but no one seems to care. In some such way I predict that under present arrangements one of the best fishing resorts in Maine will, in five years, have become one of the poorest.

Of the five trout I spoke of saving, I caught a double of half-pounders, one a silver trout and the other a blood red fellow. One was hooked through the back and the other through the belly. They made things lively, and I felt that I had done well when I landed them. Madame fished for two days with fair success, using bait; then she laid down her rod and said she was through fishing until she could use a fly, like other folks. She stuck to it, too, and this spring I am engaged to give her lessons in casting.

One evening after supper we went out for a little while, and saw what I had often read of, but had never been lucky enough to see, the water "alive" with fish. This evening every trout seemed to be feeding upon the surface, and I tell you, I flew around. As a natural consequence I broke the tip of my rod the first thing. It was too late to go to camp and rig another, so I was compelled to quit or do the best I could. But it was one of those scarce days when the fish are looking for you, and will bite at anything. Fancy casting wasn't needed, and I would point out the fish I would take next, and then get out my line as best I could, and I generally got him. Darkness came altogether too soon to suit me, but not before I had gathered in a couple of dozen. Fish are freaky creatures. The best day's brook fishing I ever had was one when, according to all traditions, I ought not to have had a bite.

Madame's vacation ended before we were half ready. She had been perfectly happy, and I was a false prophet. If it rained and camp leaked a little she moved her chair and kept on with her work or reading, and let it leak. In short, she took things as they came, like an old camper. The result of my experiment was a conclusion that any woman almost can not only take such a trip, but will enjoy it and be benefited thereby as much as her husband or brother, if she can only get the chance.

I was very glad that I gave one woman a chance, and that is not all, I shall never go again without her.

– A. G. MCK., MIDDLETOWN, CONN.

ON MOOSEHEAD WATERS

By T., from *Forest and Stream*, August 28, 1887

Northwest of Moosehead Lake, in Maine, lies a tract of country well suited to the production of trout and game. It has not the great extent of uninhabited forest found further east in the Aroostook country, but the trout average larger, and in some sections the larger game is, perhaps, as likely to be seen as in any part of the State.

It was the fortune of the writer to spend two weeks of summer in canoe and camp in this region. Although I had caught thousands of trout in Connecticut, during more than twenty-five years of fishing experience, I had never been into the wilderness to leave all other affairs and betake myself wholly to sport and recuperation. The friend who induced me to take the trip had been in this country many times, and was almost as familiar with its lakes and streams as the guides. Leaving Boston at 8 o'clock, Friday morning, July 2, we were at Skowhegan, Maine at 6 o'clock in the evening. Here we hired a livery team, and the next night were at the forks of the Kennebec, forty-six miles away. The road follows the Kennebec River all the way, is in good condition and affords a very pleasant drive. There are comfortable hotels every ten or fifteen miles. A stage runs each way between the Forks and Skowhegan every week day. At a farmhouse about fifteen miles below the Forks we saw a young yellow and white "coon cat." The large bushy tail was ringed with alternate yellow and white bands. We stopped and tried to effect a purchase, but the lady of the house told us there was "not money enough in the country to buy him." She said this cat was sent to her from Fairfield, Me., when a kitten.

We found that our guides, who had previously been engaged by letter, had everything in readiness, and at an early hour Monday morning we bade farewell to the last settlement and, by the silent and steady strokes of the paddle, were borne away to find what of interest the forests, lakes and streams might afford.

We spent an active week, and although we caught only a moderate number of trout and no large ones, we were very fortunate in seeing an unusual number of the wild life of the wilderness. There were seen one caribou, five deer, including two fauns, five beavers and three otters, all in six days. We had all the trout we needed and or guides salted and brought in perhaps 20lbs. The largest trout taken weighed 2lbs. Our guides took us to a lake which they had discovered the year before, and which they believed was rarely visited. The canoes had to be carried a considerable distance through the forest to the lake. This genuine lake of the woods covers seven or eight acres, and is mostly shallow and overgrown with lily pads. At one end there is an old beaver house, and around this some clear water of considerable depth, and here the trout lie. In three hours' fishing we took 18 1/2 lbs. of dressed trout. The largest weighed 22oz. according to my friend's estimate, which he backed up by his pocket scales; and at this and other times during the week he gained great respect from me by the accuracy with which he could name at sight the weight of a trout. The scales never failed by a single ounce to agree with his estimate. I, however, learned later that these were peculiar scales. They would make a trout weight anywhere from 3/4 lb. to 1 1/2 lbs. at the will of the manipulator. The mountains rise abrupt and rugged from two sides of the lake, and all its shores are covered with the primeval forest. A small family of beavers live in a house at the mouth of the little stream that feeds the lake. Tracks of caribou and deer were numerous, and a moose had worn almost a path where he came to the water. Three otters were fishing and came within three or four rods of our canoes.

One night we camped in a hunter's lodge on a little island in a lake near the Canada line. While it was still daylight a doe and fawn came out and on the sandy head opposite our camp. The fawn was in the red coat mostly and was as playful as a lamb. We watched the antics of this little fellow for a long time, till he followed his doe into the woods again. Along this same beach we saw traces of a moose. He had walked along the sand for half a mile. Setting out from the shore is a great rock known to the woodsmen as Gull Rock. Here there is each year to be found a gull's nest. Some gulls were circling around the lake. We climbed the rock and found a deserted nest only.

Shortly before our trip two woodsmen going over our route had the fortune to get from one tree an old she-bear and three yearling cubs. We found this tree, which was a good-sized pine, well scratched with the claws of bears. The partly devoured body of a deer, upon which the bears had been feeding, lay under the tree, and nearby were the carcasses of three of the bears. In the sand banks of the adjacent stream were the fresh tracks of a very large bear, doubtless the father of this unfortunate bear family. The old fellow was seen at the time the others were killed, but kept himself out of danger.

Of grouse we saw very few; they seem to have disappeared from this region, where I am told they were very numerous in years since. At one place we went ashore to see the work of bank beavers, and saw stumps a feet or more in diameter from which the beavers had felled the trees. Our guide told of having measured one stump 22in. in diameter.

As our trip was in July we found black flies, minges and mosquitoes. As a protection against the former we carried a "fly cream" that is freely advertised. I gave it a trial all the first day, applying it with a liberal hand and was slow to believe there was no protection in an article so confidently puffed and backed by testimonials. By night I was so bitten by black flies as to show the marks a month afterward. Had there been no other repellent in the party I should certainly have been driven out of the woods; fortunately there was plenty of a mixture of sweet oil and tar, and this really gives protection and comfort. This, however, fails as a protection against the mosquitoes at night. We had two covers of cheese strainer cotton arranged to go over the head and arms and kept away from the face by hoops. But the nights were hot, and the heated breath being thrown back in the face by the too heavy cloth, made the arrangement intolerable. Then I had a canvas hat arranged with vents and this I could fasten over my head, and by putting some twigs to keep the veiling away from my face so the mosquitoes could not reach me, found protection. The hat was too warm. Arranging this headgear with care and covering hands and feet with the blanket, I listened to the buzz of the baffled insects with serenity and soon fell asleep. After an hour or two I would awake to find I had in sleep thrown off the covering, so as to expose my face, or the twigs had become displaced so as so let the veiling fall on an ear or nose and the exposed member was being worked by as many mosquitoes as could find room. When I go to the woods again I shall have covering of silk veil arranged over hoops and long enough to tie under the arms. With an arrangement of this kind for protection at night and plenty of tar and oil for use by day I shall have no fear of insects. My companion said there not only black fly this year where sometimes there were a million, but even his pocket scale won't back that statement.

The second week we camped in a "head-works" on Long Pond, fifteen miles above Moosehead Lake. A head-works is a small shanty built on a raft, and is used by the lumbermen in the spring when they are engaged in rafting logs across the ponds by means of a windlass. Here we found a stove, a good protection from the rain, and there were few flies or mosquitoes. Fires had run through the timber along the shores and there seemed to be no large game in the vicinity. We saw one otter, and making an excursion up one of the streams flowing into the pond found a beaver dam about 30ft. long and 3ft. high, setting back the water for over a mile. Our guides cut a path through the brush till they could get their canoes in the still water above the beaver dam. Working the canoes noiselessly up the stream we soon heard the loud reports, such as are made by a beaver as he strikes the water with his tail in diving, and coming around a point saw a very large beaver plain in the water. He would swim a little way, then dive, striking the water with his tail in such a way as to make a report like a pistol, and throwing the water several feet in the air. Our canoes drifted with perhaps 30 ft. of him before he took alarm, and disappeared. The trout were very numerous in this beaver pond. The largest we took weighed a pound, but most of them were from 3 to 5oz. Our best fishing from this camp was at the mouths of streams flowing into Long Pond, and this sport grew better as the water became warmer. One night we built a fire on a point of rocks near camp and fished for eels, baiting pieces of chub. No eels were caught, but a fine trout of 1 ¼lbs. came almost ashore in front of the fire to take the bait. He was taken about 9 o'clock and after the last of twilight was gone.

Our custom here was to start out about 8 o'clock in the morning and paddle up some stream or to a place in the lake where the entrance of the stream attracted the trout. We took with a broiling iron, tea pail, some coffee, bread and bacon. After catching a supply of trout, we started a fire, made some coffee, broiled some trout and bacon, took our dinner leisurely, and perhaps by 2 o'clock launched our canoes again for exploring or fishing, or more likely both, and by 5 or 6 o'clock were back in camp.

Here we just rested and grew fat and rugged every hour. None of our friends knew where we were and no telegram or letter could be sent to us. That is the way to throw off all business. Get where no reports, either good or bad, can come, and if your business place burns up you won't know it till you get out of the woods. My mind was here as free from every care as that of a child.

We captured a young loon about as big as a goose egg. He was a sleek little fellow and was caught in a landing net after being tire out by continued chasing. He would dive as an old one, only he could not stay under so long nor go far. When released he went under and only showed his head at intervals till a long way from our boats. Then we secured two young black ducks. These would weigh about a pound each. They could not fly, and when we gave chase in a canoe they ran ashore and hid in the grass and bushes where we caught them. As they were well matched and seemed able to make a race on their merits, we decided they should have a swimming match. Placed side by side in the water, the birds at the word were released. No sooner were the ducks at liberty than they went down like loons. One we never saw again, and the other showed his bill and the top of his head only, at intervals of two or three rods, till beyond our sight.

The second day of our rest at Long Pond, we met near the foot the pond two young men, with a birch bark canoe. They evidently looked on us as at least doubtful characters and did not want much to do with us. Our canvas suits did not look particularly clean nor knobby; we had not been shaved for ten days, and the frequent and free application of tar and oil with plenty of sun, gave no doubt some grounds for their evident suspicion. By persistent questioning we learned they were part of a company of four from West Newton, Mass., and were camped in a log-driver's camp at the foot of the rapids about a mile below and had a canvas canoe at their camp. We did not wait for any invitation, but having caught trout enough for all, we went to their camp, turned in our fish and had dinner with them. They had hired their canoes at Moosehead Lake and had come up without guides. The birch canoe they had carried a mile through the woods to avoid the swift and broken water, but on the advice of our guides decided to try running the canvas up the river. Taking a part of their luggage we pushed on ahead. After catching as many trout as were needed for supper and breakfast for our whole party, and waiting their appearance until we grew uneasy for their safety, we sent our men back in one canoe to learn the cause of the delay. In about an hour our guides returned with the young men and their canoe. At the first quick water the Massachusetts men attempted to run, their canoe tipped over throwing two of their number into deep water. Everything that had been in the canoe was soaked–blankets, provisions, and extra clothing. The party had one good fly-rod and that was lost, also a knapsack containing all their flies, maps, and many little articles the loss of which was an inconvenience. We piloted them to our camp, where there was room enough for all, and did what we could to make them comfortable. They were with us as long as we remained in the woods, and retained possession of the camp a week after we left. I learned by a letter received from one of the party after their return, that the men who guided us ran their canoes back to Moosehead Lake for them, and in an eddy below the rapids where their canoe was capsized, found the fly-rod and most of the other property which had been lost in the catastrophe.

I think it a mistake for inexperienced men to try to canoe without guides through waters with which they are not familiar. These young men when we met them had not been able to catch many trout, and were very short of provisions. They had nearly half a barrel of had tack, which was spoiled by the upsetting of their canoe, and that is about all they did have. They would had been forced to make a few meals of had tack only before they could get to where they could replenish their supplies if we had not succored them.

One little stream flowing into Long Pond was completely covered up with bushes, but by running a canoe up the stream a little way some short casts could be made under the overhanging brush. The water was clear and shallow, and from his position in the canoe the caster could see the movements of every fish. Usually a dozen or more trout lay just where the flies could be dropped over them. Sometimes twenty casts would be made before a trout would take any notice of the flies, then a trout a quarter or half a pound weight would come up as if that particular fly was what he had been looking for a long time. In this way a half dozen or more would be caught, after which no more could be coaxed to rise. Off the mouth of another stream I hooked a trout showing such energy and strength as to convince me I had the largest fish of the trip. The canoe was run away from the weeds and grass into the deeper water where the trout was hooked, and the 6oz. rod bent nearly double as it checked the rushes of the gamy fish. When this trout was netted he weighed only a pound, but the cause of his apparent strength was manifest. He was hooked through the back in such a way as to give full play to all his strength.

At an early hour on the Friday morning or our second week in the woods, we packed our camp duffle and turned our faces homeward. That night we were at the hotel at the Forks. The next day Skowhegan was made in time for an easy supper, and Waterville, eighteen miles further, in time to take the train for Boston, which was reached at 6 o'clock Sunday morning.

I had seen a bit of wild nature, and although the 3 and 4lb. trout I had hoped and expected to see did not show themselves, I was satisfied with the trip. The experience of the friend who took me to his favorite outing place served to make sure a reasonable degree of sport, and the kindness and generosity that are as natural to him as the love of the woods made him the king of camp companions. I shall not soon forget the special care he took that I might not, by my inexperience, lose any part of the sport or fail to see everything of interest. Our guides were skillful canoemen, cheerful, tireless, uncomplaining workers and pleasant companions. They did all they could to make pleasant our vacation, and more than earned the moderate wages they asked. A canoe trip is from the fatigue of tramping; and never being tired; the canoeist is always in condition to enjoy all the pleasures of the wilderness.

The trip of which I have written occupied sixteen days from Boston. The cost was about $75 apiece exclusive of money spent for tackle, etc., before starting. In a trip of this kind one learns much about the lumber business and the mode of life of the people engaged in it. Another summer I hope to start again, rod in hand, for the Maine woods.

– T., PROVIDENCE, R. I.

AN ENCOUNTER WITH A MOOSE

By Macannamac, from *Shooting and Fishing*, Dec. 12, 1889

Early in October, this last fall, I had been hunting for nearly a week in the Moose River Valley of Northern, Maine, and although the weather was anything but fine, had succeeded in bagging two caribou, a large bull with a fine set of antlers, and a cow with antlers about six or eight inches long. The day following my good luck, my guide and I started for the place where the caribou were left, to get out the antlers of the bull and some more of the meat. I had the skin of the bull tied on my back and shoulders, and the head and antlers on top, which the guide threw two hindquarters over his head with one leg projecting out forward from each shoulder and steadied them by an arm slung over each leg. In this manner we started for the camp, about two miles distant. Before proceeding half a mile along the side of the mountain, we came upon another cow caribou, possibly one of the herd of four that I had shot into the day before, but only stopped a moment to look at her and see her get out of the way.

I started along a few steps in front of my guide, and we trudged along quietly under out loads for nearly a quarter of an hour, when I was suddenly halted by a cautionary signal from the guide. "Did you see hear anything?" said he. "No," I replied, and asked him if he had. "Yes," he replied, "big game ahead; I heard a heavy step." I waited a moment, but thinking him mistaken, passed on; but his practical ear was not deceived, for I had not taken half a dozen steps before I heard a noise ahead distinctly. I looked in the direction for a moment, then toward the guide, who was standing transfixed, pointing in a certain direction. I shall never forget my sensations as I looked in the direction and saw the immense head, antlers and shoulders of a bull moose. It is a situation we all hope to take in as the zenith of our ambitions,–to face a bull moose in his native element and within sixty yards' range.

Instinctively I raised my rifle and drew a bead upon him, then I thought of the 700 pounds of caribou meat laid out, and fifteen miles from the nearest settlement. I felt it would be a wanton act to fell that huge monster and leave his carcass to rot in the woods, and I lowered by rifle. I already had a fine set of antlers on my back, handsomer than those on the moose, who antlers, though large and long, were tined and not palmated like those of an older moose.

"Why don't you shoot?" whispered the guide. "Too much meat," I answered. "You better shoot; you may never in your life time have another such a good opportunity to shoot a bull moose." "But we have got more meat now than we can save and carry out," I added. "Never mind: shoot him quick, he is moving away; the moose meat is much better; we can throw away the caribou and take out the moose." I raised the rifle the second time, and if the antlers had come up more to my ideas, would have fired, but held to my first intention. The moose, in the meantime, moved leisurely, at a tangent, toward us, if anything, presenting his whole frame to view. He looked the size of a mountain. I shall never forget how tall he appeared. He was looking upon us with considerable curiosity, and I do not blame him, loaded as we were. My guide, afterwards remarked that he didn't think the bull had ever before seen anything, in his travels, that looked exactly like us. He would turn his head first one side, then the other, his antlers describing the arc of a large circle; then he would stick his nose out as if to sniff us, and lay his big ears back, and his mane would rise like the hair on a cat's back, and his antlers rest back upon his shoulders. At one time I did not know but that he was contemplating a charge upon us. He looked a veritable "monarch of the forest." (The guide estimated him at four years old and over 900 pounds in weight.) He must have stood, trying to "take us in," for several minutes, or until my guide, rather piqued that I should not take the prize, remarked that if I was going to stand there and look at him all day, he was not going to hold the caribou meat, and giving himself a lurch sideways, landed the hind-quarters upon the ground. This motion and sound startled the moose, and he gave three or four mighty jumps, at each plunge producing a thud I shall never forget, and which actually jarred the ground from the heavy concussion, and then struck into a trot down the side of the mountain.

He was now thoroughly scared; as the guide said, he must have scented the caribou meat and blood. His wake was simply terrific. I cannot describe it; only those who have seen or heard a moose running away can appreciate it. It sounded like a cyclone passing down the slope of the mountain; or like (as I read recently in a paper, describing, very fittingly, a moose running in the woods) a locomotive engine plunging along, off the track. He seemed to pay no attention to small growths in his way, such as small maple, ash and spruce, but would break them down like reeds. Some I afterwards measured between two and three inches in diameter, his tracks, which were deeply sunken in the earth from his ponderous weight, were between five and six inches across. As he ran off he carried his head a little lower than the upper line of his body, his nose straight out and antlers snug upon his shoulders. For full twenty minutes we could hear him, long after he had reached the valley below.

Once before I had heard the same effect, but in a less marked degree. My guide and I were following in a canoe, a cow moose in and out of small bogs and along the river banks in a district not far from this same place. It was a calm, clear night in October, and the cow had given several "calls." I thought I could distinctly hear the wind blowing over an adjacent mountain, accompanied by the creaking of trees, and remarked to the guide that the wind was rising, but to my surprise he informed me that what I heard was the bull in the distance coming down the side of the mountain to the "call" of the cow.

My encounter with the moose afforded me the most intense enjoyment I have experienced in the woods, and I felt well paid for having spared him. I have often thought of the satisfaction it would have given me if I had had my camera with me and could have snapped it upon him in his various positions. Of what value would the results have been as studies of this noble animal so fast becoming extinct.

– MACANNAMAC

HUNTING THE MOOSE, PART II: UNCLE HOWARD'S DREAM AND WHAT CAME OF IT

By R. V. McBain, from *Shooting and Fishing*, October 2, 1892

Robert V. McBain (1858-1932) was born on a farm in Pennsylvania, but left at a young age, and moved to Boston. Here he worked as a clerk for many years, then as an insurance agent. Spending his summer vacations in the woods, he loved hunting and it was while living in Boston that he wrote the following

Water Warrior
(Currier & Ives)

account. McBain removed to Montana by 1910, living first in Hamilton, then in Missoula. He died in 1932 at Idaho Falls, Idaho at the age of seventy-four.In his long article about a trip called "Hunting a Moose" he and his brother-in-law went to Camp Hurricane in the Kibby Valley of the Dead River Region. Here is the story he related about his "well-loved, fat and jovial Uncle Howard."

On the morning of our second days residence at Camp Hurricane–as Ellsworth had named our woodland retreat, whether on account of the decidedly stiff gale that had swept under its walls during our first night beneath its roofs, or because of its proximity to Mt. Hurricane, I am unable to state–Isaac James, guide and moose slayer, put in an appearance. The manifestations of delight with which we greeted him seemed to make the old man very happy. But I must confess that if the said Isaac had not been the bearer of our lost blankets, our reception of him probably would not have been so heartfelt and sincere. Please do not understand, however, that we were not glad to have Mr. James among us for his own sake, for such was not the case. Like Brutus, it was not that we loved Isaac less, but the heat and comfort of our blankets more.

Upon the arrival of Mr. James, the man who had hired himself out to us as guide, although not acquainted with the country, packed his knapsack and turned the toes of his moccasins towards Camp Douglas.

The next day Ellsworth had the good fortune to kill a fine, fat doe, and as ducks were quite plentiful on the lake, Camp Hurricane was the scene of many a feasting during the remainder of the week.

On Tuesday morning, October 20, breakfast was served at an early hour by our guide, and as the sun painted the rock-capped, hoary head of Mt. Hurricane a delicate orange, and tinted the bank of clouds floating in the east a fiery crimson, three Nimrods armed to the teeth, or thereabouts, and led by the redoubtable James –not Jesse, however–emerged from Camp Hurricane, and gliding noiselessly along a well-beaten deer path, soon reached the base of the mountain. Here a halt was called, and, after a few minutes consultation, Ellsworth and the guide began the ascent of its rugged slope.

Ellsworth was very anxious to try the killing powers of his new .40-calibre Winchester, and as the guide reported having seen many fresh deer signs on the second bench of the mountain, he decided to go where the slender-limbed, soft-eyed, round-bodied creatures were said to congregate. Howard, however, refused to accompany him in his hunting of the deer; and, as I did not care to have either one of them prowling through the vast wilderness alone, I concluded to stay with Howard, while the guide accompanied Ellsworth.

As my worth brother-in-law and the guide disappeared among the thick underbrush that covered the base of the mountain, Uncle Howard turned towards me, and, laying a fat hand on my shoulder, said in a confidential tone;–

"Let 'em go, Bob; you stick to me, and instead of fooling our time away in search of such small game as deer, we'll turn our attention to the lord of the forest–the mighty moose. If I should chance to kill one of those great creatures my cup of glory would be filled to overflowing, and I actually believe that I would cut the tail from the huge animal, and, placing it in my cap, wear it proudly as the red warriors who formerly owned the land we now stand on, did the scalp-locks of their enemies killed in hand to hand conflict. I feel in my bones that to-day I shall be numbered among those who have killed a moose, for last night I dreamed for the third time that a great, lumbering moose, uglier than Satan, with bell a foot long, and wide-spread antlers, came down from Mt. Hurricane, and as he dashed by me I put two loads of buck-shot through his black hide, and a bullet through his heart. Come on, my boy, and see your old Uncle Howard do that which has been the subject of this dreams for many years," and, shouldering his three-barrel Daly gun, he stole cautiously along the base of the mountain.

Laughing slyly to myself, at the confidence Howard placed in his dreams, I followed him, and although I did not share with him the belief that on this day he would be numbered among the moose slayers, I kept a pretty sharp lookout for big game, for as we skirted the mountain I had seen the imprint of the cloven hoof of a large moose–judging by the size of the track–also the round-toed tracks of several caribou.

All day long we moved cautiously through the forest, occasionally coming across a moose bush, whose lacerated bark gave evidence of having lately been visited by the object of our search; but as his mooseship failed to materialize in the flesh, and I struck some fresh signs of deer about three o'clock in the afternoon, I concluded to switch off from the moose hunt, and try my skill at deer stalking.

I had not been on the track of the deer more than a half hour when a large doe and two yearlings jumped from behind a fallen tree-top, and, running at their best speed, dashed towards a patch of laurel to the right of me. Leaping on the trunk of a fallen hemlock, I drew a bead on the shoulder of the larger of the fawns, and, as he sped into a little opening between two large spruces, I touched the trigger. At the crack of my rifle the little buck–for such he proved to be–sprang high in the air, and jerking his feet upward as though preparing for another spring, fell to the ground in a lifeless heap. Rushing forward, I quickly bled my prize; and then calling loudly for Howard several times, and receiving no answer, I bent down a sapling, and with the aid of a couple of forks soon had the little buck hanging head downward.

It was the work of but perhaps fifteen minutes to dress the deer. Then unsheathing my hunting axe I began blazing a line due east, in which direction I knew there lay an old logging road, running north and south, upon which we traveled considerable in our trips to and from camp. I had blazed but a short distance when the report of a shotgun came booming through the air from the direction in which I was travelling. An instant later it was repeated, then all was still. Recognizing the voice of Howard's three barrel, from the reports, I pulled back the hammer of my Winchester, and keeping a sharp lookout, stood motionless for probably five minutes. Nothing larger than a saucy red squirrel, however, put in an appearance, and concluding that my estimable uncle had either killed that which he had shot at, or that it had taken some other direction in its flight, I resumed my occupation of marking a pathway. Twenty minutes later I came in sight of Uncle Howard. He was moving listlessly along the logging road. In one hand he carried his gun; in the other a brace of partridge. By way of stirring the old man up, I shouted:–

"Hello, Uncle; have you killed your moose yet?"

"Moose be d——n," he growled. "I don't believe there is a moose in the State of Maine. I grew disgusted with the whole business some time ago, and exchanging my buckshot for bird-shot, turned my attention to getting enough partridges for your supper. But say, young fellow, what in the Sam Hill was you popping at down there in the woods?" he inquired, extending the hand holding his gun, in the direction from which I had come.

"What do you think, Uncle?"

"A chipmunk I should judge; and more'n likely you missed him," he answered sarcastically.

"Wrong again, my revered and portly kinsman, " I responded, patting him on the back. "True, the animal that fell before my deadly rifle was a coat not dissimilar in color to that worn by the rodent mentioned by you. But I assure you that his tail wasn't any way near as long as his body. It was a fine young buck, Uncle, and fat; but, hold on there, I see a partridge setting on yonder hemlock. See me knock his head off," and stealing quietly up the slope of Mt. Hurricane, I threw the rifle to my face; but ere I could line the sights on the slender neck of the bird, he flew farther up the mountain. I followed him with my eye, and seeing him alight on a tree on the next bench above me, I determined to have another chance for my "white alley," as the boys used to say in school. Creeping up the mountain as cautiously as possible, I soon got within shooting distance again, and sinking on one knee, I dropped my eye into the sights, and lining them carefully on the distant bird, touched the trigger. Bang! and a few brown feathers floating on the air told graphically the story of the bird's downfall.

As I rose to my feet a long, thin whine or whistle closely resembling the singing of a bullet when in transit, came to my ears, and an instant later came the sound of breaking brush, the cracking of dry twigs, and the rattling of broad, hollow horns against limbs of trees and underbrush, then a great, black, moose, with broad, spreading antlers, dashed by within fifteen feet of me. As I whirled quickly to give him a shot, my feet slipped from under me, and I fell to the ground on the broad of my back. Scrambling to my feet as quickly as I ever did in my life, I leaped on a fallen tree-trunk; but alas! the moose as out of sight. However, I could still hear him crashing through the bushes, and thinking to warn my companion, I sped down the mountain, shouting like a mad man. Suddenly the roar of Howard's shot barrels tore the air asunder. An instant later, the sharp whip-like crack of the rifle barrel, came ripping through the atmosphere. Then I heard Howard shouting at the top of his voice;—

"Hurry, Bob; for God's sake hurry, or we'll lose him,"

On I dashed, and within a few seconds leaped into the road. There a sight met mine eyes, which even in that moment of excitement tickled by bump of the ridiculous so much as to cause me to laugh until my eyes rained with mirth. There, before me, on the broad of his back in a tree-top which had fallen to the right of the road, lay my poor, unfortunate kinsman. His heels were caught on the limb; his head on another, and in such a manner as to bring his extremities close together; while that portion of his body which is covered by his coat-tails when he is on foot, hung far below the level of his head and heels. He still grasped the old three-barrel in his right hand, while with his left he was vainly attempting to extricate himself from the uncomfortable as well as ridiculous position into which he had fallen.

Oh, if I had been the possessor of a Kodak for a few minutes! I could have taken a snap-shot at the moose slayer and sold the pictures and film to Howard for a hundred-dollar bill at least. But such has always been my luck. When opportunities have offered to make money easily I have never been prepared to take advantage of them.

I soon relieved my well-loved kinsman from his cramped position, and as soon as he had inhaled a sufficient supply of the piney air to express his feelings, and had given himself that satisfaction in language more forcible than elegant, I ventured to inquire if he had seen the moose, and why he had not put two loads of buck-shot through his black hide and a bullet through his heart, as his dream had prognosticated he should do.

"Did I see the moose?" he ejaculated fiercely. "What the d—n do you take me for, a blind man? Of course I saw him and heard him too," he continued, coming close to me; "and if I had not leaped backward into that thrice-accursed tree-top, he probably would have run me down. When you began climbing the mountain after the partridge, I stopped in the road to await your return. Before long I heard you shooting; then I heard something coming through the bushes. At first I thought you were trying to play some trick on me; but the noise kept increasing in volume. Then came the rattling of those broad horns on the young trees–a sound like of which I had never heard before, and which, if I live to be as old as Methuselah, I shall never forget. Almost directly a great, black, bull moose–the one of my dreams–dashed from the thicket, and, with the speed of the wind, came tearing towards me. I forgot all about what my gun was charged with; and, pulling back both hammers, poured the birdshot into his breast. This appeared to have no more effect upon him than so much sand thrown against his hide. As the smoke cleared I saw that he had lowered his huge head and was rushing at me in a manner that meant business. Then I thought of the rifle barrel, and throwing the lever over quickly I yanked the hammer back, and without stopping to take aim, pulled the trigger. At the crack of my piece, the great beast swayed and staggered as if struck, then fell upon his knees; but in a second he was on his feet again, and as he dashed blindly upon me I leaped backwards, alighting in that tree-top where you found me. And after all this to think that you would ask me if I saw the moose. It is too much," he groaned, sitting down on a tree-trunk and mopping his face with a large red handkerchief.

"Come, Uncle," said I, "don't be downhearted. Let us take a look at the trail; for if the moose staggered, and fell to his knees, as you say he did, probably you have killed him, and we may yet be able to find his carcass."

My words seemed to fill the heart of the would-be moose slayer with hope, for, leaping to his feet, he began following the trail. It was a very easy matter to do this, for the ground over which the moose had passed was soft and marshy, and his great weight had forced his cloven hoofs far below the surface at each step. The huge animal seemed to be heading for some high ground on the opposite side of the marsh, and as we reached the elevation and began the ascent of its slope, I noticed by the tracks that his toes were spread far apart. By that token I knew he was badly hit. Soon we reached the top of the high ground, and as we pitched over the summit and began to descend the opposite side, we discovered the object of Uncle Howard's dream lying on a flat rock–dead.

THANKSGIVING IN THE WOODS

By George A. McAleer, from *Forest and Stream*, December 1, 1894

George McAleer

Dr. George McAleer (1845-1923) was born in Henryville, Quebec, graduated from Stanbridge Academy in 1863, taught school for two years, and then removed to Worcester, Mass. Employed as a bookkeeper, he studied medicine at night, then in 1866 enrolled in a medical course in Philadelphia, graduating in 1869. Having made several inventions that were pirated, he finally won his lawsuits and went back to Worcester, working as a bookkeeper for his brother Reynolds, who operated a successful saddle and harness business. He and his brother went into business together, creating R. McAleer & Company, which ran successfully for over half a century and in 1895 he became the first treasurer of the Bay State Savings Bank, a position he held for over 20 years. An author of several works of fiction and history, Dr. McAleer was also an avid outdoorsman, writing for numerous outdoor magazines and was one of the first members of the Megantic Club, becoming a director of their clubhouse on Spider Lake.

"Snowing, come."

Our winter's hunt for 1893 had been planned many months previous and all preparations had been made for a hasty departure when our guides should summon us, and now in the latter part of November came over the wire the short but welcome message which appears above. Next morning our party, made up of Dr. Heber Bishop, of Boston; Harry S. Steeley, of New York, and the writer, and generous supplies for such an expedition were being hastily transported toward the mountain fastness of northwestern Maine, where the beaver builds his dam and the lordly moose has still a home.

For hours we had journeyed away from civilization, and late in

the afternoon we arrived at the terminus of the regular gauge rail-
way where transfer is made to the diminutive narrow gauge road,
its rails being but two feet apart, and room for but a single passenger in each seat.

We follow the devious pathway of winding stream, climbed
over mountain spurs and finally alight at the little station of Dead
River, in the forest where but a single house is the only habita-
tion. And yet our journey is not ended, nor will it be until we
have gone into the denser forest some fifty miles beyond, where
the shriek of the locomotive is not heard and the dilletanti do
not come. Here teams are taken for an eighteen mile driver over a
primitive road to our destination for the night.

Before the sun appeared above Mount Bigelow the next morning a buckboard team with the party and supplies on board took
its departure over the unequalled blue-ribbon corduroy, boulder
and bog road of Maine for the camps of the Megantic Club, on the
Chain of Ponds some twenty miles away.

We had planned to reach these camps soon after midday and
our permanent camp beyond Mount Pisgah, in the Moose River
Valley, the same night.

But the weather grew sunny and warm with advancing day,
and the melting snow and previous rains had so filled the bogs
and worked such sad havoc with much of the corduroy, that our
progress was slow indeed. It was late in the afternoon when we
reached Shaw's farmhouse, some seven or eight miles this side of
the Megantic Camps, and as far as it was possible for the buckboard to go, that we decided to stay there over night and push on
to our destination the next day. Shaw's farm is simply a clearing
in the wilderness to grow hay to feed the horses and oxen used in
lumbering operations during the winter season, and it would be a
very expensive luxury to transport it in from the settlements.

As frequently happens in this northern country at this season,
when the sun went down it grew intensely cold and the next
morning a sheet of solid ice covered the ponds.

Our guides looked crestfallen. The ice was not thick enough

to be safe, and to go around the shore to the other side of the pond to the trail was entirely out of the question, because of dense water brush, boulders, overturned trees and trap rock rising sheer 50 ft. and over, out of the water. And besides, such crust had formed upon the snow that the most careful, stealthy footstep could be heard a hundred yards away, making successful still-hunting of big game absolutely impossible.

A council of deliberation was convened, when the guides suggested that the trip be abandoned or postponed to a more favorable season. It was announced to them that we were out for big game, that we had proceeded too far to back out, that the weather bureau probably had some more snow to distribute, that we would await its arrival with becoming complacency, and that the problem now pressing for immediate solution was how best to get an early view of Camp Taylor over in the valley beyond the mountain.

Our guide of endless resources, Herb Heal, child of the forest, lithe and sinewy, as willing as strong, and whose burden never tires, skilled with rifle and rod, grand master of paddle and frying pan, clear of eye and steady of nerve, and whose footprint in the pathless forest makes a bee-line to destination, proposed that he and Jack Boyle, a fellow guide well-schooled in woodcraft, make an opening for a canoe, and then proceed to chop a canal through the ice, and for the rest of the party to follow after the lapse of a couple of hours. This plan being the only way out of the dilemma, was adopted, and at once put into execution. We returned to the warm farmhouse and whiled away a generous two hours and then embarked in frail canoes and followed in their wake.

The ice was so thick it could not be broken with a pole, and with axe only a narrow channel could be cut, so that our heavily laden canoes had to be paddled with the utmost caution to prevent the sharp, jutting corners of ice from penetrating their thin sides and giving us an icy bath, and possibly sending us to the bottom.

Going around a bend about a mile from the landing, we see

the ice choppers still at work, and a very considerable part of the task yet to be accomplished. We overtake them and are chilled to the bones before reaching the shore, an hour and a half later. Packs are shouldered and the trail taken along Clear Water stream for Camp Taylor, some ten miles beyond. Ascending the stream to its source, we reach the summit of the Boundary Mountains between Maine and the Province of Quebec, overlooking Spider and Megantic Lakes in Canada, and many miles of beautiful mountain scenery in Maine.

Our trail follows the crest of these mountains for several miles, and furnishes such wealth of panoramic splendor as might well enlist the pencil of artist and pen of poet. But to human mind and human skill it is not given to portray adequately such beauty and loveliness, and fortunate indeed is he whose privilege it is to gaze upon the fascinating scene.

To some the journey may seem long and rough, and that fatigue would dull the edge of romance, but he whose ear is attuned to nature's symphonies and whose eye appreciates the beautiful and grand, has a thousand compensations, and the trip ends all too soon.

Gong over a ravine we encounter an enormous track of a bear, around which we gather and note that it must belong to an animal of huge proportions, and all resolve to go in pursuit the next day. The shadows are lengthening and we hurry on. Fatigue says tarry, but enthusiasm prevails, and soon we are on the downward slope toward Moose River.

Another mile and a half and we are crossing the beaver dam now in possession of a colony of these interesting quadrupeds, a few rods beyond which is Camp Taylor, our haven of rest and abode for the next few weeks, hidden away in the forest and unknown to all save its very few owners and some trusty guides.

A roaring fire is soon giving needed warmth and a cup of bouillon paves the way to a well-earned and bountiful supper. Far away as it is from sources of supply, Camp Taylor is not without most of the necessities and many of the luxuries of civilized life, and the spring mattresses and soft wool blankets were not among the least highly prized.

The fatigue resulting from the unusual experience of the past few days was so great that an adjournment was made from the table to bed, nor was any practical joker inclined to indulge in levity. Political ambition, financial depression, professional obligations or business cares troubled not the dreams of the sleepers. The weather had moderated during the afternoon and night, and with the break of day the camp resounded with the enthusiasm that greeted the announcement that six inches of snow had fallen during the night and that it was still snowing. This prevented following bruin's trail, for which, no doubt, he was thankful, but all started out in pursuit of moose, caribou and deer, the three members of the party, each with a guide, taking different directions.

As the day advanced the snow fell thicker and faster, until the great, soft snowflakes filled the air so full as to limit the vision in the mountain defiles to a few yards, and at midday it seemed as if night was at hand.

It was a slavish day to be out and all made an early return to camp, three deer having been seen but none were killed. The storm grew in volume during the night, and it was snowing in such abundance as to shut out the view of a neighboring peak not a mile away. It seemed as if a large snowball might be made by simply clasping the hands together in the air.

But venison was wanted, for the camp and all sallied forth, Dr. Bishop and Herb, Harry and Latty, and the writer and Jack.

Well, perhaps it is not best to tell all the happenings of that day. Some things are too sacred to tell and should be kept as family secrets, and so I believe my readers will pardon me if I respect this custom that boasts a venerable antiquity, and give but a mere outline of this day's doings.

I had tramped up an down the mountainside, and wallowed and floundered about in soft snow two feet deep and over, until after midday, and was thoroughly fatigued with the exertion and wet with sweat and the vast quantity of snow dislodged from the spruce and fir trees, now bending under its weight and looking like huge ghostly pyramids, without getting a shot or seeing anything to shoot at, and so I informed Jack that I was going to give it up and go back to camp.

Now, if there is any one thing that Jack likes to do better than another, after pleasing his employer, it is to bring in his share of game to camp. Admiring his ambition and desire in this, and telling him I could certainly follow my tracks back to camp, we parted, Jack carrying the compass and I without one.

For a time everything went well with me, but I observed that the tracks were rapidly growing indistinct, the snow was falling so fast, and so dense was the snow cloud that no familiar peak or mountain top was discernible to aid in locating myself.

Hurrying along as fast as my weary legs would carry me, I soon arrived at a place where other tracks intersected, and making a close examination I was puzzled to know which were mine, all being well filled the snow.

Discovering what seemed to me satisfactory evidence, I again took the trail and hurried on. Feeling entirely confident I journeyed on and on, until I encountered a great windfall, around which the trail deflected, when it dawned on me that I had not been that way before, and that I was upon the wrong trail, and that when I returned to the place where I took it all tracks would be so obliterated that it would be impossible to tell one track from another.

Like a flash it passed though my mind that I would probably have to pass the night upon the trail, and I felt in every pocket for matches. Not being a user of tobacco I found none.

Thinking whoever made the trail which I was following might still be within hearing distance, I fired the signal shots agreed upon for "help wanted, but got no answer.

Gathering myself together I started back. Hurrying along with anything but welcome thoughts passing through my mind, I had covered about three-fourths the distance, when I saw the welcome form of Jack coming along the trail. He had heard my signal shots and answered them, but the wind being unfavorable for me and his rifle of smaller caliber than mine I did not hear them. Jack understands human nature too well and is too astute a diplomat always to say what he thinks, and so his innocent query now was: "What did you shoot at?"

Rather an awkward question to be sure, but well calculated to let me down easily.

We hurried back, and when nearing the intersection of the trails we met Herb who hurriedly asked, "Have you seen the Doctor?"

Well, perhaps the rest hadn't better be told here, but after a time we got together and struck a beeline to camp by compass, where we brought up at without any desire for more exercise that day.

We were much surprised not to find Harry and Latty in, and knowing our experience, I proposed to fire the signal shots. In this I was overruled on the ground that Latty was at home on every foot of this territory, and that he couldn't be lost. Darkness soon setting in, and knowing Harry would not stay out until that hour whether successful or not, if everything was all right, I stepped out and fired the signal shots. No answer was returned. After ten or fifteen minutes more Herb fired another volley, and was answered from afar off. Later another signal brought answer from near by and soon two forms, nearly resembling animate piles of snow, came tumbling into camp the very personification of despondency and fatigue.

Latty being asked where had been all day nonchalantly replied, "Oh, just up there in the edge of the woods."

This answer was so transparent and evasive that it became a standing jest during the remainder of the trip, and it found a place on our thanksgiving bill of fare, by way of embellishment.

Tending to mitigate the misadventures of the day, Harry made the best shot of the trip. Locating a deer far up on the mountain side, looking directly at him, he took hasty aim and planted his bullet exactly in the median line where the neck joins the body. The bullet passed directly through the heart and out under the tail, the deer falling dead in its tracks. They attempted to bring the quarry to camp, but had to abandon it because of the severity of the storm.

Herb and Latty went out next morning and brought it in, Latty finding a stream that was turned around the wrong way "up in the edge of the woods."

It was still snowing, but the abated fury and the hunters were content to spend the morning hours in camp, enjoying much needed rest; but two more deer fell to different rifles before night.

The succeeding day broke clear and cold, the curing smoke from our cozy camp was soon lost to view, the bark on the trees snapped with the keen frost, the forest seemed dressed as a bride in costliest laces, which the rising sun decked out with gorgeous sparkling gems, and all were enraptured with beauty, stillness and grandeur of the scene.

Much as the summer camps may be enjoyed and praised, he has missed much novel and pleasant experience who has never had the pleasure of a sojourn in the wilderness when the snows of winter still the footfall and nature sleeps.

As the day wore on one hunter and a guide, then another took their departure, and lastly the writer and Jack sallied forth.

Going but a short distance from the camp, following the course of a mountain brook, we came upon a birch tree nine inches through and some sixty-five feet long, that had been cut down the night before by beavers. We had encountered many beaver cuttings almost ever day, but had never before seen any tree so large as this felled by these diminutive rodents. Human skill could not better plan to fell the tree, nor to fell just where it was wanted. The principal gash had been cut more than half way through the trunk upon the side on which it was to fall, and upon the opposite side a smaller gash higher up, felling the tree directly between two other large trees, into one which it must have lodged had it varied but a few feet either way in its descent.

After duly admiring for some time the patience and skill manifested here, Jack at my suggestion returned to camp and procured the saw, and sawed out a section, showing the cutting, and it has now a conspicuous place in my valued collection of trophies of the trip.

The others of the party returned to camp with two magnificent bucks and a splendid bull caribou, when hilarity and good cheer reigned supreme.

Thanksgiving was drawing near, and our *chef* was instructed to do the occasion honor, and to tax to their utmost the resources of the camp. Whether or not he succeeded we will leave our readers to decide when they have read the *menu*, which was emblazoned upon birch bark, and which is reproduced here. With but a single exception, every dish and articles thereon was served, and all received due attention.

But why recount here in detail all the fun and frolic of the trip? Every incident had an individuality and pleasure all its own, but to enumerate them here would extend this article to undue length, and overtax the patience of my readers.

To sum up briefly, our two weeks of camp life in the deep snows and cold of winter was made up of fun, frolic and incident which gave to each day an individuality all its own, and rounded out into a prized remembrance the most pleasant time we ever spent in camp.

Our unconventional and unusual exercise soon gave energy to nerve and strength to muscle, and made easy the task which at first would seem impossible. The fascinations of our environment, the absolute whiteness of the snow, the deathly stillness of the woods, the delicate tracery of the evergreens and towering forest trees lent an added charm and made a beautiful picture of the woods in winter.

Our killing comprised two does, five bucks and a bull caribou. Slaughter being the lesser object sought, our killing was much less than it might have been. We endeavored to spare all females and those killed would not have been shot had their sex been known.

Our ambition was to secure a lordly moose, and while we were in their country of "at home," and saw their track several times, the continued snow blotted out at night the trail picked up and followed during the day, and so we got none. But this will be an impending incentive to another trip, and will give added zest to anticipation.

Cheery Bob Phillips, superintendent of the Megantic preserves, did us the honor of accepting the hospitality of Camp Taylor during the last few days of our stay, and to show him our apprehension of his condescension and presence, and to aid in holding him down to *terra firma,* we kindly allowed him to put upon his shoulders two saddles of venison, weighing 110lbs., and carry them out over the mountain trail to the Chain of Ponds, the little distance of some ten or a dozen miles. Such honors seldom come to him, and he is so highly pleased when they do, that his elation knows no bounds, and his best friends say he a decided lump upon his back ever since. This dangerous experiment, which has ruined many a beautiful character, is mentioned here, that others may profit by, and avoid our mistakes.

– GEO. A. MCALEER, WORCESTER, MASS.

CAMP TAYLOR, MOOSE RIVER, MAINE: THANKSGIVING DINNER, NOV. 30, 1893

MENU

SOUP
OX-TAIL – TOMATO – CONSOMME

FISH
FRIED DACE DRAWN BUTTER

ENTREES
CARIBOU STEW A LA NASH – LOIN OF VENISON
WITH CIDER JELLY
LARDED GROUSE – JUGGED HARE A LA James O. Gray
DEERS LIVER AND BACON – DEER'S FRIES BREADED
PORK AND BEANS – DEVILED HAM

BOILED
SUGAR CURED HAM MARTIN, SAUCE
CARIBOU AND DEER TONGUES

ROASTS
SADDLE OF VENISON – RIB OF CARIBOU
PARTRIDGE STUFFED – DEER'S HEART

VEGETABLES
POTATOES ALA NATURE – LYONAISE FRIED
BOILED ONIONS – CORN
HUNGY-GUNGY A LA HASTINGS

RELISHES
MIXED PICKLES – PICALILLY – WORCESTERSHIRE
SAUCE
SHREWSBURY KETCHUP

DESSERT
HOT BISCUIT WITH CREAMED BUTTER
CORN FRITTERS WITH MAPLE SYRUP
FLAP JACKS AND MOLASSES – DOUGHNUTS
GINGER BREAD – APRICOT SAUCE – STEWED
PRUNES
FROZEN APPLE SAUCE – JOHNNY CAKE
PUMPKIN, MINCE, APPLE AND PRUNE PIE
RAISINS AND NUTS
TEA – COFFEE

MARYLAND CLUB RYE – OLD TOM GIN – VERMOUTH
MARTINI AND MANHATTAN COCKTAILS
OLD MEDFORD RUN
CIGARS – CIGARAETTES

DR. GEORGE MCALEER   ACK BOYLE
HARRY S. SEELEY   WM. E. LATTY
DR. HEBER BISHOP   HERBERT L. NEAL

A MAINE HUNTRESS

By William H. Allen, from *Shooting and Fishing*, January 3, 1895

William H. Allen, (1869-1918) resided in Livermore, Maine where he was employed as an Insurance Agent and occasionally as a reporter for the local newspapers. An avid sportsman he would often take the train to Farmington and beyond to hunt and fish.

The year just passed, when Mr. D. S. Thompson, the well-known optician and jeweler, of Livermore Falls, Me., started on his annual hunting trip to the Dead River region. Mrs. Thompson, who has usually accompanied him on his fishing excursions, and has a 5 pound salmon and two 5 pound trout to her credit, besides numberless smaller ones, decided to go with him and try her luck at hunting. Not long after arriving at this decision, Mr. and Mrs. Thompson, with Mr. Bert Eaton, a young man from Boston, were on their way to Kingfield. Leaving the Maine Central railroad at Farmington, they transferred their baggage to the little Sandy River railroad, a 2 foot gauge which runs through one of the most picturesque sections of Maine, and in time found themselves, after a most enjoyable ride, at the town of Strong, where they changed to the Franklin and Megantic railroad, another diminutive train similar to the one they had left, and were soon being whirled along to Carrabassett station, at the foot of the far famed Mount Bigelow, through a country noted from Maine to California for its woodland scenery, reminding one of a most beautiful panorama. From Carrabassett they were conveyed by stage to Eustis, where civilization in that direction ends, and after a night's rest at the Shaw House, their baggage was loaded on to a buckboard and they started for Barnard pond, six miles distant, where a camp had been engaged of the noted guide and trapper, Moses P. Scribner.

They did not encounter any large game on the trip into camp;

in fact, were not on the lookout for any, as it was one of the last days of September and the open season had not begun, so Mrs. Thompson, who carries a Winchester repeater, made to order for her by the Winchester Repeating Arms Co., and is an excellent shot, contented herself and enjoyed rare sport, bagging partridges enough to last the party a day or two.

Upon arriving at the camp, which was a very comfortable one considering its environment, and is constructed of logs, with a good apology for a piazza on the front end, Mr. Thompson and Bert, after building a fire, began to put thing shipshape about the cabin, which was to serve as their home for several weeks, while Mrs. Thompson busied herself getting tea, which did not take her long, as she very readily adapted herself to the conveniences at hand; and notwithstanding the many disadvantages she labored under, a supper soon served that would have tempted the appetite of a king. And so began one of the most enjoyable outings the party ever experienced.

Those who have passed their vacations in the Maine woods realize how quickly the time passes, how short the days seem, and Mr. Thompson's party were soon brought to a realization of this fact after a few days had passed and no venison had been secured, although the surrounding country was teeming with large game.

A number of deer had been sighted each day, but as is frequently the case (as my readers will testify to this), they were unable to get within rifle shot. Once day Mrs. Thompson, who is a very fine shot with a rifle, and had defeated her husband and Bert at target practice and in shooting partridges and other small game, said that her appetite craved a nice juicy piece of venison, and that if Mr. Thompson and Bert could not secure it, she was going to shoot a deer herself, and shouldering her rifle, after dinner she struck out, accompanied by her husband, who chuckled to himself occasionally at the idea of her, a woman, shooting a deer, after he and Bert had scoured the woods and swamps for several days without being able to obtain a shot. They soon reached the swamps, and after hunting through both the lowlands and the highlands, they decided to return to the camp, as it was getting quite dark, and turning about, struck out, as near as Mr. Thompson could estimate by his compass, on a bee line for camp. The route back took them through a swamp and along the shore of a pond. It was too dark for hunting, for they had considerable difficulty in groping their way along in the darkness and so Mr. Thompson persisted in talking to make the time pass quickly, but every time he uttered a word above a whisper, Mrs. Thompson enjoined silence; finally he gave up trying to talk and picked his way along ahead in silence. He had not proceeded far, however, when crack went a rifle, and glancing quickly around he saw a deer jump about 20 feet and fall dead, and another glance revealed his wife standing with a smoking rifle in her hand, and he realized that Mrs. Thompson had shot her first deer, while he and Bert had not secured a single shot at one. Leaving the deer where it had fallen, marking the spot, they kept on to camp, which was reached long into the night.

The next day the deer was toted into camp and hung up on the piazza.

While Mr. Thompson and Bert were greatly pleased at Mrs. Thompson's having shot a deer, they were somewhat chagrined to think they had not secured one; but their courage was good, and Mr. Thompson was soon rewarded by a shooting a fine deer, while Bert secured several shots at a large bear, which he was unable to bring down, owing, so Mrs. Thompson claims, to buck fever. Bert, however, declares that it could not have been buck fever, for it was a bear he was shooting at; but Mrs. Thompson persists that the symptoms were very much similar to those attending the well-known disease, and I guess she is about right, for bruin was not more than eight or ten rods from Bert when he fired.

On a later trip into this same section, Mr. Thompson, accompanied by Mr. Scribner, the guide; Hon. Frank L. Noble, of Lewiston; Hon. J. F. Lamb, Dr. C. E. Knight, and Frank A. Millett, of Livermore Falls, shot two more deer, and says that he could have secured as many more had the law allowed, so plentiful were they. Dr. Knight and Mr. Millett secured a deer apiece on this trip in a few days' hunting.

– WM. H. ALLEN, LIVERMORE FALLS, MAINE

AMONG THE TROUT OF THE KENNEBEC

By J. C. Bodwell, from Frank. M. Johnson's *Forest, Lake and River: The Fishes of New England and Eastern Canada*, 1902.

Brook Trout Fishing: An Anxious Moment (Currier & Ives 1874)

Rev. Joseph Connor Bodwell (1840-1913) was born in Weymouth, England and came to America with his family 1850. In 1862, while living at Framingham, Mass., he enlisted in the 7th Squadron of Rhode Island and was captured at Harper's Ferry, later being released. He graduated from Dartmouth the following year, was admitted to the Massachusetts Bar in 1864 and finsihed his studies at the Hartford Theological Seminary in 1871. In the next few decades he served as minister of churches in Thompson, Connectincut, Stockbridge and Bridgewater, Massachusetts and finally in Lydonville, Vermont. He died in Machiasport, Maine.

Rev. Bodwell, not a fisherman, was vacationing in the Kennebec Valley when he was introduced to the gentle art of fly-casting and was instantly hooked. When Frank M. Johnson edited his popular book in 1902, he included the Reverend's article of that experience.

Spring has opened her sleepy eye to the delight of all who live in this beautiful world. If "in the spring of a young man's fancy lightly turns to thoughts of love," the heart of an older man opens and perhaps, more wisely, to another of nature's impetuous invitations. He hears and heeds a voice that stirs a fever in his veins,–a voice from out of the forests and streams, a resistless voice that he is all too glad to obey.

> Do you know the blackened timber—do you know
> the racing stream,
> With the raw, right-angled log jam at the end;
> And the bar of sun-warmed shingle where
> A man may bask and dream
> To the click of shod canoe poles round the bend?

It is there that we are going with or rods and reels and traces.
To a silent, smoky Indian that we know,
To a couch of new-pulled hemlock, with the star-light on our faces,
For the Red Gods call us out, and we must go!
And we go — go — go— go away from here!
On the other side of the world we're overdue!
See the road is clear before you when the
Old Spring fret comes o'er you,
And the Red Gods call for you.

With the ring and rhythm of these words my heart turns towards the head waters of the Kennebec, as they flow with a rush and a roar through the gates of the dam at old Moosehead.

For ten years, I have stepped from the Canadian Pacific train, and gazed with delight upon the great lake lying in its beauty, one thousand feet above the level of the sea, and buttressed in the distance by Katahdin, whose crest, one mile nearer heaven than the lake itself, looks calmly down on Moosehead. As I draw nearer the hotel on the lake shore that for so many years has sheltered so many enthusiasts in the pursuit of big trout, I hear a murmur, ever growing louder. It is the music of the great stream,–a stream bordered on either side by forest primeval, and by a woodland road for five miles southward, to the Indian Pond.

In a few minutes from the hostelry, one finds himself on the delightsome pathway, amid a solitude,–and the great trees arching overhead, and here and there footpaths through the woods to the river and its pools. Once seen, that river with is ever-varying vistas of beauty, with its rounding bends, its peeps of purple mountains, its picturesque shores, its murmur and hiss and roar, its mysterious and deep-toned chug! chug! chug! as it passes toward the sea, now with wide level sheets of water, and now in swift rapids, broken by falls and whirlpools into which strong men have fallen and slept their last sleep–that river, with its beautiful pools that quicken one's step and fill his heart with hope as he draws near,—who having once seen it at its source can ever forget the Kennebec!

I came, years ago, to that river as a tyro, never having made a cast, never having seen a fly, but soon received some kindly instruction from the men who were there, for all masters of the gentle art will meet even a neophyte upon the level, act toward him by the plumb, and part with him upon the square. One of them, a distinguished clergyman, was fishing a certain pool, day after day, but without success, the Red God being sometimes capricious in his bestowal of favors. In my ignorance of the laws of the game, I conceived that pool to be the minister's especial preserve, and religiously kept away from it. Upon his departure I eagerly started for the pool, and wading in, took my place at its head,–a swift strong current on the one side and shallows on the other. Making an awkward cast, to my surprise and delight, a great head popped up in the strong water, but I failed to make connection. With nervous haste I made another bid for the big trout; this time there was no "going–going–gone!" The bid was taken at once, and my work was cut out–the fight began. Owing to my inexperience, it took me fifteen anxious minutes to land that fish. I could not guide him with my tip; first, he rushed across the deep pool into the swift water where I feared his pull would break away, then, down and up the pool, and then across to the shallows, where he thrashed so vigorously that I thought he would free himself; but amid all my excited errors there was one I did not make, that of giving him any slack. Being an Englishman, I instinctively held on with bull-dog tenacity that at last brought him in triumph into the net,–a four-pound trout, a thing of beauty, with dark-green back, mottled sides, and a belly of brilliant red. With hands that, wielding the rod, trembled like a leaf with excitement, I had started my reputation as a fly fisher, and was happy.

The next season, a half-hour's visit to the pool weighed my net with a three and a four pound trout. From that time on I lost that miserable feeling of inferiority that troubles a tyro among experts.

Perhaps I have caught enough big fish to permit me to give a bit of advice to beginners. Don't be so anxious to hear the singing of the reel as to allow our fish too much line; shorten your line, as soon as possible, without stopping to play your fish; when he is a heavy one, haul in your line, hand over fist, as fast as he gives you opportunity, accommodating yourself to his rushes this way and that, with the tip, and as short a line as possible. Your tip will do the business. I have seen many a fine trout lost by too much finicky play.

Last season, going a mile down the river, by a charming leafy path through the forest, I waded out with difficulty to a little ledge, peeping above the water far from shore. It was treacherous footing to that ledge, and I had the pleasure of seeing a dignified clerk of the United States District Court of Portland execute a frantic dance in the ford, to keep his feet; this way and that he tumbled, with arms waving and a tremendous splashing. I laughed till I ached, and having sat down myself several times in that river, I hoped to see this official take his seat; but, alas, he didn't. Making the ledge, I began fishing. The beauty around me on that September morning was enough, but after a little casting I had a lively one–a half-pound trout. Having no basket, and unable to place him on the ledge, I had to wade all the way back to place him on the shore; this I had to do each time, as I successively caught three more trout, from two pounds and an ounce to three pounds and a quarter in weight. Tired out and bearing a heavy net, my homeward steps were elastic; for, as every angler knows, the heavier the burden, the lighter the steps for home.

Once more and I'm done. The last day came, a day of tender regret for the angler who must leave divine nature for the man-made town. Just one more cast, and then for home. With this feeling I went to an old mill that stood at the intersection of the lake and the dam,–a point so difficult to land a fish that but a few days before my ministerial friend lost both fish and leader through the gate.

Taking my station on the platform, I made a long cast, and struck a heavy fish. The water was pouring with a powerful swing through the gates at my left into the river. I must pull that fish toward me, past the heavy currents, and not let him get the better of me. To add to my trouble, a storm had brought in a large tree, and placed it ten feet in front of me, so I must also guide the fish around that tree, and then past me to the right until, getting him alongside the wharf to my right, I could reach down and net him. With several narrow escapes that quickened my heart, I at last, got him to the wharf, and, having neglected to bring my net, raised a yell for help that, heard above the roar of the water, brought a net in which I landed a handsome two-pound-and-nine-ounce trout.

With this last triumph, I took the midnight train for home, content, and in the hope that a kindly Providence will allow me to visit that beautiful Kennebec for years to come.

Chapter 4

MOOSEHEAD LAKE AND
PISCATAQUIS REGIONS

The early history of Maine's largest lake belongs with the Wabenaki people, settlers not arriving until the early 1800s.

In the summer of 1828, a year after the town of Greenville was incorporated, Hiram Rockwood, a surveyor from Belgrade, and for whom the Rockwood Strip is named, made a trip to the lake and explored Moose island (now Sugar Island), Deer Island, Farm Island, Mt. Kineo, Sand Bar Island and the Moody Islands. In November he submitted his work to the State of Maine as "A Geographical Description of the Principal islands in Moosehead Lake," describing their approximate sizes and the kinds and amounts of timber on each island. In the next few years Rockwood surveyed and described Frenchtown (Town A), Tomhegan Township, Letter A Township and others along the shore of the lake.

Rockwood explored the Debsconeag region in 1832, surveying Debsconeag, Pemadumcook and Rainbow Townships. Traveling up the West Branch, he stayed in Mattawamkeag, then went up the river to Pemadumcook Lake and through the woods to First Debsconeag Lake, where they found rock placed in a strange formation. Staying at Grant's lumber camp, he then explored Rainbow Township, estimating over 34 million board feet of lumber available. He reckoned that 5,000 acres had pine on it.

William Cummings arrived in Greenville about 1828, removing from Parkman. On April 28, 1835 he was returning home from the outlet of the lake in a terrific windstorm and mistakenly went down the west side of Deer Island, where he encountered open water. On the other side of the island he encountered a blinding snowstorm, lost his horse, and finally crawled to an old hovel, where he spent the night, wet, cold and hungry. Three local men signed an affidavit which Cummings sent to his employers, hoping to get some money for his trouble and his loss.

In 1836, James Hall, an engineer was commissioned by the State of Maine to produce a preliminary survey of the possibility of locating a canal from Moosehead Lake to Great Moose Pond in Harmony, since the Kennebec River above The Forks was not navigable. After months of tramping, exploring and working with the local residents, he found that a canal could be cut from the foot of the lake three miles to the Wilson Ponds, then by utilizing "the North Branch and Wilson Stream," it could follow down through Shirley Mills and empty into Sebec Lake. He noted that he was accompanied by several men "who were desirous that the route should pass through Kingsbury and Wellington, and follow down the Hegan Stream," but he noted there were too many mountains in the way. Instead he suggested that the canal follow the Piscataquis River to Guilford, then turn south to a small pond, over the small rise between the watersheds and descend through Cedar Brook and Main Stream to the Great Moose Pond. In November of 1836 he submitted his report to the State of Maine, estimating that it would cost over $239,000 to build the canal. Evidently nothing ever became of it.

In 1838 the State made appropriations for a road to be built "from the head of Moosehead Lake to the Canada line, a distance of about thirty miles." Unfortunately it was not maintained and soon grew back into forest.

Three boats loaded with lumbermen and supplies left Greenville in late October of 1843, to build a lumber camp further up the lake. One batteaux, a little leaky and loaded with heavy chains went ahead of the other two boats. When they arrived at the designated building locale, there was no third boat in sight.

Evidently, once out of sight it sank, the men not able to get to safety.

That same year 40 to 50 oxen were turned out near the lake, but could not be located for two years, but were then accidently found near Mt. Katahdin in good health, having lied on grasses and brakes. Two years later in February of 1845 *The Gardiner Blade* reported that there were over three thousand men engaged in obtaining lumber about the lake, and in February of 1848 small pox broke in around the lake and a number of lumber camps had to close.

A grand hunting excursion took place on November 12, 1848 on Sugar Island, the party consisting of over one hundred hunters. They formed a line and made a clean sweep of the island. To prevent the bears, deer, moose and smaller animals from escaping into the water, they had a string of boats ready, resulting in great slaughter.

In 1849 John Townsend Trowbridge made a trip to Moosehead, his narrative being second only to Thoreau's trip in 1846. They travelled to the lake through Kingsbury, first staying in Greenville. Later a party took the steamer *Moosehead,* up the lake and stayed at the Kineo Hotel and climbed Kineo Mountain. That same year the *Barre Gazette* of Vermont, reported that five tons of salmon trout were taken from Moosehead Lake the past winter-some weighing 30 pounds each. The *Pittsfield Sun* reported that the total trout taken amounted to two thousand dollars' worth of fish. The following winter a trout fishery, or hatchery, was established at the lake and trout was selling for seven cents a pound, being shipped to Portland and Boston, where they got ten cents a pound.

In 1853 the citizens of Belfast voted to establish a railroad north to Moosehead Lake in order to take advantage of the lumber and slate available in the area. In 1855 the Bangor Journal published a long, anonymous journal called "A Birch Bark Journal." In it, the traveler, who called himself *The Forest Ranger*, detailed his time spent at Grant & Batchelder's Camps on Pemadumcook Lake. In

September, a bear was killed in Foxcroft that measured seven feet in length; it having made great havoc with the corn fields.

The Piscataquis Observer noted in 1858 that "Mr. J. G Lyford of Sebec was said to be the greatest hunter now living; he has a record of three hundred and twenty-four bears killed by his own hand since the year 1804.

MOOSEHEAD LAKE AND THE KENNEBEC

By Charles Lanman, from *Letters of a Landscape Painter*, 1845

Charles Lanman

Charles Lanman (1819-1895), an early American explorer and artist loved to travel and paint. During his several trips to Maine and Quebec, he wrote about his adventures and chronicled the people and characters that he met along the way. These writings were published into two books, "Letters from a Landscape Painter" (1845) and "Adventures in the Wilds of America" (1854).

In "Letters of a Landscape Painter" Lanman first spent a few weeks in Portland before he headed north into the Kennebec Valley. In his book he gives an early and valuable picture of Moosehead Lake as it appeared in 1845.

Moosehead Lake is the largest and the wildest in New England. It lies in the central portion of the State of Maine, and distant from the ocean about one hundred and fifty miles. Its length is fifty miles, and its width from five to fifteen. It is embosomed among a brotherhood of mountains, whose highest peak hath been christened with the beautiful name of Katahden. All of them, from base to summit, are covered with a dense forest, in which the pine is by far the most abundant. It is the grand centre of the only wilderness region in New England whose principal denizens are wild beasts. During the summer months tranquil waters remain in unbroken solitude, unless some scenery-hunting pilgrim, like myself, should happen to steal along its shores in his birchen canoe. But in the winter the case is very different, for then, all along it borders, may be heard the sound of the axe, wielded by a thousand men. Then it is that an immense quantity of logs are cut, which are manufactured into lumber at the extensive mills down the Kennebeck, which is the only outlet to the Lake.

A winter at Moosehead must be attended with much that is

rare, and wild, and exciting, not only to the wealthy proprietor who has a hundred men to superintend, but even to the toiling chopper himself. Look at a single specimen of the gladdening scenes enacted in that forest world. It is an awful night, the winds wailing, the snow falling, and the forests making a moan. Before you is a spacious, but rudely built log cabin, almost covered with snow. But now, above the shriek of the storm, and the howl of the wolf, you hear a long, loud shout, from a score of human mouths. You enter the cabin and lo, a merry band of noble men, some lying on a buffalo-robe, and some seated upon a log, while the huge fire before them reveals every feature and wrinkle of their countenances, and makes a picture of the richest coloring. Now the call is for a song, and a young man sings a song of Scotland, which is his native land; a mug of cider then goes round, after which an old pioneer clears his throat for a hunting legend of the times of old; now the cunning jest is heard, and peals of hearty laughter shake the building; and now a soul-stirring speech is delivered in favor of Henry Clay. The fireplace is again replenished, when with a happy and contented mind each woodman retires to his couch, to sleep, and to dream of his wife and children, or of the buxom damsel whom he loves.

The number of logs which these men cut in a single winter is almost incredible, and the business of conveying them to the lake upon the snow gives employment to a great many additional men and their oxen. The consequence is, that large quantities of flour, potatoes, pork, and hay, are consumed; and as the farmers of the Kennebeck mostly supply these things; winter is the busiest season of the year throughout the region. When the lake is released from its icy fetters in the spring, a new feature of the logging business comes into operation, which is called rafting. A large raft contains about eighteen thousand logs, and covers a space of some ten acres. In towing them to the Kennebeck, a small steamboat is employed, which, when seen from the summit of a hill, looks like a living creature struggling with a mighty incubus. But the most picturesque thing connected with this business is a floating log-cabin, called a Raft House, which ever attends a raft on its way to the river. During the summer, as before stated, Moosehead Lake is a perfect solitude for the "log chopper" has become a "log driver" on the Kennebeck,–the little steamer being moored in its sheltering bay, near the tavern at the south end of the lake, and the toiling oxen been permitted to enjoy their summer sabbath on the farm of their master.

The islands of Moosehead Lake, of any size, are only four; Moose and Deer Islands at the southern extremity, Sugar Island in the large eastern bay, and Farm Island in a north-western direction from that. All of these are covered with beautiful groves, but the time is not far distant when they will be cultivated farms. Trout are the principal fish that flourish in its waters, and may be caught at any time in great abundance. And thereby hangs a *fish story*.

It was the sunset hour, and with only of my companions, I had gone to a rocky ledge for the purpose of trying my luck. We cut each of a long pole, to which we fastened two immensely long lines with stout hooks. Our bait was squirrel meat, and I was the first to throw my line. It had hardly reached the water, before I had the pleasure of striking and securing a two pound trout. This threw my friend into a perfect fever of excitement, so that he was everlastingly slow in cutting up the squirrels; and it may be readily supposed that I was somewhat excited myself, so I grabbed the animal out of his hands, and in less than a "jiffy," and with my *teeth*, made a number of good baits. The conclusion of the whole matter was, that in less than forty minutes we had caught nearly seventy pounds of salmon trout, and some of them, I tell you, were real *smashers*. But the trout of Moosehead are not to be compared with those of Horicon in point of delicacy, though they are very large, and very abundant. The reason of this is, that its waters are not remarkably clear, and a good deal of its bottom is muddy. Moose River, which is the principal tributary to the Lake, is a narrow, deep, and picturesque stream, where may be caught the common trout, weighing from one to five pounds

In this portion of Maine every variety of forest game may be found, but the principal kinds are the grey wolf, the black bear, the deer and the moose. Winter is the appropriate season for their capture, when they afford a deal of sport to the hunter, and furnish a variety of feed to the forest laborers. Deer are so very plenty, that a certain resident told me, that, in the deep snow of last winter, he caught some dozen of them alive, and having cut a slit in their ears, let them go, that they might recount to their kindred their marvelous escape. But the homeliest animal, the most abundant, and the best for eating, is the moose. I did not kill one, but spent a night with an old hunter who did. During the warm summer nights these animals, for the purpose of getting clear of the black-fly, are in the habit of taking to the water, where, with nothing but their heads in sight, they remain for hours. It was the evening of one of those cloudless nights, whose memory can never die. We were alone far up the Moose River, and it seemed to me, "we were the first that every burst into that *forest* sea." On board a swan-like birch canoe we embarked, and with our rifles ready, we carefully and silently descended the stream. How can I describe the lovely pictures that we passed? Now we peered into an ink-black recess in the centre of a group of elms, where a thousand fire-flies were reveling in joy;–and now a solitary duck shot out into the stream from its hidden home, behind a fallen and decaying tree' now we watched the stars mirrored in the sleeping waves, and now we listened to the hoot of the owl, the drum of the partridge, the song of a distant waterfall, or the leap of a robber-trout. It was not far from midnight when my companion whispered "Hush, hush!" and pointed to a dim spot some hundred yards below. The first fire was allotted me, so I took the best aim I could, and fired. I heard the ball skip along the water, and coming near, found my mark to be only a smooth rock. Two hours more passed on, one small moose was killed, and at day-break we were in our cabin fast asleep...

AN EVENING WITH THE LUMBERMEN

By Laura J. Curtis Bullard, from *Now-A-Days*, 1854

Laura J. Curtis (1832-1912) was born in Freedom, Maine, married Enoch Bullard, a merchant, and resided in Brooklyn, New York. A strong women's advocate, she was an associate of Susan B. Anthony and Elizabeth Cady Stanton, and would often host gatherings at ther home of dignitaries and activists in

Life in a camp (Scribner's Magazine June 1893)

the cause. Having the support of her husband, Laura was one of the founders of Sorosis, a women's club, and was an active leader in the Women's Bureau and the Working Women's Association.To promote the independence of women, Bullard wrote two novels, Now-A-Day in 1854 and Christine, or Woman's Trials and Triumphs, in 1856. She was also associated with The Revolution, a weekly women's newspaper begun by Susan B. Anthony, and when the paper had financial difficulties, she purchased the enterprise and edited it from 1870 to 1872, making it more literary in its style.

While both her novels are set in Maine, "Now-a-Days" tells the story of young Esther Hastings, who when her father's death leaves her family in dire straits, she accepts a position as a teacher in a backwoods school in Aroostook County. An important part of the plot involves young Esther making up her own mind about her future, declining an offer in a lucrative marriage, something that was not considered rational in the mid eighteen hundreds. In the following section of the novel, Esther and her friends visit a lumber camp, a place considered off-limits to women.

"It was terribly cold out of doors; one of those still, freezing nights, that does so much greater execution that the wild and blustering ones; just as a self-willed, though quiet man can effect so much more than an impetuous, but unsteady one.

But the cold did not penetrate into the camp, where it stood surrounded by snow-covered stumps and trees, whose evergreen hue contrasted well with the white surface around them; the clear moon lighted up with a silvery tinge their boughs, laden with feathery flakes, for there had been a violent storm, and the flakes had not yet fallen from the branches.

It was not a night which would tempt one out of doors, but within the log-camp all was light and cheerful.

The men, having had their suppers, were gathered round the blazing fire, some sitting on the deacon seat, others on the stools, in different parts of the room. A rough, but manly-looking set they were! Dressed in their somewhat picturesque costume of red flannel shirt, and a pair of pantaloons, their vigorous forms unfettered by suspenders, or anything binding, they looked well fitted to be the pioneers of civilization—well suited to their work in the free, broad forests—each looked every inch a man. The voices of most of them were deep and clear, like the ring of their own axes on the stout pines, and nearly all had shrewd and intelligent faces, that fitted well in their powerful and muscular frames. Many of them were smoking, but the greater number were chewing tobacco. They were talking cheerfully together on various subjects.

"Talk about trees!" exclaimed an athletic fellow, rather below the middle height, emitting a whiff of tobacco smoke from his nostrils, as he took his pipe from his mouth, "that haint a circumstance to one that Bob Sykes and I felled last winter. Why, it scaled nine thousand feet—a pumpkin pine, none of your confusy stuff—clear as a ten-foot snow-drift in the middle—-"

"Caan't you make it ten, Bill, so's to make it even numbers?" asked a tall, fine-looking fellow, in a tone that indicated some little doubt of the truth of the last speaker's story. "Neow dew, jist to accommodate!"

"It's true, as I hope to holler, Tompkins," replied Bill, "I'll take my Bible oath on't."

"Oh, I haint no sort o' doubt on't," replied Tompkins, "fur I see a tree on et that sealed twelve thousand—"

"Phew!" interrupted Bill; but Tompkins proceeded, "and Sam Slocum and I chopped that one down in less than an hour; to be sure he was a d——-d smart chopper, and if I dew say it myself, I'm some."

"Rather smart, I should say. Neow, what's the use o' lyin'!" exclaimed Bill, as a loud shout from all present, indicated that the object of this extravagant story was appreciated, "but if you dew lie, 'taint no sign that everybuddy else does. Talk about choppers!—I've seen Sam Slocum."

"Then you've seen a devilish smart feller."

"He's wall enuf, but he haint a primin' to Bob Sykes."

"Neow, git out with your long yarns, and all-fired stories," interrupted Tompkins.

"Tell as big a one as I'm a mind ten, you allus beat it," rejoined Bill, "but that's eoz I stick ten the truth, and yeon draw on your imagination, and there's a never-failin' spring thar, I swan to man."

"Bill, you must do as the Yankee that went to New York did," said a man who had been reading a newspaper, and who had not before taken part in the conversation.

"How as that, Clark?"

"Got a patent right for lyin' I s'pose," exclaimed Tompkins.

"No," said Clark, "he advertised that he'd got the biggest oxen in the world. Somebody asked him how much they measured. He straightened up in his boots—six feet two, he stood in his stockings—and says he, "Cetch me to tell that! Guess I'm cuter than that comes teu! Ef I was to say one on um girted twelve feet, some long Yankee or nuther would be sayin' he'd got a pair that girted fourteen. Neou, I say, I've got the biggest in the world; if any Yankee kin beat that, let him come on.""

Bill did not appear at all dismayed at the hits of his companions, for he was a notorious "bragger." The story only diverted his attention to oxen, and he began, "Wall, I hev seen some mighty poor cattle in my day."

"So hev I," interrupted John, the teamster, "but I'll stump anybody to keep a team in better order, and do more work with um than I kin with my critters; them's as likely cattle as ever was in these diggins."

"Hosses is better than oxen, in the woods," said Bill.

"Wall, neou, they haint, in my way of thinkin'; they may be spryer, but they hain't got the wear to um that oxen hev."

"Oh, wall," replied Bill, "use um up, and get more, that's what I say."

"Neou that's what I call abusin' God's creaturs," exclaimed the teamster, who, like many of his class, would have infinitely preferred overtasking himself, to his cattle.

"Wall," interrupted the newspaper reader, "if it hurts your feelins so, to use up dumb cattle, what do you say to some of them slave-holders that do the same to men and women?"

"Oh, d——d them, replied John, "you're allus luggin' them in; can't you let one night go, without going' over that old story?"

"No, I can't, nor I won't," answered Clark, his bronzed face lighting up, "when that infernal system is being helped along by the votes of such men as we are, when men with just such bodies and souls as we have, are sold like brutes, separated from their families, and dragged the Lord only knows whare."

"Oh, be hanged to it! It haint none of my business! I haint got nothin' to deu with it, nohow. I don't buy um or sell um, nor wouldn't have nothin' to deu with um, nohow yeou can fix it," said John.

"But do you support the system by voting for men who do their best to extend it, by annexing Slave States, and all such measures," replied Clark.

"Oh, I'm a democrat, dyed in the wool, and I go fur the reg'lar nominee—no splittin' fur me—union is strength; and as to my vote, 'taint of no great account here—why did you hear how Josh Emerson got 'lected?"

"No! How was it?"

"Why, he kept a kind of a shanty, where the lumbermen stowed their supplies, and the 'lection was that, and between votin', they would liker up, you see. Wall, they kep one man watchin the hat where they threw their votes, but onct the feller left it and kivered it up with a pocket-handkerchief. Wall, some-buddy, unbeknownst, watched their chance, and when the assessor got back, the hat was rammed full of votes for Emerson. 'Oh, that's too devilish bad!' says the assessor, so he put in his hand and took eout a decent handful, and sez he, 'I guess that's about right; count the rest.' So Josh got in by a swampin' majority. They set out to contest his seat, but he hed sich an awful majority that they gin it up. So, one vote that didn't amount to much."

Tompkins squirted a vast amount of tobacco juice between his teeth into the fire with excellent aim.–"My opinion on slavery," said he, "is jest this—I ask, is it allowed in the Constitution? Ef it is, I go fur it, ef it 'taint I don't. Neon, I say it was; all the old patri-ots, great men like Washington and Jefferson understood that it was so. Neon, don't you think yourself, Clark, that, notwith-standin' the word slave haint mentioned in the Constitution, it was a mutual understandin' that the South should keep their slaves?"

"Wall, I might screw around that," replied Clark, "but I'll come to the pint; I do think so, but I think too, that it was looked upon as an evil by those men, and as inconsistent with their views of a republic, and they would hev been glad to hev got rid on't, but they didn't know how; they thought 'twould die out; they all said as much, and if the Constitution don't condemn holding slaves, it taint for extendin' the d—d system, nuther, and I'm down on that, and, furthermore, as to ketchin' their slaves as run away, I'll be d—-d if I do sich dirty work as that."

"Wall, I'm with you that," said Tompkins, "fur I'll be hanged, if arter a feller has got pluck enuf to run for his life and liberty, ef he shouldn't hev it fur all of me. But the most of them slaves is lazy, shiftless, cowardly dogs."

"Who wonders at it!" asked Clark, "I guess you'd be lazy teu, if you only go what you had to eat, and drink, and wear fur your work, and not allus enuf of that!"

"Oh, the devil! There haint many of the slaves treated that are way, and ef they was, that is all I git for my work—jist what I kin eat, drink, and wear—neou, ef I was rich, like some of these ere fellers that live like pigs in clover, why then yeou might talk; but I'm a slave myself—I hev to work like a dog, and don't get no great pay."

"Pshaw! you get good wages—then, the work suits you.—Why, you'd rave like a tiger, to be shut up in a store, measurin' tape, or sellin' barrels of flour, ef you was a rich man. Rich men are slaves to their money bags; twistin', turnin', screwin', plannin' to make more, and keep what they've got. They haint no happier than we are."

"Wall," said Tompkins, "I wouldn't object to tryin my hand at it a spell, anyhow: wouldn't I cut a dash!"

"I cum plagney nigh bein' rich onct, myself," said Bill.

"How was that?–A speculation?" asked Clark.

"Not 'xactly," replied Bill. "Not the ushil kind of speculation, though it was rayther in that line. Ye see, I cum mighty near marryin' a rich gal, and a pooty gal, teu."

"Well, what hindered you?" inquired Tompkins, looking at Bill's huge and awkward frame, as if he thought him better suited to any character than that of a lady's man.

"Why, ye see, I got acquainted with a gal of that kind, and arter stayin' around a spell, and doin' up the courtin' a leetle, I cum to the pint—I axed her ef she'd have me—sez she, "I'd rather be excused,' and I, like a d—d fool, excused her."

A roar of laughter greeted Bill's brief account of his love-affair, and the conversation turned on the beauty of women.

"Wall, neou, that's a pooty gal eout to Simpson's; that are schoolmarm, that was eout here yesterday with the old 'ooman," said Tompkins, "she's a trig-build, good-lookin' gal; got a dreadful footy foot, teu."

"Wall, I don't say but what she hez," said a man who had not taken much interest in the previous conversation, "but I've seen dreadful many enuf sight pootier than her. She can't hold a candle to a gal that I know on. That are gal is as straight as a pine tree, and her skin and teeth as white as the heart of one, and jist the pootiest pair of eyes that ever you did see; as smart as a steel trap, teu, she id, I tell ye."

"Oh, git eout!" exclaimed John, the teamster, "the wimmin is jist like colts: look dredful pooty and frisky in the fields, loose; but the devil and all in harness. Take my advice: don't hev nothin' to do with um! Let um alone! Don't hitch yourself to none on um!"

"Break um in!–break um in!" said Tompkins. "Them frisky ones is just the best kind, ef ye only keep a taut rein on um."

"Taint so easy doin' on't, "replied John, shaking his head, sorrowfully; "they're the head-strongest jades! They'll take the bits right into their teeth, and off they go, and ef you holler whoa ever so much, they'll kick up their heels the more, and tear off the Lord only knows whar."

"I guess John speaks from experience," said Clark.

"Wall, I don't say but what I deu. When it cums to breakin' in critters, horse or ox, I won't giv in to nobody; but ef anybuddy kin head off, my old woman, when she's go sot a sartin way, I'll giv in beat, fur he kin deu more than I kin."

John settled back in his seat, whistling in true Yankee fashion, while he whittled out a goad stick. A man near him, was fitting a handle to an axe, as the original one had been broken; he felt the keen edge, and looked at the polished steel with no little pride. "Neou, that are, is what I call a good axe," said he, "though 'taint quite ekil to one I had onct. I don't like braggin, but I will say, give me that are axe, and I'll agree to take the heart of any tree from any man, I don't kear who he is."

Wall," replied Bill, "'taint so much the axe, in my way of thinkin', that makes the odds, as the man that stands behind it; though tools does a good deal, arter all."

"That are axe I was speakin' on," continued the speaker," is layin in the Penobscot, I spect, there to Passadunky; that's an all-fired place fur jams. Did you ever drive, on that are river?"

"Wall, I rayther guess I hev," was the reply, "and I guess I've worked some getting off jams that. It's a ugly lookin' sight, enuf to make a saint swear, to see them logs pile up every way; standin' up straight, in the air, and the water fizzin' through like a milltail, frothin' and roarin'. Taint so pooty fun, nuther, to stand up to your waist in stun cold water, workin' and pryin' them are logs till you don't know whether you've got any legs or not."

"Wall, that haint so pooty," said his companion, "but I like river-drivin', howsomever; it's lively-like, and I allus like to strike the blow that starts the jam; but I cum mighty nigh loosin' my life, that time that I lost my axe; I thought then, sure enuf that I was a goner. I hedn't gin but one blow, when snap, crack went the log that hung up the jam, and all the rest came whirlin' and rushin' ahead, end over end, some on um snappin' like pipe-stems. I was master sorry to lose that axe, but I gin it a fling and sprang for my life. I've seen many a jam, but that was the beatemest. There was ten acres of logs, and we had been to work most three days tryin' to get um off, and ye see the water hed riz behind um mighty high, so when they did go all of sudden, it was some, I tell ye. I guess I made some mighty smart leaps from one teeterin', whirlin', slippery log to another; wall, none of the fellers ever expected to see me ashore alive agin, and I was as much astonished as they was, to git out safe. 'Twas a narrow squeak, I tell ye. But I 'spect my time hedn't cum, "he concluded.

"River drivin' is the pootiest part of loggin' I think," said one.

"They haint no kind of work that suits me better," said Tompkins. "It looks so good to see um sailin' along, clean out of sight; and ef the jams is bad, why I spose we should git tired of chasin' arter a drive, and never havin' no variety. I never git used to a jam. It allus make me as lively as a cricket. I don't get as mad as a March hare, like some of your fellers, if they do happen to git hung up, that is, if taint out of all reason afore they start agin."

"Hark!" suddenly exclaimed Bill; "I heerd sleigh bells;" and almost before he had ceased speaking, the rapid tread of a horse, with the jingling of sleigh-bells, was heard, and with a loud whoop, the driver reined up at the camp..."

A MOOSE HUNT IN MAINE

By Senarius, from *American Sportsman*, January 31, 1874

 *In this short story the anonymous author gives us one of the earliest accounts of a fishing and hunting trip made to the wilderness north of Moosehead. The writer, remembering back twenty years to the mid 1850's, was apparently a little confused as he reiterated his account; from Moosehead Lake a traveler crosses into the West Branch, not the East Branch as he mistakenly called it. Also, to "pole up the river" would have taken them in the direction of Seboomook, not east and north to the infamous "Mud Lake Carry," the early entrance to the Allagash region. In spite of his geographical errors, he does give us a wonderful account of fishing and capturing a moose in the water.*

Some twenty years ago, while visiting my native town, in one of the New England states, I received an invitation from two of my old schoolmates, who had never left the shade of their paternal tree, to join them in an expedition to the wilds of Maine. Glad enough was I to become one of the party, as after the excitement of meeting old friends, had passed my time hung heavily on my hands.

We left for Bangor by rail, thence by stage to Moosehead Lake, where our guides joined us with the boat and camping utensils. I well remember the excitement of our first camp on the east branch of the Penobscot. The efforts of the guides to make my two companions comfortable for the night, as it was their first experience in camp life; the novelty, together with the imaginary fear of some nocturnal visitor, keeping them awake, far into the night. The next morning we started in our batteaux, pushing up the river. When nearing a carry, so called, where we were to leave the river and strike the shores of Mud Lake, we came upon a party of twelve lumbermen, stopping for dinner near the mouth of the brook.

After dinner, one of them told us that he had discovered a hole in the brook, full of trout, and we had better stop long enough to capture enough for supper. I looked round for their fishing rods to gain some insight into the way they took these highly esteemed fish. What was my astonishment, when I saw them jump into the water, splashing, and making as much noise as possible. Presently the trout by the dozens, threw themselves upon the stones in the shallow water where they were gathered up by one of the men stationed there. Then the others, by feeling among the rocks at the bottom, seized those that had taken refuge, and threw them on the bank. I must confess, unsportsmanlike as it was, my companions and myself, joined in the melee, and that night we supped upon delicious trout, some of them over two pounds of weight.

We accomplished the carry, and presently noticed one the guides coming toward us in the canoe, seemingly in great excitement. When within hailing, he cried out "There's a moose in the lake." I caught up Boston's rifle, R. his double gun loaded with No. 4 shot and we, with the other guide, jumped into the canoe. What was my chagrin to find, upon examination, the rifle empty and the bullets ashore in Boston's pocket, there was no time to return for them, as the moose was making tall traveling for the shore, and it would be only by great exertion, that we could get near enough for a shot before he landed. Fortunately as I then thought, I found a lead sinker in my pocket, large enough for a slug, and soon had the rifle loaded, and here we were, four men in a birch canoe bearing down to attack a bull moose, not exactly upon his native heath, but in one of his familiar lakes.

By hard paddling we succeeded in turning him from the shore, and when near enough, the guides said fire. After a quick aim, I saw my slug strike the water a foot over the moose's neck, while R.'s charges of No. 4, only made him more determined to land in spite of us. What were we to do? A noble moose within shot, a chance coming to one probably but once in a life time, and we with empty guns. R. however, soon found some buck shot cartridges in his pocket, and nervously succeeded in leading both barrels, then handing the gun to me, he said the game is too large, I feel that I shall miss, and he will escape. The moose was now perfectly enraged, and forced us to make way for him to the shore. I waited till his side appeared above the water, when the cartridge, bursting only as it reached him, let out his life blood, coloring the water for yards around. The second barrel, fired in mercy, extinguished his life, and we soon drew his eight hundred-pound carcass ashore.

SAM'S LAST BEAR FIGHT, AND HOW HE KILLED THE BEAR

Anonymous, from *Piscataquis Observer*, February 4, 1874

The story I am about to relate, is not a got-up affair, but a real occurrence—a fact recorded in the minds of many who remember well, the person and the time. Though not myself, one of the principal characters in the fight, yet "all of it I saw and part of it I was."

The location, on the banks of the Piscataquis, near a small village, where on either margin fine well-cultivated intervals greet the gazer's eyes. Here, in said village lived a middle-aged man, quite a fellow to talk of his hunting, though not boasting of any exploits, yet ever throwing out unmistakable hints, that it would fare hard with a bear or other wild varmint should one cross his path. No children ever reposed on, or rolled themselves up in, a bear-skin of his; one reason was, Sam (he was known by that name) had no children; another was, no bear ever put in an appearance when he was out hunting, and, of course he could carry no bear-skin home as a trophy.

Well, Sam had talked so much of seeing bear signs, their tracks, where they had dug wild turnip, or torn in pieces some old hemlock log in search for ants, that the people of the neighborhood, moved doubtless by a desire to prove all things, wished greatly to know, should a Bruin put in an appearance and Sam have his gun charged with a bear charge, whether he would show himself true grit or not.

As in the course of events there is a time for everything; so came a time to try our hero's courage. A little way down the river lived a farmer, his buildings on the left bank and his sheep pasture across the river opposite. The pasture was somewhat grown up to clumps of bushes, and many an old monarch of the forest in the shape of down hemlocks strewn over the opening, dense woods around. A number of sheep were reported missing, supposed killed by bears. This was an opportune moment for our bear hunter.

A party was easily mustered to go there and watch for the sheep killer; time, early autumn, weather mild, and a good moon. In the evening some half a dozen, headed by our hero were on the spot, each bearing a gun, and Sam's charged with a bear charge.

After a time an object was pointed out in the distance and decided to be a bear. After a few discharges, Sam fired. Just at this moment appeared another character on the scene. Our Si, enveloped carefully in a bear-skin, was seen approaching. Sam, now his own gun being empty, took another gun and blazed away, his comrades loading the guns, the bear all the time advancing, and the bear-hunters retreating at first in good order, through bushes, over cradle-knolls and down trees, firing at every good view, and the skirmish ending in a complete rout, and our marksman finding himself, so hard pressed under one bush, jumping into the river down a steep bank some twenty-five feet.

The forces are at length rallied together, a counsel is held, and it is resolved there shall be no more retreat; for is there is no bounty on bears? This season of the year they are fat, and their fur robes valuable. And then, the name of getting driven from the field! Up to this time all has been on the defensive. Now of the offensive.

The little brown jug was found and duly welcomed. (This was more than forty years ago.) Sam never imbibed, for which reason his nerves were steadier, and he was the fitter person to take deliberate aim. Already search was made, and the bear, not very comely in appearance, is found. "When Greek meets Greek then comes the tug of war." Old Bruin sees by the determined front there is more fighting to be done, and the attack commences in earnest, our hero at times, not ten feet from the bear.

"Now the battle's growing hot, my boys,
I don't know how 'twill turn."

Powder burns well now, and soon the black varmint is in full retreat, over logs, through brush, &c., and is driven at length, much against his will, over the bank, down through the bushes skirting the river, splash into the stream, and, as he swims slowly down, the mark for a few parting shots, he is seen to lodge on a sand bar below, and the party cross over to the farm house, where all the principal events of the hunt, the retreat with its disasters, the "deeds of daring done" and all the successful termination are all rehearsed by our hero to Si and the farmer's family. After this who could doubt the courage of our hero?

He raised no more parties to go watch for bears.

TROUT FISHING IN MAINE

By Nedlam, from *Forest and Stream,* May 24, 1877

Nedlam was the pen-name for Charles A. J. Farrar of Jamaica Plain, Massachusetts, who produced guide books to the Rangeley Region and to the Moosehead Region. This is one of the earliest tales he wrote about his own experiences at Moosehead.

Moosehead Lake
(Currier & Ives)

I often see an inquiry in your valuable paper from some sportsman, asking where good trout fishing can be had, easy of access, and propose giving you the benefit of a trip I took in the fall of 1874, and from which I derived more pleasure than any previous search after the speckled beauties, although I had previously visited the Middle Dam, Richardson Lakes, Moose River, from Holden towards Canada line, and several times to the Pleasant Ridge Ponds–my experience, as you see, having all been in Maine.

In the early part of September of 1874 my friend B— (an ardent lover of "chucking the bug") and wife, and self and wife, left the Hub in the morning train, ticketed for Mount Kineo and return, but not quite sure where we should stop, as our "objective point" might be changed if sufficient inducement should offer.

We thought seriously of making a short stop at Monson, Maine, when we started, but our hopes were almost dashed when we were approaching Portland, and had just lighted our pipes in the smoking car, to be informed by a gentleman who was enjoying the same luxury, who was visiting Maine for the same purpose as ourselves, that 1st, there were no trout in Monson, and 2d, that they were not good for anything if there were; and 3d, that they could not be taken with a fly, all of which tended to make us think our original informant (who fishes entirely with a gun) must have been mistaken.

After parting with our friend (on short acquaintance) we concluded to "stick" to our original plan of campaign, no matter what stories we might hear. Our conclusion was badly shaken many times before we reached our destination, and we came to the wise conclusion that the waters of Maine had a varied reputation, even with the residents and lovers of sport with a 10-ounce rod.

We spent the first night out at the "Exchange," in Bangor, and after a good night's rest, breakfast, etc., proceeded to the depot of the Bangor and Piscataquis R.R., and were shown to a car attached to a baggage train, which gave promise of a long and tedious ride.

In answer to our inquiry of the conductor about the time required to make the trip, he informed us that "When he went, he went," and we fully agreed with him before our arrival at the end of the road.

At that time the employees of the road (so we were informed) sold peanuts along the line, and would stop any time to sell a pint, and it seemed to us that the story was true; but they do much better now, as a strictly passenger train runs over the road in the sporting season.

We arrived at Monson in time for dinner, after a pleasant ride of fifteen miles in the stage from Guilford, and devoted the first hours of the afternoon in getting our rooms at the hotel in order, so that our ladies could be comfortable in our absence, and make us comfortable when we returned. About four P.M. the pale portion of our party started out to deliver the letters of introduction to a gentleman who could "tell us about it," and were sadly taken aback when he informed us he had not caught a fish for twenty years; but before we had quite recovered from the shock, he informed us that he would introduce us to the postmaster, who was the "boss" fisherman of the place.

On our way to the post-office he informed us that "Ed," could catch them anywhere, and if he couldn't assist us we might as well move on.

We found Mr. Haynes a very pleasant gentleman, and kindly disposed to render us any assistance we might require, but check our enthusiasm by informing us that trout could not be taken with a fly in the waters of that vicinity, as it had been tried over and over again without success, except in the case of one little fellow about four inches long, and he was thought to be too small to know any better. We, however, decided to give it them a chance to refuse us at once, and proceeding to the hotel, strung our rods, and at just five P.M. were in a boat on the lower part of Hebron Pond, just opposite the hotel, say ten rods away. My friend insisted upon taking the paddle, and my string of flies were soon in the water, without much thought of striking a fish in the lower end used as a mill pond, as we were told there were none there, and my companion was using his paddle freely, forcing the boat rapidly through the water, when a fine fish rose at my fly, which I failed to strike, and before I could cast again the boat was upon him, and I was unable to raise him again.

This gave promise of adding something to the little fellow before mentioned, and our spirits were raised several degrees in a few moments after. Again starting for the pond proper, I struck a fish, and after a few minutes sharp play landed a beauty "tipping the beam" at 1 ¼ pounds. During the handling of this fish, we shot into the pond proper, and the wind being off shore, we put our boat broadside to, and both commenced work in earnest. In a moment another greedy fellow had my fly, and after a contest of about ten minutes my second fish was in the boat, weighing 1 ¾ pounds, and we were obliged to "pull for the shore," as it had commenced raining, and at just six P.M., we landed with enough for supper, having demonstrated that the trout would rise to a fly, and about seven o'clock we sat down to our frugal meal of fried trout, baked potatoes, etc., giving us a foretaste of what was to come.

We made up our minds not to work too hard, and to take things just as easy as possible, so the next morning we did not get on to the pond until nine o'clock, and having made a few inquiries of the postmaster, thought we could find where the trout were, and were not disappointed, as when the horn tooted at twelve P.M. for dinner, we had twelve trout, running from 1 ¾ to 2 pounds 9¼ ounces, almost filling my landing net. And we settled one thing very satisfactorily, viz., that they would only take a very large and bright red fly, as B. insisted upon using such as he had used at the Richardson Lakes, and for a large portion of the forenoon would not accept any from my book, but he soon came to it, and made good use of them the balance of the time.

The people of the town were rather astonished, the postmaster with the rest, and he went out in the afternoon, as did our ladies, to see how it was done, and had a chance to be satisfied, as we added nine to our catch, all of good size.

We spent three weeks at this place fishing every day the weather would allow, except Sundays, and our smallest catch for any day was twelve. Some days when we visited a pond where they were small, running from a quarter to a pound and quarter, we would catch at least a hundred.

Every day we had many things to remember, and which would doubtless prove interesting, but I will only relate one more day's experience, and then begin where I started, by giving you the information indicated.

We had become quite intimate with "Ed," whom we found one of the jolliest fellows we ever met, and one morning, he started for Monson Pond to show us where the fish could be found. The fish not being in the right mood, he suggested we should go through the woods about a mile, to No. 18, a small pond rarely visited, and where he very much doubted if a fly had ever been cast. We had been at work there an hour at least without a sign, when I saw a break close to my raft, and proceeded to put my flies "where they would do the most good," for me at least, as I thought, but in an instant my "split bamboo" was shivered, the second joint being in "fiddle strings," from the sharpest strike it has ever been my lot to receive, although my score shows one of eight pounds. However, I saved my fish, after a very long and hard fight; but somewhat surprised me by only weighing two pounds.

Shortly after B. had a rise near him, and at once put his flies over the fish, and with a rush and a splash his rod was in the same condition as mine. He also saved his fish, which weighed 2 ½ pounds.

Our spare rods being at Monson Pond, where was nothing for us to do but to return. After returning we strung new rods, and insisted that Ed. should commence using the fly, and finally prevailed upon him to do so, although we thought he only did so to keep us from teasing him. Everything being ready, we shoved from the shore, and commenced our sport, the wind, to our ideas, being just right. When perhaps an eighth of a mile from shore the wind ceased instantly, and we decided to start for home at once, when the air seemed full of flies, which settled upon the surface of the water. Almost instantly the pond seemed full of fish, jumping out in all directions, and such a sight I never expected to see again.

We struck them right and left, and landed them as fast as possible, and the mouth of every fish was full of those black flies, about the size of our common house-fly. Our guide caught his first fish, and he will never catch one what will give him more play, and tax his skill more than that one did. After the fish were netted, he carefully laid the rod down with the remark that, "He would paddle us just where we wanted, as he had had fun enough for one day, and more than in all the fish he had ever caught with bait." He had made two fine "hornbeam fly rods," and can now hold his own with any one.

Within a radius of seventeen miles there are thirty-two ponds all full of fish; and right here I wish to say that the trout from Monson Pond are finer than any I have ever seen. The names of the ponds are: Hebron, Monson, Spectacle, Doughty (2), Bunker (2), Bog Stream, Bell (2), McLane, North Moors, Bear, South Senior, South Junior, Meadow, Meadow Stream, No. 18, Grindstone, Buttermilk, Benson, Ship, Greenwoods (3), Long Hedgehog, Big Indian, Little Indian, Herring and Greenleaf. The country is mountainous, affording some of the finest views possible, and any one loving nature cannot help being pleased by a visit to that section, and especially if combined with the above is a love of fishing.

I am informed from perfectly reliable authority that Ship Pond contains land-locked salmon in abundance, but cannot speak from my own knowledge; am reserving that pleasure for my next visit.

The greatest drawback at Monson is the lack of suitable boats, which difficult can be readily overcome; and I would recommend any one going there to obtain a birch or a light boat, which can be had at or near Bangor, or at Moosehead Lake.

Any one calling upon E. R. Haynes, postmaster, will derive what information they may require, and make the acquaintance of one of the best fellows to be found, ready to meet a brother sports-man, and assist his on almost every occasion.

– NEDLAM, BOSTON, MARCH 17, 1877

VACATION ON A WAY-BACK FARM

By Chas. Winthrop Sawyer, from *Forest and Stream*, February 25, 1899

American Homestead (Currier & Ives)

Charles Winthrop Sawyer, one of the well-known experts on firearms in America, wrote several books, which have become classics in that field. They were "Firearms in American History 1600 to 1800" (1910); "United States Single Martial Pistols (1913); and "Our Rifles" (1920).Calling back over the years, Sawyer wrote this tale, apparently autobiographical, about a trip he once took to Maine. Needing a good vacation from his drafting work, he took a boat to Portland and a train to the interior, where he stayed with a family at a remote farm.

...The farmer's wife was at the door to meet us, but the boy was too shy, and was waiting in the barn for me to make first advances. Many are the delightful, natural country people I have lived with, but none as retired, quaint and old-fashioned as these. There is no neighbor for nearly two miles. From there to the next neighbor is four miles. A caller during the year is a rarity. The farmer's wife is about sixty years old and never has been further than twelve miles from this house, where she was born. Forty-seven year ago, when the farmer was twenty-one years of age, he "went up to Bostin" and now remembers every incident of that remarkable adventure.

Think of a boy of fourteen years old, man grown, who never rode on a railroad, never heard of an electric car, never ate nor heard of oysters, lobsters, ice cream, chocolate, or tropical fruits, and can't imagine the sea, a tall building, or a theater. Do you say, "What an ignoramus?" Not a bit of it. There never was a more agreeable companion than he. He wasn't much of a talker, and for a week never said much but "Yes" or "No." But what he didn't know about all out-doors was hardly worth knowing. Always good-natured, always quiet, never tired, we tramped the forest and fields, fished, hunted, camped and sketched together. After making his acquaintance at the barn I asked him to go to the house with me to help me carry in my trunk to my room; but my secret motive was to make him forget self-consciousness in curiosity to see my things. I thought his tongue would be loosed by questions; but therein I was mistaken. He sat and looked with evident interest; heard my explanations about a jointed fishpole, artificial flies and rubber worms; handled my rifle with deference; smelled my Java coffee and looked amused at the filter coffee-pot, but never opened his mouth.

Meantime the sun had gone behind the clouds, and I proposed that we try to catch some trout for supper. We moved a portion of the woodpile and dug him some worms–he said "No" to my offer of a rubber one–then went to the meadow southwest of the house, where a number of deep, bubbling springs gave rise to a brook. The brook appeared but a thread among the stubble, but was mysteriously wide and deep, for it had but beneath the sod on each side. Here were abundance of greedy trout. Trout are light or dark in color, according to whether they live in sunshine or shadow, and dark trout are the most beautiful fish in the world. Their backs are a very dark, rich brown-black; their sides a trifle lighter, with many brilliant, jewel-like spots of bright red, surrounded by yellow and light blue; the brown background shades to tawny yellow below and then blends into flashing silver on the belly. All trout are very shy and suspicious, and if the ground shakes, or they see the fisherman, or a moving shadow, or the bait is out of season, or looks suspicious, Mr. Trout coolly and persistently refuses to become acquainted with Mr. Fisherman.

We walked quietly and softly to the meadow, where we separated by a few hundred feet and approached the last 10ft. to the brook on all fours, taking up and putting down hand and knee with utmost caution. I felt again, as in boyhood, the intoxicating, wild instincts of the hunter. The gentle breeze blew in my face, and brought to my nostrils the sweet smell of the peppermint and spearmint, which trailed its stems in the water. Lying on my stomach, I used my utmost skill to fool the wary beauties, and was rewarded by occasional struggles with strong and desperate fish, trying to escape, or to rub off the hook, or break the slender line or pole. Out of skill and a real bait, an alder pole and a stout line, was putting two fish into his old burlap bag for one that went into my creel. When I hooked a fish I had more fun with it than he had with his, for my fish had a chance to escape and cripple my fishing apparatus, too, and I had to put my skill against the fish's to see who should be victor. Which would you prefer, more fun or more fish? Why not combine both by putting a live bait on my hook? There was no other reason than that when we went fishing together we caught all that the family could eat, and that was enough. We fished down the stream to the road, where alders overhung little water-bright pebbles and moss-covered boulders. I watched to see if Almon would jerk his fish out and tangle his line and dangle his fish on the bushes overhead, and get mad and use country swear words. No he. A little motion of the wrist and a slight lifting of the pole sufficed.

When, toward evening, we returned to the house, the setting sun was sending long bars of light through the cloud banks. We set three chairs on the grass by the back porch, and while Almon called the hens I put a pan of trout in the left-hand chair, an empty pan in the right chair, and sat in the middle one, with a board on my knees. Around us were three cats, five dogs and a hundred or more hens. Every time a fish head was thrown there was a wild rush from all sides converging on the bait. The dogs and cats reached it first, hens flying, scratching and chucking on top of them in a rough and tumble scramble. The hens always finally secured the morsel, generally by picking it out of the dog's mouth. The dogs and cats were persevering and contested as gamely for the fiftieth morsel as for the first. I called the largest cat and gave her a morsel from my hand. Instantly the cat was the center of a struggling mass of hens three deep on top of her. The cat rolled on her back and scratched for dear life, and the hens made a fearful racket. A hen which had been standing by dashed in and got the fish head and ran away, followed by a string of others. She had to fly to the house top to get a chance to eat it. We watched her swallow it whole, after many gulps and gasps, and then we went in.

The large, dim kitchen was a most delightful room at night. In the middle of one side was a great open fireplace, where a glowing bed of coals lighted the pots and pans set on them, or hanging by hooks or chains from a long crane. Beside the fireplace were the iron doors of a brick oven. The ceiling was but a couple of feet above the head, dark with age and smoke, and hung around the fireplace with strings of onions and dried apples. A long table stood in the middle of the room, set for supper. Opposite the fireplace an alcove between two large corner cupboards showed two doors leading to the family sleeping rooms. The two ends of the room had two windows each, and between the windows of one end was the sink. Here the fish were washed and rolled in corn meal, and soon we had the pleasure of seeing them curl and brown in boiling salt fat. Most of the good odor went up the chimney. We gathered at the table. A small lamp in its middle lit the white cloth, and left the rest of the room vague and shadowy. The dish of trout passed from hand to hand. We helped ourselves from a milk pan heaped high with your string beans and peas, crowned by a great lump of melting butter. Corn bread, tea and milk went with them. Then a great, steaming bean pot was brought from the brick over, the lid removed, a long handled spoon stuck in, and I was helped to the most delicious Indian pudding I ever tasted; soft, jelly-like, wheyey, rich and satisfying.

After supper three of us sat before the fire and two of us talked. The farmer's wife was doing the dishes at the sink. The farmer sat at my right with his feet on a stool, head bent forward and grizzly beard reaching down his vest. Almon sat on an uncomfortable chair at the left, heels on the top round, bent forward, with hands clasped around his knees. The farmer smoked his clay pipe and watched the fire, and talked at it to me, and mostly asked questions. The farmer's wife soon joined us. We put a fresh stick on the coals and watched the ever-changing flames, and talked of the years gone by. The farmer told stories of his boyhood. I supposed the region was then one of bears and wolves and wildcats, but he told me that it was then well dotted with farms. The companions of his boyhood had died or moved away; their children had gone to manufacturing towns, and the farm lands had merged into his or gone into the hands of the great landed proprietor who lived next down the road. The farmer's wife soon fell asleep in her chair, and I took the hint that these people usually retire and rise with the sun.

My bed was a great foot-poster in the clean-smelling spare room at the other end of the house. How delicious was the feeling of that crisp, firm, corn-husk mattress under the smooth sheet. Once in the night I was awakened by the rush of barking dogs past my window, the sound growing fainter in the distance and finally dying away down the road. I spoke of it in the morning while I was watching Almon and his father milking in the barn.

"Might hev be'n a fox, or a coon, or mebbe somethin' bigger," said the farmer. "One year we was mighty pestered with some critter that kept ketchin' our hens an' clawin the cats. My wife got so scared that she didn't dare venture outside the door nights. Finally we ketched him in a steel trap, an' what do you think it was?" I guessed a fox. "Nope, it was a whoopin' big black stray tomcat, an' he was so fit we smashed the trap tryin' to kill him. The curis' thing is, whar he came from. They ain't nobody within twenty miles ever had such a cat." I had my private suspicions that he didn't always know cats from "somethin' bigger."

A horn sounded from the house. "Breakfast," said the farmer. We turned the cattle out into the lane, whose low stone walls, overhung by raspberry bushes, and shaded on one side by overhanging boughs of apple trees, directed them to the forest-girt pasture that occupied the hill slopes on all sides except toward the road.

Milk pails in hand, we repaired to the house. An enormous pewter coffee-pot stood by my plate.

"I b'lieve you said you wanted to make your own coffee," said the housewife.

"I think I have an improvement over the old method," I replied, and brought my nickel apparatus. While all stood watching, the coffee was put in the filter, set in the pot, boiling water was poured in the strainer and upon the coffee, and the apparatus assembled air-tight.

"I guess you are mighty fond of coffee," said the farmer

"I guess so to," I replied, and smiled at the recollection of the great yellow package the farmer had brought from the village and exhibited to his wife with the remark: "How much do you suppose I giv' fer that?" She looked it over, read all the printing, hefted it, and guessed. Said he: "Fifteen cents, and this spoonholder throwed into the bargain." "Let's have that kind right along," said she, "and mebbe we'll get some dishes." "Then if you don't need the dishes," said I, "you can sell them to Elmiry and have the coffee for nothing."

While we were eating breakfast the farmer said: "That remark o' yourn yisteddy about sellin' Elmiry the dishes an' havin' the coffee for nothin' minds me of the way Hi Robinson got somethin' fer nothin' out er the storekeeper at the village. You 'member Hi, don't you? He's kinder slow spoken, 'n some folks calls him foolish. One day I was settin' in the store a spell with a lot more, an' in comes Hi. He goes up to Lish, who keeps the store, an' takes an egg out o' his pocket an' says: "How'll yer swap?" 'Oh, I don't knows I want to swap fer one egg,' says Lish. 'What do you want for it?' 'A darnin' needle.' 'Well, I'll swap with you,' said Lish, an' took the egg and giv' him the darnin' needle. Hi stood 'round a while, 'an then he says, drawlin' like, 'Say, ain't yer goin' ter treat?' 'Treat? On one darnin' needle?' says Lish, 'not much,' 'Feller cross the way will,' says Hi. Lish grinned. 'All right, says he, jest ter humor him, 'what'll you have?' 'Cider and an aig,' says Hi. That tickled the rest on us, but Lish brought the cider, and broke there egg into it–Hi's own egg–an' Hi see it was a double yolker. He took up the glass an' looked at there egg for some time. Then he says, says he: 'Say, hadn't you better gimme 'nother darnin' needle?'"

Stories and breakfast ended, I took the rifle from its rest above the mantel shelf and followed the road toward the next neighbor's. The clouds were high and fleecy, the sun in full splendor, but for summer time not very hot. In that altitude the heat is never very intense. Going down the knoll toward the first bridge presented the picture of a yellow road cut in the turf, winding, and undulating, full of light and shade and color, softened by bordering vegetation, and disappearing in shadow. A gentle breeze brought sweet country odors. All about, birds, trees, grass and flowers. I walked softly, drinking enjoyment. The woods approached, and their dim recesses seemed black by contrast. What is that dim form? It may be the next neighbor's red setter dog. So vague were the outlines that I stopped to await a motion. There was no motion. I opened the rifle and snapped the breech down. At the click the shadowy form became a fox on the gallop to circle past me. The fox kept steadily to his path, and a bullet from the rifle began a cross path. The two paths and the two bodies, the big soft one and the little hard one, instantly intersected, and I held a harmless fox in my arms and stroked his soft fur. Shall I go back to the house with him? No; I will put him in a tree out of the way of harm.

The forest path lured on. Patches of sunlight moved on the forest floor, golden bright lighting green moss and checkerberry plant, brown twigs, dark red and russet leave. Vistas in half-light showed between the tree trunks. Red squirrels chirred, occasional gray ones ran along nearby boughs, deer had left frequent evidences. The lives of all were safe; the rifle was not for them during this season. The road led on and on, with delight at every step. Finally, sighting a telescope straight down the dark road was a bright picture of a large white farmhouse, with outbuildings attached, a garden, a woodpile, and a great protecting tree. From the upper windows of the house everything the sight could reach belonged to this proprietor: hills and valleys, forest, field, stream and meadow. Truly, he could say, "Monarch of all I survey."

I found him seated at the grindstone in the shadow of the barn, sharpening a scythe. He reached for my rifle and looked it over critically. "That's a might pretty gun. It' about the size and heft of my grandsire's pea-rifle, only it's a got a smaller hole. Seems to me 'tain't much more'n a toy. You calc'latin' to shoot any b'ars with it?"

"No, I guess not. I haven't lost any bears. I brought it along more for company than for game. The game law is on now, you know."

"Game law? Humph! A'in't nobody around here to touch you if you shoot anything you want. Ther's plenty of deers around, 'n pa'tridges is thick's hens up in the parsters. Help yourself."

"I shot a fox coming down here."

"Did you, now? With that little gun?"

"That little gun has more business to it than you think. With a soft pointed bullet and a high pressure powder you could make beef of one of your cows at 50 yards, first shot. But I'm looking for woodchucks this morning. Got any chucks hereabouts?"

"Chucks enough to fill the barn right out in that field beyond the orchard."

To the field I went at once. It reminded me of a stiffened sea or a rolling prairie. From the highest ridge I could see the whole of it at once, about half a mile wide by a mile long. Yellow and brown stubble shone in the sun. Scattered apple trees dotted one end. Woods bordered all around. A trickling stream sparkled and disappeared amid long grass and tufts of bushes. Within range of the rifle I counted fourteen black dots, each with a red patch in front. There are the holes, anyway. Now for the chucks.

I stretched out at full length on the side of the ridge away from most of the holes and waited. The sun warmed my back and the breeze cooled one side of my face. Rising heat-waves made the air shimmer, and distant objects seemed to waver. In the blue distance above the woods rose the outlines of distant hills. There patches of bare rock shimmered like gray steel were outlined by shade lines of deepest purple. Clumps of small trees presented soft forms of yellow-green. Old trunks of dead birches made vertical lines of white. A long time passed in the enjoyment of nature. Solitude, quiet, peaceful, and richly beautiful, brought to the imagination romance and vaguely drifting stories. I rested my head on my outstretched arm and luxuriated in the beautiful pictures that, without effort, formed and changed and passed before the mind's eye, an involuntary nature's drama. From my revery I fell to watching the ants that were investigating the Gulliver who lay over their tiny nests. Their little feet and antennae tickled my bare skin, and I started to rise, and then I recollected why I was there. Probably that motion had sent every woodchuck head back into its hole. Now, there sat three chucks upright, each on his earth-patch. Several holes were gray with heads, and I knew just how all the noses were working and smelling for a scent of the intruder. After a while I rolled a green apple down the opposite side of the ridge. The smallest chuck ran for it at once and sat up in plain view and ate it. More chucks appeared. Any one of them was an easy shot, but I decided to give them a fair chance for their lives. I selected one which I judged to be a fat young female, and waved my hand on high. Instantly every chuck ran for his hole. Most of them halted at the entrance and turned their heads around in my direction and waited to see if they were pursued. I whistled and in they dived, turned around, and almost immediately stuck their heads out to look and sniff. I guessed my younger one to be 75 yards distant, took out the long-distance cartridge and quietly substituted a soft-nosed short-range one, raised the rifle sight two notches, took a careful bead on the center of the forehead and gently pressed the trigger. Every head but that one disappeared at the report. That one stayed just where it was. I didn't need to go get it, for it would certainly wait for me, so I gently put another cartridge in place and kept quiet. In a few minutes another hole became gray. A change in the rifle sight, another report like the crack of a child's whip, and the hole remained gray.

A much longer wait, and then another substitution of a gray spot for a black one. Another crack, and one more chuck became mine. Three chucks and an 8lb. rifle were enough to lug on a warm day, so I went from hole to hole and drew out the limp occupants by the ears. I called with them at the great farmhouse. They were having dinner, and I gladly accepted an urgent invitation to "set up to the table."

Master and mistress, farm hands and maids, all put their knees beneath the same broad board. The jests were merry and personal, and the beans, boiled pork, cucumbers, "white cake," "sweet cake" and pie, as good as they smelled. Cheese and cider, after the meal, were passed as we tilted back in our chairs for the noonday rest. The afternoon was spent in the hay field. The men took turns in pitching on and raking after, while I trod the load. In the shadow of a haystack was a jug of cider wrapped in a wet cloth. We all took care not to let it get lonesome.

In the cool of the late afternoon I started home with two of the woodchucks, and gathered the fox on the way. The dogs spied me from afar, and the game had to be put in a tree to keep it whole, while I shouted for the dogs to be called home and shut up before I could go on. The setting sun was richly coloring the clouds beyond the house as I toiled up the knoll with my burden, and supper and rest were pleasant prospects.

No church bells broke the stillness of the next morning. Neither did any crack of the rifle, or cast of fly or bait. But we did desecrate the early Sabbath morning by preparing the game. Seated on a couple of great peeled hemlock logs, Almon dressed the fat young woodchuck for roasting, and tacked the skins on the wood house door, while I deprived the fox of his robe. The hens recognized no Sunday, and were as amusingly frantic for morsels of meat and fat as they had been before for fish cleanings. The hen house, in front of us, gray and weatherworn, was a most interesting example of how twisted and rickety a hen house can be and yet stand. The farmer came and sat on a log and whittled for the sake of doing something.

"I kinder think we'll hev comp'ny this arfnoon. The store-keeper seed ye when ye come, an' he's prob'ly told ev'rybody 'round that there's that same city feller up here, an' some on 'em 'll be up to see you."

Sure enough, dinner was hardly done when the dogs set up a chorus and rushed away down the road. We all went to the door and peered down the road after them. Soon a team emerged from the woods and rattled down the road to the accompaniment of flying gravel and barking dogs, bounded across the bridges, and crawled slowly up the knoll. "Kin you make out who it is?" said the farmer to Almon. "Link Belknap," said Almon. Now I knew that Link lived fully ten miles away, and I appreciated this kindness in coming so far to see me, and concluded that I would treat him to the best cigar he ever smoked. By this time the wagon came into view again, and I saw there were Link, his wife, two daughters and a man I didn't know. They drove up to the door and proceeded to climb out. "How-y-yer," said the farmer. "How-y-yer," said Link, and that was all the greeting that passed between them. They seemed drawn within themselves, like a quiet tortoise drawn within his shell because of something unusual in the vicinity. The woman greeted the farmer's wife in the same shy way, by smilingly. I tried to make up for the apparent lack of cordiality, but I knew enough not to say much at first. The horse was hitched in the shade, and we all repaired to "the settin' room" which was a great room taking the whole width of the house between the kitchen and my room, and here all drew chairs against the walls, and sat stiffly in the embarrassment of strange surroundings. The women seemed able to find a little something to say, and I tried city talk on the men, to draw them out, but soon found they preferred crops, the weather, farm work and things they knew about. Another chorus from the dogs announced Lish, the storekeeper, and his "wimmin folks." We now made quite a party, and pretty well filled the wall space; but when another ferocious outburst and other "Whoa" brought a man, his wife and baby, the men naturally stayed out of doors, and left the women to keep house.

We drifted along to the orchard gate, and sat on the wall and the bars, and smoked my cigars, and heard about everybody's business, while I wondered what to do about all those women who had come so far, some of them from sheer friendliness, some of them for the ride, and the rest out of curiosity to see a strange "city feller." What would you do in a case like that? The problem finally solved itself, and the wild strawberry patch in the afternoon shade of the woods knows the story of the city man's attempt to look unconscious under covert observation.

All hands stayed to supper, although one and all made show of protesting, for politeness' sake. The piece de resistance was a baked stuffed woodchuck garnished with water cress. Cold beans and brown bread, "white cake," "dried apple sweet cake," pie, preserved plums, cherry jam, and the ever-present stewed leaves called tea were consumed in wholesale quantities. All the women felt it their duty to compliment the hostess on her "white cake"–known to city people as hot saleratus biscuit–and pan after pan of light, fluffy, red-hot cakes disappeared into dyspeptic stomachs. The correct way was to put a lump of butter on quarter of a biscuit, stuff it all into the mouth, fill any remaining space in the mouth with tea, and swallow both at once. Supper produced good cheer and heartiness and loosened all tongues. One after the other, in a string, the three teams rattled away after cordial invitations to visit each family.

"Well," said I when we were again by ourselves in the cozy kitchen, "this has bee a red-letter day for you."

"Yes," said the farmer. "I've gin away a good many meals in my life, an' I never make no 'count of it. I like to see folks around, an' I hope there'll be some come every Sunday. I ain't goin' to let you go home before winter." I smiled in the darkness for a long time.

The next day broke dark and cloudy. At breakfast I got permission for Almon to accompany me to Rattlesnake Pond, and he was so pleased he opened his mouth several times to speak, but thought better of it. We got a couple of gunnybags from the attic, to carry a spare flannel shirt apiece, lunch, bait and fish lines, hung them over the shoulders and tied them around the waist to keep them in place, and gun in hand, we went across the pasture and took an old trail through the woods. Up hill and down dale, over crags and through glades we hurried. An hour and a half of fast traveling brought us to a beaten road. We followed it a good many miles, and then took into the woods again. Another couple of miles, and we came suddenly to the shore of a large pond. It was long and wide. Rocky, wood-covered promontories extended out into it, cutting it into bays, and adding to the delight of exploration by continually offering new points of view. In most places the woods grew to the water's edge. Where we were was a grassy beach. We crossed a ridge and saw a fence running far out into the water, and a cow trying to wade around it. That meant a house was near by. We sought the house, and gained it after a dispute with the dog.

The owner was willing that we should take his boat, and between us we lugged it to the water. Almon had never been in a boat, so we tied the guns by long ropes to the thwarts, so as not to lose them if we upset. Almon cut a fish pole, while I put mine together. Then we went along the shore with a stick apiece and whacked a few dozen frogs on the heads, for bait for the 2ft. long pickerel we were looking for. Incidentally we secured a pretty, black turtle with bright yellow spots on its back. Then we pushed off and I paddled gently along the lily pads while Almon trolled. The water was placid, the air was quiet, the boat glided noiselessly. The peace of gentle Arcady brooded over all. Two-foot pickerel, or any other pickerel, didn't seem to want our acquaintance. I turned the boat's prow out into the pond and started slowly across. Suddenly a peculiar whoa-hoo-hoo-oo seemed to waver in the air all over the water. Almon caught my eye questioningly. Pretty soon we heard it again, but couldn't locate it, for it seemed to be all over the pond at once. "What do you think it is," I asked, "a bear or a panther?"

"Ha, ha, that's the time you got fooled. It's a loon. Watch the bays near shore for a black speck. That's about all that shows, he swims so deep in the water. We will try him with a rifle, and you will see he will dive as a flash, and be safe under before the bullet gets to him."

Just then a sounding splash was heard, and Almon's pole was jerked from his careless hand and rushed away up the pond like an arrow from a bow. Away we went after it as fast as I could paddle, and after many trials caught it. Some monster at the end of the line pulled and struggled with tremendous strength and darted hither and thither with such speed that the taut line cut the water with the sheer noise scissors make running through cambric. The boat rocked and pitched, and Almon pulled and pulled and held on for dear life, and the thing tried to dive and down it went in spite of his efforts until the stout pole bent half a circle, and the point was under water. Suddenly the strain relaxed and Almon's strength threw high in the air the biggest pickerel I ever saw. It seemed as if he went above the tree tops before he turned and came down. He fell flat on his side with a resounding splash that threw the spray in every direction, and we picked him up stunned and limp. Didn't we gloat over that prize?

I laid down the paddle and we both set to fishing in earnest. Pretty soon I had a fish on that made the reel sing, and I played him until he was tired, and then lifted him to keep the first one company. He was a big fish, but he looked like a baby alongside the other one. We caught one more, and not another bite could we get. Even the loons had stopped hallooing to us. So we went where the water sloped sharply down a bank with pond lilies growing in a neighboring shallow. There we put on smaller hooks and baited them with worms, with a sinker just above, and caught perch, small bass and sunfish about as fast as we could pull them in. A mink ran along the shore near by. A flock of partridges came to the water and drank without seeming to mind us in the least. Pretty soon a hedgehog looked out at us and tried to catch a breeze from our direction. "Try your gun on him,: said I. "Too far," said Almon. So the rifle sent its message and he joined the party.

Then we went ashore and built a fire, and broiled some fish, and ate our hard-boiled eggs, cheese, fish and gingerbread. Robins, bluebirds, yellow birds and a scarlet tanager watched us from above. Squirrels and a woodpecker were tamer and showed a desire to be friendly. We took our luxurious ease and watched our wild acquaintances, and looked out over the pond now rippling in an afternoon breeze, gray and blue-gray from cloud reflections and brown in quiet places. Then we fished again. Pretty soon we saw a very large bird flying on the water with wings flapping it at every stroke, tail and legs dragging as if it was held from below. "There's your loon," said I, "trying to rise with his head to the wind. He is so heavy for his wing size that he had hard work to get out of the water, and if he were in a very small pond with high trees all around he would be obliged to stay there, as if he were in a trap." The loon, free above the water, circled the pond twice to get above the tree tops, long neck out-stretched and wings going like a blur. "That loon comes here to feed, and the chances are that he goes to some other nearby pond to sleep, and that reminds me that with the distance we have to go, we better be starting for home." I looked at my watch and it was 4:30.

We hurried the boat shore and tied it where we had been told, divided the fish, hedgehog and chipmunks between us, and found we had a pretty good load apiece. We could not go home at the speed we had come, and darkness and imminent prospect of rain overtook us on the beaten road. We had difficulty in finding the path into the forest, and greater difficulty to keep the path, which wasn't much of a path in the daytime. After a time we concluded we were lost. I had a few matches, and we lighted one. No sign of a path. "Well, my boy, I guess we had better find the nearest place and camp." But Almon was afraid his parents would worry, and thought we had better push on a little while longer. When only one match was left we saw a blazed tree, which Almon recognized and from which he thought he could go home. On and on we stumbled, with frequent falls in inky darkness, which I dreaded for my gun's sake. Yet the poor gun would be about as badly off if we camped and rain came on. So we kept pushing ahead,

Almon leading, until I ran into the roots of an upturned tree, which struck me at once in the knees, stomach and head. That struck me as a familiar bump, and I spent my last match to look at it. Yes, I knew that tree, and we were going wrong, for the fallen trunk ought to point nearly home. On we went again with hopes renewed, and soon we reached the pasture. I know that one of us at least felt like singing.

Down the pasture slope we went, with lights in the windows in full view, and cool breeze feeling good to the face, for we were bathed in perspiration from hard traveling and extra shirts n. What's that odor? That's the very odor that has haunted me for years. I have a curious knack of never forgetting a smell, and the remembrance of odors, like other recollections occasionally come to mind. This particular smell was apparently a recollection of childhood, and had come to memory many times, and bothered me a good deal, for, try as I would, I could neither associate it with subject nor place. It was only a delightful fugitive trick of memory. Now here it was in reality. I started on a run for the house, and it grew constantly stronger, richer and more alluring. I threw open the porch door, and without stopping to greet the anxious inmates, "What's that smell?" I asked. The room was fragrant with it, but it was strongest in one direction, and I traced it right up to the brick oven, where a thin steam came through the crack at the top of the door. "What are you baking?" I queried. "Cake pudding," said the farmer's wife. Instantly a flood of recollections came over me, and I remembered that delicious dish I had had once, and only once, in my life, and never could recollect where. Supper was a delight, not only because of hunger, but because of that dessert of the queerest, richest sticky paste of a pudding, eaten with cream, that ever a mortal put into his watering mouth. Like the Indian pudding, it was baked in a closely covered pot. Why is it so good I cannot tell, for it is made of common scraps of cake, gingerbread, "white cake," butter and molasses. What else the farmer's wife alone knows, and it is her secret of manipulation that makes it what it is, unique, delicious, and what it is.

Well, I wish that I could tell of all the pleasant incidents of the weeks at this charming old-fashioned farm. I would love to tell the story of how Almon and I fell over a sleeping bear, and the way Almon told the adventure afterward, for the fright loosened his tongue, and he thereafter forgot his bashfulness. But stories and vacations must come to an end sometime, and the day finally came when I was to return to the city. Our next neighbor, who was going to the village, offered to take me, and at the appointed time drove up to the house. We put the trunk aboard, while all stood around to say good-by and have the last handshake.

"Now you be sure to come down this fall, when pa'tridges is good," said the farmer.

"Indeed I will try to," said I.

"Tell your father to come down," he called, as I was getting into the wagon.

"Tell your mother to come down," called his wife as I rode away.

"Say, bring your woman down," he called as loud as he could when I was getting far off.

Then as we rolled over the bridges, Almon came running after as if he or I had forgotten something. "Good bye, come soon," he called at the strength of his lungs. And I stood up in the wagon, and making a trumpet of my hands, at the full strength of my lungs I called back, "I will."

– CHAS. WINTHROP SAWYER

ANGLING FOR EASTERN TROUT

By Mary Trowbridge Townsend, from *Outing Magazine*, May 1899

Mary Leavenworth Trowbridge was born in Barbados in 1851, while her father was employed there, but the family returned to New Haven in 1866, where she completed her education. In 1874 she married William K. Townsend, who had graduated from Yale in 1871 and Yale Law School in 1874. After working a few years as a successful lawyer, Townsend became a professor at Yale, a position he held til his death in 1907. He was also a Judge for the First District Court and was considered one of Yale's "most brilliant sons." Mary accompanied her husband on a number of trips to the Maine Woods and after a vacation at Moosehead Lake in 1899, she composed the following account for Outing Magazine, recounting a day on the lake. It was during this time that more and more women were going to the woods with their husbands, but Mary went a step further, offering advice to fishermen, a subject that had been held sacred among fishermen for centuries.

There are two requisites for the art of angling, one being to buy your tackle and the other to find the fish. The combination of tackle and fish is what makes up three-fourths of the fun. I had not read this sage advice when a misguiding friend started me with an outfit which included a polished twelve-foot bass pole, with shining brass ferrules, a fine white twisted silk line, a brass multiplying reel, a paper of split shot, and a varied assortment of gorgeous flies. Days were spent in lassoing the spikes or in disengaging the twisted knots of my silken line, but still no fish. One day and Indian boy stood grinning at my feeble efforts, swinging his catch of trout before my longing eyes. For a dime he sold his secret: a creature half fish, half lizard; he called it a cockadouche.

My dainty flies were replaced by this reptile, which was flung into the current near the boom. Then the water seemed to become one great yawning mouth. My start set the hook, and with that first rise was born a determination to sink or swim with that fish. My wonderful multiplying reel was tangled, my shining ferrules split, and my rod went to pieces, but I gained the twisted line, and pulled it in, hand over hand, until I grabbed my captive and fell with its shiny body on the pier.

To be sure, my tackle had gone for experience, but as I proudly walked through the little village with my two-and-a-half-pound trout, there entered into my soul that keen subtle love of the woods with its free, restful, joyous life, where you come so near to Nature's heart, and where, on her peaceful bosom, she

"Leads us to rest so gently, that we go,
Scarce knowing if we wish to go or stay:
Being too full of sleep to understand
How far the unknown transcends the what we know."

Ah me! That was many a long day ago that I took my first trout. Since then my rods have been shorter, but they sway and curve with every movement of the fish, and the whir of the click sets the blood coursing in quicker rhythm through my veins.

Could angler have a more delightful spot in which to camp than the region around Moosehead Lake? What good guides you found among those north-woodsmen; strong, unswerving as the pines of their own hills, canoemen by right of inheritance, quick to see, alert to avoid dangers. Their flapjacks are crisp and brown; their bough beds loaded with hours of dreamless sleep, and, above all, they can "smell" fish. Think of the start from Kineo with birch loaded with a goodly supply of luxuries besides the necessary flour, bacon and coffee; the paddle to a comfortable "chance" up the stream bordered with balsam and spruce and dotted with those picturesque sentinels of the forest, the white birch, with the blue-crested kingfisher zigzagging from tree to tree as advance guard.

In the early morning we glide by the lily-padded "logans," and in the long grasses that fringe the deep spring-fed stream, drop an occasional fly as we pass some tempting spot, but the fish are epicures and scorn the early breakfast which they force us poor mortals to take in order to take them. As the white mist rises in fleecy clouds before the glory of day, the water is broken in swirls and spray from the antics of trout rising to grab whatever is floating on its surface. Frank holds the canoe within a comfortable casting length, and gently we lay the brown hackle and grizzly king upon the ruffled water.

Only two casts, then with savage haste our fly is seized, and cautiously we back down-stream drawing our captive from the school, for we hunger for more of their gamy number, so must not disturb the pool. Then come the frantic dart under the tangled roots of the bank, the boring into deep water, the wily twisting around the water-weeds, the headlong leap in the air, when our tip must be lowered to prevent a broken shell. It is a fair fight bravely fought, until the lithe body with its steel-like muscles is netted, and a well-placed blow ends its struggles.

Oh! Misery, you are fitly named, for well do I remember other times when, toward the close of the day, with the gentle breeze just rippling the golden sunset mirrored on your bosom, I have cast so tenderly into the schools tolling their great silver bodies in your cold waters, and no fly could tempt, no skill allure them from their wanton revels.

Or go with me to the Outlet, the headwaters of the Kennebec. You will never come back supperless, for under one big rock about a half-mile down the rushing rapids there waits a big red-bellied fellow. It takes a skillful canoeman to reach him, one who can hold his canoe where the water breaks in white foam over the sunken rocks. But cast across the river, letting your flies float down with the current until they reach the eddy near the big rock. It is no lazy strike this time, but a desperate plunge in the air as the water for another cast; then a glorious headlong struggle with the rushing river to help him. Big fellows, these. What matter if you are drenched with spray from the rapids as your birch dances like a cockle-shell upon the seething waters. You must reel in as you can, and snub him willy-nilly when your line grows small upon the reel, until, exhausted, you coax him to net in the quiet waters of some bend in the river.

Again at the Outlet, crawl out on the boom above the dam; you can count a hundred pounds distributed among some twenty-five or thirty trout that lie with heads up stream and fins lazily fanning the water. You may unsuccessfully temp them with Montreal or Ibis or Parmachene belle through the long bright hours of day, but let twilight come, put on a miller or royal coachman, and cast so that your fly will fall on the edge of the logs, then roll gently into the deep water, and your work is done. The proud fellows have lost caution with the daylight.

Those busy lazy days in the woods, when your world is bounced by the spruce-rimmed dancing stream, and your mind refuses to grasp more than the play of sunshine on the water or the deep swirl left by some passing fish! The early catch, the paddle back for breakfast–but first the fish must be laid on the grassy bank, their points noted the big ones carefully weighed–then rest under the leafy shadows with the chattering squirrel for company, until the sputtering red-spots are laid before you enfolded in strips of crop brown bacon.

Toward evening the refrain is repeated, only this time the shadows lengthen and the woods grow strangely silent save for the weird cry of the distant loon as you float back to camp. Now comes the evening sacrifice to the nymphs who rule the woods, when the pyre is laid of curly-barked birch. As the sparks float upward tangled among the glittering worlds above, the rough clay pipes are lighted, and John and Frank and Albert live over their hardships to the snow-bound lumber camp, or tell of the lonely trapping trip where an accident meant facing death alone in these grim forests. So, lulled by these unceasing tales, you crawl into the fragrant balsam boughs, and the day is done.

There are rainy days in the woods when the firs won't burn, when the bushes spitefully drop their burdens of water down your devoted neck, when even the trout leave the broken, sputtering surface of the stream and seek stiller depths. Other days when the mosquitoes transform the music of the woods into the discords of sheol; when black flies close your eyes and midges drive you to the shelter of the smudge, where, weeping in its stifling smoke, you see visions of the morrow with clear weather, a gentle breeze and a well-filled creel.

I can hardly write of trout without speaking of the playful little pest, the chub that are always ready and waiting to seize your fly, are always where the trout are wily and hard to coax. What a trial of faith it is as you cast under the shadow of the lily-pads where a tremulous wake tells that a trout is lurking, to have your hook swallowed by a leathery-mouthed chub. You can't shake him off; he's too heavy to haul in, so after you have pulled up the lily-pads that he had carefully twisted himself around, the water is churned up, and your trout is laughing at you from some safe hiding-place.

Angling for trout develops an instinct by means of which you unconsciously learn where to look for them and what kind of fly to use. Given a rocky ledge near the mouth of a stream, a deep bend below a cliff overhung by a perversely crooked bough–he may not be there today or to-morrow, but some day you will find him. I recollect a forcible illustration of the fulfillment of faith in the trout's sense of the eternal fitness of such things. It was at the close of our Moosehead season. As we passed Socatean Point, after a day of head winds, with a beggarly half-dozen fish, the beauty of the spot arrested me, and although we had often unsuccessfully tried the fish at that particular spot, the present conditions seemed so perfect that we felt they must be there. We stopped paddling. A few casts developed the fact that the trout with his artistic eye, also loved that ledge. We increased our catch by three fish weighing eleven pounds. The following day surrounded by an advance guard of jealous-eyed guides, we beat the record with eighteen weighting forty-three pound.

...There is a peculiar aesthetic satisfaction in the sight of a day's catch of Eastern brook trout. The small-mouthed black bass may fight more vigorously, the ouananiche startle you by his quick runs and dashing leaps; but what crude colorings they wear as compared with the rich salmon, bejeweled armor of the trout of the deep pool, offset by the silver livery worn by his neighbor from the lake. Can it be true, as Mr. Lanman says, that "one principle cause of the great variety in the color of the brook trout is the difference in food," or has he power, like the chameleon, to change his color to suit his surroundings, and thus elude his enemies?

Whether you cast your fly for him among the snowflakes of Lake Edward or among the rocky torrents for the Blue Ridge, where you find him an important visitor among his brethren, the rainbow and the cutthroat trout of the Yellowstone or the Rockies, to your cast respond the eager strike, the quick rush, the sharp run, and the tough, determined fight, and all the inherited artifice that mark the aristocratic lineage of the crimson spots, square tails, and the white-lined fins of Salvelinus *fontinalis*.

LOST

By Joseph A. Thompson, from *Forest and Stream*, April 13, 1901

 *Joseph A. Thompson, an experienced lumberman, scaler and surveyor, had been asked many times if he had ever been lost in the woods. He told about once being lost in the region around Baskahegan, when he was much younger, in one of its many bogs that surround the lake.He wrote, "A few years later I was destined to meet a man in a very wild and remote part of the State who neither then, nor since has ever had a shadow of a doubt as to whether he was lost or not."*

My story

It was late in the summer of '79 that I was at my camp on the beautiful Ebeeme Lake, entirely alone, making preparations for my fall hunting and trapping, meanwhile awaiting the arrival of my hunting companion, Joseph Rollins. I spent the great part of my time in filing the teeth of the massive bear traps, looking for signs of bear and occasionally catching a string of brook trout.

On the last day of August I decided to follow Babel Brook away upon old Ebeeme Mountain, and besides catching some brook trout, look for signs of bear. Putting a luncheon in my pocket and a notice on the door of the camp, written on birch bark with a small piece of charred wood from the fireplace, notifying any hunter or woodsman, who happened that way, that I would be back at night, and launching my canoe, I paddled up the lake, singing as I went.

How little did I realize what an experience was to come to me that day, and how different would be the conditions of my return!

Arriving at the outlet of the brook, and drawing the canoe out of the water, I slung my carbine on my shoulder and cut a small alder pole for fishing. I remember distinctly looking back over the pond as I adjusted my fishing line, and thought what a glorious day it was, and how beautiful to be alone with nature. There was not a man within five miles of me who did not think as I did that day. Fishing the brook, pool after pool, I soon caught my string of fish.

Hanging them to a low bow of a tree, as I expected to return that way, I struck off for the mountain, looking about for a chance to set a bear trap later.

About four miles from the canoe, and in one of the most inaccessible parts of the mountain, I heard a faint halloo. As the halloo of a bear is almost identical with the halloo of man, my only thought was, "Perhaps, old fellow, later on I'll have your pelt.

"Hall-oa!"

"Holler away old fellow."

"Hall-o-a!" again comes floating to me through the clean air.

"Can that call be that of a bear, so very human in its sound? I almost fear not; and if by chance any one should be lost in this wild place I pity him.

Unslinging my carbine, I shoot.

"Halloa!—Halloa!—Halloa."

No bear would call after a hearing a rifle; so advancing and shooting occasionally after traveling a long distance I caught sight of a white object away up on the mountain. Behind a tree I remain perfectly silent and watch. Can that man possibly be sane? Coatless, hatless, vestless, he looked, as his eyes bulged out his head, like a raving maniac, and so weak that he could walk only with difficulty. On my approaching him he broke down and cried like a child.

His Story

"Stopping at the Katahdin Iron Works for a few days to recuperate my tired body and mind, and hearing you were in this locality, I engaged a man and team to take me to the Prairie, a settlement seven miles this side of the iron works. Here my man and team left me and I started to try to find your camp, much to the regret and notwithstanding the remonstrance of the two men who lived nearby.

"You will never in this world find that camp—never! There is no road leading to it—no trail. He gets there by canoe as well as by land. It is a blind trip for a stranger, and you better let one of us guide you."

"Thinkin they were after the money more than anything else, and in order to obtain the job, were perhaps trying to scare me a bit, I decided that I was competent to find you myself. So bidding the men good-by and getting the general course to your camp, I started. Traveling for a while on an open ridge or horseback, as they had directed, I looked off to the left and saw a body of water, which I took to be the Ebeeme thoroughfare, so leaving the ridge I struck for it. No sooner had I got down into this low, boggy land than I was completely turned around. My reasoning faculties left me. I shouted. I hallooed. All to no purpose. I was terrified. Starting on with no fixed point in view I would travel on a while and then stop and halloo. To add to the horror of the situation I had only a small luncheon; no gun, no axe.

"I traveled on in this manner till dark. The night was not very cold, but oh! The lonesomeness of it! Alone, and with the fear of so remaining as long as my strength might hold out, and then starving to death. The morning found me weaker from exposure, loss of sleep and lack of nourishing food, but I felt as though I must keep on. About an hour ago I reached the climax, and in sheer desperation I threw away my coat, my vest, my hat and ran I knew not wither, hallooing as I ran."

For a long time I could not convince him that I knew the way out myself. Travelling short distances at a time and resting often, we finally reached the canoe. I paddled out onto the lake, well pleased with my day's work, if my string of fish was left hanging on the tree.

Before I got to camp my man was sound asleep—completely worn out. For two days he did not leave the bunk, and in two weeks he had hardly regained his equilibrium. Night after night he would moan and halloo in his dreams. During the day he was my shadow, and when at last he was well enough to return home he begged me to come out of the woods, or fear that some time I might meet with an experience similar to his own.

He has never been in the woods since then.

– JOSEPH A.THOMPSON, BANGOR, ME.

A CRY IN THE NIGHT, A STORY OF THE MAINE WOODS

By Holman F. Day, from *Forest and Stream*, Jan. 4, 1902

Holman Day

I place this on record as the most remarkable story that has ever come out of the Maine hunting woods-and I know considerable about the stories of the Maine woods. If it were not vouched for so eminently I would not tell it. It would be too much for credulity and wouldn't be worth the telling. I believe it, for I know that men who tell it to me, even though they cannot explain it. They believe it and do not try to explain it, for they cannot. Here it is. If the thing seems too much to believe, then don't believe it. But the facts are facts just the same.

On the north side of Boarstone Mountain, in the town of Elliottsville, in Piscataquis County, Maine, lives Trustrum H. Brown, who calls himself "The Mediator." He entertains the harmless vagary that he is the mediator between man and God. For some fifteen years since his retirement to the wilderness of northern Maine he has been writing what he calls a new Bible, and he has a mass of manuscript piled a foot high. By the way, I have examined the Mediator's manuscript considerably, and it is far from being balderdash. Much of his writing indicates real thought and considerable ability. The Mediator is in no sense of the word a crazy man despite his hallucination on the subject of religion.

Brown has a bit of a farm and raises potatoes and vegetables enough to last him through the winter. He traps a little and hunts a bit and never goes hungry.

Early in December, just after the first snow of the season, he discovered one morning the fresh tracks of a moose near his house. By the manner in which the creature's great feet had splayed into the snow, Brown saw that the moose was a big one.

In his capacity of mediator he asserts that there are ten thousand spirits about all the time. He alleges that he asked one of these spirits to tell him how big the moose was, and that the spirit skipped along ahead and then came back and rendered him the information that the moose was none other than the Ambejejus Giant that had defied the rifles of hunters for years. The spirit further declared, so Brown avers, that the moose didn't have much of a start.

So the Mediator tied on his snowshoes, grabbed his rifle and a bit of a snack, and started away on the lope into the forest. That was early in the morning. Well, The Mediator scuffed along till noon without coming up with the moose. But the tracks still continued fresh, and his spirit guide, so he says, kept breathing into his ear that the animal was almost in reach. He ate his lunch of cold venison as he walked, for in a stern chase of a moose no time is to be wasted. His keen woodman's eyes noted that the clouds hung low and were massing darker and darker. Had he not been so confident that the moose was just ahead of him and would "yard" at the coming of nightfall he would have abandoned the chase. But his hope toled him on.

At 4 o'clock it was dusk, and still the splay tracks were stretching on ahead of him. Then he could see them no longer, and regretfully he was brought into a ravine and abandoned the chase for the night.

He had not reckoned on the long pursuit, and therefore had not provided himself in the usual cautious manner. Above all, he had not brought his woods axe.

Only a man accustomed to the woods realizes how serious an omission this is. The Mediator was able to collect some dry kye or limbs that had dropped from the trees and he hewed off some low branches with his hunting knife. He kindled a bit of a fire at the foot of a tree. He did not dare to go to sleep, for the cold was raw and piercing. So he stood and turned himself before the fire like an animated spirit, moving constantly to keep awake.

In the morning there was nothing left of his provender except one flat-chested biscuit. Had he not been unduly fired with zeal to catch that moose he would have retraced his steps. But he felt that probably the animal had yarded a little way ahead, and so on he went. He did come across the trampled place where the moose had spent the night, and with its great teeth had ripped off the twigs and bark. By the mighty reach The Mediator saw that the animal was a monster, and on he drove eagerly in a scurry of snow from his broad shoes. Still those monstrous splotches in the snow kept trailing away ahead of him.

Then some unkind weather sprite joggled the clouds overhead. The snow commenced to come in the fine, driving flakes that indicate a protracted storm. Then, and not till then, did the reckless hunter turn about. But before an hour had passed the snow, driving faster and faster, covered his tracks. Night came on again. Once more he lighted his fire, and, dizzy for want of sleep, staggered about it, struggling to keep awake. The Mediator is nearly seventy years old, but his little thin form is inured to hardship by many years of woods life. A less experienced man or one with less vitality must have succumbed.

The snow came down damp and heavy, and the sagging boughs above kept dropping clumps down on to his shoulders and into his neck.

At the first lightening that showed that morning was approaching, he ate the last crumbs of his biscuit and started away. But the snow drove hard in his face. He was weak with hunger and sick for sleep. His limbs were stiff and his whole body ready to sink with fatigue. Accustomed though he was to the woods, it is not surprising that in a few hours he knew that he had lost his way. But still he kept on, hoping that he might come across some trail or water course, his chief hope of rescue, some logging camp.

The snow ceased in the afternoon, but a sharp and driving wind succeeded. It flung the driving snow and shrieked with it through the trees and clearings. The fine particles cut his face like the dust of a sand storm. Few men have made a fiercer struggle for life than he. It is probable that partial delirium overtook him, for he insists that he could not only hear his spirit guides, but could see them as they flocked about him and beckoned him on.

At dusk he was in a country wholly unknown. There were mountains to the right, but he did not recognize the peaks, nor the surroundings. About an hour after the dark came down, with the wind still driving the snow into his eyes, he came out into a section that he recognized at last. It was "The Gulf." This is a canyon about three miles long, through which the west branch of Pleasant River rages. The walls are precipices. But along the north side skirts a wood road leading to camps three miles above, and into this road The Mediator staggered.

Now, he was desperately weak. But he knew that if he could round the foot of the canyon and scramble for three miles up the side of the first Chairback he would come to Long Pond, where there were camps.

It was now a race for life. He stood his dear old rifle against a tree and hung his cartridge belt on a limb. Then he cinched the belt around his thin waist and started. He was in a half-stupor when he came down to the frozen ford at the foot of the canon. He crossed, and striking the corduroy road that leads up the first Chairback he plowed on. He fell a dozen times, but he had sense enough to struggle up and dig to his task again.

When he made Long Pond his strength was nearly gone. But he knew that across the pond lay Hall & Davis' sporting camp, three miles away. The wind was still driving the snow, and he miscalculated his route across. When he came to shore he peered in all directions and listened. There was no glimmer of light anywhere, and no sound indicating that any camp was near. His knees were doubling under him by this time. His strength was gone; his eyes would not stay open, and he gave up. He stumbled and crawled up on the shore and fell across a log. His tongue was swollen in his mouth and his throat was dry. He says that he tried to shout but he could utter no sound but a gurgling whisper. Then he became unconscious.

Now comes the strange part of the story.

There was at the Hall & Davis camps at that time a hunting party from the town of Dexter. Among them were N. E. Meigs, the leading clothier of the place, and Walter Abbott, one of the proprietors of the large Abbott woolen mill. Mr. Meigs had been out that day with the party, and in trying to cross the pond had frozen both his ears, so bitter was the cold. He would have perished had not his guide beaten him to make him walk. He had desired to lie down and go to sleep on the snow, and had begged the others to go away and leave him.

On this morning he was lying in his bunk wondering whether or not he was going to be able to save his ears. They were wrapped up and were aching fearfully, and Mr. Meigs wasn't taking the intense interest in any outside matters. The others were playing pitch-pede before the fire.

Suddenly Mr. Meigs raised himself on his elbow and cried, "I hear some one shouting for help."

The others stopped their play and listened. Beyond the moaning of the wind in the chimney and the sough of the big trees outside there was no sound.

"Folks with frozen ears can hear 'most anything," remarked one of his comrades.

"But I certainly heard some one shout," persisted Meigs.

"Do you believe for a moment," said his friend, "that a man with his ears done up like a pound of pickled tripe could hear a sound that we didn't?"

The clothing man admitted that it didn't seem very probable, but still he persisted in his opinion strenuously. At last one of the guides went to the door and shouted into the night. There was no response.

"It couldn't have been," he said, returning.

"I don't want to be stubborn in this matter," said Mr. Meigs, "but I do think that we ought to make some investigation. I can't go to sleep with the notion that some poor cuss is out here in the cold. Somehow or other I can't reason myself out of the notion that there is something the matter outside, and I wish you would look it up. I'd go myself it weren't for my ears."

After poking some fun at the persistent man arguing from his nest in the bunk, two of the guides put on their clothing and went out.

"Of course it may be that someone has dropped into the water hole down here a piece," said one of them, "but as that's more than a mile away it don't stand to reason that you could have heard any shouting with your ears done up in that manner."

In the course of fifteen minutes one of the men came running back, and those in the camp heard him pulling that moose sled out of the lean-to.

"There is something the matter after all down at the water hole," he cried to those within. "Ed was ahead and he hollered back to me to bring the moose sled."

And in a little while they came tugging into the camp a stiff figure that the guides, as soon as the man was in the lamplight, recognized as Mediator Trustrum H. Brown, of Elliottsville.

At first they thought that he was dead. But they undressed him and set him bodily into a tub of ice-cold water. They rubbed him with snow and after some work he commenced to revive. Then they poured whiskey and brandy down his throat, and at midnight he was sitting up and telling them his story.

In two days he was all right and lively once more, and it may be stated here while I am on the subject of recoveries, that Mr. Meigs saved his ears.

Now The Mediator swears that the sound he emitted when he sank down on the log was only a whisper. Even a shout as loud as a foghorn would scarcely have ben heard a mile away by the men inside a log camp heavily banked with snow.

That the sound should have been heard by a man with his ears frozen and wrapped in bandages is more curious still. But for that I have authority that cannot be disputed. Both sides have told me their stories.

They do not try to explain it-neither will I.

But, as I remarked in the first place, I set this down not only as one of the more remarkable stories of endurance that the Maine woods have ever reported, but as a mystery that is almost uncanny.

– HOLMAN F. DAY

Chapter 5

THE WEST AND EAST
BRANCHES OF THE
PENOBSCOT RIVER

One of our first recordings of a trip along the West Branch was in 1804, when Charles Turner and others made the first known climb up Mt. Katahdin. From 1819 to 1826, the mountain was visited by Colin Campbell, Daniel Rose, Joseph Treat and Joseph Turner Jr., who were on the Monument Line, and trying to work out whether old British maps showed the mountains north of Katahdin that the British claimed as proof of their domain over northern Maine. However, those mountains didn't actually exist.

Hiram Rockwell, a surveyor for the State of Maine, made several early trips to the West and East Branches of the Penobscot. In July and August of 1826 he worked his way up the East Branch, passing Grindstone and Whetstone Falls, where five barrels of bread got wet. Taking time to dry it all out, they camped above the falls. The next day they arrived at one of Rufus Dwinal's lumber camps, then worked their way up the East Branch to Grand Falls, where they left baggage and returned to the camp for their other supplies. From here on it was a strenuous repeat of portaging back and forth with so much gear, but they finally arrived at "Metagarmin Lake," as he called it. They first poled up "Nalumscitaqua Stream," but found it dry, so they went back downriver for all the supplies, then began a long portage north across to the Aroostook River.

Rockwell made another trip to the Chesuncook region in

March of 1828, spending time at Moosehead Lake, then working his way down the West Branch to Ripogenus Lake. From here he headed north to intersect with the Monument Line that had been laid out previously.

Between 1833 and 1846 Katahdin was climbed and chronicled from the West Branch route by Edwin Rose, Joseph Blake, Jacob Bailey, Charles T. Jackson and Henry David Thoreau. Due to lumbering, the route to Katahdin via the East Branch and Hunt Farm opened up and was used as an approach from 1845 to 1853 by Edward Everett Hale, Dr. Aaron Young, Rev. Marcus Keep, Rev. John Todd, William M. Jones and Col. Thomas L. Higgins.

In 1841 the ninety-two mile Chesuncook Road, which led from Sebec to the foot of Chesuncook Lake, was opened. The road, which was laid out under the direction of Rufus Gilmore and Noah Barker and others, intersected the Lily Bay Road near Grants Camps on Black Brook, and was built at a cost of $2,000. Already four or five teams had passed along it, taking supplies into the lumber operations around Chesuncook Lake.

Otis Eastman, a young New Hampshire lumberman, was working on the West Branch in 1845, left the lumber camp with his team to secure some logs, but was gone too long, Going out to find him, the lumbermen found that two logs had rolled onto him, killing him instantly.

A law was passed in 1847 provided that the Chesuncook and North Twin dams on the West Branch, shall, after they have paid certain amounts to the proprietors, go into the hands of the Penobscot Log Driving Company.

It was reported in 1850 that the body of a lumberman was found on Ragged Brook on Penobscot waters. William Mains of Dexter had left the tavern of Mr. Grant in the company of a man named Frost of Bangor, each having a jug of rum in their pockets. The next morning Mains was found dead on the ice. His clothes were nearly all torn from his body, which was considerably bruised. It was supposed that he had inflicted this on himself while in a delirious state. It was later explained that they were both at work for H. P. Blood and Co., at Lobster Lake, and had left camp to go to Mr. Grants to get some blacksmithing supplies, when this occurred. It appeared to be foul play, but a coroner's report could not be sure, and they felt assured that Mr. Frost had not murdered him.

In 1850 a company of river drivers in the employment of E. A. Reed & Company, who were on their way to Sandy Stream at the base of Mt. Katahdin, when they met with several adventures. At Medway, after a long parley with a hotel landlord, he agreed to keep them overnight. However, they had a little too much sport, resulting in knocking down banisters and raiding his stash of lemons and oranges, but the proprietor was well compensated in the morning. The next night, having arrived at a lumber camp at the foot of Millinocket Lake, they laid down to rest after their hard tramp, when the alarm of fire was given. They all made it out alive, but the entire camp was burned down, along with many of the clothes and boots. Without food and exposed to the elements, they finally made it to their home camp at three the following afternoon.

In 1854 Ansel Smith, the veteran lumberman and guide of Chesuncook Farm, billed the Cartland & Berry Company for accommodating their men. Not receiving any payment, Smith then brought a suit against Asa T. Cartland and Tristram Berry, at the court in Dover. Cartland and Berry were unable to pay the bill immediately, so relied on William Strickland and Company, for whom they had been employed, to pay the bill, which was now $274.14, but Strickland refused, so the court case was set for a future date.

Frank Ellison of Waltham, Mass. made a trip Maine in 1858 and left a journal of his adventures. At Moosehead Lake they hired John Ellis as their guide and crossed over Northeast Carry into the West Branch, camped at Lobster Lake, then up to Umbazooskoos Stream. After visiting the farms of Peter Walker and Ansel Smith, where they purchased a basket of potatoes. That evening Uncle John, as they called their 68-year old guide, and Jim went moose hunting and were successful. After a few days at Caucomogomoc Stream and Lake, they poled back up the West Branch, passing "The Moose Horn," Asa Fox's camp, and Lobster Lake outlet. Back at the carry they stayed at Mr. Mitchell's Carry House, then took the steamer back to Kineo.

AN EVENING WITH A CATAMOUNT

Anonymous, from *Farmington Chronicle*, January 5, 1871

 *This exciting adventure with a catamount, a local name for a mountain lion, takes place near Katahdin Pond and the East Branch of the Penobscot. There are a number of tales of woodsmen and trappers seeing and encountering these large, carnivorous creatures up to about 1860, but, like the wolf, they were forced out the Maine Woods by heavy logging.*

It was our fifth day in an old logging camp near one of the Katahdin Ponds. Clives had got his cordon of traps set and had gone that afternoon on his first round to visit them, telling me I need not expect him till late. I had been fishing along the shore of the pond for nearly a mile from our camp, when turning into a little nook in the shore, overhung by alders, under which a small brook came in, I espied a raccoon digging in the mud.

The recognition was mutual. He eyed me a moment, with his cunning visage turned askew, then scuttled away among the bushes. Hoping to make him take up a tree, I dropped my pole and gave chase. But there were no trees to his liking very near, and I was about giving up the race, when Mr. Graycoat stopped at the foot of a yellow birch, and looking round at me as if he thought it a more than usually good joke, suddenly disappeared.

Coming up, I found there was a large opening in the trunk near the ground, and looking in, saw that the tree was entirely hollow–a mere shell some three or four feet in diameter, lighted by several other holes and clefts up and down the trunk. I could see the coon up some fifteen or twenty feet, clinging on to the side, and peering curiously down to see what I was about.

I had stopped to pick up a pole to knock the coon down, when there was a cry so chilling and piercing that I involuntarily cried out. On glancing up to the treetops, I saw a large gray creature crouched upon a limb, and about to spring. In an instant there was another shriek, followed by a heavy spring among the leaves that shook the ground. I sped into the tree and scrambled up it like a chimney sweep. I went up with as much alacrity as the coon had done, he meanwhile, going higher, throwing a shower of dirt into my eyes, which were open to the fullest extent. I was scarcely up before the creature was at the hole. Perhaps the dust and dirt blinded him, for he was snuffing and purring at the bottom. I managed to wriggle up some twenty or thirty feet to where a large limb had grown out. Here with a long sliver or shim in my hand, I sat prepared to act upon the defensive.

I did not have long to wait. For the cloud of dust subsided a little, the creature perceived me, and uttering another scream, began climbing after us. The sliver I held was six or seven feet long and sound, though covered with rot and dirt. I got out my pocketknife and quickly sharpened the hard wood down to an acute point. It thus became quite an effective weapon. And as soon as the catamount—for such I judged it to have been—came within reach, I gave him a "jab" in the face with my spear—then another, dealt upon him with all my strength. His claws were occupied in holding on. A new shower of dirt rattled into his eyes.

I redoubled my thrusts. It grew too hot for him, and I had the inexpressible pleasure of seeing him slide to the bottom, growling and snarling with rage. But in a moment he was up on the outside. I heard his claws in the bark, and could see him as he passed the rifts and holes in the old trunk. But the aperture at the top was too small to admit anything but his head or one paw at a time.

Seeing the coon he commenced a series of cries and screeches, and thrusting in first one paw and then the other, tried to reach him. When the catamount's claws came too near he would shrink down a little towards me, keeping an eye on both of us, with a coolness that struck me as rather remarkable under the circumstances. Finding that he couldn't get in at the top, the panther began to descend and coming to the hole just above my head, looked in. Quick as a flash his long paw popped in and clutched up my cap with I don't know how much hair. I had to crouch close to keep my head from following it. Withdrawing his foot, he would eye me a moment, then thrust it in again and strain to reach me. But taking out my knife I gave him such sharp pricks that he soon got sick of that sort of exercise; after glaring at me awhile he went down to the bottom again. Lying stretched out on the ground, he would fix his eyes first on one then on another of the holes along the trunk, and at the least movement, spring up, and in a moment be at the top looking down at the coon, till, finding us all still beyond his reach, he would go back and watch again.

I could see him quite distinctly through my loophole. A long, lithe body–six feet, I thought, with the large cat head, strong legs and broad feet, from which his claws were uneasily protruding and receding, and a long tail to and fro with restless impatience–the very embodiment of strength and ferocity.

How to escape was the next question, after the momentary peril had ceased. Would the catamount go away of his own accord? He didn't act like it. His movements seemed to indicate that he meant to try a siege.

Night had come on–but the moon was rising over the treetops. I looked up at the raccoon; he was reconnoitering through a crevice. Suddenly the idea struck me that if I could force the coon out the panther might seize him, and perhaps be satisfied with one of us. But I confess that it was not without some self-reproach that I began to put this plan into operation. We were companions in danger, and to drive him out to certain death was truly the very climax of selfishness. But the instinct of self-preservation is not to be subjected to moral tests.

Again sharpening my stick, I stood up on my seat, and drove the coon before me. He offered no resistance, though manifesting the greatest reluctance to go out at the top. But I forced him out. The moment he appeared in sight, the catamount leaped up after him.

Poor fellow, he made one frantic attempt to get back into the tree, then turned to battle with the ascending monster. One sharp cry of fear and agony and his lifeblood was feeding our savage besieger. After sucking at his throat for a few moments, the cougar sprung down and ran off into the forest, with the coon in his mouth. I saw him disappear among the shadows, and heard his footsteps die away in the distance.

It was an opportunity not to he neglected. I was not long getting down. Crawling out of the tree, I made a beeline for the camp, in nearly an opposite direction, at about my best paces. It was ten o'clock when I got in. I found Clives wondering at my absence, and considerably alarmed. I told him of my adventure, and the next morning we moved our camp down to the Millinocket Lake. We didn't like the neighborhood. A catamount is not, in my very humble opinion, a very agreeable companion to spend an evening with.

MY FIRST MOOSE

By Corp'l Lot Warfield, from *Rod and Gun*, February 26, 1876

Corp'l Lot Warfield was a name used by an unknown Maine man who often wrote articles in the various sporting magazines about his experiences. In this story we learn about one of his earliest experiences in the woods while working at a logging camp Near Lobster Lake.

The winter of 1835-6 found the writer, then a lad in his teens, serving as cook in a lumber camp on the south bank of the west branch of the Penobscot, a few miles below the Moosehead "carry." The principle articles of food were pork, salt beef, beans, corn-meal and flour, and needing but little culinary skill to become palatable to the hearty choppers. The "Boss" had confidently counted on securing a moose occasionally to vary the diet, but up to the New Year not one had been brought to bag.

In those days moose were very plenty, though even then the Old Town Indians had penetrated that section of the country in their hide-securing, slaughtering excursions. Every Sunday would see the old flint-lock "Queens-arm" taken in hand by some one of the gang, who, accompanied by one or two others with axe and moose-sled, would pay a visit to some one or more of the many moose-yards in the vicinity, and as often return empty handed. The moose would take alarm and flee, or the 'blamed' gun would hang fire. Several moose had been wounded and followed in the soft snow for weary miles, but without successful issue.

I had, from the earliest recollection, a strong penchant for a gun and burning powder, and though forbidden to touch the gun by its owner, my uncle, resolved on seeking a moose the first opportunity. I had not long to wait, as a thaw set in long enough to soften and settle the snow, succeeded by severe cold weather without wind, forming a firm crust, except in the densest thickets of soft timber. The gang had just commenced work at a point so distant as necessitated carrying their dinners. This was in my favor, and I started out early in the morning, taking my sled and ax, with no ammunition save the charge in the gun—all else being under lock and key—laying my course to a yard I had once visited with one of the gang. On arriving in the near vicinity, I proceed with great caution. Leaving the sled and drawing my yarn mittens over my boots to muffle the sound, with gun at cock, I stalked carefully along till I saw a young bull moose lying broadside toward me some sixty paces distant. Ere I could overcome my trembling he arose, looked alarmed—evidently he had wind of me—and taking a quick aim, I fired and had the mortification him seeing dash out of sight. But a trail of blood showed he was hit, and returning my sled I was soon on the chase. The crust breaking under his weight must have greatly impeded his progress, yet I failed to sight him until a "barren" on the north shore of Lobster Lake was reached.

Here, on a slight elevation, I saw him lying down; but on seeing me he was up and soon out of sight. It was now noon. I had not been a bit disheartened till now. Right here, on the ice to my left, a poor chopper had be overtaken and devoured by the wolves of the winter previous, and the thought that the trail of blood would soon bring the savage brutes upon me was terrifying; but I pushed on and about two miles further discovered him standing in an open space in the river. His eyes were blood-shot, and at every approach he lowered his crest and rushed as far as the open space permitted.

How bitterly I regretted the want of ammunition. Tears sprang to my eyes as I aimed and snapped the empty gun at his breast, thinking how easily I could shoot him.

The wound, low down in the belly, was scarcely a mortal one, though it had evidently weakened him. I was about concluded to return to camp and had descended upon the ice as the easiest route to camp, when a happy thought occurred. Cutting a sapling and binding my sheath knife in a split at the small end with the leather tongs tied around the top of my boots was the very thing. With this improvised lance I approached, and as I expected, he made a charge. The impetus carried his body well up on the ice, and as I struggled to regain the water I improved my opportunity and severed the jugular. I could scarcely repress a shout of joy; fear only of awakening wolves prevented. In a few minutes I had a shoulder of moose on the sled and was dashing wildly downstream. At the junction of the Penobscot the ice was broken, so I was obliged to make a laborious detour in the tangled brush. Once again on the river, and the few miles to camp was soon accomplished. I had ample time to prepare my feast, and two large pans of fried steak were smoking on the table as the hungry choppers arrived, one of whom asserted that he had scented it half a mile distant. Down the vista of forty years comes the sweet smell upon my olfactories causing the mouth to water. I was questioned as to who had brought in the meat—it being taken for granted that some lucky hunter of a neighboring camp had called; such courtesies being not uncommon in those days. I gave an evasive reply at first, being fearful of a chiding for my disobedience, but finally owed up, and my success gained for me immunity. Ere the report was finished there was the howl of a wolf in the direction of Kineo, which was immediately answered in the direction of Katahdin. Gradually more tongues joined in the chorus, as they drew nearer together toward the dead moose.

In the morning, it being Sunday, several of the men returned with me to save what, if any, was left by the wolves. One submerged hind quarter was all that remained but bones; and one of the men was mean enough to scold me for not having the forethought to pry back the carcass into the water. For many years after that my lot was cast with the hardy sons of the backwoods, as chopper, hunter and trapper, and many a moose and other wild animal fell before my aim, but of no other exploit was I half as proud as the one narrated.

CORP'L LOT WARFIELD

THE BEAR TRAPPER'S STORY

By Old Isaak, *from East Branch of the Penobscot: Searching for Salmon in Maine, in American Angler*, February 7, 1885

 *The unknown author, a man from New Jersey, describes a very long trip he took with three other men in the fall of 1884, in search of large salmon in the East Branch of the Penobscot. In the long article, the writer gave us much detailed information about the river, the earliest sporting camps and waterfalls.*

Their guide was Alec McLain who they had hired at Mattawamkeag. McLain and his son Will opened up the famous Phoenix Camps on Sourdnahunk Lake about 1896. Here is the story their guide told around the campfire.

"Well, you see boys I had some traps set not far from my house, about two or three miles, and foolishly went to visit them without either gun or knife. I found a big bear caught by one paw in the trap. The paw was pretty well skinned by the struggles of the blank, blank brute to get loose, and I was afraid he would get away. I picked up a good big stick of hardwood about as big as a fence rail and I let him have it right across his eyes four or five times as hard as I could strike. I've killed a lot of bears, boys, but this was the blank, blank biggest and blank, blank toughest brute I ever saw.

"The clog was fast between two saplings, but I'm blanked if he didn't drag them saplings down and get loose. I wasn't going to run. I hadn't time. I let him have the club again and skinned one side of his head, but before I could jump to one side he had me by the left arm with his blank, blank teeth, and his hind claws stuck into my leg. I jumped back and the clog catching between two trees, I tore loose from his clutch by the leg and wrenched my arm—yes, tore it right out of his blank, blank, mouth.

"That was more than two weeks ago and it ain't healed up yet, though I can use a paddle and setting pole by resting them on my wrist. You see I can't shut that hand very well, the tendons are so blank bad strained."

Alec took the bandage off his arm, and while the doctor dressed it, he finished his story.

"I thought I was done for and that I never should see my folks again, and I wondered how long it would be before they found my body. You see a man thinks awful fast when a big bear has him by the arm. When that clog caught and I tore loose I just stumbled over and laid there. I didn't lose my senses, not by a blank sight, but I got awful riled, for that bear was making desperate efforts to get at me again. I saw that he would likely tear his foot off and get away, so I got up and went to the nearest house. It was only an Indian's hut, but I knew he had a gun. I wanted to shoot that bear the blankest worse kind. I found the Indian at home smoking his pipe. I told him about the bear and his squaw bound up my arm. The squaw wanted to see the bear and would go along. I found I could not use my arm at all, so I told the Indian he would have to shoot. We found the bear still to the trap, and the clog held by the two saplings.

"Now," said I, "give it to him quick for I am afraid he will tear loose."

"No, no," said the squaw; "don't shoot yet; I want to see him, he acts so funny.

The bear was making desperate efforts to tear his foot out of the trap or get the clog loose. The squaw drew near laughing and poking a stick at the beast to make him dance about. The Indian drew his gun, but the squaw got in his way. Just then the desperate struggles of the bear tore his foot from the trap, leaving his skin in it. His rush knocked the woman sprawling against the Indian, upsetting him, and they both rolled together on the ground, each apparently trying to see which could kick the highest. The bear went off in the underbrush, and that was the last I saw of him."

"So, you did not kill him after all?"

"No, he got clean away; but I'm sure to get him if he don't leave my neighborhood."

"Clarence," said Julius, "have you had a bear fight?"

"No, Mr. Wheeler, but I've killed a good many. The last one I caught in a trap. I picked up a clog and walked right up to the bear, which backed out as fast as I approached. I had a young friend with me who had never shot a bear. He carried a rifle, while I only had a knife. I got close up to the bear and put my knife twice into him. I called my companion to come quickly, for if he wanted to shoot a bear he must hurry, as this one would be dead in a few moments. He came up and put a bullet in its head, so he can make his brags that he shot a bear."

The Doctor was getting sleepy, so we retired to our tent, and in a few minutes I was dreaming of bears.

BRUIN IN THE BUTTERY

By William A. Brooks, Forest and Stream, July 15, 1893

Canoeing down the West Branch, Brooks and his companion, with two guides, long for the comfort of a cabin at the end of the day's paddle. Unfortunately they had to carry their canoes and outfit around two falls and were drenched by the impending rain by the time they reached the camp.

Black Bears   We were wet, cold and hungry, so that with visions of warmth and plenty at the camp, we paddled vigorously. The banks stretched away on either hand, the same two unbroken lines of forest trees, which all day long we had been passing; but at three o'clock in the afternoon we saw a clearing on the right, in which was the house where we intended to spend the night. It was a low, unpretentious structure standing with its adjacent log hovels, in the middle of the clearing several rods back from the stream, but to us it was as welcome as the most magnificent of city hotels could have been.

On landing we placed our goods under the canoes as before, and then hurried to the house, taking with us our rods, rifles and personal luggage. We were given a hearty welcome by the old backswoodsman who lived there, and he soon had a roaring fire blazing like a conflagration, around which we grouped ourselves, enjoying the genial warmth. Our saturated garments hung from the hooks in the beams overhead, but in various nondescript, but dry substitutes furnished by our host we were very comfortable.

In a short time he announced that our dinner was ready, and in a very much shorter time we were discussing the venison steak and other viands set before us, with appetites rendered keen by life in the open air and the long fast and exertion of the day. After our meal we again sat around the fire chatting with our host and with each other.

"There seems to be plenty of game this fall. Two deer came out into the clearin' t'other day, 'n we sat on the porch 'n watched 'em a spell afore they went back into the woods. We didn't shoot, for we had plenty of fresh meet in camp. Did you boys see much game on your way down stream?"

"Yes," one answered, "we saw plenty of deer and moose sign, as well as several deer themselves, and there are fresh bear tracks up at the carry."

"Yes, bears are pretty thick this year, but it's rather cur'us fact that people don't see much of 'em in the woods. As a gin'ral thing bears are pretty shy and don't want much to do with humans critters, if they can help it, thought they'll fight if cornered, and a she bear don't want much foolin' round her cubs. Its surprisin' too, how quick one'll git out o' sight if ye do run across him. He'll give one tremendous jump into the bushes, makin' noise and crashing enough for an elephant but after that first jump when he gits out o' sight, you won't hear another sound. They slip away dretful quiet like."

"Me and my brother, we come across bear in the woods las' winter," said my Indian guide, "he had hole under the roots where big spruce blow over, and we kill him with axe. We been in woods choppin' and don't have no gun."

"Well, we had a scrimmage with one, two or three years ago last spring, without goin' very fur away from home," continued the old man. "One night I had gone to bed and was jest settling down to sleep when I heard an awful racked down below, and a boy who was workin' for me came and said there was a bear in the buttery. There was an Indian here that night named Mitch, and after I turned in he and the boy sat here by the fire talkin' and smokin', when they heard a sound of somethin' or other movin' round in the butt'ry. Then some tin pans tumbled down, makin' a terrible din, and they jumped up and opened the butt'ry door to see what was the matter. They thought perhaps one of the dogs had got shut up in there, but they slammed that door to a good deal quicker 'n they opened it, 'cause there was a big black bear in there, and thy didn't have no idee of tacklin' him bare-handed, and their guns w'ant loaded. They didn't even have no axe handy to swat him with, as you and your brother did, Sebattis." Here the old man paused to light his pipe, for, like any other old sailor or backwoodsman, he could spin a yarn much better with the help of the narcotic weed.

"I dressed myself as soon as I could and we loaded our rifles. I told old Sam, the boy, to open the door quick after we were all ready, and Mitch and I took different positions in the room here, so that one or t'other of us could send a bit of lead where it might do the most good. You see, the butt'ry is a pretty big one, but with Mitch over there, and I about where I be now, we could cover the whole of it.

"Well, when we got all ready Sam, he slipped up to the door, yanked it wide open and jumped back. But by that time the bear had gone. The butt'ry winder had been left open and he had climbed out the same way as he got in. I guess the things he knocked down frightened him, for they made noise enough, and the butt'ry was a sight to behold.

"He had knocked two pans of milk and a mess of corned beef and pork and had made a dretful muss of it. He didn't seem to have eaten much, so we thought perhaps he might come back if we kept quiet, and I told Sam and Mitch that if he did for them to slip out the door and each one go round the house. One was to go round one side, and one round t'other. Then if he got away from me one o' them would be plenty sure to get a shot.

"So we sot there, keepin' quiet and not saying a word and after a while sure enough we heard him climbin' in agin. Sam and Mitch went out and I opened the door jest in time to see him disappear through the winder.

"I yelled to them to look out for him, but it was an awful dark night, and they couldn't see him. As he ran round the corner of the house he went plump into the Indian, who was going round from the other way. He pretty near knocked the wind out of Mitch and I don't know which was the most frightened. The bear got off with a whole hide that time, however, and disappeared in the darkness.

"Mitch came in puffin' and we sat down again to wait. We didn't much think he would come back, but we'd wait and see. After a while we heard him, but he was pretty wary, and we could tell he wasn't climbin' in but was sniffin' round outside. Then he seemed to move away and Sam got up to peek out the winder in this room. The winder was down, but all of a sudden Sam up with rifle and blazed away right through the glass.

"The bear had run right by the wood pile out there, where the ground was all white with the chips that were strewn about, and as his black hide showed up agin 'em Sam drew a bead on him. We rushed out and when and we got there, the old feller was kickin' his last kick. It was a pretty shot, but I guess there was some luck about it too. Sam got the bounty and sold the hide, so the shot was wuth somethin' to him anyway, luck or no luck. The two was wuth $25 to him and that, with what I paid him, he spent for schoolin' down to the settlements the next winter. He as a good boy, Sam was, and was tryin' to save some money to get an eddicaiton, so I was glad he got the bear."

We spent that night beneath his humble but hospitable roof, and in the morning continued our journey beneath the sky as blue and serene as if clouds and storm had never been.

– WM. A. BROOKS

MOOSEHEAD LEGENDS: 1.–SUBOOMIAK.

By Frederick Howard, from *Forest and Stream*, **August 10, 1895**

Forest Fire

Frederick Howard of Augusta apparently intended to write more fictional stories, but only completed this first tale. It takes place on the upper West Branch, where in 1906 a dam was put in above Northeast Carry, creating a lake named Seboomook. There are varying meanings projected, but it is clearly a water based word, not a proper name, and derives from "Sebem," the original name of Moosehead Lake, which means, "moose."

Calling his hero a Tarrantine Indian, suggests he was a member of the Mic Mac Tribe, as "Tarrantine" was the name the early Basques sailors gave to that tribe, especially when they became war-like, aggressively moving into neighboring Passamaquoddy and Penobscot territories in search of beaver hides.

On the West Branch of the Penobscot River, north of Moosehead Lake, between Elm Stream and Chesuncook Lake are a series of falls or rips, necessitating a carry by any one journeying the stream in a canoe. There is a legend that Suboomiak, a Tarrantine Indian, once ran the rapids in a frail birchen craft, hence its name at the present time, "Suboomiak Falls." The range or township as surveyed out is known as Suboomiak, and includes the territory that was one the hunting ground of the Indian whose name it bears.

The beautiful West Branch of the picturesque Penobscot never looked fairer than on that June afternoon so many years ago. The soft haze of spring twinkled in the vista, the stream opened among the gigantic firs that diffused their balsamic odors on the sweet-scented air. The gay carol of a robin was heard in the little clearing where stood the rude cabin of Eldridge, the trapper, the only reminder of his motherless children of their home in the distant settlement, from which their nomadic father had brought them to this forest wilderness. For three days the robin had been their only companion, save for the midnight prowling bear or lynx. The father was absent on a trip, to dispose of his season's stock of furs at the traders, leaving the sturdy boy of 9 to care for his toddling sister of 3.

On the opposite bank, where a graveled bar had formed against the prostrate trunk of some forest giant, was drawn up a birch-bark canoe. It was fashioned by a master hand, and at either end was a rude drawing on the birchen surface of a Beaver–the totem of the Tarrantine, and Suboomiak, the last of his tribe, who had seen his comrades exterminated from their home among the lakes and streams of these forest wilds. Alone, he had clung to his old hunting ground, trusting to remain in peaceful posses-sion until he should be called to a better place by the Great Spir-it, whose presence was visible to him in every mood of nature, whether mountain storm, or solitude of the dense evergreen woods, that surrounded his lonely tepee. With eye as bright and form erect as ever, the aged Indian stood by the side of his canoe gazing in bitter resentment at the cabin in the little clearing, which bespoke of encroachment of the white hunter on the territory so long his sole privilege and in which his totem had ever been respected. The rifle of the pale face had driven away the deer once so easily stalked and slain by his swift arrow, and the traps of the invader placed on otter slide and beaver dam destroyed the furry occupants that had provided his wigwam with protection from the fierce blasts of the winter. Dark thoughts surged through the brain of the swarthy Tarrantine: "Why should not he assert his right to the grand old forest with its network of streams and lakes? Did not the unconquered spirit of his fathers, who had fought and died in defense of their homes, move him to perpetual hatred of the white race, and the blood call to him for vengeance?

The voice of conscience pleaded for kinder and nobler impulse. He was known as Suboomiak "the Faithful." The prospectors for the lumber camps and the hunters from the great cities–in which he had heard the white men were thicker than the leaves on the upland maple–had entrusted life and property to his care in the untracked wilderness he knew so well. Never had he betrayed a trust or shirked a task; should he now stain the record of an honest life with a savage act of personal revenge? Yet his rights had always been respected, until the hunter from the lake settlement, covetous of the game and fur, had trespassed on the range, and surily ordered him to move further north, to the cheerless bogs of the boundary marshes. Now that the opportunity to destroy the deserted cabin and clear the virgin woods of every taint of foe lay before him, why should he hesitate to grasp it?

As he stood racked with the mental tumult of emotions a full dull sound fell on his ear, causing him to start in alarm and scan in the direction of the wind. Was it the roar of the great falls below? And what meant the thickening of the haze on the river surface? To his ear and eye trained in forest lore it was a more evil sound than the troubled waters of the river at the long rips; more than a spring atmosphere that dimmed the landscape, and it needed not the glimpse of rushing deer and swift flying birds to tell the dusky hunter the terrible death they were seeking to escape. It was that horror of the dense resinous wood, a forest fire travelling before the wind with race-horse speed.

A grim smile settled on the stoical features of the Indian; by no act of his, the desolation he had contemplated would be most thoroughly complete and vengeance be wrought, while from his canoe in midstream he could watch the scene of destruction and then escape in safety, for none were so swift with the paddle than he.

The roar of the advancing fire now became more distinct, and the smoke dimmed the sun as to scarcely show the Indian's shadow behind him. At the window of the cabin a white baby face was pressed against the single pane and a pair of innocent eyes appealed to the silent dusky form, standing motionless on the opposite bank, watching intently the approaching fire. Now the flames shot up over the tops of the tallest firs, leaping forward and catching ablaze its neighbors of less stature, and thick black smoke rolled over the clearing, obstructing it from the Indian's view. As it was lifted by a puff of wind the children were disclosed crouching at the river's bank awaiting the fearful end that was so swiftly and surely approaching. At sight of the doomed children the Indian leaped hastily into his canoe, and with a deep sweep of the paddle directed it toward them. Gone from that savage bosom was all desire of vengeance, gone all the thirsting for blood, all memories of hatred.

The totem of the beaver so long the symbol of integrity and friendship must not desert the faith so implicitly given in face of an awful death. A few quick strokes and he reached the bank in front of the cabin which he was now in flames, the little ones were grasped by a single movement of the strong dusky arm, another plunge of the paddle and the frail craft with its precious burden had begun its race with the fiery element now raging on either bank. The muscles of the sinewy back of the Indian rolled into the great cords as he bent to his task. Like an arrow the canoe shot ahead in mid-stream keeping pace with the death on either hand. The thick smoke, black from the consuming pitch, was so dense and stifling as almost to suffocate the occupants. Directing the children to lie on the bottom the Indian dipped his blanket in the stream and covered them with its safe protection.

Ever nearer and nearer, the roar of the "great rips" ahead rose above the crackling of the flames. No canoe had ever passed in safety over its dangerous vortex of cross currents and whirlpools, but it was the only path from the fire-fiend that so fiercely pursued them.

The sun had long since set behind the western woods, and the fitful glare of the flames gave an uncertain light in which to combat with the treacherous stream and half-sunken rocks. Throwing aside his paddle and grasping the tough setting pole, he threw all his strength and alertness into the task before him. The canoe, caught by the swift descent of the current, poised on the smooth surface of a rock and then, caught at the stern by the on-rushing waters, swept broadside on toward the brink of the first fall. With a firm brace in the bow, the Indian hurled his weight on the pole against a projecting boulder; the light craft swayed an instant, trembling like a dry leaf in the autumn breeze, then swung around and shot over the edge, and dropped to the pool below down into the semi-blackness of the rips beyond. The stream grew narrower and blazing branches dropped around and on them from the fiery towers above, thus adding another danger to the horrors of the elements. On dashed the canoe, skillfully deflected from death-dealing rock or whirlpool by those keen eyes and tense muscles of steel. The fire now leaped from bank to bank of the narrow stream, it singed the hair of the Indian's head and scorched the hands that held, as in a vise, the faithful pole. More than once it caught in the blanket that screened the children from the fiery blast, and which was now dried from its immersion by the intense heat, necessitating the holding of the craft in the on-rushing stream by the strength of a single arm, while the blanket could again be plunged in the seething waters; then onward the mad rush would continue toward the lower falls.

The fire almost blinded the Tarrantine as it played before his face, and his brain whirled as the deadly flames swept into his set, determined face, while again and again the scorching air was drawn into his laboring lungs; but not once did he flinch from his erect position, gazing steadily the canoe was poised for the last leap at the lower falls, and held again so steady for the fearful plunge. As the fragile craft struck at the base of the falls it was swept by a strong current toward the bank, the sturdy pole failed for the first time to hold on the slippery rocks, and the canoe with a quick lurch hurled the dusky pilot into the boiling whirlpool. With a superhuman effort the Indian gained rock, regaining his grasp on his pole.

The canoe with its precious freight had disappeared in the gloom of the forest-shadowed stream, now tranquil for the remainder of its course to the broad, safe expanse of the lake below. The fire had been outdistanced in the fearful run of the rapids, and the impetus of the falls had carried the birch bark and its occupants to safety. The limit of ordinary human strength had been passed long ago; only one trained to undergo the tortures of pain could have held to such endurance; but at last the tremendous exertion tells, and the pole on which the Indian leans heavily slips from his grasp of those nerveless fingers and the river sweeps without obstacle over the smooth surface of the rock.

At dawn next morning a canoe was found by the log drivers on Chesuncook against the shore. It as of Indian design, of handsome build, and on its fire-blackened sides could be traced the rude outline of a Beaver. Lying under a seamed and scorched blanket were the two children of Eldridge, the trapper, asleep, locked in each other's embrace, safe through the baptism of fire.

Near the foot of the lower falls on the river was found later, where whirlpool had cast it, the body of an Indian–Suboomiak, the Faithful.

– FREDERICK HOWARD

THE MOOSE WARDEN'S STORY

By Charles A. Stephens, from *The Youth's Companion*, October 7, 1897

A prolific writer of children's tales, Charles Asbury Stephens began writing under a number of pan names including Stinson Javis, Marcus Vanderpool, Charles Adams, Henrietta Crosby and Charlotte H. Smith. Many of his tales were written as series, the Knockabout Club and the Moose-Hunters.

A View of the West Branch

Borrowing from his childhood farming experiences, Stephens produced several other series set in a more rural atmosphere. The Old Squire and the Grandfather's tales series were very popular children's books for many years. While staying at Grandfather's farm, each evening the children would gather around Grandfather and request a tale. Stephens, who wrote many odd tales, used this form to introduce a number of unconnected stories.

On the night of the thirteenth of September, while we were camping at Abol, Maine, on the west branch of the Penobscot, a canoe with two men appeared in the river and drew in to shore a few rods above us. Our two guides, Charley and Steve, exchanged a queer look. "We're took!" said Steve. "That's Newcomb the Moosehead game-warden, and his guide, Jack Holder!"

Whit, my fellow-tourist, laughed uneasily. When game-warden and sportsman meet off in the wilderness in "close time," they scan each other curiously, the one thinking, "Has this fellow been shooting deer or moose out of season hereabouts?" the other, "I wonder if this game-warden thinks I am a poacher?"

In truth, we felt a little queer, for the game laws of Maine are strict; any man worthy to be called a sportsman will observe them strictly, and we had a quarter of "lamb" in one of our canoes. A suspicious warden might call it venison; it was, in fact, part of a deer that one of the guides had shot before we joined them, and the season for deer and moose does not begin till October 1ˢᵗ. To be fined for shooting out of season would be bad, but the disgrace of seeming to have done so, or of consenting to our guides doing so, would be worse. A true woodsman would no more shoot out of season than he would pick pockets, though many "cads" who try to pass as gentlemen and sportsmen are always ready to poach.

Scarcely had the game-warden's canoe landed before another canoe suddenly emerged from the mouth of the Aboljacknegesic and crossed over to our side of the river, and Charley muttered, "That's Hollins—the downriver warden! He must have come through from Ktaadn Ponds."

But the measure of our surprise was not yet full. Hollins had scarcely landed, evidently to camp a little way below us, when the sound of paddles came again to our ears and a third canoe, also containing two men, shot up the river. These men passed us, but landed to camp hard by.

"And if that aint McAllister, the Allagash warden!" Steve exclaimed.

"All the game-wardens in Maine will be here in ten minutes more!" he added, guiltily. "I'd better bury that 'lamb' 'bout as quick's I can. Come, Charley."

While the guides were thus employed, Whit and I strolled along the bank to exchange courtesies with the wardens. Then we learned that their meeting us or each other was wholly chance, and due only to the fact that Abol was a favorite camping-place with game-wardens as well as with tourists.

Good specimens of the better class of backwoodsmen are these game-protectors; strong, observant men, bronzed from sun and wind. Later in the evening, after supper, all three of them, with their canoemen, returned our call and sat down to chat and smoke before our campfire. The conversation naturally turned to game, for in a few days more the "law would be off;" and the beginning of the "open season" is the event of the year in these wilds. Who better than a warden would know if moose were likely to be plenty? The answer to that to that question my friend and I were very anxious to know.

Meanwhile our young guide, Charley, who had been practicing for several nights with a "moose horn" made from a roll of birch bark, had stolen down to the river-bank unobserved, and suddenly woke the forest echoes with a doleful, long-drawn bellowing, in imitation of a bawling cow-moose in autumn.

"Pretty well done, the Allagash warden said, laughing. "Not quite the tone though. I doubt if a moose would come to that, unless possible a spike-horn, or prong-horn. The old males have grown mighty cunning and suspicious. Only an Indian, or a practiced hunter, can now draw them with a horn."

Whit suggested innocently enough, that the warden should take the horn himself and give us a lesson regarding the proper note and intonation.

"And enable Charley and Steve to go away and say they heard a game-warden calling moose here in 'close time,' hey!" rejoined McAllister, with a knowing laugh, in which Hollins and Newcomb joined. "Oh, no, we game-wardens know very well how many hands and voices are against us. There are guides and even fellows calling themselves 'sportsmen' who will get a game-warden into a scrape if they can."

This seemed to indicate a suspicion on which did not think well to comment.

"But if it wasn't for us," McAllister continued, "there would be no game in the Maine woods. But for us, poachers would kill every deer and every moose in Maine in three years. Every sportsman and every tourist ought to stand by us and help us, instead of treating us as enemies."

"That's true," said Whit.

"Then why don't they do it?" exclaimed the warden, warmly.

"All who are fit to be called sportsmen do."

"Huh!" said McAllister.

"Mac feels a little strongly on that subject," remarked Hollins, apologetically.

"Yes, Mac and a New York 'sportsman' once called a moose near here," said Newcomb, with a wink around the fire-lit circle of faces. "The New Yorker came out ahead. Mac lost his job."

"Oh, yes, you all know about it," muttered McAllister, shortly. "It's a standing joke in these parts," he added to Whit and me.

"But we never heard it," rejoined Whit. "Tell us about it!"

McAllister seemed not much disposed to do so. His brother wardens sat and grinned across the fire at each other; and the silence ended by nettling the Allagash warden.

"The story was against me," he remarked. "But I was merely trying to do my duty. You see, I had one of the cunningest old fellows to deal with that ever came into these parts.

"He was a New York doctor, who had been spending his vacations in the Maine woods for years. McMartree his name was; "Doc" McMartree they called him. I don't like to call him a sportsman. And yet the "Doc" was an educated man, and would pass for a gentleman when at home.

"He was of the kind who are always for having the game laws enforced against others and never against himself—that's about the meanest kind of poacher. He knew the whole country around Ktaadn like a book, and every little pond and logan in it. He camped three falls up at Sourdnahunk Lake, and few sportsmen ever go up there.

"The old "Doc" was one of those men who are always trying to 'make themselves solid' with the wardens and guides by presents and good whiskey, so that they would wink at his poaching. His favorite dodge was to come down here about a fortnight before the season opened and take his pick of the deer and moose, particularly of the moose. He nearly always had an Indian named Joe Barley to 'guide' him; and Joe was one of the best moose-hunters that ever came up the West Branch. If there was a moose around Joe would call him.

"You all know Sourdnahunk dead-water, four miles above here. The river spreads out there in a kind of pond; very pretty place, and on the south shore there is a gentle slope now covered with white birch growth. Doctor McMartree used to camp there, a little way back in the birches. I could easily show you his old camp-ground, although it wasn't everyone who knew about it; for the 'Doc' would never take other sportsmen and hunters with him if he could help it He wanted everything to himself.

"Just to the north of his old camp-ground there is a brook running through bushy meadow-land from a little pond two miles back in the woods; and across the brook there is a grand belt of woods on higher land that rises up to a long mountain-ridge. That bushy meadow-ground and the forest beyond was then good moose-pasture; moose always came out to the deadwater there, to grub for lily root.

"The Doc knew all about it, and for four or five years he had gone there a week ahead of the season and 'called' a moose. Other sportsmen with their guides came to know something about it, and certain hints came to the ears of the game commissioners. I was warden here at that time, and a commissioner told me that I must be careful to look out for McMartree.

"The Doc is a jolly old fellow," said he, "but you must fetch him to the book. He must be made to mind the laws."

"Now I was well acquainted with Doctor McMartree. We had known each other for years, and it was disagreeable to be obliged to watch him. He always used to go up the West Branch by way of Mattawamkeag and Medway; and that fall when he and his young son, Lincoln, came to Maine about the tenth of September, I gave his Indian guide a friendly word to keep within the law.

"I heard afterwards that the doctor did not take it kindly; his view of the matter was, that he had come to Maine a long time and spent a good deal of money freely, he ought to be allowed to do about as he pleased. That is quite characteristic of many fellows; they expect their money and their patronage will make everything all right for them.

"But I had my duty to do—for which the State of Maine pays me three dollars a day. There was no other way but for me to keep an eye on the doctor and his party. They went up the river to their old camp-ground on Sourdnahunk dead-water; and a day or two later I went up there, too, and camped at Sourdnahunk falls, a mile below them.

"I had hardly made my camp and got supper that evening, when I heard the doctor's Indian calling moose. It was a sweet night for it; no wind, but just a light air from the west; and the soft, long-drawn-out bellow came so naturally on the evening stillness that I should have supposed it to be a cow-moose if I had not known that the doctor's camp was up near there.

"It nettled me. 'Aha old cock!' I thought; "now I'll trap you. You had your hint to quit, but wouldn't take it. You must be hauled over the coals.

"As it grew dark I got into my canoe and paddled up the dead-water. As I crept along the west shore in the shadow of the trees I heard the Indian call again—for he was too good a hunter to keep bawling often. The wild, lonesome-sounding bellow came floating on the still water, and I knew that he was holding his horn close down to the surface, to make the sound like a moose cow feeding on lily-root with her head to the water.

"The call came from the little bushy, boggy meadow to the northwest of the dead-water; and I was as certain as need be that they were lying in the rushes and alders over there, expecting that a moose would come down from the little ponds to the west of them; the 'air' was just right to carry their scent off on the river-side.

"I landed about half a mile below, went slowly around through the birch growth and entered the meadow at a distance above where I had heard Joe call. I made my way very carefully, for I did not know exactly where they were lying; and, of course, if I were to stumble on them in the dark, I might get a bullet intended for a moose; for a moose will sometimes steal up as sly as a fox, though usually they make racket enough, in conscience.

"After a time the Indian called again, and I found that they were lying nearly a quarter of a mile off, near where the swamp terminated on the dead-water.

"This time they got a response. The quavering echo of the Indian's horn had scarcely ceased on the mountain-side above us when I heard a crash in the under-growth at a distance of half a mile or so along the brook—a moose was coming!

"It gives a person a queer sensation, when off in the woods at night, to know that one of those big black brutes is heading in his direction My present business, however, was to keep quiet, and, if possible, surprise the doctor and his boy when they had shot game unlawfully.

"After that first loud crash, I heard nothing further for several minutes. Evidently the bull moose had stopped, as if suspicious that all was not right. Not a sound broke the night quiet for at least ten minutes; meantime I crept down a little nearer the place where I concluded that the hunters were lying, and sat down on a log to watch.

"I had my carbine with me; I did not expect to use it, but had taken it along, as one naturally will in the woods.

"After a time the Indian bawled again very softly—aar-oo-oo-oh!—the most peculiar wild sound imaginable, as if the moose's mouth were nearly filled with succulent lily root; a sound which only an Indian could have imitated.

"The bull heard it, and responded with a short, startling note, like the first cough of a locomotive moving a heavy train. Immediately I heard him coming again, *crash, crash* through the under-growth—a terrific noise, so really frightful that I involuntarily gripped my carbine and stood to cover of a swamp ash. Evidently this was no spike-horn, but a savage old bull; and I wondered what little 'Link," the doctor's boy, thought of it! I imagined that the lad must be not a little excited, if not frightened.

"The moose did not come straight through the swamp. Most old moose are now wary, having nearly all of them had some experience with hunters. This one coursed through the woods along the border of the swamp, then doubled back and tore past us again, grunting hoarsely as he went by. He had not approached within a hundred yards, perhaps not within two hundred; and it was far too dark, and there was too much thick alder and willow, to gain sight of him.

"But I could hear him plainly, even after he stopped racing to and fro, as he stood stamping and thrashing the brush with his antlers. In the course of ten minutes the Indian gave still another low bellow; I heard him swash the water in the brook, as if a moose were wading there, and he made a sucking noise as of hoofs in soft mud.

"That started the moose afresh, and he coursed back and forth as before, tearing through the brush and grunting fiercely. But even then he was wary to rush directly down on the hunters; again he stood at a distance, thrashing the underbrush to splinters.

"Now the doctor was a skillful hunter, and he knew that sometimes a moose can be 'drawn' by jealousy of a rival, when nothing else will fetch him up within shooting distance. A moment later I heard stealthy sounds behind me on the other side of the brook, and was pretty sure that either the Indian or the doctor, or perhaps possibly another moose, was over there.

"Before I had time to think it out, or even creep away, there came a crash over there. In fact, it was the old doctor himself, smashing a clump of dry willows to bits with the butt of his gun—to fool the moose and make him think he had a rival at close hand!

"The ruse worked like a charm, for I heard an awfully savage grunt from the moose; then he was coming *crash* straight for that moose—coming like a mad rhinoceros! I jumped to my feet to get away to one side, but before I had taken two steps that moose was close upon me.

"I saw the black outline of his huge body bound out between two alder clumps, and actually the brute looked ten feet tall! I did what anybody would do in such a predicament—fired at him pointblank and jumped aside for dear life.

"I cannot say that I took much aim, but one could not easily miss a creature of that size not two yards off! My bullet tore through the moose's throat, and he nearly fell on me, uttering a horrible gurgling bellow.

"I jumped plump into a clump of alders, and before I could extricate myself, there came a dazzling flash of light full in my face. It quite blinded me. I stood, blinking in the sudden brightness, and had scarcely made out that it was the beam of a dark-lantern from just across the brook, when I heard a voice, the voice of the old scamp of a doctor:

"Why, Mr. McAllister! I am indeed astonished! A game-warden shooting moose in 'close time!' This is in very truth a bad example! If I hadn't seen this with my own eyes, I could not have believed it. And much as I have always liked you, McAllister, I fear that it will become my painful duty to enter complaint against you!"

"Such sarcasm was hard to bear, and I answered angrily, 'You're the one against whom a complaint will be entered, and that straight off!'

"But, my dear fellow, we have shot no moose," replied the doctor, in his politest accents. "It is you whom we have caught red-handed. It is you whom we have surprised poaching. My guide here can testify in support of what I have seen, also my son Lincoln."

Young McMartree had been standing at his father's back with the dark-lantern, ready to open it for a shot at the moose. The Indian, who had now come up, stood laughing softly on the other bank.

"I was so angry that I gave them all the rough side of my tongue, promising them that they should not get off half as easily as they imagined. But I had much better have accepted the situation good-naturedly; for fearing, probably, that I would begin legal proceedings against him, the doctor set off down the river next day, and entered formal complaint against me!

'When the case came to trial, all three of them testified simply that they had heard me fire and seen me standing beside a dead moose. I could not deny the shooting of the moose. My explanation was so long and tedious that I was laughed at. The net result was that I lost my job as warden; and it was two years before the commissioners became so far convinced of my honesty as to reappoint me.

"And Doctor McMartree. Have you been able to square accounts with him?" Whit asked.

"No, siree! The old rogue was much too cunning ever to come up here again. He knew that I should be on his track. I hear that he now spends his vacations in Canada, away up the St. Maurice River, where there is fine hunting; and I will warrant you that he is as great a poacher as ever."

– C. A. STEPHENS

CHRISTMAS AT PERRY'S

By Edward W. Frentz, from *Shooting and Fishing*, December 15, 1898

Edward W. Frentz, who was born in Maine, grew up in Melrose, Massachusetts and attended Phillips Exeter Academy. Graduating from Colby College in 1886, where he was captain of the football team in 1883, he returned to Melrose where he became a master archer and helped start the Massachusetts Rovers Club.

Frentz worked as an artist, journalist and editor, eventually rising to the position of editor of Youth's Companion. He wrote one book, "Uncle Zeb and His Friends," and numerous articles, many of them similar to his fellow writer, Charles A. Stephens.

It was Christmas Eve at Perry's, though the only proof of it lay in the old Winchester calendar on the wall and the log under the window in which Johnnie had faithfully cut a daily notch. Certainly all the outward signs which have come to be associated with the great festival were lacking. There were no lights in the window; no bright fire roared upon the hearth; no stocking's hung by the chimney; no laughing children excitedly discussed the probability of a visit from Santa Claus, or the possible contents of his pack. There was only a woman crouching—a discouraging heap—on one side of a pathetic little blaze in the fireplace and a boy, weak with hunger and half sick with fear, on the other.

The last candle had been burned a week ago; the last of the wood, which Perry had cut and brought in before he left, had cooked their breakfast early in the day. The little blaze on the hearth was now eating up the charred and half burned brands which had been carefully raked together, and the mocking flame, as it rose and fell, painted huge distorted, ominous shadows on the cabin walls. The blizzard, which still tugged at the door and threatened at the window, had been raging for three days and nights, and the snow was banked shoulder deep against the logs outside.

The cabin stood on the edge of a belt of pine in the heart of that wilderness which stretches league after league to the north and east of Katahdin. It consisted of only one room, but it was large and well built. Perry had come in there the summer before. The doctors had told him it was his only hope, and even that a small hope. He could not afford to go to California or to Colorado, so he took the advice of the Gazette, with the six month's salary, which they gave him in recognition of his faithful service, and laid his case before the great physician who has an office wherever pure waters run and fresh breezes blow and pine trees exhale their wholesome fragrance. This great physician, though not a "regular practitioner," has cured many a case which the other doctors have given up, and Perry's promise to be one of them. Not that he was cured yet—that would take time—but already he was so much better that he knew he should be cured if he took the medicine long enough.

It was, in fact, because he felt so much stronger that he had put the thong of his sled across his chest and started four days before for Henshaw's, twenty miles out, but the nearest place where he could buy provisions. The larder had got dangerously low before he knew it, for flour and beans and sugar and bacon go fast when there are three to feed and the cold breath of the northern woods sharpens the appetite.

He had started early in the morning, after a good natured argument with his wife about the snowshoes. She had insisted that he take them. The ground was almost bare then—just enough snow to let the sled slip along with reasonable smoothness—and he had laughed at her; but he took the shoes.

He got out to Henshaw's that afternoon, and after buying his provisions, spent the night with Townsend, the storekeeper. When he awoke the next morning the blizzard was raging at its height, and had already sifted a foot of snow over the wilderness he must traverse on the return trip. He had been determined to start, however, and almost lost his temper with the kindly intentioned men who had come stamping into Townsend's during the forenoon, and who tried to dissuade him. Finally old John Blanchard put his big hand on Perry's shoulder and said:

"See here, Mr. Perry, don't be a fool. I've lived in this country, man and boy, for sixty years, and I've hunted and trapped and guided over every foot of it. Now I know how ye feel; I know you're frettin' 'bout the wife and boy. But jest listen ter me a minute. I couldn't git inter your camp today if I should start without a pound o' stuff to hinder me, an' I s'pose I'm 'bout as husky a feller as you be; howeversome, I'm a leetle older. Yet you talk 'bout goin' in and totin' two hund'ed poun's o' grub! What's goin' ter become o' the woman an' the kid if you start an' don't git through. S'pose some of us fellers find ye side o' the trail when the snow goes off next spring—will yer wife and boy be any better off then? I say, don't be a fool. Stay here till the storm lets up, and then I'll start in with ye an' see ye through."

Perry could find no convincing answer to the old man's argument, and so he waited; but hour after hour he stood at the window, silently watching the whirling whiteness without, and chafing till the kindly men at Henshaw's took turns in watching him lest he start in spite of them.

And that is why the woman and the boy crouched alone on Christmas Eve, cold and hungry, by the dying embers in the cabin in the "black growth."

The little blaze on the hearth at length flickered out for want of further fuel. When there was nothing but a glow left in the embers the woman roused herself and recalled the boy to consciousness of the present by a touch upon his shoulder.

"Come Johnnie," she said, "We must go to bed to keep warm." And then, in the attempt to be cheerful and with that fine courage which women so often display in the face of disaster, she added, "I guess father will get in tomorrow. We can hold on till then. If he doesn't come, perhaps you may be able to shoot something."

He who sleeps, sups," the French say. It is a shrewd saying, and recognizes one of God's great mercies to his children. Rolled in their blankets and cradled in fragrant hemlock boughs, Johnnie and his mother forgot their hunger and were warm. When they awoke, the bitter wind was dead. The snow had ceased and the sun was shining upon a world decked all in white. In the south-west towered the mighty mass of Katahdin, sharp and clean-cut against the cold, blue sky. On every side the trees and bushes sparkled with a wealth of diamonds and gleamed with countless millions of pearls, till the sight was dazzled and the hand involuntarily went up to shade the eye.

Already the surface of the snow disclosed the lace-like tracery of partridge feet and squirrels'; and as Johnnie and his mother stood in the open door of the cabin, looking down the trail in the hope—which each at heart acknowledged to be vain—the hope of seeing a familiar figure—there before their very eyes were the tracks of a great buck, plain as a military road. From the shelter of some hemlock thicket he had started, no doubt, as soon as the storm had ceased, impatient to break his long fast. The tracks passed close to the cabin, and even to one unused to the woods, showed that the buck had sunk almost belly deep in the soft snow.

Johnnie pointed to the tracks, and without a word stepped back into the cabin. He put on his old mackinaw coat and larrigans, took down the rifle from its pegs, pulled his cap over his ears, and started. His mother helped him eager and sympathetic interest, refraining , lest she discourage the boy, from expressing what he knew as well as she—the difficulty, if not the hopelessness, of coming upon a buck under such conditions and without snowshoes.

At first stop Johnnie sank above the tops of his larrigans, and often waist deep; and weak as he was from hunger, his breath came hard and his knees trembled before he had gone a hundred yards. But the possibility of venison steak, the thought of his mother's hunger and his own empty stomach kept him at it. By the time he had gone half a mile he came upon droppings so fresh that they were still steaming, and this gave him new courage, and enforced increased caution.

The trail crossed the big ridge, went down the other side, and then started up a second incline beyond. It was all the boy could do to reach the top of this second knoll. His feet were lead, his rife weighed a ton, and his breath came in gasps. But as his head rose above the ridge and his eyes roved ahead down the long slope, they rested upon the buck, browsing quietly, back to, and unconscious of his pursuer—a magnificent sight; a prize any sportsman would have worked hard to win, and to this tired, starving boy, a prize the winning of which might almost mean life itself, both for him and for his mother.

There was too much at stake to risk an offhand shot. Johnnie crouched slowly in the snow till only his cap showed above the ridge, and his rifle rested in the fork of a yellow birch sapling. He could not shoot for the heart, for the buck stood back to him; so he drew down the bit of ivory toothbrush handle—from which, in leisure moments, he had made his muzzle sight—till it rested squarely on the point where the buck's neck joined his body. But it was a very erratic piece of ivory. It wavered and wobbled and wandered about till Johnnie's heart almost stood still. But at last it settled motionless in its place for the least little fraction of a second, and the boy pressed the trigger. The woods reverberated with the roar of the report. The hills especially that upon the right, threw back the echo with startling distinctiveness, so that even in the overwhelming interest of the chase, Johnnie marveled at the clearness of it. The pungent blue smoke rose and drifted slowly away, the buck gave one mighty leap and fell and then lay still.

With a yell of exultation, Johnnie, no longer mindful of cold or hunger or fatigue, started toward his quarry, leaping, wallowing, and staggering, through the snow. Before he had traversed half the distance to the buck, another figure emerged from the heavy growth on the right—the figure of a tall young man in a gray frieze reefer, knee breeches, and fancy golf stockings. Upon his feet were snowshoes decorated with tufts of red and blue worsted; and although at every step he sank several inches into the light snow, his progress, when compared with Johnnie's was as the flight of a bird beside the gallop of an elephant.

He went straight toward the buck, and even before Johnnie could reach him, had begun to dress it. As the boy came up panting, breathless, hot with anger, at the prospect of losing the fruits of his labor, the stranger turned toward him with a smile and said, "Well, son, if you had got around a little sooner you might have done me out of my buck; but I'm glad you didn't. There aren't many finer fellows in the woods that this—"

"Your buck!" broke in the voice of the boy, sharp with anger, and with a note of terror in it, too. "Your buck! I'd like to know how he's your buck when I followed him an hour through this snow and plugged him fair and square in the neck. He's my buck, and you'll just let him alone."

"Why son, you seem to cherish hallucinations. I'm afraid you have wheels, so to speak. If you'll kindly examine the buck I think you'll find a large hole in his heart. It is my impression that I made the hole with my .45-90, and don't believe that in such a case a coroner's jury would claim that death due to natural causes."

The young man's good natured banter, above all, his air of calm confidence, cooled Johnnie's anger and chilled him with a sense of helplessness and defeat. For the first time he looked closely at the buck. There was, indeed, a hole just over the heart, and the red stain spreading in the snow beneath the carcass showed that the bullet had gone through. He could see no wound in the neck.

The puzzle was too much for him, and without attempting to solve it he threw himself face downward across the body of the buck and began to sob as if his heart were broken.

The stranger laid a kindly hand upon his shoulder and lifted him up. "What does all this mean, mu boy?" he asked. "Why do you care so much about this buck? Aren't there plenty of other deer in the woods?" And then Johnnie broke down again, and the stranger gradually drew from him the story of the last few days; of the father's enforced absence and the mother's hunger and his own; of how he had seen the tracks in the morning and followed them; of how the buck had fallen when he fired; and as if to convince himself of the truth of what he was saying, Johnnie lifted the buck's head and turned it, and there on the underside, was a bloody crease along the neck—his bullet mark, which he had not seen before.

When he had finished the story, the stranger patted him kindly on the back. "It's all right son. Now you stay here while I go over to our camp. I'll be right back, and when I come, you and your mother shall have such a dinner that you can't walk for a week."

With peace in his heart Johnnie waited. When the stranger returned there were three other men with him, and the arms of all of them were loaded. Dunbar, of the Journal—the man who had shot the buck—had the coffeepot, full and steaming, just as he had snatched it off the fire. Hawkins of the Times, carried a bag of beans and a bag of potatoes, and his pockets bulged with cans of condensed milk and packages of sugar; and Jim Coleman, the guide, bore a hindquarter of venison and five pounds of dried peaches.

And so, without stopping to dress the buck or to discuss the question of property rights in the carcass, the little procession started, with Johnnie in the lead. These newspaper friends of his—newspaper men who had come into the woods for a Christmas vacation—had no idea whose cabin it was they were going to; but then they reached the door and met Johnnie's mother and found out that this was the spot which Perry—"Jack Perry of the old Gazette,"—had chosen for his fight with consumption; that here was his cabin and this was his wife and boy, they set to work as only newspaper men will when they find a newspaper man in trouble. Dunbar went out with the axe, Mitchell cut up the bacon, Coleman mixed up a batch of biscuit, and Hawkins attended to the coffee, so that almost before you knew it a meal was on the table that would have tempted less hungry people than Johnnie and his mother.

Having done there work promptly and well, the "boys" left Mrs. Perry and her son to eat their meal in privacy, but instead of going back to their camp, they all started on their snowshoes down the trail to Henshaw's. Before dusk Johnnie and his mother heard a great shouting outside. It did not need much imagination to guess what it meant, and they rushed to the door. Sure enough, Perry was coming with his sled-load of provisions. But instead of pulling on the line, he sat, laughing and protesting, on the front of the load, while the three newspaper men, with their guide and old John Blanchard, with strong hands upon the rope snaked the sled along at a merry pace.

That night a Christmas dinner was served for eight in Perry's cabin. There was no roast goose or celery or cranberry sauce, but there were plenty of other things just as good, and the best appetites in the world to eat them.

And when the meal was over, and wreaths of fragrant blue smoke floated up from the group on the deacon seat before the blazing logs, Dunbar went down into his hip pocket and brought up a flat bottle with four x's on it; and Hawkins went down into his pocket and brought up another bottle with four x's on it. But no one of those x's indicated any unknown quantity, nor did anyone have to solve any algebraic equation to find the value of them. Instead, they took some hot water from the tea kettle and a dash of nutmeg, and with a few of the x's they produced something which steamed famously and with a fine fragrance and they all drank standing up, out of tin dippers, after Hawkins had said something. Even Johnnie was allowed to try a little, because, as Dunbar said, he had shown himself to be a game little chap, and, after all, had made a pretty good shot, considering. Besides, it was Christmas.

MAINE BEAR TRAPPERS

By John B. Burnham, from *Forest and Stream*, August 26, 1899

John Bird Burnham (1869-1939) was born in Delaware, attended a military school and graduated from Trinity College in Hartford, Conn. As a young man he moved to Essex, New York, near Lake Champlain, where he obtained a position as a journalist, and from where he would frequently take trips to the Adirondack region, as well as the Maine woods and would write continuously about his adventures. In 1904 he was appointed as Chief Game Protector for the State of New York and in 1911 became president of the American Game Protection Association, a position he held until 1928. He later retired to his home in Westboro, New York on the shores of Lake Champlain.

John B. Burnham from his biography (Courtesy of Ernst Mayr Library, Harvard)

The many adventures of this avid sportsman and the account of his involvement in the fledgling conservation movement were chronicled in "John Bird Burnham-Klondiker, Adirondacker, and Eminent Conservationist," By Maitland C. De Sormo in 1978.

Here, Bunham reiterates a bear story he heard while visiting Capt. Wing in Dead River, a venerable old sportsman, guide and camp proprietor.

"Four years ago," said Mr. Wing, "I made $120 in ten days' time trapping bears. I got four old bears and two cubs. One of the cubs was alive. On this trip I got a bear every other time I looked my traps over.

"I started from home and went into my camp on Pray Hill in the northeast corner of the town. It was about the 1st of May. I went out and set four traps and then went home again. In about a week's time I went back to look at my traps. The first trap I came to was gone. I hunted for it for two hours and couldn't find it. The trail was an old one, and it rained since it was made, and I couldn't follow it good.

"I was looking off through the woods uncertain which way the trail went, when I happened to see a bear's head cocked up looking at me. I knew well enough the bear was in my trap, and I walked right up to it to get a good shot. I saw a couple of small animals that I took to be rabbits run off in the bush, but I didn't pay much attention to them, being so hard upon the bear. I got where I wanted, and knocked my bear over, and set to skin her. When I turned her over I see she was suckling cubs, and that reminded me of the small animals I had seen run off, and I knew well enough then what they were.

"After I took the old lady's hide off I spent the best part of an hour looking for the cubs, but I didn't find them, and I had to give it up as I had the other traps to look over.

"The next trap I visited was gone, too, but the bear had got into it since the rain, and left a good trail, and I soon found him.

"The bear kept head on and would not give me just the shot I wanted, so I gave him one through the head and knocked him down. When I worked the gun for a new cartridge there was nothing there. For some reason or other my magazine was empty, and I could find no more cartridges in my pockets. About the time I found this out, the bear rolled over and got on his feet and stood there looking at me to see what I was going to do next. It was kind of aggravating, and I says to myself, 'Your hide's going back with me to Flagstaff, Mister Bear, some way or 'nother.'

"You can bet I wasn't going to lose my bear just because I had run out of ammunition.

"I looked around for something to kill the bear with, but couldn't find anything till I got clear back where the trap had been set, a matter of a couple of hundred yards or so. There I go a chunk of wood 6ft. long and 3in. through that I'd used setting the trap. It was heavy rock maple, and I says to myself, 'This is good enough for a cartridge, and it won't play out.'

"When I got back to the bear he set there winking and blinking and showing his teeth, telling me he didn't like me trying no more experiments on him. I crept up behind, and swung my club, and the very first clip I drove the skull full in, and after that I had no more trouble taking off the pelt. The rifle ball had hit him in the nose and missed the brain, and only stunned the bear temporarily.

"I generally figure to get a side shot on the skull between the eye and ear. I look the bear in the eye, and after a while he turns his head and looks away, and that gives me my chance.

"The next day I thought I'd see what I could do to get the cubs, so I took my boy with me and went back to where the old bear lay. When we got near to the carcass we saw two cubs going up a big spruce tree, snake fashion, circling round and round the tree as they went up. I brought my rifle up and took a quick shot and put a ball right through the head of one of the cubs, and that was the end of him.

"Then I thought of catching the other one. I asked the boy if he thought he could climb the next tree to the big one, for that had no limbs. He said he believed he could skin it, and started for the tree.

"Hold on,' I said; 'I want to rig you out.'

"I went and cut a crotched pole 10ft. long and fastened the crotch to his belt so he could climb with hands and feet, and told him to go ahead and skin up the tree.

"He got up 30ft. or so, carrying the pole with him and then he was on an even height with the cub in the other tree, and only about 10ft. off. I told him to take the pole and put the crotch on the bear and shove it off the limb it was sitting on.

"The boy gave the bear a punch and knocked him off the limb, but he hung on underneath. 'Now," I says, 'you give him a good big punch and knock him off anyway.'

"The boy gave him a good punch and knocked him off. The cub made himself round like a bat-ball coming through the air, and he struck on his rump right at my feet. I grabbed him by the nape of the neck and back and he turned like a flash and began scratching like a bag full of cats.

"I sang out to the boy to hurry up and come down or I'd have no flesh left on my hands, and when he got down had him tie the forward feet with a piece of string and help me get the little devil under control.

"All this time the cub was making the most unearthly noise, and I thought to myself if there were any old bears around I should have company. I kept the bear till he was six months old and then sold him. When I got him he weighed 5lbs., and when I sold him he weighed 50.

"I had put the old she bear in for bait, and about a week after I got the cubs I went back to the trap and caught another old one, and a little after that I got my fourth grown bear in the trap where I had knocked the bear over with a club.

"Bear meat makes as good bait as anything. The secret in catching bears is to select the right spot for setting the trap. One man may set a trap in one place and never catch anything, and another man may go fifty or a hundred rods to one side and get a bear right off the first thing.

"Some bears are mighty smart. I tried three years for one, and had the blacksmith make me a special heavy trap. He was a monstrous big bear, and you could follow him through the woods by his track just as easy as you could an axe. I put out a dead horse weighing 1,000lbs. for him and he hung around till he ate him all up, and it didn't take a great while either. I covered the horse with brush and hid the trap in different places, but he'd paw the brush away till he'd located the trap before he'd take a bite of the horse. I've known bears to walk round and round a trap till they'd worn a regular ring in the ground. At last I took bee's honey and smoked herrings and that was too much of a temptation for him to go by, and I got the old fellow.

"As a rule bears, when they get in a trap, they fight themselves and get set up so they choke themselves. If one gets in a stream or pond, where he can keep cool, he'll live for quite a spell."

THE KNIGHT OF THE SPIKE-SOLE BOOTS

By Holman Day, from *Pine Tree Ballads*, 1902

Holman Francis Day (1865-1935), a noted Maine poet, was also known for his many novels about the State and its people. He began writing novels in 1900 and wrote about twenty between that date and 1936. Many of his novel were set in towns, but his books on the north Maine Woods were the best remembered – King Spruce, The Ramrodders, The Red Lane and The Rider of the King Log, wonderful romantic stories of logging, river-driving and prohibition.

The Hulling Machine (Courtesy of Ernst Mayr Library, Harvard)

Day, seeking a warmer climate, moved to Mill Valley, California and about 1920 opened a film company known as Holman Day Productions. Over the next five years he produced two dozen short films and one feature film. Most of his films were based on his novels, such as Knight of the Pines, King Spruce and Rider of the King Log. At least two of his films, My Lady of the Pines and Wings of the Border starred Mary Astor, one of the most noted silent film actresses of that time. Day died in Mill Valley in 1935, but was buried in his native Vassalboro.

Among his wonderful poems is "The Knight of the Spike-Sole Boots," which he set at the Hulling Machine, a set of falls on the East Branch of the Penobscot, so named because the violence and turbulence of the water, and the many rocks resulted in much of the bark being taken off the logs as they passed through the falls.

> They had told me to 'ware of the "Hulling
> Machine,"
> But a tenderfoot is a fool!
> Though the man that's new to birch canoe
> Believes that he knows, as a rule,
> They had told me to carry a mile above
> Where the broad deadwater slips
> Into fret and shoal to tumble and roll

276

In the welter of Schoodic rips;
But know it all, as a green man does,
And lazy, as green men are,
I hated to pack on my aching back
My duffle and gear so far.

So, as down the rapids there stretched a strip
With a most encouraging sheen,
I settled the blade of my paddle and made
For the head of the "Hulling Machine."
It wasn't because I hadn't been warned
That I rode full tilt at Death–
It was simply the plan of an indolent man
To save his back and breath.
For I reckon I'd slice for the left-hand shore
When the roar of the falls was near,
And I braced my knees and took my ease–
There was nothing to do but steer.

(There are many savage cataracts, slavering
for prey,
"Twixt Abol-jackamegus and the lower Brass-
u-a,
But of all the yowling demons that are wicked
and accurst,
The demon of the Hulling Place is ugliest and
worst.)

Now the strip in that river like burnished steel
Looked comfortable and slow,
But my birch canoe went shooting through
Like an arrow out a bow.
And the way was hedged by ledges that
Grinned
As they shredded the yeasty tide
And hissed and laughed at my racing craft

As it drove on its headlong ride.
I sagged on the paddle and drove it deep,
But it snapped like a pudding-stick,
Then I staked my soul on my steel-shod pole,
And the pole smashed just as quick.
There was nothing to do but clutch the
thwarts
And crouch in the birchen shell,
And grit my teeth as I viewed beneath
The boil of that watery hell.
I may have cursed–I don't know now–
I may have prayed or wept.
I yelled halloo and I waved adieu
With a braggart's shamming mien,
Then over the edge of that foaming ledge
I dropped in the "Hulling Machine."

(*A driver hates a coward as he hates diluted
rye;*
*>Stiff upper lip for living, stiff backbone when
you die!*
*They cheered me when I passed them; they
Followed me with cheers,*
*That, as braces for a dying man, are better far
Than tears.*)

The "Hulling Place" spits a spin of spume
Steaming from brink to brink,
And it seemed that my soul was cuffed in a
bowl
Where a giant was mixing his drink.
And 'twas only by luck or freak or fate,
Or because I'm reserved to be hung,
That I found myself on a boulder shelf
Where I flattened and gasped and clung,
To left the devilment roared and boiled,

To right it boiled and roared;
On either side the furious tide
Denied all hope of ford.

So I clutched at the face of the dripping ledge
And crouched from the lashing rain,
While the thunderous sound of tumult
Ground
Its iron into my brain.
I stared at the sun as he blinked above
Through whorls of the rolling mists,
And I said good-by and prepared to die
As the current wrenched my wrists.
But just as I loosened by dragging clutch,
Out of the spume and fogs
A chap drove through—one o' Connor's crew–
Riding two hemlock logs.
He was holding a pick-pole couched at Death
As though it were lance in rest,
And his spike-sole boots, as firm as roots,
In the splintered bark were pressed.
If this be sacrilege, pardon me, pray;
But a robe such angels wear
Seemed his old red shirt with smears of dirt,
And a halo his mop of hair;
And never a knight in a tournament
Rode lists with jauntier mien
Than he of the drive who came alive
Through the hell of the "Hulling Ma-
Chine."

He dragged me aboard with giant swing,
And he guided the rushing raft
Serenely cool to the foam-flecked pool
Where the dimpling shallows laughed.
And he drawled as he poled to the nearest

Shore,
While I stuttered my gratitude;
"I jest came through to show that crew
I'm match for a sportsman dude."

There are only two have raced those falls
And by lucky chance were spared;
Myself dragged there in a fool's despair
And he, the man who dared!
I make no boast, as you'll understand,
And there's never a boast from him;
And even his name is lost to fame–
I simply know 'twas "Jim."
If Jim was a fool, as I hear you say
With a sneer beneath your breath,

So were knights of old who in tourneys bold
Lunged blithesomely down at Death.
And if I who was snatched from the jaws of
Hell
Am to name a knight to you,
Here's the Knight of the Firs, of the Spike-
Sole spurs,
That man from Connor's crew!

Chapter 6

THE NORTH MAINE WOODS

In 1838, Dr. Charles Jackson, the State Geologist, made a trip to northern Maine, observing the geology and geography of what he called the Aroostook Mountains. He climbed Sugarloaf Mountain, near Shin Pond, and said that he could count over "fifty lofty peaks and seventy mountain lakes, cascades of 200 feet fall, etc."

That same year Milford P. Norton and a group of young men from Somerset County, purchased two lots of land in Townships 11 and 12 of the 5th Range, now Masardis and Ashland. And it was observed that people passed through Bangor every day on their way to the Aroostook territory.

Dr. Holmes, another Maine geologist made a trip north in 1838, remarking that the Aroostook River was the handsomest steam of water in Maine, with many intervals that would make excellent farms. He also noted that it was not uncommon to find cedar trees with a trunk from one foot to one and half feet.

That winter an eight-year-old boy, James Saunders of Linneus, was headed for his father's barn to feed the cattle, when he encountered a large black bear. Giving a screech, the boy ran to the barn, pursued by the bear, and just as he got to the barn the bear caught him with his front paws and headed for the woods. Three men in the house, heard the boy and ran after the bear, catching up to him in a quarter of a mile. Two of the men had axes, and when the bear turned toward them. They found the axes useless, so they quickly got a gun and returned to the woods, where they shot the bear through the left side. This forced the bear to fall dead dropping the boy, who returned home, more frightened than hurt. After skinning the bear, they found that it weighed 362 pounds, the largest ever killed in that region.

In 1839 the Sheriff of Penobscot County with 150 men, left Bangor on a long trek to Madawaska, to arrest trespassers on the public lands and put a stop to the plundering of the valuable timber that grew there.

Later the Land Agent of Maine auctioned off the trespassers logs, hoping to, but not covering the costs of the expedition.

Another group of men from Sangerville set off for the headwaters of the St. Croix River, intending to purchase lands on which to settle. When they arrived they could find no board for their horses south of the Aroostook River, and were advised by the locals to build a raft to cross. Completing the raft, they got the horses on board and headed across the river, intending to land a mile and a half downriver. However, the water proved to be too swift, and quickly coming upon a submerged tree, the horses and men went overboard. Mr. Hardison clung to the raft, George W. Fowler disappeared, and Parsons swam after the raft, a distance of one hundred rods, when his strength failed and he sunk. E. S. Fowler by extreme strength stayed afloat and was rescued when Hardison held out a pole. The horses made it to shore, but tragically two men were lost.

With the opening of the Military Road, by 1841 Houlton had two churches, a courthouse, three inns, and ten or fifteen stores. In 1842 McCary had a lumber operation at Fort Fairfield with two hundred men and 80 horses the past winter. Capt. Van Ness, commander of the fort, had the heads of moose, caribou and deer that some of his men had shot near the garrison, and Colonel John Hodsdon, the proprietor of the town of Hodsdon, had no doubt but 1000 deer had been killed within a circumference of six miles of his house. Wolves were not known in that region until about two years earlier, when they were pushed south by settlements on the St. John River, and the previous year the wolves had killed almost half of the sheep on the Aroostook River.

In March of 1855 Senator Blake of Aroostook was in Augusta securing money for the settlement at Madawaska, which was in dire straits, having little to no food and an outbreak of smallpox. Several had died, and one women, in order to save her children, made a tea from hay, which sustained them until aid arrived. The money appropriated was insufficient, so Mr. Blake furnished them grain from his own farm, on which he had seven or eight hundred bushels of wheat, and for which he refused to take any pay for the grain.

Rev. Marcus Keep, who made the first trail up Katahdin, wrote in 1860 that when Madawaska was first settled some eighty years previous by the French, that moose were so thick that the settlers never wanted for meat. A tradition says that the Indians were displeased with the practice of French hunters killing them for their hides only, and in revenge killed hundred for less than their skins, to lie and rot. Soon after that no moose track was to be found for a hundred miles or so.

In 1862 three young men visited Aroostook County collecting specimen of birds of Northern Maine. One of the men was collecting for the New York cabinet, the other two securing specimens for the Natural History Department at Cambridge. The woods of northern Maine were very quiet in the winter of 1862, many of the men being off in the Civil War, and the Indians predicted a cold winter that year, but many moose.

Dry hardwood was selling for $4 a cord in Presque Isle in 1863, and a large amount of freight from Aroostook County was being shipped by way of the St. Francis Railroad. Lumbering supplies from Boston were coming north to Calais and thence by railroad to the north woods.

In February of 1866 Mr. Butler of Ashland, who was lumbering on the Fish River, cut a gigantic pine tree. They first cut a log which scaled at 1,000 feet; from that to the branches 1000 feet more. Soon after that N. S. Lufkin killed a monster caribou near Van Buren Plantation, noting that caribou were seldom seen in the Aroostook woods.

THE DEATH STRUGGLE

By John Neal, from *The Moose Hunter, or, Life in the Maine Woods.*
Beadle & Company, The American News Company, 1864

John Neal

John Neal (1793-1876) was a novelist and writer, born in Falmouth, Maine. Removing to Baltimore, in 1815 his dry goods business failed, so he read law and was admitted to the Maryland Bar in 1819. He worked at intervals as editor on several newspapers and magazine and began writing novels, one for which he was accused of libel and challenged to a dual, which he declined. Neal went to England in 1823 where he became a literary critic of American literature, but returned to America in 1827, settling in Portland, where he became editor of the "Yankee," for many years. Neal, a very physically fit man, opened the first gymnasium in the city. A man of talent and ingenuity, he never became famous or achieved great success, mostly due to his having too many varied interests, which never allowed him to focus on one area of expertise.

"The Moose Hunter" was published as a dime novel, the early form of paperback novels. We pick up the adventures of the heroes as they encounter a moose...

...Again the far-off yelping of dogs in full cry was heard, but in a direction opposite to that which they were taking. The next moment a signal was made by one of the Fraziers, who was on the look-out. All hurried up to find out what it meant. Before they had reached him, however, the Brigadier, who had been so startled by the sudden burst of the dogs as so lose his self-possession for a moment, made a motion for them all to separate: then he checked himself, and pointed to a dark object, which, seemed to be moving at no great distance from them, athwart a large, open clearing.

"There he goes! There he goes!" shouted all the Fraziers, greatly to the displeasure of Burleigh and the Brigadier.

"You go that way, my lads, and we'll go this. I'm sure he sees us, and the sooner we're on his track the better. You may holler now as much as you like—it will only confuse him. Oh, if we only had the puppies here!"

Saying this, he headed off in full sight of the moose, followed by Burleigh. The others continued their course along the outer edge of the woods, gradually contacting the circle as the creature moved about, evidently bewildered by the number and position of his enemies. At one moment he seemed resolute on crossing the open pasture, with his long, shambling trot, and the next to go back to the cover of the nearest wood. That he was not seriously hurt, was evident enough by his motions.

"Halloo!" shouted the Brigadier, as the creature came out in full view, but after a moment's pause, he dashed headlong into the nearest undergrowth, crashing through it like a river-horse through the reeds of the Nile. "Halloo! That's the very boy we're after! Jest look at his horns!"

They were magnificent, to be sure—among the largest ever seen by the oldest of the party.

"Hurrah!" there goes the puppies!" and sure enough they were heard in fully cry, not half a mile off.

The old man hurried forward with a tremendous swing in the direction they seemed to be going, while the school master took a shorter cut for the woods, hoping to overtake the beast before he could enter the undergrowth.

Cries were not distinctly heard afar off; then the baying of a large dog; then the yelling of a wounded cur: then a shot; then all the sounds seemed to be coming nearer.

Suddenly, just as the old man was hurrying across a wide reach of glittering crust, on his way from one patch of dwarf hemlocks to another, there came a terrible shouting and screaming from two or three different quarters, which bewildered him for a moment. Before he could recollect himself, there was a great crashing close at hand. And, as he planted his left foot, with his gun leveled in the direction of the noise, there came a cry from behind, which seemed to be very near, and which, sooth to say, might well have made the blood of the most experienced hunter run cold.

"Look out, sir! Look out! Run for your life!" shouted Burleigh, with an agonizing cry. "Give him a shot, and run for your life!"

But before the old man could face round to meet a new enemy, the terrible beast came crashing through the outer growth, and steering straight for him.

Great as the danger was, and near as it was, the Brigadier waited for a chance back of the fore-shoulder, but finding the creature was coming head on, without turning to the right or the left, he let fly at the center of his chest. This shot brought the bull to his knees; but the next moment, after one or two desperate plunges, he was on his feet again and charged at a furious gallop on the Brigadier.

"Take to a tree!" shouted Burleigh; "Take to a tree, for God's sake, till I can get near enough for a shot."

The old man started, and for a few minutes, as the enraged animal broke through the crust, now and then, there seemed to be a good chance for escape; but only for a moment.

At the very next leap the creature was evidently gaining upon him. He heard the snorting and plunging, and almost felt the breathing over his shoulder. Whereupon, as a last hope, he tore off his outer garment and flung it down on the snow. The moose stopped and trampled upon it, furiously, and came on again. He now threw away his hat, which the wind took and carried out of their course: then, just as the dogs came yelling over the snow, he tripped, stumbled, and fell head long, and the furious beast was upon him before he could recover himself, encumbered as he was with his snow-shoes.

But the fearless man did not lose his presence of mind for a moment. He knew that Burleigh was at hand; he heard the baying of the large dog, which he believed to be Watch; and, as the huge animal reared to trample him in the snow, he rolled over suddenly, out of reach of the descending hoofs. The creature's fore-feet broke through the crust with his weight and momentum, so as to bring a branch of his antlers near the prostrate man. Instantly the old fellow grasped it with both hands and was lifted to his knees. At that moment, Watch rushed to the rescue, making a furious bound at the creature's throat, just as Uncle Jerry caught a glimpse of Burleigh within range, kneeling, with his gun leveled, but hesitating.

"Fire away, Burleigh! Never mind me!" shouted the old hunter. "Let him have it! Blaze away!"

The animal reared and plunged with frantic fury. The huge antler, which the old man had grasped, already loosened perhaps by the tremendous energy of that burst through the undergrowth, came off in his hands, like a thunder-blasted branch—exasperating the creature to madness. Instantly, Uncle Jeremiah transferred his grip; seizing the other antler firmly in both hands. He was literally lifted into the air, while clinging to it. It was the moment of life or death to the hunter.

Burleigh fired.

The still woods rung with the report; echoes answered from the nearest hillside, with a rattle of musketry; the enraged monster pitched headlong into the deep snow, just as he was rearing to strike the helpless old man with his fore-feet which would have settled the whole business, forever; old Watch fastened upon the beast by that hanging upperlip—the maufle, or mauflan, we have all heard so much of.

Undiscouraged, though terribly wounded and bruised and bleeding, the Brigadier threw himself upon the struggling bull, and soon finished him with a plunge of his long hunting-knife, and a wipe across the throat, before Burleigh could interfere.

Then didn't the skies ring! And didn't the woods answer to a wild hurrah! Hurrah! Hurrah. Which burst forth from two or three different quarters, intermingled with the ponderous bark of Old Watch, and the yelp of at least half a dozen scampering whelps.

"Hurrah for the old hunter!"
"Hurrah for Uncle Jeremiah."

THREE WEEKS IN THE MAINE WOODS

By Mollechunkamunk, from *Forest and Stream*, January 20, 1876

Life in the Woods, Starting Out (Currier & Ives 1860)

This anonymous author's trip is one of the first written about canoeing down the St. John River route. It probably took place many years before being published in 1876, as he chose Uncle John as his guide. This was John Ellis, who first visited Moosehead Lake about 1804 when he was a very young man. Falling in love with the region, Ellis built a camp at Lily Bay, from where he could hunt, fish and trap. He was a hunter by trade, supplying Kineo and the Greenville hotels and settlers with deer, bear and moose meat, often bartering for the things he needed. Fishermen and hunters often sought out Uncle John, for he was also one of the best storytellers in the region.

We were to go to the north woods of Maine. Imagine us, then, all prepared at the foot of Moosehead Lake, and on board the steamer which was to carry us some thirty miles towards the North Pole, and there leave us to shift for ourselves. While gliding over this charming inland sea, we will lose but little time if we introduce our guides in form.

Uncle John steps out from the admiring crown which has already gathered around him on the forward deck. Long white hair, and beard gave him a venerable appearance; a somewhat stooping form would seem to indicate that age had already undermines his strength; one eye was all he could "go" on anything, for the other had been placed on the retired list some time since. A greenhorn would decline to believe that when he looked at Uncle John he saw before him the most renowned hunter of the Moosehead country; a man who had, by mere woodcraft, conducted the surveying parties who ran the township lines through what was then literally a pathless wild; who knows every hill, stream, pond, and brook in the State so well that he not only can name them every one, but can tell the direction of all from any stand-point he may choose, and the distance of each from the other; and moreover, we verily believe there is not a good "hole" for trout in the Maine waters unknown to him. As for strength and skill, he acknowledges no superior on shore or in a birch, which he manages like a toy, and in which he will go where any living man, white or red, can float.

Ike, our other companion, is a giant, physically, for to his six feet and odd inches of length he adds breadth and brawn enough for a Hercules; so straight that he bends over backward, with an eye like a hawk and sinews like iron; quick-tempered, but good-natured, a jolly good fellow, and true as steel. Born, reared, and educated in the woods, it is only necessary to state that he is a pupil of Uncle John's to place him in a rank second to none. As for ourselves, we are modest.

The outfit which we found to answer all requirements, combining what was absolutely indispensable with the least possible weight consisted for each of an entire suit of very heavy flannel, underclothing, a heavy blue flannel outside shirt, an entire suit of "moleskin," or corduroy, a rubber coat, woolen socks, (an extra pair convenient), stout shoes, felt hat, rubber blanket, and two woolen ones; a wall tent for ourselves and a shelter for the guides, a small cooking apparatus, a shot gun apiece, one rifle, ammunition, a fly rod and tackle for each, and an opera glass apiece, with a few groceries.

Our route was that known as the "Baker Lake Route" to the few who know anything about it, and is reputed the wildest and hardest one in the State. As we were the first party who had been over it for years, and as our guides, before they reached the end, had repeatedly declared that they would never come over it again, we concluded that the reputation was just one, the more especially as F., who has seen all the head-waters of Maine, declares that he has taken no trip which can compare with it for hard work, long carries or portages, quick water, and no water at all.

Leaving Greenville, a little village at the foot of Moosehead

Lake, at about four o'clock on the afternoon of September 18th, we steamed up the lake against a miniature nor-wester, and landed at the northwest carry at about midnight. Here our woodland life began, and it was with rather a feeling of new-acquired, responsibility that we saw ourselves thrown entirely upon our own resources by the severing of the last connecting link between us and civilization by the departure of the "Governor." No time was lost, however, in a speculation as to our future; each went at once to work at his allotted task and in a short time, by the friendly light of a bright, full moon, a delightful camping ground was found, everything arranged and we in the arms of Morpheus.

At daylight next morning we were in our canoes, and soon a pair of ducks and a "musquash" gave us our first game, as well as our breakfast. A short paddle up the inlet, and a carry of about a mile and a half, brought us to Penobscot waters, a lakelet in the Seboomook meadow. While passing down the outlet of this pond, leading into the west branch of the Penobscot, we passed over the first beaver dam we had seen. While paddling up the dead water of the west branch we were at liberty to enjoy the varied tints of autumn foliage. In this latitude winter sets in early, and already the forest has begun to assume the crimson and gold, which blended with the varieties of the evergreen and the still untouched leaves of the hard wood growth, gave some of those gorgeous color pictures for which the American woods are so justly noted. The perfectly smooth waters of the stream, reflecting in the exactitude of a mirror the forms and tints on the banks, heightened the effect greatly. Having reached Big Island, we went into camp, and while the guides were preparing for the night's rest, we went off for trout, and after about an hour's fishing counted some thirty-six , all told, averaging three-quarters of a pound, the best strike being one whereby two fish, aggregating a pound and a half, were taken and landed at one cast. The favorite fly at this season, and in this water, seems to be the "green fly." The red ibis also took well, while the Long Island favorite, the brown hackle, was scarcely noticed. In short, a gaudy fly is a killing fly in the upper Penobscot waters in September. At this camp Ike set out a trap for beaver, and caught one. From here two day's hard paddling, poling, and pushing brought us to a point where we left the Penobscot, and, carrying some three miles through the woods, reached the St. John's Pond, and the first of the St. Johns waters. This is easily related, but oh! The untold trials of a carry!

We remained in camp on the St. John Pond two days, on the second of which our party started out in quest of caribou. F. and Ike went to the Abercognatic Bog, near the head of the west branch. After hunting about for some hours, they paddled down through the bog, when F., by means of his spy glass, discovered some caribou dead to leeward of him. He landed at once, and by dint of much crawling, creeping, and running managed to get to leeward of them, and was fortunate enough to find cover just when he needed it. The caribou, advancing slowly, had meanwhile come up to within what our hunter considered shooting distance. This animal possesses a great deal of natural curiosity, and the knowledge of this fact induces the hunter, whenever he can get a shot at one and kill, to lie quiet, and remain hidden after he has fired; for though the rest of the herd will run off, still if there is no sight or sound of the enemy to be had they will soon return to try to discover what the trouble is with their companion. In this manner, as many as half a dozen may sometimes be killed from the same point, simply by the hunter observing the precaution of lying still. F. then being in position, waited till the game came within range, and then, ignoring the stalking policy, stepped boldly forth from his concealment and fired at the leader, a splendid old buck, dropping him in his tracks dead. The other two, a cow and a calf, at once took up the line of march and were rushing off at a great rate, when a second shot then struck the former in the shoulder. She was staggered, but not killed, so that another bullet sped on its fatal errand, and rolled her over lifeless. By this time the calf was thoroughly demoralized, and, with his white flag hoisted, was streaking it along at his best pace, only asking to be left alone, and had gone so far that he was hidden from F. by a clump of bushes. F. ran a short distance toward the dead buck, and again caught sight of the calf, which was going straight as an arrow towards the point whither Ike had come. He was waiting to give it a warm reception when, to his astonishment, he saw F. rush out from behind the intervening bushes and throw his rifle to his shoulder, at the same time imitating the call of the old ones. As Ike was directly in range, he thought his time had come.

"Don't shoot me," shrieked he.

"Get out of the way then," came the answer, and before he had time to dodge, the rifle cracked, and the calf rolled heels overhead. Ike, as soon as he had time, discovered that he was unhurt, but badly frightened. The shots were afterwards measured. The one at the buck was 140 paces; the killing one at the cow, which struck her while running, 177 paces, and the one at the calf 198 paces–the paces those of a six footer. When it is remembered that this shooting was made off-hand, and that between each shot the rifle, a breech-loading Sharp, had to be reloaded; that the game was continually moving, and that three or of four bullets struck so exactly in the vitals as to cause instantaneous death, while the fourth only struck an inch or so too high, we think no one will dispute the assertion that it was admirable marksmanship. The late matches between the American and Irish teams developed some remarkable shooting, but, to our mind, nothing done by any member of either team excelled this; for it is one thing to shoot at a target, with the accessories of position, windage, elevation, etc., allowed for and reckoned upon, and quite another to stand up and off-hand, deliver four successive shots at moving game, loading between each, after the first. Not often, indeed, does the sportsman get such a chance, and few and far between are those who could improve it so well.

We have stated that our party separated. While two went to the bog, the other two started for a pond said to be some four miles from camp. A struggle which lasted all day landed the adventurers, after dark, in the midst of an alder swamp, where there was as much chance for game as there is on Broadway, and not till noon of the day following did they succeed in reaching the pond. A few hours' hunt was all they could spare time for, and the result was–not a sight of hide, hoof, or hair of anything in the shape of game, and they had to return, tired, hungry, and disgusted, to find their fortunate companions, and rejoice with them around the camp fire over their wonderful success. The glorious fire of giant logs, backed by the somber forest, its light playing over and reflecting all surrounding objects.

On the morning of September 28th we left the St. Johns pond, and, taking the outlet, started for Baker Lake. This was the first time we had he current in our favor, and the sensation of being helped along was as new as it was pleasant. We were, however, all day working about six miles down stream, so it will be readily seen that this sort of traveling is not the one described by the tuneful individual who informs us what he does as he

"Floats down the river in a gum-tree canoe."

Night overtook us, a jam formed by drift logs in a bend of the brook, and as we had to carry around it, and had terrific rainstorm, accompanied by flurries of snow, we were not afloat agin till the 30th, and did not reach Baker Lake till late on the afternoon of that day. On the morning after our arrival Uncle John heard caribou passing through the woods a short distance from where he was, and we at once started in pursuit, leaving the guides in camp. Knowing that there was a brook bordered by open meadow and emptying into the lake, its course being nearly at right angles with the west shore of the later, we thought it probable we should be able to find the game feeding on the meadow. So, one taking the shore of the lake, and the other a line some three or four hundred yards from it, we started. After working our way through the thick woods with the utmost caution, from nine o'clock in the morning till three in the afternoon, we reached the brook, but could find no game, and had to drag our weary legs back over the very ground we had been so joyously and hopefully traversing before. At such a time as this one is apt to think a hunter's life not what it is said to be, especially when, as in our case, the probability of a supperless and comfortless night is strong. Fortunately, however, we soon discovered one of the guides in his canoe, looking for us, and soon forgot our fatigue, disappointment, and hunger—satisfying the hunger from our well-stocked larder, assuaging the disappointment with quickly-aroused hopes and new resolutions, while boughs and blankets compensated us for the fatigue.

Leaving Baker Lake, October 3rd, we passed down into the main St. Johns River, which we found much swollen by the almost continuous rain we had experienced, and it was while coming down the steep descent from the lake to the river that we had some favorable opportunities of seeing what was meant by "running" rapids. We distinctly recall the feeling which accompanied us through one set of rapids, where Uncle John's talents shone out supreme. We had been coming down a long stretch of dead water, which for ten or fifteen minutes had been gradually changing into a very quick stream, when, coming suddenly around a point, we were startled at the appearance of a long reach of apparently boiling water directly below us, and by the sound of its rushing, then first heard distinctly, as well as the cry of "lookout" from the other occupant of the canoe. One moment we seemed to pause; the next instant the canoe, feeling the effect of a sharp stroke from the stern paddle, with a spring like that of a frightened deer, started from the comparative repose in which she had been lying, right into the breakers. A short rush, a dip, a shiver of the little boat, he calls oft and quickly repeated, of "hold," "paddle hard," :right," "left," the foaming roller as it reared itself seemingly much higher than the gunwale of the canoe, and, apparently just about to board us, then opening or subsiding as thought the touch of the stern of the craft had magic in it, the ugly, sharp, black rock dead ahead, the turn and twist of the cockle shell, the occasional scrape as he dashes madly past some half hidden boulder, the swift, wild leap as she rushes from a danger seen into one almost undiscovered, the terrific force of the falling, surging water, all combined to send the blood through one's veins with accelerated speed. With

teeth hard shut, the muscles braced and quivering with excitement, we rush on, paddle in hand, either resting quietly or working like a flail, as occasion may require, and finally just as we seem
to be surrounded by flying foam, a last, long leap over the final
fall, and the canoe glides out into the still water again, the danger all past, leaving but a realization that scarcely anything is more
pleasant to contemplate than difficulties and obstacles overcome
by strong personal effort. The effect is not unlike that of riding a
swift horse at full speed. His strength has become your own, you
hand and will his only guidance; all depends upon the rider, yet he
is almost powerless, for a mistake would probably launch him into
eternity. In both cases coolness and courage are necessary, and he
who has not both had better try neither the running rapids nor
running horses.

On the evening of the 4th we reached a large lumbering station,
with farm attached, known as Seven Islands. This was the first
taste of civilized life in nearly three weeks, and though perhaps
the accommodation would not compare with those of the "Wind-
sor," we were nevertheless hospitably entertained, and passed a
pleasant night, starting on our way next morning refreshed. On
our way down the river from this point we encountered both fog
and snow, but succeeded, on the evening of het 7th, in getting
within seven miles of Grand Falls, where we found a Frenchman,
who kindly took us in; but as the manner is somewhat peculiar,
the incident may not come in amiss.

The story of the Irishman wrecked on the coast of France, and
attempting to borrow a gridiron, is familiar. We were reminded of
it when Ike volunteered to ask for lodgings in the vernacular and
as a specimen of his knowledge of it remarked that "Donnez moi
un coup" meant "Won't you have a drink?" However, he started,
and after some moments a shout informed us that he had been
successful. Of course the Frenchman was surprised at being asked
in pantomime for a lodging by one who looked as Ike did, and who
use so little ceremony. When, after a minute or so, the second one
of the party appeared, armed with an immense ten-bore, he was

astonished. When, after a short lapse of time, the third opened the door and walked in, present with a savage looking rifle, he was bewildered; but when the fourth one put in an appearance, shouldering a delicate but wicked little twelve, he began to have an idea that he and his family were to be turned out of doors, and much of Ik's French was necessary to assure him it was all right, and that there were no more of us. So he kindly concluded to allow us to camp on his kitchen floor, and after much intelligible but well-meant jargon on both sides, he determined to retire, and all was soon quiet, the stillness only broken by the heavy breathing of our tired party.

On the 8th we started before daylight, determined to reach Woodstock and the end of our journey before sleeping. Suffice it to add we accomplished the allotted task by nine o'clock P.M., thus doing eighty-two miles in bout ten hours actual paddling. If anyone thinks that this is not a good day's work, let him try it and be convinced. We caught trout whenever we stopped long enough to cast a fly, killing plenty of ducks, (embracing four different varieties) some partridges, and incidentals, such as the "lordly heron," etc. Bear signs we saw, and had time permitted, could doubtless have added to our record the capture of a specimen of the tribe of bruin. Otter and mink were seen. One of the former was indeed killed, but as he sank in the deep water before we could reach him he was not captured.

Having spent altogether a most satisfactory three weeks, we determined to advise everyone who is fond of woodland life, and who will endure its hardships for the sake of its pleasures and adventures, to try the Baker Lake trip.

– "MOLLYCHINKEMUNK."

WINDBOUND ON CHAMBERLAIN

By Fanny Pearson Hardy, from *Forest and Stream*, November 7, 1889

Fanny Pearson Hardy Eckstrom (1865-1946) wrote hundreds of books, articles and manuscripts reflecting the areas of her expertise – ornithology, Maine Indians, Indian Geographic Names, Maine History, the Maine Woods, lumbering, log-driving, Thoreau's journeys and Maine folksongs to name a few. For her dedication to Maine history, she received an honorary Master of Arts degree from the University of Maine and upon her death, her life-long collection of material and manuscripts was given to the Fogler Library at the University of Maine at Orono.

Fanny Hardy Eckstrom

One of Maine's most noted authors and researchers, Eckstrom's major works were Penobscot Man (1904), David Libbey, Penobscot Woodman and River Driver (1907), Indian Legends of Katahdin (1924), Minstrelsy of Maine (1927), Indian Place Names of the Penobscot Valley and the Maine Coast (1941) and Old John Neptune and Other Maine Indian Shamans (1945).

This story, which was written before her marriage, was based on one of her many trips to the northern Maine Woods with her father. It appeared in Forest and Stream in 1889, one of her first publications.

It used to be the custom of the old cartographers to leave no blank space on their maps; and when their geographical knowledge gave out they filled the unexplored regions with pictures symbolical of the dangers supposed to be lurking in those wilds–lions and unicorns, dragons, griffins, wyverns, statant couchant, saltant, rampant, guardant, saliant–neither the animals nor their attitudes being calculated to smooth the apprehensions of the adventurous. In like manner we to-day imagine that the woods are full of wild creatures, yet when I reviewed my notes to find some red-letter day full of the birds and their doings, I could not think of one which compared with many spent in the field and hedgerow. There are few birds in the woods. The wilderness is a wilderness indeed, barren of life; and you can find more birds, more plants and more game within five miles of settlements that in an equal space of forest. As Thoreau says: "Generally speaking, a howling wilderness does not howl; it is the imagination of the traveler that does the howling." Since I cannot find a day which is at all note-worthy for the observations it afforded, something prompts me to select one which was wholly ordinary, and yet pleasant to remem-ber; that day when, having crossed Mud Pond Carry, we camped on the side of Chamberlain.

Those who remember the "boundary dispute" of 1842 may locate this lake, on being told hat it lies just north of the highland which the English claimed, the Dutch Commissioners debated upon, and Col. Graham surveyed, as the northeastern boundary of the United States, said "highlands" being Mud Pond Carry *et al.* Those who know the country best concede great credit to Col. Graham's ability in his survey, not only for discovering that the land here is high, but that there is any visible above water. Mud Pond Carry is the most famous road in the State. Thoreau says of it, with a pun on one of our lumbermen's terms, "This was the most perfectly swamped of all the roads I ever saw;" but the remark is lacking in originality to those who have seen the place. Mud Pond Carry leads to Mud Pond, and Mud Pond outlets into Chamberlain Lake, the largest lake in Maine tributary to the St. John.

We were belated in crossing the carry, and we delayed a little paddling across Mud Pond, for after a week of rain this morning seemed doubly fine, and the view of Katahdin–grand old Katahdin–lacking nothing of being a perfect mountain, and as savage to-day as when Leif Erickson landed, was so glorious that we could not resist it. Then there was a half a mile of quick water at the outlet, where the canoe had to be "waded" down, while the passengers went overland by the carry until they reached the meadows, where they (the passengers aforesaid) stood on stumps in order to keep out of the water, and surveyed the wide, green meadows, fair in color, but desolate to look on, because of the standing dead trees, killed by the flowage, until the canoe came down. Then there was a short voyage through the meadows, past newly-built muskrat houses. At one place the wind brought down the smell of tainted meat—some moose or caribou which had been left to spoil. All these delays consumed valuable time, and meanwhile the wind had risen as we had feared it would, when we were so hindered in crossing the carry. When at last the lake was reached, such a sea was running that it was deemed impudent to attempt to cross.

Chamberlain Lake is twelve miles long by two or three miles wide and has the honor of being a very ugly lake, which in woods parlance is equivalent to dangerous. It lies over 900 ft., above the sea, extended from northwest to southeast, without an island in it capable of affording any shelter, and not only exposed to all the winds, but subject to draughts which raise a cross and choppy sea. It is also distinguished by having two inlets and two outlets, one of them artificial. It is not a beautiful lake. There is no high land near it, and the shores, which are straight and forbidding, are even to this day fenced with the trees killed by the flowage when the locks were built nearly fifty years ago. The locks about which a word should be said, are at the natural outlet—two dams with a space between them, built for the purpose of driving logs cut on the lower lake, which naturally would go down the St. John, up into Chamberlain, thence through Telosinis and Telos, and down the artificial "cut" into the Penobscot. The locks have nothing to do with navigation, no boat larger than a batteau ever floated on Chamberlain.

We held the canoe in the Mud Brook inlet for a time, and looked at the heavy sea which was running outside; listened to the doleful creaking of the dead wood as the waves sawed one long tree against another, and subsiding showed ugly black snags sticking out, on which a canoe could be wrecked instantly; looked again at the farm opposite, and reluctantly drew back. Experience, is one of her hardest lessons, had taught one of the party not to dare Chamberlain needlessly. As we turned we saw some small duck dipping and feeding among the driftwood, but just as the gun was pointed at him he saved himself by diving. One may be a strict bird defender at home, but in the woods goes to fill the kettle.

We were more easily consoled for our failure to cross because it was dinner time. We managed with some difficulty to get ashore on the right side of the stream, in a growth of sapling birch and poplar; and, fortunately, remembered to build our fire where the smoke would not attract the attention of the men at the farm. For now, as in Thoreau's day, a smoke near the inlet is a signal for the farm to send a canoe across, some two miles and a half. Even in their great sea canoes this would have been no easy task on such a day. Mr. Coe, the owner of the farm, tells me that in winter they always leave a lamp burning all night, to guide any wandering lumberman belated on the lake.

Dinner is not an elaborate meal in the woods. Ours was soon finished, and we had the afternoon before us; for evidently we were windbound. "And yet the wind might go down," we said, watching the treetops bend, and knowing very well that there was no such happiness in store. How beautiful across the angry lake the farm looked, seated on the sloping hillside among fields colored with the soft rich hues of growing grain, of grass land and of cultivated soil. No one of the other "supply" farms compares with this picturesqueness, as seen across the lake.

These great farms are a surprise to strangers. Here is Chamberlain, some 80 miles from the nearest railroad, and 60 miles from the nearest main road, one of the only two houses on a block of twenty-eight townships–a space larger than the State of Rhode Island. What can be done with the produce of these hundreds of acres? It is all for the winter's business. For fifty years this farm has raised hay and grain for the lumbermen's cattle, and potatoes for the men themselves. It is too cold here to ripen maize, although at Trout Brook Farm 30 miles to the east a little is grown. A few staple vegetables are raised, and these, with the large quantities of grain and hay, are the objects of the farm's existence.

While we were thus forced to lie still, there was a good opportunity given to watch the birds; but except for a kingfisher which sat on the other side of the stream, and some impudent Canada jays which came *ca-ca-ca*-ing about, I saw nothing. The jays tiptoed about on the trees, bowing and bending; they fluttered down with spread wings and tails, and made themselves such nuisances, that until one of them came under the scalpel of the taxidermist there was no peace to be had. I should not omit from the list of birds two partridges, which made an excellent stew a little later, and a herring gull which sat on a rock in the lake about 200 yds. Off, and was saved only by the ball falling a little short of him. There large lakes are close reproductions of the seashore, even to the sea guns which breed here, although they are never seen between the lower end of Moosehead and salt water. It would be unkind not to mention the beautiful green caterpillar that lived on a poplar nearby, so strong, so firm in his muscles, so silken skinned, and so intelligent in his determination to go to the place he had in mind, that I remember him with pleasure. But, except for a dish of raspberries, that was all that the woods had for us. What city garden would not have yielded more in half a day?

The wind did not abate as we had hoped; so, at last, the tent was pitched on the same spot where some one else had been windbound before us. But the afternoon had not passed unpleasantly; it was too great a treat to see blue sky above us after our rainy week to demur at having to wait for the wind. And, then, we had resolved to get up before the wind the next morning. That night the woods mouse came into the tent and hopped over me, tapping my face softly. Camping out sometimes gives one strange bedfellows–toads, lizards, bats, flying squirrels, and mice to wit; but it is all part of the fun.

The next morning our first call came at 2 A.M., but this was reconsidered, and for two hours more we were allowed to sleep.

Then a hasty toilet in the dark, a cold bite, and the tent was struck, the baggage packed, the canoe loaded, and we were off before daylight. The lake was smooth as glass; yesterday's swell was lost in the calm which on fresh water follows so quickly on the subsistence of the wind. Off in the east a red line pierced the gloom, and spread until it lighted all the heavens on that side with fiery, vermilion-tinted hues, leaving the treetops black and jagged as the walls of a burning building. Overhead flew a young herring gull, and he, too, looked black in this morning conflagration.

And now the water began to curdle like hot milk. Before the sun was fairly up the wind began to ripple over the surface of the water, gathering force as it went, which was in a direction opposite from that which the curdle came. The wind was up, the waves roiled and broke, but we were across Chamberlain.

– FANNY PEARSON HARDY.

A BEAR'S FREAK

By F. T., from *Forest and Stream*, February 23, 1893

PROVIDENCE, Rhode Island–One day more and we must turn homeward. For ten days we two "sporters," with a guide and a helper, had been camped on the shores of a beautiful little lake among the Canadian mountains near the Maine boundary. We had killed a fine caribou soon after our arrival, and, our larder being amply supplied, we had taken life easy, enjoying the woods, now bright in the glory of their autumn coloring, the mountains rising in gentle slopes about us, the clear pure air, and the sense of freedom. But now we wanted some wild meat to take home, and arranged that the guide and I should hunt on the morrow.

The cold fog of morning lay heavy on our little lake as our guide paddled me across at early dawn. For two miles I followed a logging road, then turned off for a mile to a little pond where I had found our first caribou. Quiet it lay in the forest bed, with not a ripple on its surface nor a sign of life on its shores. I looked along the margin for fresh tracks, but seeing none, turned back, retracing my steps slowly thinking where I should go next, when across the pond a spot of white caught my eye. It moved, and soon I could plainly see a small caribou walking away from me. Quickly as possible I placed myself behind a point of rocks out of sight of the animal. Then I hurried to the point, and crouching low, worked my way over the rocks and looked along the shore. The little caribou, a yearling, was about 200 yards away, and fifty years nearer was a much larger one, a full-grown cow. The cow was feeding and walking slowly almost directly away from me. On one knee, with rifle cocked and ready, I waited, hoping she would turn so as to give me a quartering shot, and she did turn just enough to give me a narrow view of her side and neck. Then I fired. The 45cal, hollow-pointed ball struck the hind leg about six inches above the gambrel joint. The animal seemed crazed by the shock, falling partly down and jumping in and out of the water till I could fire again, putting a ball through her neck, when she fell dead in about eight inches of water. I was not able to move her from the place where she fell, so I went to work taking off the skin and dressing out the meat, standing in the water.

Before I had been long at this work I heard some animal make two jumps in the bushes about three rods from me. Quickly I secreted myself behind a tree with rifle ready, thinking a bull was following the tracks of the cow and might show himself. Again all was still, and I resumed my work. Just a little noise occasionally came from the bushes, a slight rustling of the leaves or the breaking of a little stick. I removed the skin with the head attached, and as it was too heavy to carry, placed it over a big log at the water's edge. Then with my skinning knife, I separated one ham to carry to camp, and placed the rest of the meat beside the skin. Back to camp I went, and before noon, our guide and his helper started to bring in the skin and as much meat as they could carry.

They returned loaded with meat, but could not find the skin. It had disappeared, the meat by its side being undisturbed. The men thought they had misunderstood me, and that I started with the hide and had left it somewhere on the way because it was too heavy.

There were fresh bear tracks near the meat, but they supposed these were made before the caribou was killed.

We had no time to investigate this mystery, as we must make fifteen miles over a bad trail the next day. This was in the fall of 1892.

Our guide recently writes that he went back to the place where the hide was lost, and by hairs on the roots and bushes was able to follow where the hair had been dragged till he found the bones of the skull and pieces of skin with quantities of hair where a bear had torn up the skin.

The bear must have been watching for me and waiting for me

to leave so that he could help himself, and it was him I heard in the bushes. But why did he take the skin and leave those fine caribou steaks?   Strange, was it not?

– F.T.

AWFULLY EASY, "DONCHERNOW"

By George F. Thompson, from *The Maine Sportsman*, January 1895

George F. Thompson (1845-1904), a steam heating engineer, resided in New Gloucester, Maine, but worked in Lewiston, where he and William H. Carmen, ran a plumbing enterprise known as Carmen & Thompson. Thompson, treasurer of the firm and an avid outdoorsman, put this humorous story into the Lewiston Journal, which The Maine Sportsman later reprinted.

Deer Hunting (Currier & Ives 1857)

It was George F. Thompson of the Carman-Thompson Company of Lewiston who told this story at the club, and it is true says the Lewiston Journal. It relates to a certain camp up in Howland, near where John A. Greenleaf of Auburn has put in a big sulphite mill and where they built that wonderful aerial railroad for handling bricks and other material for building the mill. Every fall a royal time is had at this camp and the owners, who are also in the big-mill, invite a lot of New York men down to camp. Some of them are lazy—men who would like to shoot bear if they could do it on Broadway, but most of them are indefatigable hunters.

A few years ago one of the former sort reached the camp. He was "doosid tired" before he got there and he wanted cigarettes and a brandy and soda when he arrived. When they go for deer up there they don't wait until after dinner. They go before breakfast. This gentleman said he'd "be shot f he'd get up at 4:30 A. M., begad, for all the deer, don't you know, in the state of—ah! What state is this, fellahs?"

They went without him and he awoke at eight, had the cook grill him a nice bone and made him some café royal and then he put on his corduroys, breakfasted, lit a cigar and took a couple of chairs out in the sun by the brook and sat down and smoked and read. A good many stories have been told about what happened after this, but whatever is said it can in no possible way be turned to the detriment of the lazy man, for as he sat there reading and smoking into the perfect air of a warm November day, "Crash!" and through the bushes with a snort and a leap bounded a cari- bou. The New York man jumped four feet, he says, albeit he is a philosopher. The caribou gathered for another spring when he lost footing on the crumbling earth and fell back into a pool, a deep sort of basin about fifty yards from the camp and near where the New York gentleman was sitting. The latter took in the situa- tion instantly. The caribou floundered and pounded and snorted.

A caribou, under pressure of disaster is not like a cosset or the lamb that Mary had. The New York man appreciated this and dug for the camp. Once there, he calmly lit a cigar, took out his rifle, loaded it, went back to his chair and looked for the caribou. He was still there, stuck in the mud. The New York gentleman thought it over, sat down in the chair and finally decided to kill the caribou. He was having a hunt for himself and didn't even invite the cook. He fired fourteen times at the beast and finally killed him. Then he called for the cook, and they brought the cari- bou out and hung him up on the outside of the camp.

That night a weary, disheartened, ragged, bedraggled crowd of hunters came into camp. They were met by the New York gen- tleman, who wore his corduroys still speckles and unsullied. He asked them what luck, and they said not a hair.

"Well, fellahs," said he, "you shouldn't hunt so hawd, don't you know. Occasionally, if you be seated calmly by the river's brink, the deer will come to be shot, and I have taken only one—a caribou—today, but I shall do bettah tomorrow."

Solemn was the file of hunters that passed out by lantern-light to view the big game. Many a man in the party would have given $500 to have shot the animal, but for a lazy, cynical, sybaritic duf- fer like the gentleman in corduroys, to sit in an arm chair and have the game come up and jump in the mud-puddle and wait for him to find time to shoot it, was too much. They all used language that

Noah Webster didn't put into his dictionary and they used it sixty beats to the minute.

The horns of that caribou, for it was a male, now hang in the office of a down-town broker in New York and he tells the story of how easy it is to shoot game in Maine if you only have a mud-puddle and the game close at hand.

A SKIRMISH WITH A LOUP-CERVIER

By J. W. Strout, from *Forest and Stream*, September 28, 1895

The Reverend J. W Strout, whose congregation was first at Tiverton and later at Providence, Rhode Island, took his annual vacation in 1893 to a town "thirty five miles northwest of Bangor," which was probably in the town of Lincoln, fitting his description.

I am not much of a gunner, as the reader will perceive before he has finished this sketch, only a plain minister with a strong fascination for the woods and a little shooting now and then at the swift-winged partridge or the quick-witted woodcock, so I never lose an opportunity to take my three weeks' vacation in October among the lakes and forests of northern Maine. After a close and hard summer, therefore, it was with a great sigh of relief that two years ago I boarded the train and hastened to a little town some thirty-five miles northwest of Bangor, which has always been my base of supply on these occasions. One does not look for large game in this vicinity; now and then a stray fox, as the sun hides him under the hills, runs across the path and stirs the blood a little, and once in a while a wildcat is heard and sometimes seen; the partridge and woodcock and duck often abound, and the gunning is good. Deer are often seen at nightfall drinking from the lakes, but I never could bring myself up to the point of shooting one of the graceful creatures.

The morning after my arrival in this hamlet, a fine October day, with a small fowling-piece not in very good condition, having been at rest for at least ten months, but with its single barrel very well answered my purpose. I set out for the hunting grounds. A large pond lies among the hills and sends an arm into the heart of the village here, so that one has only to spring into his boat and row away under a bridge or two a brief five minutes to find himself on the surface of a fine lake, surrounded by hills, some highly cultivated, some heavily wooded, full of inspiration and zeal. I reached the "inlet" in about forty-five minutes. It is so called because it is the entrance of a small stream into the lake, which flowing through the marshy ground, has hollowed itself into a channel without perceptible current for a mile or more. It winds around long points and through dense shrubbery, now almost hidden by the overhanging woods, now creeping from luxuriant growths of grasses, now opening out clear with muddy shores, or entering a labyrinth of fallen trees and old stumps. It varies in width from 75 to 150 ft., so that one can easily scan both banks as he rows along.

As I entered it the hush of a New England autumn was on the stream and among the woods, inviting one to dream rather than to shoot. The foliage was rich. One could count a hundred different tints from green to yellow, red to vermillion. The stream narrows down gradually, and at last I reached the old log that served me these several years for a wharf, and hiding my fishing tackle which I always carried, for sometimes the fish were more gullible that the partridge. I plunged into the forest.

Partridges and woodcocks were scarce that morning, but with little care I meandered along the old woods roads, finely shaded, among which squirrels were chattering and birds flitting. Once in a while a gray squirrel would scamper across the path and mount some old fence or tree. Most everything was there, except the game I wanted.

At last I reached a growth of spruce and hemlock and began to wake up and look about me. It was on the side of a ravine where, the previous winter, a great many hemlocks had been felled and the bark stripped from them, leaving the logs to be yarded the coming winter. The frost was still on the ground here, making it necessary to move with caution, for one was likely to slip and then to slide somewhat unbecomingly down the hill. I was stepping along thus lightly, now on a more level bit of ground, when I heard a rustling among the leaves on the opposite side of the little brook that runs through this ravine, and supposing it to be a partridge sat down on a log to await her approach. A half of a minute I suppose I waited, when, springing noiselessly upon a pile of wood not 20 yards distant, a large loup-cervier appeared in full view. I did not wait for him to see me, but fired instantly, and the next instant found myself flat on my back with my feet on the log I had so suddenly vacated, and wondering if I had hurt the animal as much as I had myself—for this gun seemed to shoot from both ends—I hastily scrambled to my feet. Well, there sat the creature in the coolest possible condition in exactly the same place I first saw him. Apparently he had watched the proceeding with some interest, but entirely unmoved. Hastily reloading, I fired again, directly in his face, bracing myself for the rebound of my gun, when, instead of getting his eyes put out or running away, he bounded toward me, but hesitated before reaching my place and looked defiant enough. Evidently partridge shot were not having much effect on its tough skin, but I reloaded and taking its gentle hints to be careful, stood cautiously on the defensive.

We stood and looked each other directly in the eyes, I guess, two minutes, when it slowly turned, and with a glance over his shoulder every now and then at me, walked the length of the long log, sprang to the ground and moved away. I did not follow for it had sat still and made itself a target for me to shoot at twice, within easy range, and now, though I bethought me of several shells, in my left pocket loaded for duck, it seemed cowardly to strike at its back. I had lost the battle in a fair fight.

I had also lost my zest for gunning in that particular place, so hurried back toward my boat; but in my haste ran clumsily into a flock of partridges, which scattered in every direction, leaving only one as the result of a startled and random shot. Being near my boat, I left this one in the stern under an old piece of canvas, and hurried after the others; and after an hours' hunt succeeded in getting one, and returned to the river. I was within 30 feet of the boat, I should judge, when to my consternation, that loup-cervier sprang from the stern sheets with my partridge in its mouth. It did not run, but sat quietly down on the opposite bank of the stream, perhaps 40 feet distant, and looked defiantly at me. My gun had only one partridge shot in it, and it would be useless to fire. But to remove the shell and substitute another with duck shot, while the work of a few seconds only, might scare the creature away or inspire it to something worse. I concluded, however, that such was the only thing for me to do, and if it fled or attacked me I must take the consequences. That exchange of shells was a quick process, the reader may be assured, and did not disturb the thief at all. I fired, and it sprang sidewise into the woods and disappeared, leaving my bird on the bank. I noticed also a good many hairs and slight traces of blood, showing that this time my shot had made an impression. I waded across the brook to the place from which it disappeared, and with extreme caution followed its trail as nearly as I could among the leaves, with a careful eye to the trees, for I suspected the creature might be in somewhat of a fighting mood now, and perhaps would take the chances at a hand-to-hand fight with me.

I might possibly have gone ten rods in this cautious manner, when apparently from directly overhead came a terrific yell that lifted my hair and started the cold shivers down my spine. It proved not quite overhead, however, but in front of me, so that I caught sight of it and had my gun leveled and ready for a spring instantly; and not an instant too soon, for it sprang at me with tremendous force. I fired and down it came, not quite where it planned—on my head—but among the rocks and leaves at my feet, with a charge of duck shot in its head. I got out of the way in a hurry, but finding there was no further danger, returned and shot it dead.

– J.W. STROUT, MASSACHUSETTS.

THAT BARREL OF SPRUCE GUM

By Charles A. Stephens, from *Youth's Companion*, 1897

After creating a number of stories for The Youth's Companion, a popular juvenile magazine of the late nineteenth century, Stephens, who often used pen manes, such as Alfred Leon Poindexter, later became an assistant editor for that periodical and was a traveling correspondent for 60 years. He also wrote many articles for both local and national periodicals and since many of these took on a medical aspect, he went to Boston University and received a medical degree in 1887.

Charles A. Stevens

Stephens was a prolific writer, turning out some 2,500 articles and 30 books during his long career. Many of his stories involve rural characters, but a few were set in the woods of Maine.

Prior to the creation of modern chewing gum, all gum was made from the pitchy sap found on spruce trees. Spruce gum was a much sought after commodity, going for a good price, the only problem was locating enough of the pitch to make the venture successful. The spruce gum gatherers had to move further and further into the wilds in search of this precious substance.

Chewing Gum is considered by many persons as a vulgar habit. Others ridicule it on account of the exercise—working one's jaws for nothing, so to speak. The fact remains, however, that very many persons, particularly the young, chew gum and appear to enjoy it.

The writer once asked a celebrated physiologist – one of the most eminent in the United States – if he could account for the gum habit. He replied promptly and with a smile that he thought he could and proceeded to explain it.

"Human beings as we at present meet them in this nineteenth century are descended from ancestors who subsisted on tougher, harder, less well-cooked and prepared food than appears on our tables today," said he, "Also they were more active, physically, and ate more food, such as it was. In consequence, they were obliged to bite and chew more vigorously and more protractedly. Of course, therefore, the muscles of mastication, attached to the jaw – masseter, pterygold, temporal, succinator, and others – were larger and more fully developed than in the modern man. Because of this we may suppose that there lies dormant in all our jaws a certain amount of unused, inherited capacity to bite and chew more than we do at present; and wherever such latent capacity exists there will be exhibited a vagrant desire to use it and a pleasure in doing so. Hence the gum industry."

"Then if I understand you, professor," I said, "the practice is natural and all right."

"Perfectly natural, possibly beneficial," he said, still smiling.

"But as to the vulgarity?" I queried.

"Oh well, "replied the professor, laughing outright, "There are a great many people among us who for various reasons quite naturally try to be finer than they have the natural basis for."

I chewed gum on the strength of this latter sentiment for several months, when it began to dawn upon me that there are undoubtedly traits descending to us from our ancestors which it is good taste and possibly good morals to tone down considerably.

Spruce gum usually retails for ten cents per ounce in the drug stores of our cities, and a superior article of ten sells for fifteen cents, or two dollars and forty cents per pound avoirdupois, which seems to be a high price. It is worth the money, however. There is a great deal of exercise for the masseter muscle in even one ounce of it. An ounce of good purple gum will keep a person with the strongest ancestral traits busy six hours a day for a fortnight, and by the end of that time his "latent inherited capacity" will need a rest.

The person who collects the gum in the great forests of Maine and New Hampshire does not enrich himself too rapidly at this price, although it should be remarked that he rarely receives more than a dollar per pound for his product, frequently less. The "middlemen" secures the lion's share of the profits. My sympathies are for the fellow who digs the gum in the distant wilderness, for I once essayed that occupation myself, for a brief period.

In the summer of 1878, being then a boy in the high school, I went to Maine for my vacation and spent a fortnight at Mt. Kineo, Moosehead Lake. Fletcher Sanderson, a classmate, whose father kept then a drug store in Boston, accompanied me.

In the course of two weeks we had tired of hotel life at Mt. Kineo, and determined to go off camping and canoeing to the more northerly lakes, on our own account. Accordingly, we bought a birch canoe, laid in a stock of provisions, and contrary to all advice, set off without a guide; for we greatly desired to "rough it," and see how it would seem to be alone in the woods at night.

I may add here –by way of parenthesis – that we had quite enough of that sort of experience before we saw human habitations again.

Embarking on the west branch of the Penobscot River, two miles from the northerly arm of Moosehead Lake, we descended the Umbazooksous, crossed the "divide" to Chamberlain Lake, and paddled northerly through Eagle and Heron Lakes.

Still heading northward, we descended the rapid Allaguash River for two days, to the beautiful Umsaskis Lake, where, on the northwest shore, near the passage into Long Lake, we camped in one of the most romantically wild spots I have ever seen.

We had been fifteen days reaching this point; we had endured not a little hardship, we had encountered some danger from wind and rapids, we had spent a good deal of time in trying to keep our birch canoe water-tight by "firing" and resmoothing the gum which protected its sewn joints; but on the whole we had enjoyed ourselves well.

While hunting in the woods to the west of Umsaskis we came upon a logger's hut near the foot of a mountain. Here, for the first time in our lives, we saw a moose. Moose tracks were visible all about this old hovel, which had evidently been deserted for several years.

Fletcher discovered in the hut several quarts of sound white beans in a nail-keg, and two or three pounds of sugar at the bottom of an old sugar-barrel; also some salt, and a box containing half a pound or more of moldy tea. There were trout in a small brook which flows down from the mountain to the lake; and we shot partridges nearly every day along the lake shore. The place suited us so well that we moved camp from the lake to the old log hovel, and had thoughts of quitting school and civilization altogether, for a life in the wilderness. All around to the west and northwest of the lake up the mountainside there was then one great spruce forest; and soon we began to notice the gum on the trunks of the trees. At first we merely dug off a few lumps of it to chew. Then we melted some of it with care and dabbed it on the seams of our canoe. It was very good purple gum. On some trees there would be seen as many as twenty lumps, some of them as large as a small hen's egg.

Moving through that dim virgin forest, peering for gum-trees, was a pleasant occupation and one requiring careful observation, for not more than one tree in twenty yielded enough gum to be worth the digging.

By the second day we spoke of collecting a lot of gum to give to our friends in Boston, made up in packages, wrapped in white birch bark, but by the third day a more ambitious project had entered our minds.

"It doesn't take long to dig a pound of gum here," Fletcher said; "and this stuff is worth a dollar and a half a pound in our pharmacy in Boston. Let's dig a lot of it to take home to sell. Wouldn't our folks be astonished to see us coming home with two hundred dollars' worth of gum to show for our trip!"

"But how could we transport such a load from the woods?" I said.

"Oh, we can get out somehow!" exclaimed Fletcher. "We can

put it in this old sugar-barrel. Fill it full and lay it in the bottom of our canoe."

We entered on the work with zeal. For a week we ranged the forest to the west of Umsaskis Lake; and each evening we cleaned and scraped the lumps of gum with our knives, clearing from them bits of bark and moss.

Fletcher had constructed a rude sort of ladder which enabled him to climb up the trunks of the spruce-trees to a height of twelve or fifteen feet, and we carried this around with us for use when the gum was too high up to be reached from the ground.

Meantime our stock of provisions was almost wholly exhausted, and but for the beans in the old camp, and the fish and partridges, famine would have compelled us to abandon our project. As it was, our meals were boiled beans and salt, fried trout and salt, and boiled partridge and salt. For the last three days we had no bread; but we "gummed" steadily, and our large sugar-barrel was full of excellent gum on the eighth day. Old gum-collectors tell me that gum is seldom found in such quantity as we found it there.

Why the sap of the spruce exudes to form gum, I do not exactly know. Some believe it flows from small punctures in the bark made by insects; others that it comes through small cracks, caused by the tree's freezing and thawing in winter. A drop of pitch must remain on the tree for a number of years before it becomes "ripe" as chewing-gum. Gum is sometimes found thirty or forty years old. It is well-nigh impervious to weather.

On the morning of the ninth day we carried our barrel of spruce gum from the hut down to the shore of the lake on a stretcher, formed by two poles and cross-sticks. It was a heavy burden. We estimated the weight of the gum at one hundred and fifty pounds, and that of the barrel at twenty-five pounds.

To transport that barrel of gum up the Allaguash, over the "carries" which we had crossed on our way from Moosehead Lake, was quite beyond our strength; but our pocket-map of northern Maine showed that by continuing on down the Allaguash we might enter the St. John River and reach Fort Kent in Maine or Edmundston in New Brunswick, where a stage connected with railroad transportation. Although we knew nothing more of the route, nor what vicissitudes might attend the venture, we resolved to chance it.

For breakfast on that ninth morning we had merely a scrap of pork, a trout and a sucker, garnished with salt. The beans were all gone, and we were so tired of them that scarcely regretted their absence.

Fortunately, Long Lake, next below Umsaskis, was calm that day; and at three o'clock in the afternoon we reached a clearing at the foot of it, where the Allaguash emerges. From a settler named Harvey, who lived there, we bought thirty pounds of flour, ten pounds of salt pork, a package of baking- powder, five pounds of cheese, and what coffee and sugar we needed. Delighted with this abundance, we camped on the river-bank a mile or two below, and indulged in a feast. At home such plain fare would certainly not have been deemed luxurious.

Next morning we went on down the river with our barrel, but were obliged to proceed cautiously, for the Allaguash was low, and one gash on the rocks might put our canoe beyond repair. There were miles of shallow gravels, with occasionally a rapid. As neither of us had acquired much skill with a canoe in quick water, we chanced to upset on running out of a strong current into an eddy, which gave us back to the current. The water was not so deep nor swift but we were able to get out; but our canoe filled, and the gum-barrel floated away.

With an eye to the main chance, Fletcher chased alongshore after the barrel, leaving me to right the canoe and rescue the provisions. I recovered the pork and cheese all right, but the flour was dough, and all our sugar went to sweeten the Allaguash.

Fletcher soon overtook the barrel, which had become water-logged and grounded on a bar. He rolled it ashore. When I reached him with the canoe and our damaged provisions, wet guns and saturated camp-kit, he was attempting to drain out the water by rolling the barrel over stones on the shore.

In fear lest moisture in the barrel might induce mold and injure the gum, we unheaded it on a large flat, ledge, and spread the gum out to dry on the smooth rock, together with our other property, including the soaked and swollen flour.

Night came on while we were laid up there; and next morning a northeast rain-storm was upon us. It continued for three days, and there we stayed, the flour gradually washing away.

To reinforce our diminished food supply, we were obliged to fish in the driving rain. There was not a dry thread in our clothing, our tent, or our blankets, and the temperature was low.

On the fourth day the sun came out, and our gum was dry enough to rebarrel early in the afternoon. Luckily for us we reached a French-Canadian farm that evening, and were able to buy bread, milk and some very strange butter which, though a rarity, we did not become fond of.

Next day we came to Allaguash Falls, a pretty cataract of thirty-five feet, and were occupied until evening carrying our barrel and canoe around it to the pool below.

The confluence of the Allaguash with the St. John River is eleven or twelve miles below the falls. The farms of French settlers are here found on both banks of the St. John, with oft-recurring hamlets, each containing its Catholic Church, store and post-office.

Eggs, brad and even poultry could now be purchased at easy prices; and as for milk and potatoes, the kind-hearted people seemed anxious to give them to us.

This land was like unto the primitive eighteenth-century Acadia which Longfellow immortalized in "Evangeline." But, oh, the butter of the country! Perhaps Longfellow never tasted that. Certainly he could not have treated Evangeline as a maiden of romance had he conceived her capable of making one pound of the kind.

The St. John, like the Allaguash, was low. There were many

slight rapids. At the foot of one of them we upset again during the afternoon, but did not stop to dry our gum; and that night we camped on the south shore of the river, opposite the French and Indian village of St. Francis. We pitched our tent among willow and hazel-bushes on the high bank of the stream, back some distance from the water, where we found hazelnuts as large as filberts.

The question arose with us whether we should fetch our gum-barrel and canoe from the water up to our camp, or leave them where they were. We had turned the canoe upside down beside the barrel, and placed both on a wide, flat rock.

"Oh, these folks are all honest!" said Fletcher. "They would not steal anything. These are Acadians, you know. Theft is unknown here—Longfellow said so."

"Oh this is a long distance from Grand Pre," said I. "And weren't the Acadians all transported to Louisiana anyhow? And if some of them did return to Nova Scotia, we don't know that any of them found their way to the St. John River between New Brunswick and Maine."

"Well maybe I am a little mixed up in my geography, but they're good enough Acadians for me to-night," said Fletcher. "The barrel and canoe are wet and heavy, and I'm pretty tired. Let's take Longfellow's word for the character of Acadians, and let's go to sleep;" which we did on short order.

The next morning I had a vague recollection of having heard a boat paddled on the river, but the sound had not fully roused me from sleep; and pity that it was so, for our canoe and barrel were missing!

Fletcher, who discovered this first, called to me in great excitement that our property had been stolen. We ran down to the place where it should have been. Not a trace of the canoe or the barrel of gum could be seen anywhere. Both had evidently been stolen, although it puzzled us to know what Acadians could want of so much spruce-gum. We concluded that they must have mistaken it, in the night, for sugar or flour.

A little way below there was a shallow. We took off our clothes and waded across the river, in about four feet of water, and then went to the village of St. Francis. As the storekeeper here could speak English, we told him of our loss and asked his advice. The man appeared to pity us, but instead of advising us, took us to the Catholic priest and told him of our misfortune. His reverence appeared to regard the case as one passing understanding, and declined to advise us, save in a very general manner.

As our guns still remained with us, we decided to go along the river-bank and search in force for the canoe; so I recrossed to the Maine side, while Fletcher followed down the Canadian bank. We marched in sight of each other for several miles, when Fletcher discovered a trail in the sand at the water's edge, where a canoe had recently been drawn up. This was near where a brook flowed into the river, and not far up the brook stood a sawmill not then in operation. There were very thick alder, hazel and willow-brushes along the brook.

After he had examined the trail in the sand, Fletcher shouted to me, and I again forded the river. We then began searching the brushes, and presently found the canoe, hidden away beneath running vines among willows and high weeds.

"The gum-barrel is not far off!" exclaimed Fletcher; and again we searched the bushes along both banks of the brook. Just below the saw mill there was great heap of yellow sawdust, one side of which seemed to have been recently disturbed. Into this I thrust an old pike-pole which I had picked up in the mill, and I had not prodded many times when the point hit something hard, which proved to be our barrel.

Whether the thief or anyone else saw us unearth our property I cannot say, but we took possession of it and poled back up the river to our tent, where we found that during our absence some-one had taken our blankets and several other articles.

"These Acadians are certainly a different breed from Longfellow's," said Fletcher.

"I told you that long ago," said I. "But we must not give them a bad name because we know there's one thief among them."

We had plenty of ammunition left, and signalized the triumphant recovery of the barrel by firing twenty shots on the river as we resumed our voyage.

At noon that day we reached Fort Kent, where we found Americans and the English language. From this place the barrel went to Boston as freight, by stage and railroad, without further adventure.

The gum sold for about what we had anticipated, nearly two hundred dollars; but Fletcher and I always felt that we had fully earned all that we received.

– ALFRED LEON PENDEXTER.

AFLOAT IN A BIG BLOW

By George E. Weeman, from *Maine Sportsman*, April 1901

George Edward Weeman (1867-1918) was born at Bridgeton and remained there all his life, working as a carpenter. For a few years he followed his favorite sport, working as a guide in the northern part of Maine and related the following story of his adventures.

American Field
Sports: An Early Start
(Currier & Ives 1863

I was engaged guiding a party of three young men from Massachusetts, through the first weeks of October. We were camped on the shore of one of the largest northern lakes. The weather had not been good for hunting. Heavy rains had kept us in the camp a great part of the time, and had driven the game back into the swamps and thick forests. The boys were beginning to get restless as the day for their departure drew near. I was familiar with all the best hunting ground in that section, and had spent several seasons guiding a party at a small pond, some five or six miles from our present camp. I had told the boys, I suppose, some rather highly colored stories of the wonderful hunting and fishing I had formerly found in the vicinity of this pond, and naturally aroused in them a great desire to visit such a hunter's paradise. It required little urging from me to consent to make a trip with them to this pond, and spend a few days in the locality. The wind had been blowing a gale on the lake for many days, making it impossible to get out with a canoe in safety, but after waiting a number of days, we awoke one morning and found the rain had ceased and the lake was calm and still. So quickly packing our canoe with tent and blankets, together with what provisions we needed, we quietly made the trip across the lake and up a shallow stream to the pond, to a place where I had decided to camp.

We arrived there about noon, pitched our tent, and prepared dinner, after which I concluded to take the boys for a tramp over the best hunting grounds and show them some of the various tote roads that would lead them to camp. We had travelled back some two miles in the direction of the mountains, when we were suddenly taken over by a shower of such violence that we were instantly drenched to the skin, and as it continued to "pour," we made our way as best we could, through the wet bushes and pelting rain, back to camp.

It was nearly dark when we arrived, wet and tired. We had no change of clothing so we ate our supper and, wet as we were, rolled ourselves in our blankets, while the rain continued to fall in torrents. It was no new experience to me, but to the others it was decidedly new and unpleasant, so much so that the following morning the three expressed but one wish, without one dissenting vote, that we get back to our more comfortable log camp without delay. After trying in vain to have them remain til the next day, I prepared breakfast, packed our "traps" into the canoe and we started on our return trip to the old camp. We passed safely down the stream of the lake, and found it as glass, without a ripple.

The rain had ceased during the night and even the lake seemed smiling its welcome, as we embarked in our canoe, which with four persons and a lot of baggage was much overloaded, even to the water's edge, yet I felt but little concern in the present calm, of safely making the three miles across the arm of the lake. Every move in the canoe had to be made with the greatest care to keep it from shipping water. Things went all right till we were about half way across, when suddenly just ahead I noticed a quick ripple shoot over the water. This was soon followed by another, and then another a little more lengthy and soon the ripples became continuous. Against my face I could feel a rapidly increasing breeze. I began to doubt my wisdom in attempting to cross with so much load in my boat, or I well knew the gales that often spring up on some of these northern lakes, without a minute's warning, and I urged the fellows to paddle for all they were worth.

The wind soon increased in velocity and in a few minutes

became a hurricane. The waves rolled higher and higher, our little canoe plowed through them—she was too heavily loaded to ride on top. Still the wind blew a gale, the waves seemed mountain high and by each one, as it came rolling mildly over us, and we expected to be engulfed. It was no use to turn back, we were as near one shore as the other. I was quite at home in a canoe and pride myself that I can ride as rough a sea or shoot a swift rapid as the best of them. I strained myself to the utmost to keep my little craft under control. We were beginning to take in water rapidly. I told one of the boys to bail, but it came in, in buckets full, he couldn't keep it out. Down came a monstrous wave and half-filled the canoe when it struck—still we floated. The fellow bailing had removed his coat and boots, determined to make a last struggle if it came to the worst. The water was ice cold, and we knew that it would almost be impossible for any of us to reach shore a mile and a half away, by swimming in such icy water. I have been in many places of danger, but can truly say I never felt myself so the dividing line between the light of life and the darkness beyond, as I did during that brief half hour, as I sat in that frail canoe, looking into the white and frightened faces of my companions, with my own face probably none too full of hope, with the foaming and angry, rushing water on every side, the strong wind taking us, faster and faster, out toward the center of the lake.

I urged my comrades to paddle as they never did before. I could do little but keep the canoe headed in the right direction. If we could only get behind a long point of timber reaching out on our left, I felt it would break the force of the wind and we would be safe; we strained every muscle and paddled like mad as slowly neared the shore. If we could only make a hundred yards more or even fifty, we would feel safe. Suddenly there was a lull in the wind, then we came into calmer water and neared the shore more swiftly; the color began to return to our faces; we could see the shiny, sandy bottom, almost touch it with our paddles; and then, at last, thank Providence! We were safely on shore.

As we climbed out of the nearly sunken canoe, with aching

arms and still swiftly beating hearts, we brushed the spray from our faces, and proceeded to turn the water from our canoe. My three young friends in turn grasped my hand, and with almost tears of gratitude, thanked me for bringing them safely out of such a trying position, and I felt filled with pride as they assured me, that should it again be their misfortune to be placed in such danger, they would not ask for more true and trusty hand at the tiller, that that of their old guide. I assured them that at the most critical moments they were cool, and never lost their heads, and that was our only salvation.

Chapter 7

DOWN EAST REGION

The earliest history of the region of Washington and Hancock Counties is along the coast as that was the place first settled. However, much of the region was claimed by both Great Britain and France, the two nations going back and forth in declarations of ownership until England defeated the French at the Plains of Abraham in 1765. However, the region went again through this problem again during the Revolution, with the British owning most of the land east of their stronghold at Castine during most of the war. Once the boundary between the United States and the dominion of Canada was established, the St. Croix River became the established line between the two owners, leaving this entire region as part of Massachusetts, then Maine in 1820. Both counties were set off from Lincoln County in 1789 and named for the nation's first president and a signer of the Declaration of Independence.

The summer of 1851 was very dry and in September, forest fires raged from Eastport to Mount Desert Island, a distance of ninety miles. Several shipyards were in peril and the smoke so thick, the residents of Eastport could not see Campobello Island.

The earliest lumbering was done near the coast, but soon the lumbermen ventured up the various rivers, ever in search of the magnificent pine trees. Little is known or recorded of the earliest lumbering and sporting of this region until the *Machias Union*, the area's earliest newspaper was established in 1852. Also, most the county's numerous lakes and ponds were simply inaccessible to early sportsmen, with early sportsmen focusing on Rangeley and Moosehead Lakes.

Interestingly, the Airline, an old stagecoach road which leads from the Penobscot River to Calais, has a very old history. In 1763 Joseph Frye, the founder of Fryeburg, Maine, and Samuel Jones ran a line from the head of the Penobscot east to the St. Croix River. This dotted path became a rough road which was followed by the earliest settlers of Eddington and Clifton, which are both in Penobscot County. Clifton was settled in 1815, a road begin completed to this town. Entering Hancock County, the next two towns, Amherst and Aurora, were both settled on the Union River in 1805, when the pioneers came up that river from Ellsworth.

The Calais Journal stated in June of 1843 that Custom House Officers at St. Stephens seized a small quantity of leather, in possession of Wm. E. Colwell, a shoemaker in Milltown. A man named John Tobin was suspected and was seized at the toll house on the U. S. side by a party of men in disguise, taken to a field, where he was tarred and feathered.

In 1846 a large freshet, or spring flood, took out 200 feet of the new dam at Milltown and the middle bridge was about to go down the river.

Mill accidents were common. In May of 1855, John Lee, a boy of sixteen years, died from the effects of a blow received while bolting slabs in a lathe mill in Machias. In October of that year, Wm. G. Lincoln, of Machias, who worked at Jenk's and Hill's door and sash factory, got entangled by a machine and was crushed to death.

In 1855, the Russian War had a good effect on the lumber business of the St. Croix River, as France and Spain were buying lumber to build ships, purchasing over one million feet from the mills at Milltown and Calais.

Mr. T. W. Briggs of Robbinson invented a new fishing fly in 1862 which was considered the best of its kind then in use. In November 1862 the editor of the St. Croix Herald was riding in Perry, when he met a woman in bloomers stacking timbers. She regularly worked outdoors, chopping wood and driving oxen. The following month sheep were being killed by wolves in Pembroke and a pack of seven wolves killed sheep and cattle in Dennysville.

On the New Brunswick side of the St. Croix, near Weston, Maine, a small settlement sprang up in 1863, known as "Skedadaddler's Ridge, "being made up of men avoiding the draft instituted by President Lincoln.

A fisherman, who went by the pen-name, Old Angler, published a long story in the Maine Sportsman magazine in 1904, detailing an early trip he took to the Grand Lakes in 1864. At that time, the only resident between Princeton and the head of the lakes, was a Mr. Gould, who cleared and built a farm at the outlet of Grand Lake Stream.

In 1866 the Granger Turnpike, a road leading from Princeton to Milford, was within three miles of being completed. That year it was also noted that bears were plentiful. In July a man was found dead in a camp on the road leading from Prentiss to Danforth Plantation. He had worked as a cook in Danforth Plt., on the drive for Mr. Charles Hathorn of Veazie, then started from the lumber camp and was not heard from afterwards.

On the 1866 spring drive, the logs of Gilbert W. Gooch, arrived at the head of Hadley's Lake, consisting of three million square feet of logs from the upper lakes. It was Mr. Gooch's second drive, bringing his total to six million square feet. Later that year, the Granger Turnpike, a road leading from Princeton to Milford, was within three miles of being completed. That year it was also noted that bears were plentiful. In July a man was found dead in a camp on the road leading from Prentiss to Danforth Plantation. He had worked as a cook in Danforth Plt., on the drive for Mr. Charles Hathorn of Veazie, then started from the lumber camp and was not heard from afterwards.

A dreadful accident occurred in January of 1869 at Perry, when Albert R. Johnson was burned to death when his lumber camp burned down.

LOG DRIVING ON MATTAWAMKEAG

By John Springer, from *Forest Life and Forest Trees*, 1851

Log Drive on Mat-
tawamkeag (from For-
est Life and Forest
Trees)

The second division of Springer's book, Forest Life and Trees, is called "River Life" and covers breaking up camp, dams, log-riding, log marks and all the trials and tribulations of getting the logs down the rivers to market. Subsequent chapters divide the State into sections with information and stories of logging in the area of Washington County, the Penobscot River watershed, the Kennebec River and lastly the many tributaries of the St. John River.

The third and last division of the book is called Trees of America, is much smaller than the other two sections. In its three chapters Spring covered the chief types of trees found in the northeast, as well as information on historical and famous trees, and the common types of trees found in Maine.

This river-driving adventure took place on the Mattawamkeag River, a tributary of the mighty Penobscot. The Mattawamkeag River, which begins in the town of Haynesville, where the East and West Branches converge, and flows over 70 miles south and west to the Penobscot. The logjam took place at the famous Slugundy Falls, which today can be accessed by several hiking trails.

...Referring to an item of experience on a drive down the Mattawamkeag, a logger says, "Our drive consisted of about thirteen thousand pieces, with a crew of thirty-two men, all vigorous and in the prime of life. Out of such a number, exposed as we were to the perils attended upon the business, a question which we sometimes inwardly pondered was who of our party might conclude the scenes of mortal life on this drive?

"We commenced about the 25th of March to drive, while snow and ice, and cold weather were yet in the ascendant. The logs were cleared from the land and stream of Baskahegan in fifty days, which brought us into the Mattawamkeag. Twelve miles down this river, below the junction of Baskahegan, we came to Slugundy Falls. There the water passes through a gorge about fifty feet wide, with a ledge on either side, making a tremendous plunge; and in immediate proximity a very large rock stands a little detached from its ledgy banks. There the whole body of logs formed an immense jam, and such a mass of confusion as then presented itself beggar's description. Logs of every size were interwoven and tangled together like heaps of straw or winnow, while the water rushed through and over them with a power which seemed equal to the upturning of the very ledges which bound it. We paused to survey the work before us, calculating the chances of success, of life and death. We knew the dangers attending the operation; that life had on former occasions been sacrificed there, and that the graves of the brave men who had fallen were not far distant. We remembered that we too might make with them our final resting-place. The work was, however, commenced; and after five days' incessant application, mutually sharing the dangers incurred, we made a clean sweep of this immense jam without accident. A short distance below are Gordon Falls, at which place there is a contraction of the channel, with high ledges on either hand, a straight but rapid run, with a very rough bottom, at once difficult and dangerous to navigate or drive. Here the logs to greater or less extent always jam, the number varying according to the height of the freshet. This place we soon passed successfully. Logs, wangan and all were soon over, excepting one empty boat which two brothers, our best men, in attempting to run, swamped and capsized. In a moment they both mounted upon her bottom, and were swiftly passing along the dashing river, when the boat struck a hidden rock, and the foremost one plunged headlong into the boiling waves. Since he was an active man, and an expert swimmer, we expected to see him rise and struggle with the tide which bore them onward; but, to our amazement and sorrow, we saw no more of him until four days after, when his corpse was discovered some distance below the place of this sad accident. At

the foot of the falls a small jam of logs made out into the channel; several of the men ran out upon this to rescue the other,
who had also lost his footing on the boat. He passed close to the
jam under water, when one of the crew suddenly thrust his arm
down and seized him by the hair of his head, and drew him to
land. On recovering from the shock which he had sustained in his
perilous passage, and learning that his brother was drowned, he
blamed the crew for not permitting his to share the same fate, and
attempted to plunge again into the river, but he was restrained by
force till reason once more resumed her sway. The body of the
other received the humble attention usual upon such interments,
as soon as a coffin could be procured. Not two hours previous to
this accident, this individual, taking one of the crew with him,
had visited the grave of a fellow-laborer nearby. During the next
hour he had left the spot, had launched his frail boat, and had laid
down in a river driver's grave.

Fourteen days from this time we drove our logs to the boom,
having passed a distance of only one hundred and thirty miles in
ninety days.

SAM SHIRK: A TALE OF THE WOODS OF MAINE

By George H. Devreux, 1870

George Humphrey Devreux (1809-1878) a native of Salem, Mass. graduated from Harvard in 1829, studied under Leverett Saltonstall and was admitted to the Bar in 1831. At the young age of 25 years he

Attack of the Wolves

served for two years in the Massachusetts House. Having invested in land in the woods of Maine, he moved there, where he lived for ten years. A delegate to the Whig Convention in 1840, he moved back to Salem in 1846, and served as Adjutant General of Massachusetts from 1848-1851. In 1856 he returned to the House.

An avid outdoorsman, Devereux later wrote a novel, setting it in the Maine Woods. The two young heroes of the story, Butler and Sam Shirk go through a series of adventures—moose hunting, log driving, fishing and being stalked by local Indians. Following is another one of their exciting adventures.

...They now picked their way across the stranded logs to the farther shore. Butler's whistle soon brought them Marquis, a beautiful white and liver-colored spaniel,—William's pet and inseparable companion. Following the dog, as he bounded on before them, they entered the forest, and soon found the lad employed in dressing a fine buck that had fallen victim to his aim.

"William has the first deer sure enough, Captain. I am not often behind in this matter; but I must be content with second for now."

"A nice fat fellow,—two years and in prime order," said the Captain, glancing at his antlers. "He will give us as much as we shall want to carry home, and a good dinner to boot."

"So he will; but I must try my hand too, if we chance upon more. We could put them in a tree and come out with a horse tomorrow. The next thing now is to choose a place to dine."

"There is a monstrous boulder over the ridge, and a brook hard by;–couldn't be a nicer spot."

"Yes, I remember it, William. Let us go there, Captain. Bill, take this fellow's fore-legs, and I will carry the hinder ones; he will be light now you have dressed him."

Just in advance of where they stood, the ground rose in a long and moderate slope, covered with hard wood, spruce and hemlock. On the further side, it descended more steeply to a narrow valley, through which ran a small brook on its way to the river. Another narrow and rounded ridge,—or horseback, as it would be there styled, from the resemblance of its conformation,—ran at right angles a short distance out into the valley, like a causeway, and terminated in a gravelly mound or knoll. Nearly upon the highest point of the little hill rested a huge mass of granite, in size and general outline resembling a small house without a roof. Its sides were nearly perpendicular and smooth, except on one end, where some slight projections, caused by the disintegration of a seam in its structure, afforded footing sufficient to enable an active man,—with the help of the contiguous branches of a cluster of birches,—to scale its top, elsewhere inaccessible to man or beast. Covered with gray mosses and lichens, the vast rock lay, like the ark on Ararat, where the waters of the primeval flood, or some travelling glacier of olden days, had left it stranded. Upon the dry surface of the knoll beneath it was a small, clear spot, well fitted for the purpose for which William Dee had suggested it.

The young men soon kindled a fire under the side of the rock, and broiled upon the coals a fat venison steak, which, with the accompaniments supplied by coat-pockets, furnished a dinner that might satisfy the most fastidious appetite. Marquis,—who had lain, during the progress of the meal, with his head quietly resting upon his paws, like a well-bred dog patiently biding his time,—had retired round a corner with a superabundant supply of bones and scraps dealt out to him by his biped friends. The Captain was enjoying his pipe; and a desultory conversation, such as suits the inert mood that follows a hearty repast, was kept up for some time. The sun was bright, and light fleecy clouds floated along on the fresh breeze, which was only recognized, however, in the shelter of the woods, by an occasionally rustling whirl of the leaves that began already to fall from the trees, and the continuous moaning of the tall tops of the pines far overhead. A merry little squirrel now and then trilled out his frolicsome chirrup, as he basked or scampered about in enjoyment of the lingering atmosphere of summer; for Marquis was both too well trained to higher game, and too agreeably occupied, to interrupt him.

All at once, the quiet scene was disturbed by a loud, sharp challenge from the dog,—who sprung round from the corner, where had been maundering over the more refractory portions of his dinner, and stood with erect tail and ears, snuffing the air and growling furiously. The little squirrel rushed in consternation up a neighboring tree; while William and Butler, springing to their feet, seized their guns, and the Captain took his pipe from his mouth.

"What is it, boy?" said William, as all three looked and listened eagerly towards the quarter to which the dog directed their attention; "what do you hear, boy?"

A moment more made audible, to their less acute senses, a pattering tramp as of many animals in rapid motion. Directly in front of them, the sound suddenly ceased, and was succeeded by a chorus of yelps and snarling.

"The wolves have smelt out the entrails of your deer, William, and are quarreling over them. We can get a good shot while they are in the muss. Your father and Marquis will do better to stay here."

With quick but careful steps, the young men ran towards the top of the ridge; thence proceeding in perfect stillness, they gained the cover of a thicket of young firs, which protected them from discovery, while, by circumspect improvement of casual openings, they could see most that was going on in their front.

In the open glade beyond, where the refuse portions of the deer had been left, were from forty to fifty wolves. Some were sitting upon their haunches; some were wandering about snuffing for a stray mouthful; and a dozen or more were still clustered where the heap of garbage had been, snapping and growling at each other, under the influence of the feelings excited by their tantalizing and wholly unsated appetite. After peeping through his loop-hole at this wild scene, William leveled his gun; but Butler laid his hand upon the lock, saying in a whisper,—

"No, no, Bill,—it won't do. There are too many of 'em; we must beat a retreat as quick as possible."

The two then stole carefully back over the summit of the ridge; and, after placing a safe distance between them and the ravenous animals, returned as quickly as possible to the rock.

"Well, Captain," said Butler, "it is lucky we have this castle at hand. There are not much less than fifty wolves out yonder. I should think nothing of half a dozen; but the pack is strong and half-starved. I believe they will dog us. The wind blows between us and them, or they would have scented us before now. We must take to the top of the rock for a while, and see how matters turn out."

"Right, James. They are cowards alone, but devils in such gangs as this. You and Bill get the venison up; the d——d rascals shan't have that to dine upon. The dog too, take him up with you. Leave your guns by me. I will keep guard till all is ready."

The youths then scrambled up the steep rock, sometimes stepping from one knob of its worn surface to another, sometimes swinging themselves up by a friendly bough, and passing from hand to hand the carcass of the deer, and assisting Marquis over the points impracticable to quadruped locomotion.

As Butler had anticipated, the wolves soon caught indications of their neighborhood; and scarcely had they reached the elevated terrace with their load, when the foremost animals began to show themselves over the ridge, snuffing the wind and yelping eagerly.

"James," said the Captain, "come down to the crotch in the birch just over my head, to take the guns from me. I will give them a salute, as they come along the horseback."

"Let me come down, Captain; and you climb up while you have time. I can scramble back quicker than you."

"No, no,—do as I say, boy. I am not too stiff for that yet. My shots will make them a little cautious about making a rush, I'll warrant it."

Dee then, placing the two spare guns behind him, stepped under the cover of the birch bushes, the tops of which also screened Butler's post upon the rock. Some of the beasts had now found the trail, and were nosing along the descent toward the party, when a rifle flashed through the boughs, and one of them was sent whining and yelping, to the rear with a broken leg. Another ball hissed sharply along the ridge, and stretched a second wolf dead upon the ground. But just as the third gun was raised, Butler exclaimed,–"Up with you, Captain, I see the heads of a host of 'em over the hill now. Give me the guns and jump up."

All three presently stood safe upon the platform, where poor Marquis, half belligerent and half terrified, lay crouching at his master's feet, shivering and growling at the crowd of advancing foes. As they came up with their lame comrade, a number began to worry him, with the well-known ferocity of their nature. He still retained, however, vigor enough to require bite with bite, and snarl with snarl. So he was permitted to withdraw into a thicket to lie down and lick his wounds at his leisure. The gaunt beasts then turned pell-mell upon the body of their dead comrade, tearing it in pieces and maintaining a running fight over its mangled remnants, till not a morsel but the skull was left upon the ground. A stout battle was held over this last by a dozen of the most powerful; which terminated in its seizure by an enormous gray old patriarch, who bore it off in triumph, followed at a timid distance by two or three, not less hungry, though less strong. These little matters disposed of, one of the leaders of the pack, whose eyes had had hitherto been attracted to the surface of the ground by the quest of something to allay his voracious appetite, perceived the little garrison upon the top of the boulder, and announced his discovery by a loud yelp. The scattered prowlers gathered directly from all quarters and formed an irregular semicircle, at a small distance around its base; expressing their ferocious interest in their coveted prey by a combination of unearthly howlings, that filled the air with its sanguinary discord. That wild, boding, infernal cry,—half moan, half savage fury, like the shriek of an angry ghost,—repeated from throat to throat and prolonged in long-drawn yelps, might have struck terror into the stoutest heart. But the hunters felt a confidence in their granite stronghold that converted the appalling sounds into an occasion of indignant contempt rather than of fear.

They eyed for a few minutes in silence the diabolical exhibition of sanguinary rage, till the stout-hearted and jolly old Captain, seating himself quietly down, said to his companions,—

"Here we are,—safe enough, and regularly blockaded by these infernal scamps. What's to be done now, James? I don't care to spend the night on this rock."

"O, I think we'll raise the siege shortly," replied Butler, laughing, "provided our ammunition holds out. We can kill or hurt half of them; and the rest will eat them up. When their bellies are filled, they won't concern themselves about us any further."

"Very likely,—that's their way. Meanwhile I go for killing as many of the rascals as we can. How many balls have you, Bill?"

"About twenty, father."

"And you, James?"

"Nearly as many, besides some slugs."

"That's well. Let me count,—one—two—three—twelve. I've a baker's dozen in my pocket. We'll do famously. Now, then, lead and fire, as fast as you can, but make every shot tell."

The Captain's advice was skillfully and energetically followed out. A rapid and sustained fire was poured forth on the devoted animals. The sharp crack of the rifles and the rounder and duller report of William's double-barrel, in rapid succession, carried death or dreadful wounds among them. The close proximity and the ample mark offered by their bodies, to men accustomed to behead a partridge at fifty yards with a single ball, rendered the

fire most destructive. The scene soon became one of intense ani-
mation. Wreaths of smoke curled up every moment into the air;
and the hiss of bullets and slugs was mingled with the yells of the
wounded and the savage howls of those still bent on the attack.
Now and then some of the older and fiercer wolves—after standing in a half crouch, with gathered haunches and extended fore-
paws, for a few moments, while they howled themselves into a
fury—dashed desperately upon the boulder in a hopeless attempt
at scrambling up its side. But the hard, perpendicular surface
afforded them no footing; and they fell backward, after an impo-
tent struggle, luck of a bullet had not meanwhile put a stop to any
further display of activity.

The ground was soon strewn with a dozen or more dead bodies; while the neighboring bushes were filled with disable combat-
ants, employed alternately in nursing their hurts and venting their
mingled rage and pain in whines and growls. The evident success
of the defense raising the spirits of the besieged, the blood-thirsty
temper of battle gained the mastery; and it began to be a source of
excited pleasure and a trial of skill, with the youngsters of the party.

"William," said Butler, "see those two stout fellows standing
side by side under that beech. I will put a ball between the eyes of
the right-hand one, and do you take the chap on your own side.
Are you ready? Now then—one, two, three."

The guns flashed together; and when the smoke cleared away,
the wolf fired at by Butler lay motionless upon the ground, a large
crimson spot on his forehead attesting the accuracy of the aim.
William's ball missed the head of its object, but, grazing under his
ear, laid open a ghastly furrow along his back. The spine of the
beast was broken, filling the air with hideous howls of agony.

"Not clean work, William! A smooth-bore is not exactly reliable. But you made a close shot. Give the poor devil another and
put his out of his misery."

Both recharged their guns, and were just on the point of firing
again, when Marquis, excited beyond measure by the commotion

of the fight, rushed to the brink of the rock, barking with all his might. But, failing to check his career in time, he lost his balance just upon the edge, and tumbled over among the bushes at its base. During the whole contest he had been gallantly darting to and fro, pouring out his defiance of the charges of his foes below; but until now he had wisely regulated his ardor and kept his ground of vantage. With a despairing whine, he slid over the verge, and now lay crouching and trembling in the thicket. Four or five of the wolves observed his fall, and dashed at his cover. But William, holding his gun in his left hand, seized the end of a long bough with his right, and swung himself off the rock. As the limb bent downward with his weight, he let go of his hold and dropped upon his feet by the side of his shivering favorite. Quick as thought, his leveled gun laid the foremost assailant upon the ground. But two more were close behind; and others still, at more cautious distance, menaced to support the attack. Before he could fire again, the second rushed in, and made his point at the dog. Fortunately for the poor Marquis, a rotten stump stood directly between him and the terrible jaws of his enemy. The enraged animal seized upon it with his teeth, and tore it to pieces with a single effort. But while his mouth was full of the rotten wood, the gallant spaniel, reassured by the timely aid of his young master, fastened his sharp teeth upon his throat, while William buried his knife twice in his shaggy breast, and, with a faint growl, he fell lifeless on his side. Butler had hastily followed William down, and the crack of his rifle sent the third wolf to the right about, with his fore leg shattered and his side torn open. Those who were coming up in the rear, intimidated with this warm reception, halted, and, crouching in a threatening attitude, contented themselves for the present with a ferocious display of teeth and a savage growl.

Butler now stepped boldly to the front and reloaded; and his intrepid demeanor, together with the severe lesson they had received, kept them in check.

"Carry up the dog, Bill. Lean your gun against the tree, and I will take it with mine. But load first. I can keep those devils back with three shots for time enough."

Loading his gun as rapidly as possible and leaving it at Jame's side, William took up the dog, and, placing him upon a spur of the rock at the height of his head, sprang himself up into the tree; and the two were again in a minute safe upon the summit. Vexed at the escape of their expected prey, the crouching wolves again threatened the charge. But Butler's cool eye was on them. The moment he saw them rise on their haunches, he laid aside his own rifle, as a sure reserve, and fired both barrels of William's piece in rapid succession. Both balls took effect, and a general retreat followed the discharge. James, taking advantage of the lull, clambered through the tree and up the rock,—William meeting him half way, and relieving him of the supernumerary gun.

"Well, Marquis, you didn't get a scratch, after all. Don't try that again, boy, however."

Marquis did not seem to need this prudent advice. He looked up into James's face and wagged his tail gently, but lay still for some time, panting and trembling, an occasional whine testifying to the perturbation of mind he had undergone.

"You managed that sally bravely, boys," said the Captain. "I stood ready to fire, all the while. But you got along so well that I would not interfere. But what's to be done next? For my part, I am tired of murdering these poor wretches. It begins to look too much like butchery."

"I think," said Butler, "that if we lie down flat upon the rock, for some time, out of their sight, that they gorge themselves upon these carcasses and be off, if they won't, I don't see but we must shoot 'em up, or stay here all night."

"Let us try your plan first. I think it will work."

So saying, the Captain stretched himself at full length, with his head resting on the unskinned deer and made himself so comfortable that he fell fast asleep. William and Butler lay down side by side, with Marquis between them, keeping up a conversation in whispers. The dog, still trembling with fear and excitement, looked occasionally into their faces with a low whine and licked their hands,—as if to express his reliance on their mutual relations of offense and defense against the brutes, whose fierce quarrelings and ravenous contentions were going on below them.

After the lapse of half an hour, Butler, on peeping cautiously over the edge of the rock, found the matters had taken very much the course he had predicted. Many of the dead and some of the most helpless of the wounded animals had been torn to pieces and devoured. Such of those hurt, as were able, had slunk away. The more fortunate survivors of the fray were roaming about, smelling after stray fragments of skin or bones, or squatting in little groups, with the lazy and apathetic air of all brutes after a good meal. Still they hung about the spot, seemingly inclined to take things leisurely.

Butler glanced at the sun, and, seeing that the afternoon was more than half gone, turned to advise with his associates as to the expediency of descending and attempting to drive them off, under the persuasion that safety, as well as the experience of hard knocks to be looked for, might have abated their ferocity. As he was about to speak, a wreath of smoke curled up among the brush-wood hard by, and two rifle-shots followed each other in rapid succession. One of the beasts dropped dead, and another, with a broken limb, hobbled off howling into the woods. Two men then pushed through the bushes with a shout, which maneuver accompanied with the fresh destruction from a new and unsuspected enemy, decided the wolves to give up the game. The younger beasts scampered in all quarters, while the veterans withdrew in a sullen trot, occasionally turning for a moment, but resuming their retreat before the ready rifles that were instantly leveled at the loiters, till not one remained in sight. One of the new-comers was Sam Shirk; the other, a tall and active backwoodsman, well known to all in the neighborhood as Joe Sibley. The besieged party came down from their fortress, and greeted their opportune allies.

"Well," said Sibley, "I should judge you'd had a considerable tall wolf-fight, by the looks o' things hereabouts. Sam and I was out, about two miles above, and heered a regular cannonading, as if 'twas Fourth of July. So arter a while, we concluded to come and see what was to pay."

"I am glad it happened so," replied Butler, "for we stood a good chance of passing the night up yonder."

"What made these chaps so darned saacy? They must have been terrible sharp-set to stand two hours before three good shots like you. But they're allers saacier when there's so many of 'em together. Your dog, too, made 'em wus. They'll allers hang on wus, where there's any brute critters they think they can get at where there's nothin' but men. By Gosh! four, five, six, twelve, sixteen carcasses, besides the one I just shot, and no partickler quantity that they's eat up among themselves. Pretty fair work,—you an't been slow,—that's a fact."

While Joe was discussing the case, Sam had set to work to skin such of the animals as had not been devoured by their comrades. Marquis, who was an old acquaintance, kept in close attendance upon him, smelling and nuzzling the warm flesh, as Shirk's ready knife exposed it to view, and starting back, now and then, with a half-frightened bark, when a sudden roll or motion of a limb recalled to his memory the fearful activity of his living antagonists. This economical proceeding, which occupied his practice hand but a short time, being finished, he threw down the skins before Captain Dee.

"There Captain, that yellerish one is the hide of the critter Joe killed. The rest is your'n, unless you'll give me one; for I want a wolf-skin bad. I've been trying to shoot one all day."

Butler and William waved their claims, and Sam joyfully bundled up the best of them, and, tying them round with a cord, placed them over his shoulder, on the end of his rifle. Two or three long tails, dangling down his back, gave to his figure an odd and comical appearance; and Marquis could not restrain himself from jumping up, every five minutes, to worry at his supernumerary caudal appendages. Joe Sibley threw the saddle and haunches of

William's deer over his broad shoulders; and all started to leave the spot...

A FEW DAYS FISHING ON THE SCHOODIC LAKES

By Thomas E. Lambert, from *Forest and Stream*, December 1874

 The accounts this year from the Schoodic Lakes, in the Northeastern part of Maine, were so grand that the writer and two Boston friends, old associates in angling excursions, determined to give this rather unfrequented locality a trial themselves.

The requisites for a few days' camping out were dispatched beforehand, and by communicating with a farmer residing close by Grand Lake, two experienced guides were engaged. The weather promised well, being during that delightful spell we had in the latter portion of the last month, and our journey was very enjoyable with the prominent exception of the last six or several miles, performed in a wagon innocent of springs over an awful road of the corduroyest pattern. It was my worst experience of this species of travel, and has fully impressed on my mind the capacity of the human frame to resist the force of shocks. Were the journey over this wretched apology for a road to continue much longer, as at the acme of the ordeal we went, plump, crash, jolt, over a dreadful piece of corduroy, I felt body and soul could not be kept together, when the joyful cry, "There they are!" reached my ear. The lovely scene there presented to our view–the calm beauty of the Schoodic Lakes, bathed in Autumnal haze–soon dispelled all thought of our late torture. In every ripple of the glistening lake fancy pictured the silvery splash of a land-locked salmon.

It was nearly 5 P.M. when we arrived at Lakeville Plantation. There something to eat was got ready for us, but our desire to do some fishing that evening was paramount to all considerations of appetite or rest, and after a hurried snatch at the viands, we were soon busily engaged in getting out rods and tackle, when a decided wet blanket was thrown upon our movements by our host, who, with sententious unconcern, coolly informed us that fishing on Grand Lake "wasn't worth a cent." With blank disappointment we looked on one another, mutely questioning. "Can this thing be?" Did this tally with Fred C.'s glowing account of his exploits on the Schoodics? Were we but the victims of a fiendish self? With tacit consent we deemed it inexpedient just then to press further enquiry on our terrible informant, beyond asking where we could find the guides. We rose full of bitterness and gall, Ned silent, but Charlie's mutterings betokened intention of going for some one's "skulp" when we got back to Boston.

Gathered together on an indicated point of the shore whence the guides could be hailed, we gave vent to our oppressive feelings in a rousing halloo, which soon met the desired answer. From behind a headland, a hundred yards or so distant, a canoe with two stalwart Indians on board shot forth and quickly reached where we were standing. One of them, Peter, was of the Mohawk tribe; the other, a white man, who had taken to his bosom a dusky squaw, and lived wholly in Indian fashion. Both, we afterwards discovered, were fully up to this business, skillful hunters, first-rate cooks, too, and withal very agreeable attendants especially Nicholas, who was brimful of humor and sporting anecdotes.

The farmer's statement, that Grand Lake did not amount to much, was fully corroborated by them, but Duck and Pleasant Lakes, they confidently assured us, would afford plenty of sport. Nothing further could be attempted that evening, and so, with somewhat restored good spirits, we retired to our night's quarters at the farm house.

By six o'clock next morning everything was snug on board the two canoes. Ned being the heavy weight of the party was left in undivided possession of one, with Peter at the paddle, while Charlie and I placed ourselves under the guidance of Nicholas in the other. We were lucky in our captain, whose amusing proclivities kept us well entertained the whole way up. Not much conversation took place, apparently, in the eternal fitness of things, he took untiring care to inform the woods and waves must occur before he would "ever cease to love."

The breeze was well in our favor and we skimmed along the waters at a rattling pace. Grand Lake has no particular pretensions to the picturesque, being an open, undiversified sheet of water, about five miles long by three in width, the shores on either side low-lying and densely wooded with pines. The monotonous said through it left us quite in a mood to enjoy a change of scene, and this was well gratified by the sight of Duck Lake. It is not more than half the size of Grand, but is infinitely more beautiful. Just at the entrance, on the right hand side, in marked contrast to the continued evenness of the lower lake, bold wood-crowned headlands jut out in all directions, forming in the numerous indents of the shore the most inviting nooks and quiet sheltered coves.

Here at the lake's outlet a short halt was called for lunch, it being our intention to proceed with the least possible delay to Upper or Pleasant Lake, as it is called. There our man said was the real good fishing of the places to be found. But the time here devoted to the meal was of the shortest duration. The splash of a salmon a little distance out made us all jump to our feet. Previous intentions were knocked on the head. We could stand suspense no longer, and in a jiffy, three sets of flies were doing their prettiest to tempt that fellow to show himself again.

For ten minutes at least we plied in vain. The speckled beauties of Duck Lake seemed to utterly disregard the city dainties we so assiduously offered. At length a decided splash was heard. An appalling stillness followed. No time for questions now. "Ha! I've got him," broke from Charlie, and so he had, and a good one, too. Out went his line with a whiz, and the quivering bend of his rod showed that the customer he had to deal with would require every care to bring him to terms. Charlie's appeal to take in my line, for fear of a possible foul, was not be resisted. I was winding up in a very miserable frame of mind at the prospect of delay until I could again commence operations, when, splash, tug, I was no longer a spectator, but in active business on my own hook. We both soon had our fish well at play, and were offering occasional consolation to Ned for the loss of the pool for first lake, when "good, sir!" ejaculated the taciturn Peter, and Ned was also in the race.

Then began in earnest the struggle for the grand prize which by the way, consisted of a purse of one hundred and fifty cents. Every move of our game was watched with an intensity that made the nerves feel as if rod and line were conductors to a first class electric battery. Charlie's enquiries for the landing net were becoming frequent; he was evidently on the home stretch. I had fair hopes of making a good second, or possibly by a sport, a rush in for first. My fish was already yielding to a slight pressure, as I commenced playing with a shortened line, when on a sudden he made for the surface and sprang clear out of the water. This well directed move to get free did not meet with success, though it was uncomfortably near it, and causing, by the sudden energy of the effort, the top of my rod to give way, left my chance of first place rather precarious indeed. The contest now lay between Charlie and Ned. But as the latter's was much the lighter fish, it was not long before the words, "Consolation boys." "Better luck next time," etc., were heard, mingled with abominable guffaws, from his direction. We suggested that a head and tail ought not count against five and six pounders, as our prizes turned out to be, but this point was not pressed, as later examination showed that between the head and the tail of Ned's fish lay three and a half pounds of good salmon. That victorious gentleman was also kind enough to commiserate me on my damaged road, which was in fact of more show than good, and had been won at some fair or other. Eyeing it, he observed it was worth about as much as it cost me, namely–the dollar for the chance–nor was he wrong.

The sport continued good and we remained here nearly two hours, hard at work, each rod in that time averaging the respective amount of about a dozen, all strong and full of play. We then resumed our journey towards Pleasant Lake. Crossing over we reached the mouth of the stream that unites both waters. There parting from the guides, who were to carry up the canoes and fire camp. We started, under full directions how to proceed, to walk the intervening distance, something close on three miles. On arriving at the shores of Pleasant, the wind was just the right thing, allowing us to fish from land. A short time at work here, and proof was abundant that the high character of it given by the Indians was every whit deserved. We met with first-rate success, as good a day as ever it was my luck to cast a line, and when the approach of evening compelled a cessation, and a return march for camp, we were laden with spoils, and in the highest possible spirits at the excellent prospects for the next day's regular set-to.

Following down the rugged course of the stream for a con-siderable distance we were glad enough at length to descry the camping ground, and the welcome form of Peter, crouched before the fire, preparing the dinner. No prettier site could have been selected, and pledging Peter's health in full pumpers of Gibson's good old Monogram, we testified our approval of his judgment. The tent was pitched in a small clearing by the stream side, the dark woods behind, and right in front a cascade, down which dashed the waters that came struggling through the boulders from the upper portion of the stream, visible some distance, till lost in among the overhanging trees; further down, below the little waterfall, was a placid pool, its somber fringes flecked here and there with the bright red of the maple's fall foliage, and over it leaned an immense old vine-tangled pine tree, as if in his quiet nook seeking rest from long continued battle against time and tempest.

We were all as hungry as hawks, and made a right royal feast. The fish was cooked in real woodcraft fashion, and, were we an exhibition jury on that occasion, land-locked salmon would stand a capital chance of honorable mention for "delicious flavor." A "little game" in which all took a hand, followed in due course, and of said little game, I must say, our noble red men showed a knowledge, which, I have no doubt, if occasion required, could be displayed even to an oriental extent. With song and story we kept it up until the "wellness" of Nicholas, as manifested in the increasing tallness of his narratives, and the miscellaneously loose manner in which another person's little dogs wagged their tails in front, gave the signal for hammock.

Among friend Ned's many little peculiarities was an alarming predisposition to cramps, which could only be subdued by a certain remedy. A violent attack came on at an admirably early hour next morning, just about daybreak. The fuss he made looking for his particular medicine soon drove sleep from the camp. He would have us also use it as a preventive. Growls and abjurations to signify he did not then, at least, require the treatment, his tender solicitude for our welfare would not let him understand. His henchman, Peter, too, by this time fortified against all danger from "cramps," so joined in the should of "tickets" that even "Old Nick" had to turn out from his birchen bark couch, though he remarked he was "a powerful sound sleeper." With a shake and a stretch, toilets were complete, and all were ready for breakfast. The amount of provisions demolished at that meal rendered it absolutely necessary to put in force the adage, "After breakfast rest a while." It was not safe to venture immediately where there was a possibility of slipping. So placing a bottle as a mark some twenty yards off and lighting our pipes, we went in for a little pistol practice. After a half an hour's shooting the target remained intact, though the trees for a circuit of fifteen feet showed evidence of our work, and we came to the conclusion that it was a pity to injure such a bottle after the noble defense it had made, and letting it remain in its glory, the subject of pistol sharpshooting was by mutual consent allowed to drop.

Now we started for the lake, but on arrival there found it as smooth as a mirror; not a ripple ruffled its glassy surface. In the still air above here and there soared a fishhawk, and now and then one came down like an arrow, dash on its prey beneath, and floated lazily off with it to the shore. These, and an occasional loon, were the only objects to break the morning quiet of the scene. Fishing for the present looked of little use. However, rather than be idle, Ned and I determined to make a circuit of the lake, and try what trolling would do. Charlie selected a spit of rock a little out from the shore to fish from, and having left him perched there, we went on our way. Our success at trolling was very poor. An occasional shot at a loon did not help in the slightest to increase the amount of our game, though unexpectedly the last shot we devoted to the black-headed diving fowl, afforded us a bit of amusement that well repaid for all the powder and shot we had wasted on them. Not far from the promontory that separated us from the spot where we left Charlie, we espied a solitary loon, banged at him, and down of course he went, but not on the 'never to rise any more" plan, for just as we were rounding the point, we heard his infernal screech as he again came to the surface, and at the same moment, to our utter astonishment, up went Charlie's arms in the air, and flop went he into the lake. We immediately pulled to his assistance, helped him ashore, and endeavored to get an explanation of the mishap. He shook himself repeatedly, but appeared totally regardless of our questions, and for some moments looked with a steadfast gaze on the water. "Well, I thought it was the devil," at last escaped his lips. The mystery was solved. The roars of laughter that followed this short speech were enough to exorcise all the evil spirits, if any there were, in that neighborhood. It was our "devil" of a loon that had done the trick. Master Charlie, finding fishing no go, had allowed himself to drift into a delicious little reverie, half in thought, half in easy enjoyment of the scene around, when his pensive lucubrations were so unceremoniously disturbed by the unexpected popping up, just under him, of the diver's ugly head, accompanied by that terrible scream.

No breeze yet springing up, we employed our enforced idleness in going about the lake. It is much of the same character of Duck, but of great extent, and a bolder class of scenery, to which is the picturesque addition of high wooded hills rolling far away in the distant background.

By the afternoon things got more lively, and soon we had our hands full of exciting business. We were into it up to the handle–chock full of occupation until almost dusk. The fish took lively, and most of them were game to the back bone, especially one splendid fellow that after a magnificent fight, that lasted, I am sure, quite twenty minutes, finally yielded himself captive to the noble Ned.

Our third day was good from beginning to end, and when next morning we had to pack up our traps for home, it was no small regret we felt that imperious business would not permit a longer stay.

– THOMAS E. LAMBERT

TWO BEAR STORIES

By Penobscot, from *Forest and Stream*, May 16, 1878

No. 1.

The true history of the bears has yet to be written. I believe that naturalists advance two theories to account for their existence through the winter without food. One is that they go into their dens extremely fat, and that this fat is slowly absorbed during the winter, thus sustaining

Bear Hunting (Currier & Ives)

life, and that the bear comes out in the spring in a lean and famished condition. The other theory is that the temperature of the animal's body, instead of being fixed like ordinary mammals, varies with that of the surrounding atmosphere, being always at a point a little above it, consequently when cold weather comes on it is cooled down to such a degree that there is no wasting of the tissues, and the animal remains dormant.

During my winter in the woods I officiated as cook to a small crew employed by my father, and as the cooking did not occupy half my time I used to join the gang in the woods between meals. Coming to camp one afternoon to cook supper I was aroused by the well-known voice of "Old Tigress," a large, black mutt, famed as a "moose dog" throughout that whole region. I knew by her bark that the game was at bay, and as she never deigned to notice anything small, I was all excitement in a moment. Hurrying into camp I seized my gun, and hastily providing myself with some buck shot, I ran down to where the dog was barking, scarcely twenty rods from camp. On reaching the spot I was greatly disappointed to see her standing alone and barking at a hole under the roots of an enormous hackmatac stub. Going up to her, I was about to reprimand her for fooling me, when I caught sight of a lot of freshly picked boughs sticking out of the hole. I had listened to too many hunters' stories not to know at a glance what that meant. Only one animal in Maine had sufficient intelligence to stop up the mouth of its den with boughs after going in.

Hurriedly drawing out the first shot with which my gun was loaded, and putting in a charge of buckshot, I stepped up to the roots of the tree, and, boy like, thrust the muzzle of my gun into the mouth of the den and pulled the trigger. The charge merely grazed the bear's thigh, cutting a shallow groove in the fat with which it was overlaid. It was a very cold day in the latter part of December, but I never saw an animal any less dormant than that bear! With one movement of his powerful hind legs he forced himself through the aperture at the mouth of his den, throwing the earth outward in every direction, and in much less time than I have taken to tell it he stood before me, one of the largest bears ever seen in that country. It was the first I had ever seen, and his enormous size, so much larger than I had ever dreamed of, appalled me; but he was within ten feet of me, and I dared not turn my back on him. Coming so suddenly into the strong light seemed at first to blind him, and he stood for a moment motionless, winking incessantly. The dog, partly between me and the bear, but a little to one side, stood like a stature with hair erect and glowing eyes fixed on those of the bear, which commenced to turn its head slowly from side to side to discover the foes who had so rudely disturbed his repose. As his vision cleared he caught sight of me, and laying back his ears and opening a capacious mouth well garnished with yellow teeth, with a snort like the puff of a locomotive, the seemingly unwieldy animal bounded at me with the lightness of a cat. With a leap that I can truly say was for life, I placed nearly the same distance between us, as that which first separated us, and, dropping my gun, sprung to the foot of a scrubby spruce close at hand, and began to ascend it with all possible dispatch. Fortunately for myself I was not pursued. Scarcely had the beast's feet landed in the tracks which I had so kindly vacated for them, when the dog, executing a skillful flank movement, fell suddenly on his rear, with a fury which completely turned his attention from myself and gave me ample time to ascend the tree, from the summit of which I watched the combat below. This however, was all one way, as it consisted of a series of charges by the infuriated brute upon the dog, which did not attempt to bite the bear after the first rush, but contented herself with simply dodging its attacks. After expending his fury in a score of vain attempts to get the dog into its power, he desisted, and walking toward the den, acting endeavored to re-enter it. Being again attacked by the dog, he turned and once more drove her back, and then suddenly retreated into the forest, closely followed by his tormentor.

As they disappeared, I descended from my perch, and, picking up my gun, proceeded to reload. By the time this was accomplished my drooping courage had wonderfully revived, and I started on the trail, determined to risk another spot, the hunter's instinct being, even then, strong within me. I soon overtook him, as he turned continually to drive back the dog, which of course rendered his progress slow. When I started I had made up my mind to advance within twenty feet of the monster so as to deliver a fatal shot, for sure. But the thought obtruded itself, as I came in sight of the huge beast, that my gun might miss fire. I confess that I had not the nerve to go so near. Turning to drive back the dog, he came within thirty paces of me. As he turned broadside to me to continue his retreat, I delivered the charge full at his right shoulder, and a tremendous charge it was, nearly knocking me off my feet. The heavy coat of hair, and the thick layer of fat arrested the shot before they could penetrate to a mortal depth; but they wounded him quite severely and roused him to a pitch of fury impossible to describe. The roar of mingled rage and pain which he gave as the shot struck him I shall never forget to my dying day. When it struck on my ear I instantly sprang for the nearest tree. The brute bounded toward me with a speed no one would have believed him capable of, and although the dog fastened to him before he had made half the distance to the tree, he paid not the slightest attention to her, but swept her along as though she had been a feather, and gained the foot of the tree before I was well out of his reach. But although the dog could not prevent his reaching the tree, she did hinder him from making any attempt to seize me. The bear, indeed, seemed to think he had a sure thing on me, and, turning furiously on the dog, he drove her before him for several rods and again rushed toward me, but the noble brute fastened to the bear as often as he attempted to return to the tree, and invariably ran away from it when he charged on her. Being defeated in every effort to return to the tree, the contest ended as before, the bear slowly retreating following the dog. By this time I had come to the conclusion that bear hunting, as a sport, was not a success, and vowed it ever I reached camp with a whole skin to become one of the most exemplary cooks ever known on the river.

On again reaching terra firma, I could not, however, resist the inclination to follow the trail for a few rods just to observe the effect of my shot. He was bleeding slowly, and following the trail for a short distance I came upon a sausage-shaped substance nearly two inches in diameter and about six in length, evidently just ejected by the bear, and followed by a stream of fluid as black as ink, which extended for nearly a hundred feet; there must have been several quarts of it. My curiosity was greatly excited. This, then, was the "plug," as the hunters called it, which I had often heard them declare the animal provided itself with before going into winter quarters. I had always supposed it to be a fable; but here was proof positive of its truth. I examined it carefully, and tried to break it in pieces, but it was as tough as copper, and almost as hard, being evidently composed principally of pitch. Since that time I have had opportunities to examine a number by dissection, while in position. It is placed at the extremity of the rectum. It not only fills the passage, but adheres to it perfectly on all sides, rendering it perfectly air-tight. I have always found the intestines empty, with the exception of the black fluid of which I have spoken, which appears to be extremely astringent in its nature. Whether it is secreted naturally, or obtained by the animal from some peculiar plant, I, of course, have no means of knowing. It is evidently slowly absorbed during hibernation, as it always occurs in less quantities as winter advances. In company with a companion, I once killed one in its den, the 18th of March. It was, I think, the fattest one I ever saw; a perfect mass of fat inside and out. As the animal would have left of its own volition in a couple of weeks, it will readily be seen that it had existed by absorption of fat. There is not the slightest doubt but the animal comes out of his den in precisely the same condition in this respect as he entered it. It is probably equally true that the bear could not exist without this mass of fat which envelops him, as it serves in some mysterious way to perfectly protect the tissues and muscles from any waste. Having served its purpose, it rapidly disappears when the beast leaves his den, and in two or three weeks after that event he is as lean as a rat, and correspondingly voracious.

Perhaps I ought to say in regard to the bear with which I began this article, that he was followed the next day by two of the crew a distance of six miles, and killed in a new den which he had dug for himself. The dog had followed him about half that distance. He proved to be one of the largest ever killed in that part of the country.

No. 2.

In regard to the changeable temperature theory, the following perfectly unvarnished statement of facts ought to settle it: A friend in Maine, being out one day with hounds, started up a buck, which, in his course, happened to run over a bear' den, scaring out an old she bear and her two cubs of the spring before. This was the 10th of December, there being eight to ten inches of crusty snow on the ground. The hunt was at once transferred to the new and more exciting game. Failing to secure them that day, a party of four pursued them all the next without success, their numbers increasing instead of diminishing, as these bears, in their terror, ran over the den of a very large male bear, which also came out and joined the others. The next day the hunters killed the two cubs. The tenth day they killed the old she bear, leaving the big male alone in his glory. During all this time they had confined their operations to a piece of woods a little less than three miles square, in the immediate vicinity of which the hunters lived, the track at night being frequently left within fifty rods of some of their homes. I reached home from a trip to Union River the day the bear was killed, and it is hardly necessary to say that the next morning the party was augmented by one. For five more days the hunt was kept up, when Christmas dawned on us, one the coldest throughout the greater portion of New England on record, the thermometer in our neighborhood at sunrise registering 35 degrees, and the opinion was expressed among the boys, as we plunged into the woods, that the "old follow would be too stiff to stir," which opinion was strengthened by the fact that he had been twice so severely wounded that he dropped in his tracks, but had once regained his feet and made off apparently as well as ever, both the men declaring firmly, however, that they had shot him through. During the hunt we had tried every good dog that we could hear of within ten miles around, but had not succeeded in getting one which would attack the bear. This was, doubtless, owing in a great measure to the cowardice of an old hound we were obliged to keep as a tracker, for it is a well-established fact that the bear leaves a fainter scent than any other animal in the State. Plenty of ordinary dogs cannot follow the track by the scent at all, even when just made, and not one in a hundred can follow it for two hours after the animal has passed. The hound in question was the best in that respect I ever saw, but would not get within a hundred paces of a bear if he knew it; and if by chance he caught sight of him making a charge he would run yelping back, and never stop till he reached some of us, even if we were two miles in the rear. This pusillanimous conduct had a fearfully demoralizing effect on all the other dogs we could get, and occasioned an amount of profanity among the boys sufficient to have run an ordinary mining camp for six months. We had long ago learned the futility of attempting to get a shot by following his track, and always after leaving him at night he would execute a series of maneuvers which would frequently take us till after mid-day to unravel.

On reaching the place where he intended to pass away the night (usually in the thickest spruce growth he could find), he would pick an armful of boughs, and carrying them to where three or four short scrubby spruce or firs grew, would lay them down in their midst, and getting on them would bend the tops of the shrubs over him, forming an arbor, under which he would remain always till we started him out, but always getting off before we came in sight of him. We had therefore adopted the plan of stationing ourselves at the various points where he would be likely to pass during the day, one man only following the tracks with the dogs. But on this Christmas morning we all followed up the tracks, for a man can't stand on a runway with the thermometer thirty-five degrees below zero, or at least he can't get off it, if he stands there long! After following the trail for about two hours we found it lead into a small opening made by the fire, the trees turning up after being killed, which rendered it extremely difficult to pass through it; so we skirted its edges, and, going entirely around it, made the discovery that there were no tracks out. This was better than we had hoped for, and we immediately disposed ourselves so as to give him a warm reception when forced to make his appearance. One of the boys had a double-barrel rifle, one barrel of which was a double shooter, thus giving him three shots. Him we placed on the tracks leading into the opening, as experience had taught us that he was more likely to come out there than in any other place. It was my turn to go in with the dogs. I had worked my way nearly to the centre of the "blow-down" with the dogs at heel, when I came suddenly on his bed, under the body of a large tree turned up by the roots. The ground was only partially clear of snow, and here he had laid through the bitter night without anything under him but the snow and frozen ground, and nothing over him but the log, at least three feet above him. I whistled forward the dogs, and almost at the same instant heard behind me the crack of Dan's rifle, making innumerable forest echoes in that cold air. The bear, on hearing my approach, had run a semi-circle, struck his back tracks behind me, and was at the edge of the opening almost as soon as I got to his bed. A second report quickly followed the first, and as I hastened back a third rang out sharply on the morning air, followed by a shout of "All right."

As I neared the spot where the shouting took place I heard some of the most emphatic language I ever listened to, and on getting there I found Dan, usually the coolest of hunters and the most placid of men, in a high state of excitement; but no bear!

It was several minutes before he calmed down sufficiently to give an account of the affair, during which time we had all collected around him.

It seemed that when he first saw the bear he was walking on a log, broadside to him, not having yet got into his "back tracks." Taking a deliberate aim just behind the shoulder, he "unhitched" and the bear "went down like a stone." He stood for a moment and was just going to call out, when he saw the bear on his feet and about striking his own trail, the log behind which he fell have concealed him up to this point. A second shot again rolled him over; but instantly regaining his feet he started down his tracks directly toward the astonished Dan, who was beginning to regard him as bullet-proof. As he approached Dan delivered his third and last charge full between the eyes. The brute pitched forward and fell headlong. Naturally supposing that an animal shot through the head must be dead, he had shouted to us, and setting away his rifle, was very coolly taking out his pocketknife for the purpose of cutting his throat, when the animal again struggled to his feet and stood reeling to and fro for a moment, so near to him that he could see him lap the blood as it ran down over his nose. Steadying himself in a moment he rushed forward on his old tracks, and not caring to be caught fooling with a bear of his size and toughness, with nothing but a pocket knife and empty rifle, Dan very respectfully gave him the right of way. A short inspection of the ground bore out Dan's statement.

In the meantime the dogs, which had gone ahead on the track

showing conclusively that the bear was still alive and able to repel all assault in that direction.

On following him up we found that he was barely able to keep out of our way, as we came in hearing of him several times, the dogs refusing to advance any faster than we did. We soon decided that it was best to leave him for that day, believing that the effects of his wounds, and the cold combined, would render him incapable of getting out of our way in the morning, so we struck out for home, the most of us going to a Christmas dance that night, so as to be sure and not oversleep ourselves. The next morning we were on hand before sunrise, the weather having moderated but very little. We soon reached the spot where we had left the trail—a very favorable place on the side of an open ridge, which they had previously avoided. The dogs, feeling unusually well, bounded forward unchecked, as we did not anticipate starting him till after the usual amount of circling, which would give us ample time to overtake them. We had gone nearly a quarter of a mile, however, before we heard a tremendous outcry from the dogs, only a short distance in advance. The uproar increased every moment; the baying of the old hound and the savage snarls of the other dogs, mingled with the roars and snorting of the bear, showing that a desperate fight was in progress. We soon reached the battleground, and were speechless with surprise to see dogs which for two weeks had exhibited nothing but fear and cowardice, attacking the enraged and foaming bear, not only with courage, but with absolute fury. Even the old hound as barking furiously not twenty feet away; and catching sight of us as we came up, he made a gallant charge on the bear, and actually scratched some hairs from his ridiculous apology for a tail. For some moments, so close was the fighting, we could not get a shot at the bear without running the risk of sacrificing a dog; but as the old fellow warmed up to his work, he soon cleared a space around him, when a shot under his ear laid him low, ending at once his life and the longest bear hunt on record. A short examination was sufficient to show that the shot between the ears, inflicting only a slight wound. On skinning him, however, four bullet holes were found in his body, two, evidently shot by Dan the day before, had grazed his lungs, and lodged against the skin on the opposite side. His lungs were very much bloodshot and inflamed, showing clearly what had occasioned his distress. The other two bullets went completely though his body, cutting the intestines in twenty places. In his normal condition they would have proved fatal in from two to six hours, and they had been shot through him, respectively, four and six days before. The plug (a name more expressive than elegant) was found intact, not having any use for his intestines, or any action in them; their being cut to pieces did not seem to affect him in the least. His coating of fat had greatly wasted away, and that which remained had totally altered in character, being of a tough, leathery consistory, wholly differing from its appearance when the animal is killed without being run. It seems incredible, and a total subversion of all the laws of nature that an animal could run sixteen days without eating or drinking, or having any action of the bowels or bladder, be shot in the meantime five times and then make a desperate fight. He would undoubtedly have whipped the five dogs easily if let alone. But all the participators in the hunt are alive, and can testify to its entire truthfulness. The conduct of the dogs was as unaccountable as that of the bear. We examine the ground with the greatest care to arrive at a solution of the mystery. The bear had gone straight from where we left him the day before to an old den that looked as though it had been used for ten years. It was dug under the roots of an enormous upturned pine. Into this he had crawled, it being well provided with dry moss and leaves, and the dogs had attacked him while in it, as could easily be told by hair lying at the mouth of it, and the furious manner in which he had torn out of it. What induced them to make the attack will always remain a mystery. They probably came upon him unexpectedly to themselves and the boldest, encouraged by the others, began the battle, upon which the others joined in.

I had just finished this article (as I supposed) when your issue of May 31 came to hand with its "Gossip about Bears." I am afraid the subject will hardly bear so much writing up, but cannot for-bear adding a few comments. So far from being "nearly extinct" in the East, they have increased rather than diminished in Maine and New Brunswick during the last thirty years, in proof of which I might cite that the payment of bounties is such a heavy tax in Maine that a bill was introduced into the Legislature last winter (and I believe passed) repealing it. I have a brother-in-law in that State who has yet to see this thirty-eighth birthday, who, when I left last fall was looking round "might pert" for two more bears to make up fifty shot or trapped by him in the last twenty years. And they are certainly not decreasing in the North Woods, for it was the unanimous testimony of guides and hunters last Octo-ber that the bears had not been so plentiful for years. In regard to this assertion that the bear, "has from two to six cubs, usually three or four." I would reply that it is doubtful if there is a single perfectly authenticated instance on record of the American black bear having more than two cubs at a birth, for it must be remem-bered that the very rare female are no proof, for numbers of bears, having young cubs, are trapped every spring. These, when pressed by hunger, give utterance to a peculiarly plaintive and pitiful cry, which, in the stillness of the forest at night, can easily be heard for half a mile. This will attract other females having young, when the cubs will naturally attach themselves to her. In a hunting expe-rience extending over many years, during which time I tracked scores, I have never found more than two following one dam; nor have I ever found or heard of more than that number being found *in utero*. Of course, I do not insist that triple (or even quadruple) births never occur, but that they are so very rare that they must, if occurring at all, be classified as exceptions.

A HOLIDAY CRUISE TO MAINE

By Digus, from *Forest and Stream*, March 1, 1883

Have you ever forgotten your first deer hunt? How every article in the outfit was examined, criticized and talked over again and again, and that rifle was in such prime condition that its various parts seemed to be out on dress parade,

(*Currier & Ives 1862*)

and had imbibed so much of your excitement that you could actually feel a tremor running its find fiber. And how–but, of course, your memory has played you no such prank, and the recollection is, undoubted, as fresh at the present time as it was on that memorable day, when you, while telling the boys that you had brought the quarry to camp, vainly tried, under an assumed air of unconcern, to hide that pardonable and natural pride of the heart which we both know.

For I have recently experienced my first deer hunt. In company with two congenial spirits and fellow students, Fred Todd, of Milltown, N. B., and Harmon J. Coulter of Georgetown, Col., I hurried away from the classic halls of the Phillips Andover Academy at the commencement of the Christmas vacation and took train for Todd's home.

We left Boston at 9 A. M., Dec. 22, 1882, and after a delightful ride reached Bangor, Me., at 8 P. M. At the latter place we transferred ourselves and belongings to a sleeper, and made all preparations for a hasty change at McAdam Junction, N. B., to the night train for St. Stephens, and then turned in; but not to peaceful slumber, for scarcely had we sunk into the arms of Morpheus, and even before a fair opportunity had been given to launch off into sweet dreams of deer, and deer hunts, in which every tree had the wonderful faculty of turning into one of those beautiful creatures, when we were roused by a Custom House officer, while "crossing the line," who went through us, and came mighty near tipping Toddy's trip in its infancy, by walking off with all his rifle shells.

It was only after the most strenuous and frantic efforts and our united persuasive powers that we three nightshirted and excited youths bore back the shells in triumph.

Upon reaching McAdam Junction, at about 2 A. M., the bracing news greeted us that the night train had been taken off, compelling us to make this our headquarters for the time being; so rousing the inmates of the Junction House, we secured rooms and finished our interrupted sleep. Making a cautious survey in the morning we found that we were anchored in the midst of about a dozen houses and an ocean of bare, blackened stumps (the result of one of those destructive fires that so often swept over these wooded countries). "Not much excitement to be found around here," thought we; so settling back with the latest FOREST AND STREAM, we gave ourselves over to its pages. But mine host, Capt. Herbert, proved himself a jolly good fellow, and entertained us with not a few stories of bear and deer hunting, a reported that deer were plenty in the adjoining country; so that the time ambled along very pleasantly until the train hove in sight. To Harmony and myself this "Down East" trip was an entirely new experience, and it was with a deal of pleasure that we took note of the country, the people, and their dress.

Have you, reader, ever been down this way? If so, you will recall the many fine specimens of manhood that appeared at the station as you hurried toward the wilderness. After leaving Bangor the great interests of the people are centered in their forests, and fully nine-tenths of the inhabitants in the immediate vicinity of the great waterways are interested, in some way or other, in the lumber trade. This of course necessitates a vast deal of out-door life; the result of this active exercise is plainly seen in the natives. They had long since donned their winter garb, and with the body snugly encompassed in numerous shirts and thick homespun, and with feet enclosed in their fancifully colored stocking and larrikins, many of the costumes were really picturesque. At about 3 P. M. of the same day we sped away to St. Stephens, a city which with two others (Calais and Milltown), constitute what is known as the Union.

These places, distributed on the east and west banks of the St. Croix, are connected by the three bridges, and with each recurring spring are the scene of bustling activity; the many thousand feet of lumber felled around the head-quarters and branches of the St. Croix are rafted down, and her meet their arch enemy, the every ready saw.

It is needless to say that at Milltown, at the residence of Mr. Charles F. Todd, a most hearty welcome awaited us, for anyone who has had the good fortune to tarry with him has always carried away the most pleasant memories. We remained at Mr. Todd's until the 26th; in the meanwhile all the necessary paraphernalia had been collected, and it was with no little pleasure that we surveyed our kit, and hastily stowing away snowshoes, axes, guns, etc., into one of those comfortable and tough little sleighs known as pungs (in which the Brunswickians dart about), we, arrayed in the prevailing mode of the country–heavy caps and mittens, each with six pairs of woolen stockings under our moccasins, deposited in the interstices of the baggage and started for Princeton, Me., twenty miles away, where we met our guide, Mitchell Sewey by name, a tall, muscular Indian of the Passamaquoddy tribe.

Leaving Princeton at about 11 A. M., we drove rapidly across Lewey's and Big lakes to Grand Lake Stream, twelve miles distant. Here is located one of the State hatcheries. We were not able to inspect very thoroughly, but found everything in excellent working order, and were gratified to hear of the good results of their work. May it keep on.

From Grand Lake Stream, under the direction of the guide, we struck off on a bark road for a logging camp, fourteen miles off, known to be in the center of a great deer country. Oh! The horrors of that bark road, the worst corduroy in the country could not equal it. After unsuccessfully trying to hang on the pung we all, with the exception of the one driving, got out and walked. The sleigh was first up, and then down, with a soul-stirring plunge, then a violent lurch to one side of the road, and after extricating the pung from the bushes, only to go ahead a few steps and strike an unexpected root, a snap and spring of the pung, and a general movement of the baggage was the inevitable result, and so it was repeated until when still far from our doubtful destination, night closed in upon us. The prospect of spending the night in these woods with the thermometer loafing around the zero point, seemed to gain ground as we went on; for the roads crossed and branched off from the one we were on in the most perplexing confusion. The thought was not at all inspiring, for we were tired after our hard day's travel, and our horse was nearly tuckered. We were more in sympathy with this faithful animal than with ourselves, and feared the night bivouac for its sake.

The guide kept far ahead, and with the aid of a torch explored most of the roads; so keeping up a steady trudging and following his directions, at about 8 P.M., the most welcome sight of smoke from a logging camp met our eager gaze; with a "view Hullo" we lost no time in ensconcing ourselves with its spacious walls.

The hospitalities of the woodmen are proverbial; rough and uncouth as they are, they always share with you a generous portion of their lot. Their welcome appeals directly to the heart, said member generally being reached through the stomach.

The cook bustled around and soon had a piping hot supper of beans, camp bread, and tea sweetened with molasses. No matter what time a man may strike one of these camps, the first question plumped at him is: "Well, stranger, had anything to eat?" Other categories seem to be of minor importance. An hour or so was spent in pleasant chat over the prospects for game, and in making preparations for the morrow's early start. The choppers had seen deer quite often while going to and from work, though many doubts were expressed as to our chances for capturing one, the snow being hardly deep enough for snow-shoeing, but making very uncomfortable walking; it would be necessary to exercise the utmost skill in still-hunting, and meet cunning with cunning.

After a pleasant talk Todd and Harmony deposited themselves in the bunk (better known as the ram's pasture) with the men.

There were ten men in the gang all told, under the leadership of Joshua Crockett, of whom I shall write hereafter. This bunk occupied the larger portion of one side of the camp, and had a thick mattress of spruce and hemlock boughs. No time is lost in disrobing in the woods, the refinements of civilization are left in the settlements–taking off moccasins, and dislodging yourself from four or five pairs of stockings completes the necessary toilet. Securely wrapping yourself in a blanket, you soon, on those aromatic boughs, sleep the sleep of the blessed.

I stayed up a while longer and buried my cranium in Hallock's "Sportsman's Gazetteer," in order to glean additional points on the nature of the animal we were in pursuit of. After finishing my reading I leaned back on the deacon's seat, and while glancing around our strange quarters spent a few moments in delightful musing. So while the heavy breathing of the sleepers and the snapping and crackling of the fire are the only sounds that disturb the silence, let me transfer a few of my thoughts to this paper, and fill in the gaps of this long-drawn narrative. First, I am sure you would have me call persons and things by their right names, it seems entirely out of place that I should so often write my friend's name, Todd, in this style. He had been with us but a short time before he was universally called Toddy, the transition to "Whiskey Toddy" was the easiest and most natural thing in the world, and thus, no matter how disagreeable the cognomen may be, it sticks. It is wonderful how nicknames will fasten themselves to a person, and really in the multitudinous cases of business, or of toil, how pleasant it is to be greeted with the old familiar name of school and college days; and so with Harmon Coulter, Harmony it is on all sides.

But the uneasy turnings of some of the men recall me to my senses, and as I turn toward the bunk, I cannot refrain from contrasting this sort of life with that of the laborers in the cities. These men come into the woods about September 1st, and stay until the rivers and lakes break up; in the meantime, day after day, great inroads are made in the forests; it usually pained me to see some powerful tree, the proudest among its fellows, seemingly conscious in its strength, leveled low to the ground.

When the men first come in they at once go to work and put up the camp, which is the work of a few hours only. The sides are generally made of straight, well-matched timber, crevices and chinks being filled with moss; a layer of bark is put up on the roof, and thickly covered with boughs. In these modern days nearly all the camps have stoves instead of an open fire and a hole in the roof for the smoke, which affords the men a vast deal more comfort.

About time to turn in, you say. Well, I shall. So, stepping over Mitchell's (the guide's) prostrate form, I hie me to my health-giving bed. In the morning a general shake and wash finds us ready for breakfast. The woodmen "chase the antelope over the plain" very early, and are always up before daybreak. No need for the cook to summon more than once to breakfast–a meal of beans (again the inevitable bean), codfish and tea. Harmony and I look at one another aghast at the prospect of this tea arrangement in store for us. Tea sweetened with molasses is far from my ideal; as long as we were in the woods, it was never without a wry face and a sidelong glance at one another that Harmony and I absorbed the compound. The "Hardy Whiskey," like a true Brunswicker, eagerly drank it at all times and seasons. To ye, O wise men! let me caution you to take in sugar, and if fond of the morning cup of coffee, convey that also.

With the daylight we hurry off on one of the logging roads, Whiskey with a new .44 cal. Winchester repeater, Harmony fondling a heavy 10-bore, double-barrel Scott gun, myself with a 12-bore, and the guide with a substantial muzzle-loader. We noted numerous tracks along the road, some comparatively fresh, but we kept on to where one of the teamsters had sent back word he had seen a very new track, and Mitchell, examining it very carefully, pronounced it the trail of a large doe; he could distinguish a buck from a doe, he said, the buck having sharp and the doe dull hoofs.

Tightening moccasins and putting BB cartridges into our guns we lost no time in taking up the trail. We had not traveled more than half a mile before we realized fully that we were in the Maine woods; the snow was about sixteen inches deep, loosely packed, making the walking very difficult, especially for still-hunting; fallen trees still further made our progress anything but pleasant. On every possible lodging place huge crowns of snow had formed, and at the slightest provocation these had the most dampening and chilling trick of sliding down a person's back.

Nevertheless, we were constantly cheered by the appearance of new tracks; never in all my life have I seen anything compare with it; the woods had the appearance of a huge sheep pasture. At every ridge we would separate and cover the ground carefully. We realized that we were coming up with the game very rapidly, having two separate spots, where, after the deer had browsed around a bit, it had laid down and rested. We were now approaching a thickly wooded ridge, so each of us, striking off in such a way that the whole ground would be thoroughly covered, went ahead as noiselessly as possible. We had passed over about three-quarters of the ridge when the stillness was broken by two reports in quick succession. Standing motionless in my tracks I listened intently for any further sound, but some little time had elapsed before I heard a cautious bark (the signal agreed to call us together). We found that Whiskey had had the honor of the first shot, but owing to the snow on the cedars and bushes he had not been able to peer ahead more than twenty-five yards and had thus been compelled to take two hasty snap shots, as the deer, discovering him, had "lit out."

From blood on the snow we thought the deer had been badly hit, but upon following the trail a short distance discovered that it had a hind leg broken, which it dragged along. Taking a hasty lunch, Mitchell, after giving us the most minute directions to the likely crossing places, plunged ahead on the trail, and we made the best possible speed to the crossings as directed. We took stations on a rise of ground, with a pace of about five hundred yards between us, and watched until far into the afternoon. I had serious thoughts of summoning the boys and with the aid of a compass pushing out for camp, when a report, which sent the blood coursing through my veins, sounded away down the ridge at Harmony's crossing—a vigorous barking made Whiskey and me scramble along as fast as possible to the place, where we found Harmony frantically embracing himself, and viewing the carcass of a well grown doe. It proved not the one that Mitchell had started after, but I suppose it had been frightened out of some favorite trysting spot by the noise occasioned in the pursuit. All speed was taken to make out of boughs a rough sort of sled so that we could drag the body easily, and with buoyant spirits we struck out; after a hard pull, about seven o'clock, we reached a well-worn logging road, two miles from camp. We were received with open arms, the men supposing that we were lost in the mazes of the forest. In about half an hour Mitchell came in, and said that although keeping pretty close to the deer, he was not able to get near enough to turn it in our direction, but thought it had crossed the logging road far down.

He, however, had started four others. Great was our rejoicing as we went over the incidents of the day, laughed at the mishaps and sympathized with the misfortunes. After supper we had a joyful talk with Joshua Crockett (the Boss); an original old fellow he is; many of his ideas though quaintly expressed, are to the point. A favorite theory of his constant injunction to the men was, "If a man wants ter smoke, let him smoke, 'en if a man wants ter chew, let him chew; the more terbaccy a man uses the fiercer, madder, angrier he gets; that's the man can slash into a tree. I tell you, I wouldn't give ten cents a day for a man that didn't chaw anything stronger 'en spruce gum." Another was, "No siree, I don't want no man 'round me in the summer time who's all the time downing ice water; it's agin natur'. Water don't have no ice in summer, never meant that man should; follow natur', says I."

In the morning we went to where Mitchell thought the deer had crossed, and sure enough there were the tracks. Despite all difficulties we determined to try the snowshoes, and found that on them we could cut out a much faster pace than on the day before. An occasional fall, as the end of the shoes caught on some unseen stump, did not cause us any deal of annoyance, traveling together one would help the other, for you know, Harmony and I were novices at it. We had gone scarcely forty yards, when we discovered the bed upon which the doe had passed the night; two hours of steady, rapid work, carried us along the trail to where the tracks seemed to have just been made. The deer had to rest often, but notwithstanding its broken leg, it was truly remarkable to notice the tremendous leaps it would make over fallen trees and obstacles of all kinds. Keeping up a pretty fair gait and plodding along, great was our surprise when we discovered that the noon hour had been passed, in fact, it was close upon 2 P. M.; this discovery made us realize that we were nearly famished. Just a few moments for a bite, and then under orders from Mitchell, Whiskey and I started back in all haste for the logging road, for, as Mitchell said, the deer was traveling in a circle, and in all probability would soon cross the road. Sure enough, Whiskey and I were not yet on the road, when we heard Mitchell's bark drawing nearer, so spurting ahead, we reached the road almost breathless. Hardly had we broken through the bushes before the deer, about eighty yards up the road, broke cover also; as it was nearer Whisky than myself, he took the shot, which had the effect only of stopping the deer, the second shot went clear through the head. Plucky animal, it deserved almost to live after such a fight, but after we knew that its broken leg was broken, we were determined to put it out of further pain. A roystering time did we have that night, the cook made some doughnuts (a great luxury in camp) especially for us, and the men did many little things to show their appreciation for the supply of fresh venison our coming had afforded them. Joshua held forth at great length upon the benefits and greatness of Free Masonry (he being a mason) and frequently grew quite eloquent in the recital.

From one of the men who had been scouring the country for hemlock bark, we learned that at Munroe Lake several deer had been seen. We decided to make this our last trip, for the season was fast drawing to a close. We were in the woods long before "sun up." When Old Sol did deign to raise himself from his icy bed, we wished that all lovers of the gun could have been out that morning; to us the woods had never looked so fine, the rays of the sun danced and gleamed from trunk to trunk, and brightened up the most somber corners, until the very air seemed to be rendering thanksgiving for this great goodness. I know that we felt the general exhilaration, for the swish, swish of the snowshoes sounded more than ever with clock-like regularity.

When about a mile from the lake we branched off in different directions; so that the lake might be approached from the best vantage grounds. Harmony and I made a long detour to the further side of the lake; Harmony posted himself, while I proceeded about a quarter of a mile up the lake around several coves to one particularly inviting spot. My choice was a good one. I had not waited long before I saw two deer coming down the lake at a brisk trot, started, no doubt, by the guide, who had gone around the head of the lake. I felt the first symptoms of buck fever, but remembering the advice of Mitchell, I looked away from the deer for a moment and tried to control myself, but it took all the will power I had. Fortunately the deer kept close to the shore, so when I thought a fair opportunity presented itself, holding my gun as steady as possible, I pulled the forward trigger on a well-antlered buck, and as soon as the smoke cleared away, saw my first deer struggling in the snow; another shot at close range gave me full possession of this noble fellow. At the first shot its mate darted across the lake in Whiskey's direction, but he being too hasty, his two shots had the effect only of making the deer take to the woods further up the lake. We had no time to take up the trail, for all preparations had been made to start at noon. Cutting up the buck and distributing the best parts among us, we pushed out rapidly for camp.

Upon settling up, Joshua said: "Well, boys, we loggers don't generally charge strangers for board en fixin's, but seen's your city chaps, and college bred, I'll put the figger at fifty cents a day for each of you, and sixteen cents a day for the hoss." His manner was so solemn, that we could scarcely refrain from giving vent to our feelings.

Bidding the crew good-by, we set out on our return trip, over that abominable bark-road. But it proved too much for the pung this time; half of the distance had been covered when the dash-board parted company, though we made use of it as a back-rest. It was with the greatest difficulty that each of us, as we took turns in driving, kept from being shot under the horse's feet. Grand Lake Stream was reached at six o'clock; there we bade adieu to Mitchell, and spent a few days longer in cruising about the country after foxes and partridges, with fair success. Thus ended one of the most enjoyable shooting trips we had ever taken. The region visited is a great one for game; the sportsman may enjoy rare sport if he uses his privileges with moderation, and does all in his power to keep down the deer-hogs. I am sure that all sportsmen will join with you in crying down the proposed amendment to the Maine deer laws.

– DIGUS., ANDOVER, MASS.

TROUTING ON THE PASSADUMKEAG

By W. G. F., from *Forest and Stream*, November 3, 10 and 24th, 1887

I.

Life in the Woods: Returning to Camp (Currier & Ives 1860)

Whoever enjoys trout fishing should not fail to visit the Passadumkeag region, Maine. Any time between June and October will be in season for the best kind of sport, either with the fly or baited hook.

My first trip to that region was in 1867, in company with five other sportsmen. We left Bangor the first day of June, at 8 o'clock in the evening, taking the European & North American express to Enfield, where we arrived at half-past 9. There we found Pettengill, whom we had previously engaged to take us across the country to Pettengill's Landing, about twenty miles distant.

Our team was a heavy three-seated, through-brace wagon, drawn by a pair of large gray horses. We passed through Lowell and Burlington, then entered an unbroken forest of nine miles, reaching Pettengill's farm, two miles from the landing a 4 o'clock A.M. Here we took a rest of three hours, after which we refreshed the inner man, and while our host was hooking up the oxen we transferred our luggage from the wagon to the ox sled, to be taken down to the landing, two miles distant. The road from the farm being only used in winter, was very rough; indeed, we had to cut away many fallen trees before the team could get through. We reached the landing after four hour's hard work. It was the first party ever known to visit that region for trout fishing. The Passadumkeag is, at low water, from 40 to 60 yds. In width, but at this season its banks are full, and the roar of the water as it ran over Grand Falls, two miles below, was tremendous.

Here we caught our first trout, and they were beauties too. We found the gray and yellow hackle to be the most enticing bait. We took ten in about twenty minutes, averaging 1 ¼ lbs. each. Our guides, Pettengill or Lord, soon had them dressed and done to rich brown. When dinner was announced, there was no need of a second call, five of us were there simultaneously. Our guides, although hungry themselves, refused to eat until all were well helped. Trout after trout disappeared, until the Doctor ordered a halt for consultation, and as he had secured the last trout from the frying pan it was unanimously decided that we must either stay proceedings or catch more trout. The vote to stay proceedings until we arrived at the camping-ground three miles up the river prevailed, and packing our outfit into bateaux we proceeded up the river to the mouth of the Nickatous, and pitched our tent on the west end of a horseback which divides the two rivers and runs nearly parallel with them some four miles.

Just in front of our tent was an immense granite boulder overhanging the river, which at this point is very deep. Along the banks of the river on the side next to our camp were numerous springs of ice cold water, here the trout seemed to congregate. Never shall I forget the sensation as we cast our first flies. The water seemed literally alive with trout, and after a few casts we stripped our leaders of all but one fly, lest in the excitement of the sport we should catch more than we could use.

The basin at the mouth of the Nickatous, twenty-five rods below us, is also a favorite resort for trout, here in 1873 I landed at one cast two trout weighing 7 ¼ lbs., one of them, 5 ¾ lbs., was the largest I have ever known to be taken from these waters. While we were enjoying an hour's fishing our guides had pitched our tent, covering the ground with a thick carpet of fragrant meadow hay taken from a stack nearby, cooked trout for supper, and we then partook of our first meal in camp.

Our table was rustic in the extreme, being made of cedar splints laid on poles and supported by crotched sticks driven in the ground, but it served our purpose well enough, our appetites were sharpened by the invigorating air of the forest.

We had agreed to catch only what fish we needed to eat while in camp. We had fished less than one hour, and after we had finished supper, we found we had twenty-three trout still remaining. These we dressed and laid in a large basket made of birch bark and carried back some twenty rods from the camp, and set them over a cool spring which flowed from the side of the horseback.

The Doctor looked glum, the fact that we could do no more fishing until these were disposed of weighed heavily on his mind. Fortune (or at least bruin) favored us, for on visiting our basket the next morning we found it empty; the tracks in the soft ground plainly indicated that they had been appropriated by a bear, and a big one, too. We gave three cheers for the bear and hoped he would call round again when we had a surplus of trout, which he did not do, however.

The second day we divided our party, part going further up the Passadumkeag, myself, and two comrades, with Lord as guide, going up the Nickatous, intending to go as far as the falls, some six miles up, but on reaching the timber we came to a rocky tumbling stream, which Lord informed us was the Pistol, the outlet of a chain of lakes some three miles above. The view of the Pistol from our boat resting at its mouth was grand, the stately forest on either side, the huge boulders lying in every direction, the water foaming and dashing past them and forming into deep eddies afforded most enticing lurking places for trout.

We decided to land here and explore this stream to the headwaters, so drawing our boat well up on the south bank we proceeded to try the trout in the first eddy at the mouth of the Pistol. Our first cast proved our predictions to be true; we each landed a fine trout weighing about three pounds. These we turned over to Lord and proceeded up the stream, only occasionally stopping to make a cast, which invariably proved the stream to be literally alive with trout. After following the stream for half a mile or so, myself and Heald decided to take a trail which we found a little way back from the south side of the stream, concluding that it led to the lakes, leaving Hunter and Lord to follow up the stream and intersect us at the outlet of the lower Pistol lake. We loitered along for an hour or more enjoying the strange wild scenery and wondering at the strange stillness, when suddenly we heard way off up the trail a growl that dispelled our reveries, and nearly paralyzed us for a moment. The growl was repeated at frequent intervals, and we thought we could distinguish a human voice. Thinking our comrades must have been assailed by some savage beast (although unarmed, save a hatchet and hunting knife) we rushed forward to the rescue. As we approached the snarls and growls became more frequent, and the voice more distinct; we distinguished words which sounded like "Oost yer black varmint." Just as we were rounding a bend in the trail we heard two shots in rapid succession, followed by a gruff voice saying, "Thar, darn yer picter, ye miserable varmint, ye wanted me ter drag yer out didn't yer." Arriving at the spot we found a dead bear and an old man trying to remove a heavy trap from the bear's foot. The old hunter at first seemed disinclined to be communicative, but after assisting him to remove the trap and drag the bear out a little further in to the trail, we elicited from him the facts concerning the outcries we had heard. He had trapped the bear some rods from the trail and had probably been in the trap several days or until, as he expressed it, "the varmint had been caught long enough to become supple." He wanted to get him out to the road (before killing hm) and had driven him as one would drive a pig. To the trap was attached a heavy wooded clog, which catching in the brush from time to time would make the bear cry out with rage and pain, and by the time they had got to the trail both man and bear were thoroughly exasperated. He had attempted to kill him with his axe, but on coming near enough he showed so much fight, that he was obliged to settle him with a couple of shots from his old gun, the stock of which was tied on with rope yarn and wire. We judged the bear weighed about 400 lbs. We secured some of his claws as trophies and proceeded on to the headwaters of the Pistol. We found Hunter and Hall already there; Hunter had just struck a large trout, which engaged our attention for some thirty minutes.

Lower Pistol Lake is two and one half miles in length and about a mile wide. On the south side and extending out into the lake, half a mile or so, are hundreds of huge granite boulders reaching above the surface, the north and west side are bordered by high bluffs of granite.

These lakes with the Nickatous, four miles above, are favorite resorts for deer; we saw one noble buck with large spreading antlers (now just in the velvet) quietly nipping the lily pads near the outlet and about forty rods from us. He fed on and allowed us to look at him with apparent unconcern for several minutes. At last, raising his head and sniffing the air, with a loud snort bounded away up the rocky shore and out of sight.

Sportsmen from Boston and New York now make annual visits to this region. Most of them are entertained by our old friend Joe Darling, whose camps on the Nickatous are noted for their luxurious appointment.

At 2 o'clock our guide invited our attention to a dinner of broiled trout, hardtack and hot coffee. Our table was a broad, flat stone close to the water, and shaded by the branches of an immense oak. After dinner we took an inventory of our luggage and found we had 34lbs. of trout to carry to camp. On our return we found in a ravine near where we left our boat a considerable quantity of clear blue ice. With our hatchet and knives we soon broke off as much as we could carry in the boat to camp, which we reached just at sunset. As our friends had not yet returned from up the river, we set to work getting together some dry logs for our evening camp-fire, while Lord prepared supper. Just as the shades of evening began to deepen around our camp we heard the voices of our comrades in jubilant tones far up the river. As they approached we concluded that something quite unusual had elated them, and as they reached the canoe landing we saw at once the cause of their noisy demonstrations, and we added our voices to theirs in three rounding cheers for the Doctor as he stepped from the boat with a scratching, struggling cub in each hand. They had killed a bear, and captured her two cubs. Enough sport for one day at least.

II.

The Doctor declined to give any account of their trip up the river until after supper, as they had partaken of nothing but a hasty lunch since leaving camp in the morning; so securing the cubs with our bundle straps we all sat down to supper, well knowing that it would be useless to try to elicit any account of the day's doings until the rigid, determined expression on the Doctor's countenance cleared up, and he considered it his duty, however, to inform us that the bear must be skinned the first thing after supper, and the ownership of the same decided by lot; as for the cubs he thought he had a legal right to one of them at least, as they had nearly ruined what little wearing apparel he had, to say nothing of sundry scratches about the knees, somewhat deeper than the clothing.

Supper being finished and our duty having been made plain to us, we proceeded to move the carcass of the bear from the boat to the light of our camp-fire, and under the direction of Adams, who was well up in the art of preparing skins for ornamental purposes, we decided that this skin would be the most useful as well as ornamental made into a mat, as the fur was fine and glossy-black, so in skinning we took great care to remove the feet and claws with the skin intact, as well as the head, leaving the upper part of the skull with the jaws attached to the skin. We cut loose some still slender poles which were quite springy; and proceeded to stretch the skin by placing them lengthwise and crosswise, bending each pole so the spring would stretch the skin in the right directions. This being accomplished, preserving compound was rubbed over the flesh side, and it was hung up to dry. Lord and Pettengill had in the meantime prepared such part of the carcass as they considered the most edible, and consigned the remainder to the river.

Our work being now done the Doctor informed us that the

laborer was not only worthy of his hire, but the late worker was entitled to an extra supper, and although not up to all the mysterious arts of cookery he had prepared with his own hands a lunch which he now proposed to stake his reputation upon, whereupon he proceeded to rake from the coals of our camp-fire three lumps about the size of a man's head' they resembled rocks, but after brushing the ashes from them we found them to be composed of blue clay and were informed that each lump contained supper for two. A few smart raps with the hatched sufficed to break the lumps into halves, first disclosing a mass of feathers embedded to the insides of the clay ball, then the body of a—"can it be a partridge?" No, but they were done to a rich brown and fragrant with appetizing odors, "truly a lunch fit for the gods."

After lunch we repaired to our tents to listen to the Doctor's account of the capture of the bears:

"We paddled up the river as far as the Lower Taylor Brook, which we reached about noon, only stopping once to try the trout at cold springs, where we caught several very fine ones. While we were quietly resting on the right bank at the mouth of the brook, our attention was called to a strange whining noise in the river a few rods above us. On looking, what was our surprise to see a large bear swimming across the Passadumkeag from the opposite side, followed by her two cubs, which were whining piteously, evidently disliking their cold bath. The bear was heading for a point about three rods above, and evidently had not seen us, as she manifested no fear. Heald, with his Ballard across his knee, quietly waited for the bear to reach the shore. Heald raised his rifle to his shoulder, and at the same time giving a sharp whistle to attract her attention. She raised her head to listen, and on the instant the crack of Heald's rifle echoed among the hills. The bear made one convulsive struggle and sank to the ground just at the edge of the river, the ball had entered her brain just forward of the ear. Heald and I sprang to the shore to intercept the cubs while Pettengill took to the boat to head them off should they attempt to recross the river, a precaution which saved us the cubs, for as we reached the bank they turned and swam for the opposite shore. Pettengill was on hand, the bow of his boat not 6ft. from them, the stern near the bank. I sprang aboard, at the same time giving the boat a vigorous push in the direction of the cubs. We were upon them before they reached the opposite shore, and succeeded in getting a rope around their necks without much trouble while they were in the water. We then lifted them into the boat regardless of their teeth and claws, and hitched them up closely. They were sorry-looking objects, their resistance seemed to be wholly defensive. It was not without a pang of regret that we lifted the carcass of the dead bear into the boat. The cries of the little ones was distressing, they were trembling with fear, or the effects of their cold swim, but the warm sun soon dried them off, and if it did not elevate their spirits it certainly improved their appearance. We decided to return to camp at once, concluding that paddling a boat twenty miles and capturing three bears was a day's work not be grinned at."

The Doctor's account of their day's doings, being thus briefly told, we retired to our couches, a tired but happy company.

We arose the next morning feeling none the worse for our hard jaunt and tiresome work of the day before. Our breakfast consisted (in addition to our usual fare of fried trout, baked potatoes and coffee) of a bountiful supply of broiled bear's steak, which our guides declared to be very toothsome. We decided, however, that an appetite for bear's steak would have to be acquired, and as time with us was precious, we concluded that trout were good enough for us. As the day promised to be lousy, we decided to remain about camp, as we had much to do. We first made a rude cage about 2 ½ ft. square, in which to keep and transport the cubs. We found it no easy job to remove them from the box (into which we put them during the night) but with the aid of the straps which we had put around their necks, as a second precaution against escape, we finally succeeded in dragging them out without injury, and placed them in the cage. The Doctor proposed to devote the day to civilizing them. They were not at all inclined to be petted at first, but after two or three hours' persistent and gentle stroking about the head and face with a smooth stick, scratching their ears and rubbing them under the jaws, the Doctor so far overcame their fears that they allowed him to stroke them with his hand, and even seemed to solicit it. We then prepared some condensed milk by diluting it largely with warm water, and making it quite sweet, which, after a little patient coaching, the Doctor succeeded in making them eat from his hand. While lapping the milk they kept up a constant purring noise, loud enough to be heard for several rods. After eating the milk, they went into the nest of dry moss which we had gathered for them, and soon were oblivious of all the restraints that civilization had placed upon them.

As the day advanced the clouds began to clear away, and by noon the sun was shining bright and warm. Heald suggested, "that as we were all languishing for something to do," we avail ourselves of this opportunity to pot our trout, which we had promised to take home to some of our friends (we had taken into camp several two-gallon stone pots for this purpose, together with such other materials as were needed to preserve trout in this manner). This suggestion was approved by the whole party, as this would call for more fishing, about seventy-five being required to fill our pots. The first thing to be done was to prepare our ground oven for cooking the fish. This Lord and Pettengill knew just how to do, and they proceeded at once to dig a trench six feet long by eighteen inches wide and one foot deep, this they filled with dry wood and set a-fire, which was left burning for two or three hours. As soon as the sun began to cast shadows upon the river, we each selected a favorite locality for casting our flies, and commenced the exciting sport. Lord and Pettengill were to dress the fish as fast as caught. The trout, if possible, seemed more plentiful than on the preceding day, the river seemed fairly alive with them. I believe it was possible for one man to have caught one hundred in two hours, with tackle and flies of suitable strength to permit of landing at once. Fishing as we were with single fly, and being from five to fifteen minutes in landing each fish, we had at half-past six caught seventy-three, an average of twelve to each man in little over one and a half hour's fishing. Our guides had them dressed and all ready to pack into the pot.

Our method of potting was to pack the heads and tails, as closely as possible, sprinkling over each layer a handful of whole spices. When the pots were full we put into each 1 ½ pints vinegar and 2lbs. of butter or olive oil, then putting on the covers and stopping the joints with clay, we raked open the coals, and placed the pots near the bottom of the trench, covering completely with ashes and coals, where they remained without further attention for six hours, Lord engaging to remove them at the proper time. Prepared in this way trout are simply delicious, and may be kept for months if not disturbed. It being now 7 o'clock and our "labors," or rather pleasures, of the day done, while supper was preparing we listened to a brief lecture by the Doctor on the training of wild animals, with practical illustrations. After supper we mapped out our trips for the next two days, and wrapping ourselves in our blankets, were soon enjoying undisturbed repose.

III.

We were awakened the next morning by Pettengill, who told us that the morning was fine, and as the day was likely to be a hot one, we must be ready to start by sunrise if we wished to travel with any degree of comfort. We had planned a trip of twelve miles up the Passadumkeag to the Upper Taylor Brook, intending to go across from Maple Ridge to Spring Pond, and remain all night in a lumberman's camp, which we were informed we should find there.

The object of this trip was to become familiar with the country, as well as to test the trout fish at the mouths of the several streams emptying into the Passadumkeag. We had noted quite a difference in the color and flavor in the trout taken from the Pistol from those taken from the main river, and we wished to determine if they were the same in smaller streams, considered from the standpoint of edibility. We intended to do our fishing on our up trip.

Partaking of a hasty breakfast, we packed what articles we should require in the batteaux, not forgetting to take along the cubs also, as they were of too much importance to be left to themselves; besides, having slain their natural protector, we had, as it were, adopted them into our family.

We had a most delightful row for eight miles up the river, stopping from time to time to try the trout in the most favorable places. We passed Duck Stream, which our guide informed us was a great resort for black ducks in the fall, on account of the great abundance of wild rye which grew along its banks (I thing the wild rye is much like the wild rice which grows so abundantly along the Upper St. Lawrence).

Just above the stream we surprised a doe with two fawns at her side. Heald involuntarily raised his rifle as the deer sprang to cover, and as quickly lowered it again as she came into full view. The fawns were beautifully spotted with white and appeared to be four or five weeks old.

We cast our flies for a few moments at the mouth of Spring Brook, and were surprised at not getting a rise. This was indeed strange as the place seemed especially favorable, the water being clear and cold, but there were none there, for us, at least.

We proceeded on to the mouth of the Lower Taylor, where Heald shot the bear, and examined the place with considerable interest, as we listened again to the Doctor's account of the adventure. Here we found the trout very abundant and beautifully spotted, and almost as light as silver in color, of the average size, varying but little from three-fourths of a pound. Here we intended to go across Spring Lake; but after going a short distance we found the trail rough and obscure and the older members of our party declared it a failure; and we decided to go back to the boats and continue our trip up river to the Upper Taylor and return to camp that night. Reaching the mouth of the steam we disembarked, and as it had become very warm, and each of us having taken a turn with the oars, we were inclined to rest, for we had found the current quite strong in several places, which made vigorous pulling necessary. We had rowed twelve miles in seven hours, including the stops, and although we had enjoyed every moment of the time, we were, as the Doctor expressed it, "beat out."

Pettengill and Lord soon prepared a dinner for us which made us feel sorry for our friends at home, who were restricted to home fare, and thank our stars, we were here. After resting for a couple of hours, we began our return voyage, which was uneventful, save the killing of a fine specimen of the great gray owl (*Syrnium cinereum*), the only specimen I have ever seen alive, and a pair of pileated woodpeckers, the latter of which seemed to be quite abundant in the vicinity of Maple Ridge. Stevens was much elated at receiving the birds as a present, and at once prepared their skins for mounting.

Our trip down the river was as pleasant to the sight as it had been going up, and vastly more agreeable, as we had little pulling to do, the current favoring us. We reached camp at 7 o'clock, feeling that we had accomplished a day's work that would count to our advantage in the future.

The next morning we decided to break camp and start for home, determining to stop at Enfield for a day if possible and try the togue and trout in Cold Steam pond.

Reaching Enfield we chartered the little steamer Fairy, owned and commanded by Mr. Treat, whom we found to be the right sort of a man to fall in with, and disposed to take us where we could find good fishing and enjoying it with us. We went to the east inlet where we successfully landed seven trout, that weighed in the aggregate 21 lbs., and three togue the largest of which tipped the scale at 14 lbs.

We left the fishing grounds with great reluctance. Our trip had been full of enjoyment from the start, and we had left all our business cares behind us; but now our vacation was ended and we must return to them again, but we returned invigorated in body and mind.

We made annual trips to this region for several years, then varied our trip to other fishing grounds, more remote from civilization. Our trip this year, 1887, was to the old camping ground, and on the 20th of September, after an absence of ten years, we found ourselves again in camp at he mouth of the Nickatous. Very little save the river itself looked natural. The forest had been stripped of its magnificent growth of timber, fire had laid waste thousands of acres, the logging road, over which we traveled on our first trip with so much difficulty, had been transformed into a turnpike.. The roar of the Grand Falls was still to be heard as of yore, and the trout were there, "not the old residents," but their descendants, in sufficient numbers to give us all the sport we desired. As we revisited old localities along the river, and sought for old and cherished landmarks, and found them not, we were filled with regret that the progress of civilization and the want of mankind make it necessary for him to take from nature so much that is grand and beautiful, without a possible restriction.

– W. G. F., UNITY, ME.

AN EASTERN MAINE BEAR STORY

Anonymous, from the *Madison Bulletin*, April 25, 1889

Somewhere about 1850 there settled on the backwaters of the Machias River, near what is now termed the Air Line road, two brothers, named Eben and Hiram Bacon, says a writer in the Portland Transcript. Going back into the woods thirty or forty miles, they selected a tract of land near the river, built a camp, and began clearing up a farm and planting crops, in the meant time subsisting principally upon such game as the forest afforded. Deer, moose, bear and caribou were abundant, while small game could be taken plentifully all around them.

As the winter approached the bears entered their dens and disappeared until the following spring, at which time would come forth hungry and ravenous and range the county over in search of food, which consists of ants, frogs, refuse food thrown out from the logging camps and any wild animals that were not smart of cunning enough to elude them. At such times it is very easy to trap them, they readily taking bait.

Late one spring while the Bacon Brothers were attending their planting, they were greatly annoyed by the depredations of an old bear, a huge monster that made a track in the soft earth as large as the bare foot of a man. He stole provisions from the camps of the log drivers who were at work on the river. Not a round of pork, or keg of molasses, or sack of bread, could be left over night, but would be carried off by bruin, in fact he often revisited the camps by day, while the men were absent, and carried off anything eat-able that he could lay hold of. He had paid the Bacon Brothers several visits at the clearings, each time laying a heavy tax on them, when one night just as the brothers were about retiring, they were startled by an outcry from the pig-pen, a short distance from the cabin. Rushing out they were just in time to see bruin making off with their only pig, but a hot pursuit by the brothers soon caused him to drop his prize and hasten off into the woods.

The next morning one the log-driving crew missed their molasses keg, a stout, five-gallon keg, secured by iron hoops, and on following the trail a short distance, the keg was found, with one head knocked in and the molasses eaten or spilled by the bear. The day as Hiram came in from work, he said to his brother that he was determined to catch that bear if he had to sit up all night and watch for him. "I shall set a trap for him tonight and one that will be sure to take him."

The next morning quite early, Hiram arousing Eben, said he wanted him to go with him to the trap which had been set the previous night; at the same time remarking that he believed he had caught the old "pig-stealer," fast and sure. Hiram leading the way, they passed down by the pig-pen and a little further on to a clump of bushes, Eben with his rifle in his hand. "Well," exclaimed Hiram, "the trap is gone sure enough." On all sides were marks of a severe struggle, the ground was torn up, the trees scratched and the bark torn off, and for some distance through the woods and bushes could be seen the trail of his bearship, till they emerged upon an open piece of meadow land, and there, standing on his haunches and wildly beating the air with his fore paws, was a huge black bear, with the molasses keg hauled down over his head and securely held there with long, sharp-pointed nails in slanting from the outside. Hiram had conceived the idea of filling keg with nails and baiting it with a quantity of molasses, of which bears are so fond. The bait has proved too tempting for bruin, and crowding his head into the keg, he did not feet the sharp nails until he attempted to withdraw it, when he discovered his mistake. In this condition, he was easily dispatch.

ATTACKED BY WOLVES

By Edwin J. Miller, from *The Adventures of Ned Minton, A Story of Fact and Fiction*, 1904

 *Edwin Jabez Miller of Whitneyville (1837-1909), spent the better part of his life working in the woods of Down East Maine and near the end of this fruitful life, he decided to chronicle some of his experiences as well as those of the people of the Machias River Valley. Since juvenile fiction was a popular medium at the turn of the 20th century, he created a fictional young man, Ned Minton, and sent him through a series of adventures in his small book. His object, quoted in the preface of his book, was "to give a plain and correct account of some of the more important facts, with just enough fiction interwoven to make the story interesting..."*

Mr. Minton's team had been in the woods about four weeks, when there came on a very severe snow storm, nearly three feet, piling down and clocking the roads. In the parlance, "a bob-sled full:" meaning enough to form a smooth surface over the bob-sled in the camp yard, where it was usually left over night. This storm came on unexpectedly, and at a time when the cattle were nearly out of hay. Mr. Minton doubted if his truck team would be able to get in the hay from Wesley, the nearest town, for a week or more, hence he was under the necessity of getting a supply elsewhere to last until the roads became passable. He had a few stacks of meadow hay on Crooked River, five or six miles distant, which he thought might be reached, and after due consideration, he ordered Jack Strong, his head chopper, and his son Ned, to take "Old Mike" and break a track to the stream, and if possible, haul in a small load.

Ned was delighted with this opportunity to get a respite from barking logs from day-break until dark, for the job had not become somewhat irksome to him, as well as laborious. As soon as he received the order to go, he began shoveling the snow from the horse-sled, while Jack put up the grain for the horse and food for himself and Ned. Then he got two hay-forks, a shovel and an ax, and after lashing everything securely to the sled, Ned led old Mike from the hovel, and in a few moments he was harnessed and on the road to the stream, which lay in the direction of the settlement.

The snow was deep, and the horse floundered along laboriously, stopping frequently to regain his wind, so that when they arrived, where the stacks were, it was nearly sunset. Ned loosed the horse from the sled and led him around to the lea side of a stack; then he removed the harness, and buckled on the blanket, for he was perspiring freely. Next he secured him to the foundation stake of the stack, and gave him a liberal feed of grain, and free access to the hay. Jack then mounted the stack and pitched down about two hundred pounds to Ned, who stowed it on the sled; then Ned brought up the pail of food, and they too ate their lunch, while the horse was eating.

They had scarcely finished, however, when a wolf down the stream, but a short distance away, commenced to howl dismally. In a few moments an answering howl came from the opposite direction, then there began a sound most doleful and terrifying, evidently from the throats of a large and hungry pack. A streak of pallor overspread Ned's face, and as he looked at Jack inquiringly, he uttered the one word "Jimminy!"

Jack spoke assuringly to Ned, telling him that they need not fear, for they would remain where they were until morning, and with a position on the top of the stack, and armed with their forks, they could successfully defend themselves against a score of wolves even though they were ravenously hungry. It was an easy matter to get fuel to build a fire, there being plenty of small, dry hackmatack trees, nearby, which had been killed several years previous by the flowage of the stream. Jack knew that wolves were usually cowardly, in daylight, hence he began chopping downs the trees, as fast as he was able, while it was yet light. He told Ned that he did not fear an attack until after dark, and to tote the wood to the stack as fast as he could. Ned worked busily. His first poles were cantered against the stack, that he and Jack might make a speedy climb in case of need.

In an hours' time enough wood was prepared and carried in to keep the fire burning brightly through the night. The job was accomplished none too quickly, however, for the gloom of night was gathering, under the tree tops, and the wolves had closed down near enough for Ned and Jack to occasionally catch a glimpse of their movements and sense their near presence by the sound of their jaws, as they snapped them together, tapping time, as Ned expressed it, to their song, which sounded fearful enough to raise ones hair on end. Old Mike had long since ceased to eat and was snorting and tugging at his halter in his efforts to break away.

While Jack shoveled the snow from a spot on which to build a fire, Ned put the forks and ax on the top of the stack, where they would be in readiness. After fastening the horse more securely, he pulled an armful of hay from the stack and crowded it between the logs, laid for the fire, and set a match to it. Immediately the landscape lighted up, then even the bravest of the wolves fell back out of sight; but the pack continued to howl ever more frightfully than before. Later in the night, their howls turned to snarls as if they were fighting among themselves; then the sounds became more indistinct and finally ceased.

In half an hour an owl began to hoot from his perch on the limb of an old stub, at the further side of the stream, and old Mike, contentedly resumed eating, which was taken, by the boys, as an indication of safer conditions.

The danger of an attack having apparently passed, Ned grew very sleepy and began to nod. Jack told him he thought they could now venture to take a nap; so after piling a fresh supply of fuel on the fire, they ascended the hay-stack and dug a hole next to the stack pole, into which they slid and in half a reclining position soon fell asleep.

How long they slept they could not afterwards tell, but they were suddenly awakened by old Mike, who was snorting and tearing around in greater terror than in the early evening. Jack and Ned sprang up quickly, each grappling his fork and assuming a position of defense. The fire had burned low and in the dense darkness no moving objects were discernable. Fortunately the smoldering embers were not far distant, so Jack lifted a large fork full of hay and cast it upon the coals. A dense smoke arose followed by a bright blaze. The light seemed to give Ned more courage and he slid from the stack and quickly raked the brands together and topped them with a fresh supply of dry wood. This was scarcely accomplished when it seemed, to Ned, that all the inmates of pandemonium had broken loose; for a dozen wolves, which were within a few feet of old Mike, and were about to tear him to pieces, set up a howl of disappointment more terrifying than any other sound ever heard, by Ned, before. When this dreadful din commenced, Ned dropped the stick which he was about to cast upon the fire, ran to the stack, seized the end of the fork-handle reached him, by Jack, who quickly drew him to the top. The fire was now burning brightly, but Ned had been so thoroughly frightened that he could not be induced to descend to the ground again until the gloom of night had been fully dispelled by the rising sun.

When the morning came quietude pervaded the forest, and surrounding country, the wolves evidently having taken their departure. A little more hay was then pitched on the sled and after freeing the horse, Ned and Jack lunched on frozen doughnuts, washed down with cold water dipped from the stream.

Breakfast over, they took their forks and visited the spot where the wolves had held their orgy the night before. They found the snow trampled, to a solid mass, and stained with blood. A deer had been killed and the flesh and bones, save the skull, had been devoured. Evidently the flock had fought over the remains, for the snow was tinged with blood from this spot to within a few feet of the hay-stack.

After satisfying their curiosity, Ned and Jack harnessed the horse and started for camp. When they had driven about three miles of the way, they met several members of the crew, coming to their relief, with guns and axes. These men said that the wolves had been plainly heard at camp, six miles distant. They were almost surprised to find both boys and the horse alive and unharmed, for an old hunter, in the crew, had pronounced the varied tones of the pack indicative of victory over either man or beast.